How to
Master Skills for the

Second Edition

TOEFL® iBT

READING

Basic

DARAKWON

How to
Master Skills for the

TOEFL® iBT

READING Basic

Second Edition

Publisher Kyudo Chung
Editor Sangik Cho
Authors Timothy Hall, Arthur H. Milch, Denise McCormack, E2K
Proofreaders Michael A. Putlack, Will Link
Designers Minji Kim, Yeji Kim

First Published in January 2007 By Darakwon, Inc.
Second edition first published in November 2024 by Darakwon, Inc.
Darakwon Bldg., 211, Munbal-ro, Paju-si, Gyeonggi-do 10881
Republic of Korea
Tel: 02-736-2031 (Ext. 250)
Fax: 02-732-2037

ISBN 978-89-277-8085-4 14740
978-89-277-8084-7 14740 (set)

www.darakwon.co.kr

Photo Credits
Shutterstock.com

Components Main Book / Answer Key / Free MP3 Downloads
7 6 5 4 3 2 1 24 25 26 27 28

Table of Contents

INTRODUCTION

1 Information on the TOEFL® iBT

A The Format of the TOEFL® iBT

Section	Number of Questions or Tasks	Timing	Score
Reading	**20 Questions** • 2 reading passages – with 10 questions per passage – approximately 700 words long each	35 Minutes	30 Points
Listening	**28 Questions** • 2 conversations – 5 questions per conversation – 3 minutes each • 3 lectures – 6 questions per lecture – 3-5 minutes each	36 Minutes	30 Points
Speaking	**4 Tasks** • 1 independent speaking task – 1 personal choice/opinion/experience – preparation: 15 sec. / response: 45 sec. • 2 integrated speaking tasks: Read-Listen-Speak – 1 campus situation topic reading: 75-100 words (45 sec.) conversation: 150-180 words (60-80 sec.) – 1 academic course topic reading: 75-100 words (50 sec.) lecture: 150-220 words (60-120 sec.) – preparation: 30 sec. / response: 60 sec. • 1 integrated speaking task: Listen-Speak – 1 academic course topic lecture: 230-280 words (90-120 sec.) – preparation: 20 sec. / response: 60 sec.	17 Minutes	30 Points
Writing	**2 Tasks** • 1 integrated writing task: Read-Listen-Write – reading: 230-300 words (3 min.) – lecture: 230-300 words (2 min.) – a summary of 150-225 words (20 min.) • 1 academic discussion task – a minimum 100-word essay (10 min.)	30 Minutes	30 Points

B What Is New about the TOEFL® iBT?

- The TOEFL® iBT is delivered through the Internet in secure test centers around the world at the same time.
- It tests all four language skills and is taken in the order of Reading, Listening, Speaking, and Writing.
- The test is about 2 hours long, and all of the four test sections will be completed in one day.
- Note taking is allowed throughout the entire test, including the Reading section. At the end of the test, all notes are collected and destroyed at the test center.
- In the Listening section, one lecture may be spoken with a British or Australian accent.
- There are integrated tasks requiring test takers to combine more than one language skill in the Speaking and Writing sections.
- In the Speaking section, test takers wear headphones and speak into a microphone when they respond. The responses are recorded and transmitted to ETS's Online Scoring Network.
- In the Writing section, test takers must type their responses. Handwriting is not possible.
- Test scores will be reported online. Test takers can see their scores online 4-8 business days after the test and can also receive a copy of their score report by mail.

2 Information on the Reading Section

The Reading section of the TOEFL® iBT measures test takers' ability to understand university-level academic texts. This section has 2 passages, and the length of each passage is about 700 words. Some passages may have underlined words or phrases in blue. Test takers can click on them to see a definition or explanation. Test takers have to answer 10 questions per passage. 35 minutes are given to complete this section, including the time spent reading the passages and answering the questions.

A Types of Reading Passages

- Exposition: Material that provides an explanation of a topic
- Argumentation: Material that presents a point of view about a topic and provides evidence to support it
- Historical narrative: An account of a past event or of a person's life, narrated or written by someone else

B Types of Reading Questions

- Basic Comprehension Questions
  - Vocabulary Question (1-3 questions per passage): This type of question asks you to identify the meanings of words and phrases in the reading passage.
  - Reference Question (0-1 questions per passage): This type of question asks you to identify the referential relationship between the words in the passage.
  - Factual Information Question (1-3 questions per passage): This type of question asks you to identify specific information that is explicitly stated in the passage.

- Negative Factual Information Question (0-2 questions per passage): This type of question asks you to check what information is NOT mentioned in the passage.
- Sentence Simplification Question (0-1 question per passage): This type of question asks you to choose the sentence that best paraphrases the essential information in the highlighted sentence.

• Inference Questions
- Inference Question (0-2 questions per passage): This type of question asks you to identify an idea that is not explicitly stated in the passage.
- Rhetorical Purpose Question (1-2 questions per passage): This type of question asks you why the author uses particular words, phrases, or sentences.
- Insert Text Question (1 question per passage): This type of question provides an example sentence and asks you to decide where the best place for that sentence would be in the passage.

• Reading to Learn Questions
- Prose Summary Questions (0-1 question per passage): This type of question asks you to complete a summary chart with major ideas from the passage. It is worth up to 2 points, and partial credit is given. This type of question does not occur with a Fill in a Table question in one passage.
- Fill in a Table Question (0-1 question per passage): This type of question asks you to identify and organize the major ideas of the passage into table categories. It is worth up to 3 points for tables with 5 correct answers and 4 points for tables with 7 correct answers. Partial credit is given. This type of question does not occur with a Prose Summary question in one passage.

C Question Formats

• There are three question formats in the Reading section: Four-choice questions with a single answer in traditional multiple-choice format, four-choice questions with a single answer that ask test takers to insert a sentence where it fits best in a passage, and Reading to Learn questions with more than four choices and more than one answer

HOW TO USE THIS BOOK

How to Master Skills for the TOEFL® iBT Reading Basic is designed to be used either as a textbook for a TOEFL® iBT reading preparation course or as a tool for individual learners who are preparing for the TOEFL® test on their own. With a total of ten units, this book is organized to prepare you for the test with a comprehensive understanding of the test and a thorough analysis of every question type. Each unit consists of seven parts and provides a step-by-step program that provides question-solving strategies and the development of test-taking abilities. At the back of the book is one actual test of the Reading section of the TOEFL® iBT.

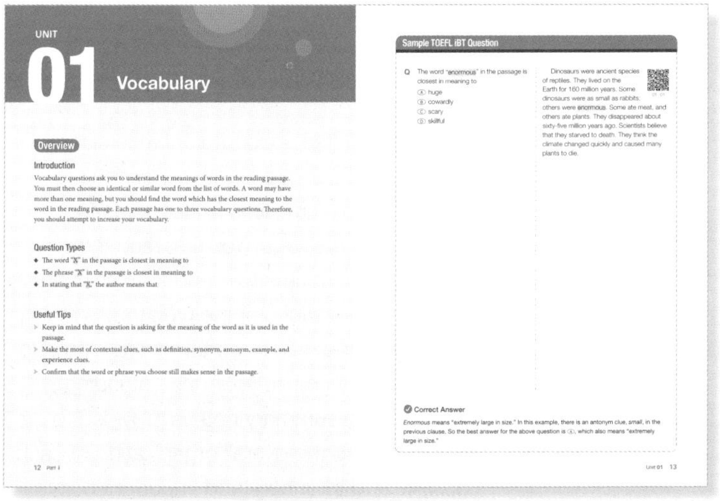

❶ Overview

This part is designed to prepare you for the type of question the unit covers. You will be given a full description of the question type and its application in the passage. You will also be given some useful tips as well as an illustrated introduction and sample.

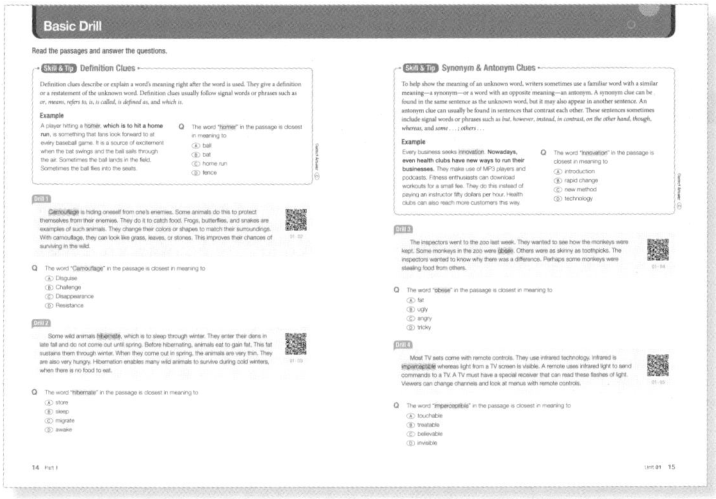

❷ Basic Drill

The purpose of this section is to ensure that you understand the new types of questions that were described in the overview. You will be given a chance to confirm your understanding in brief texts before starting on the practice exercises. You will read some simple passages and answer questions of a particular type. This part will help you learn how to deal with each type of question on the Reading section of the TOEFL® iBT.

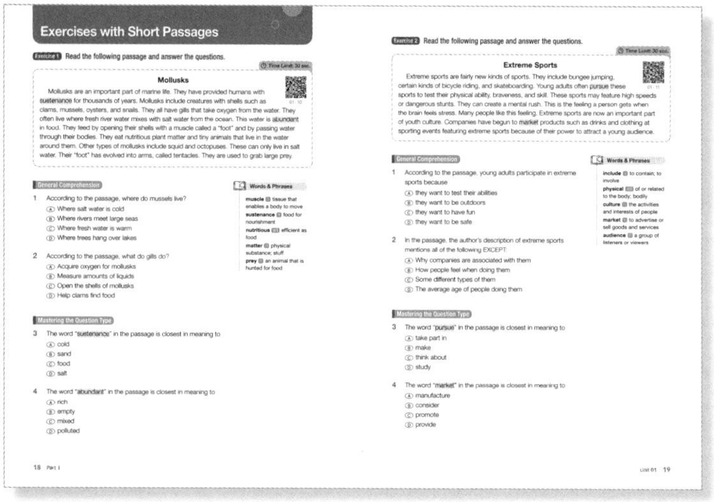

❸ Exercises with Short Passages

This section is the first of the exercises in each unit. It is a halfway step before exercising with the mid-length passages. Four short passages are offered, and a time limit is given for reading each passage. After reading each passage, you will solve some general comprehension questions as well as other questions of the type that is dealt with in the unit. Definitions of difficult words are offered to help you understand the material better.

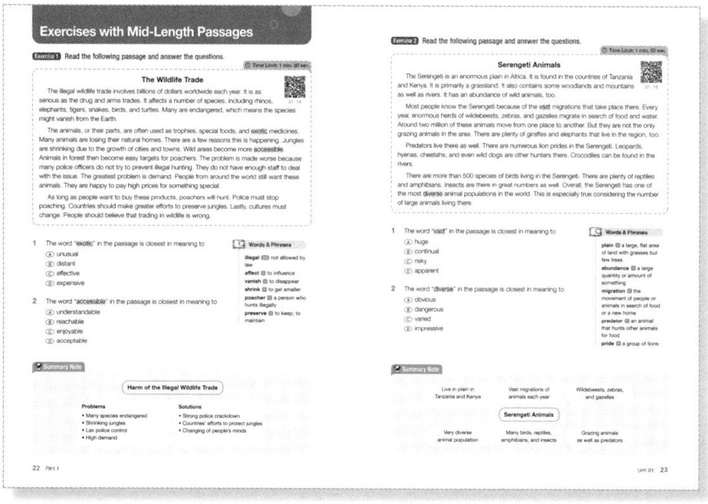

❹ Exercises with Mid-Length Passages

This section is the second of the exercises in each unit. Four mid-length passages are provided, and a time limit is also given for reading each passage. You first read the passage within a time limit and then solve the question or questions of the type that is mainly dealt with in the unit. Important words are also listed to help increase your understanding. Additionally, a summary note is provided to help you grasp the overall organization of each passage and to understand important points.

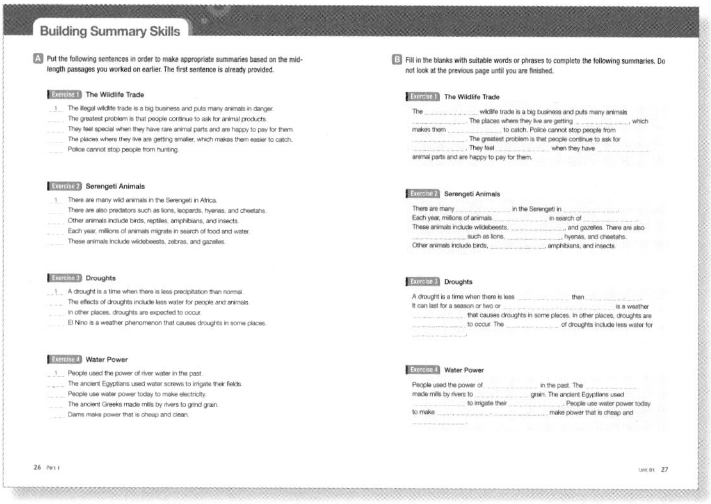

❺ Building Summary Skills

The purpose of this part is for you to understand the previous mid-length passages thoroughly by completing the summaries of them. This will also help you enhance your paraphrasing skills, which are strongly recommended to those who are preparing for the TOEFL® iBT.

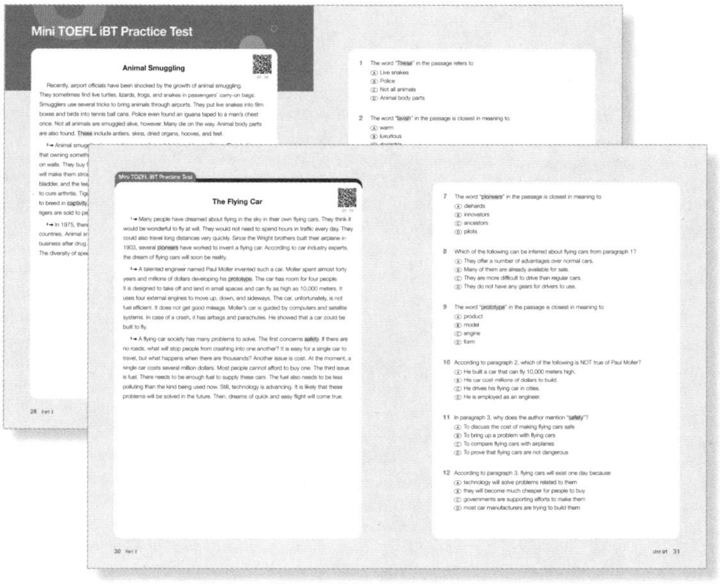

❻ Mini TOEFL iBT Practice Test

This part gives you a chance to experience an actual TOEFL® iBT test in a shortened form. You will be given two passages with 6 questions each. The topics are similar to those on the actual TOEFL® test, as are the questions.

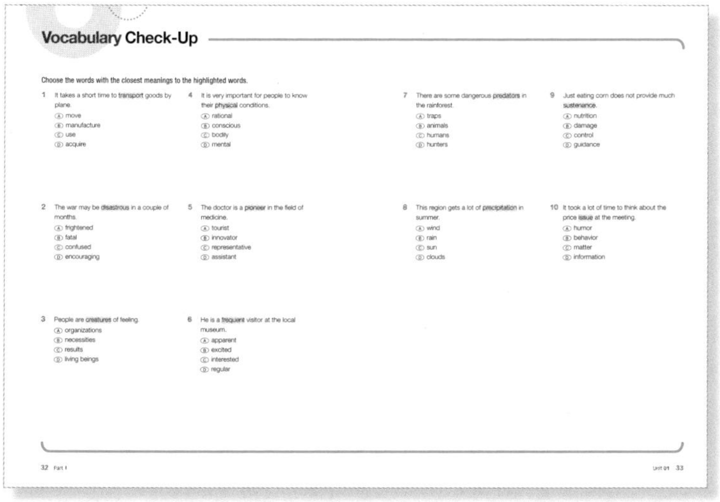

❼ Vocabulary Check-Up

This part offers you a chance to review some of the words you need to remember after finishing each unit. Vocabulary words for each unit are also provided at the back of the book to help you prepare for each unit.

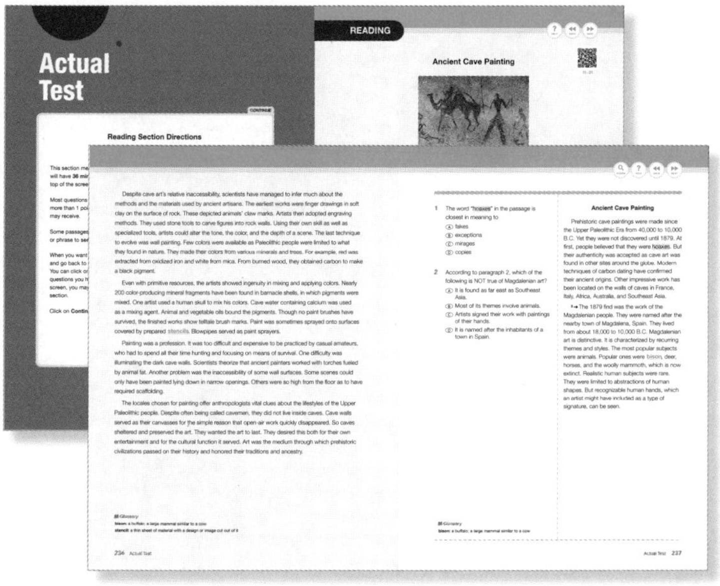

❽ Actual Test

This part offers one full practice test that is modeled on the Reading section of the TOEFL® iBT. This will familiarize you with the actual test format of the TOEFL® iBT.

PART I

Basic Comprehension

In this part, the reading comprehension questions include vocabulary, reference, factual information, negative factual information, and sentence simplification. The learning objectives of these reading comprehension questions are to identify individual words, referential relations between words in the passage, factual information, and essential sentences.

UNIT

01 Vocabulary

Overview

Introduction

Vocabulary questions ask you to understand the meanings of words in the reading passage. You must then choose an identical or similar word from the list of words. A word may have more than one meaning, but you should find the word which has the closest meaning to the word in the reading passage. Each passage has one to three vocabulary questions. Therefore, you should attempt to increase your vocabulary.

Question Types

- The word "X" in the passage is closest in meaning to
- The phrase "X" in the passage is closest in meaning to
- In stating that "X," the author means that

Useful Tips

- Keep in mind that the question is asking for the meaning of the word as it is used in the passage.
- Make the most of contextual clues, such as definition, synonym, antonym, example, and experience clues.
- Confirm that the word or phrase you choose still makes sense in the passage.

Sample TOEFL iBT Question

Q The word "enormous" in the passage is closest in meaning to

Ⓐ huge
Ⓑ cowardly
Ⓒ scary
Ⓓ skillful

Dinosaurs were ancient species of reptiles. They lived on the Earth for 160 million years. Some dinosaurs were as small as rabbits; others were enormous. Some ate meat, and others ate plants. They disappeared about sixty-five million years ago. Scientists believe that they starved to death. They think the climate changed quickly and caused many plants to die.

01 - 01

Correct Answer

Enormous means "extremely large in size." In this example, there is an antonym clue, *small*, in the previous clause. So the best answer for the above question is Ⓐ, which also means "extremely large in size."

Basic Drill

Read the passages and answer the questions.

Skill & Tip Definition Clues

Definition clues describe or explain a word's meaning right after the word is used. They give a definition or a restatement of the unknown word. Definition clues usually follow signal words or phrases such as *or, means, refers to, is, is called, is defined as,* and *which is.*

Example

A player hitting a homer, **which is to hit a home run**, is something that fans look forward to at every baseball game. It is a source of excitement when the bat swings and the ball sails through the air. Sometimes the ball lands in the field. Sometimes the ball flies into the seats.

Q The word "homer" in the passage is closest in meaning to

- (A) ball
- (B) bat
- (C) home run
- (D) fence

Correct Answer (C)

Drill 1

Camouflage is hiding oneself from one's enemies. Some animals do this to protect themselves from their enemies. They do it to catch food. Frogs, butterflies, and snakes are examples of such animals. They change their colors or shapes to match their surroundings. With camouflage, they can look like grass, leaves, or stones. This improves their chances of surviving in the wild.

01-02

Q The word "Camouflage" in the passage is closest in meaning to

- (A) Disguise
- (B) Challenge
- (C) Disappearance
- (D) Resistance

Drill 2

Some wild animals hibernate, which is to sleep through winter. They enter their dens in late fall and do not come out until spring. Before hibernating, animals eat to gain fat. This fat sustains them through winter. When they come out in spring, the animals are very thin. They are also very hungry. Hibernation enables many wild animals to survive during cold winters, when there is no food to eat.

01-03

Q The word "hibernate" in the passage is closest in meaning to

- (A) store
- (B) sleep
- (C) migrate
- (D) awake

Skill & Tip Synonym & Antonym Clues

To help show the meaning of an unknown word, writers sometimes use a familiar word with a similar meaning—a synonym—or a word with an opposite meaning—an antonym. A synonym clue can be found in the same sentence as the unknown word, but it may also appear in another sentence. An antonym clue can usually be found in sentences that contrast each other. These sentences sometimes include signal words or phrases such as *but, however, instead, in contrast, on the other hand, though, whereas,* and *some . . . ; others . . .*

Example

Every business seeks innovation. **Nowadays, even health clubs have new ways to run their businesses.** They make use of MP3 players and podcasts. Fitness enthusiasts can download workouts for a small fee. They do this instead of paying an instructor fifty dollars per hour. Health clubs can also reach more customers this way.

Q The word "innovation" in the passage is closest in meaning to

Ⓐ introduction
Ⓑ rapid change
Ⓒ new method
Ⓓ technology

Correct Answer Ⓒ

Drill 3

The inspectors went to the zoo last week. They wanted to see how the monkeys were kept. Some monkeys in the zoo were obese. Others were as skinny as toothpicks. The inspectors wanted to know why there was a difference. Perhaps some monkeys were stealing food from others.

01-04

Q The word "obese" in the passage is closest in meaning to

Ⓐ fat
Ⓑ ugly
Ⓒ angry
Ⓓ tricky

Drill 4

Most TV sets come with remote controls. They use infrared technology. Infrared is imperceptible whereas light from a TV screen is visible. A remote uses infrared light to send commands to a TV. A TV must have a special receiver that can read these flashes of light. Viewers can change channels and look at menus with remote controls.

01-05

Q The word "imperceptible" in the passage is closest in meaning to

Ⓐ touchable
Ⓑ treatable
Ⓒ believable
Ⓓ invisible

Skill & Tip Example Clues

Example clues provide examples of unknown words. An unknown word and its examples have a part-whole relationship, so the unknown word is usually a more general word which can represent its examples. The clue may be introduced, but is not always, by signal words such as *include, for example, for instance, such as,* and *like*. The clues are not always in the same sentence.

Example

In spring, many people suffer from **coughing, itches, sneezes, runny noses, and watery eyes**. People may think these are indications of a cold. If these symptoms last for a long time, they should see a doctor. It could be allergies caused by dust, mold, or pollen. They can cause a lot of irritation.

Q The word "symptoms" in the passage is closest in meaning to

Ⓐ signs
Ⓑ symbols
Ⓒ patterns
Ⓓ phenomena

Correct Answer Ⓐ

Drill 5

The northeast part of the United States gets the most forms of precipitation. The region is subject to rain, sleet, and snow. Some years, there is so much that it may damage crops. This causes many farmers to borrow money from banks to pay for their expenses. It can also cause damage to buildings.

01-06

Q The word "precipitation" in the passage is closest in meaning to

Ⓐ changes in temperature
Ⓑ water from the sky
Ⓒ dust in the air
Ⓓ clouds above mountains

Drill 6

The wolverine is a hardy animal. It is strong and can survive in places with cold temperatures. It is able to catch large animals. It lives in the forests of Canada and the United States. The wolverine is able to walk up to 100 miles per day while hunting for food. It is strong and aggressive enough to steal food from bears.

01-07

Q The word "hardy" in the passage is closest in meaning to

Ⓐ horrible
Ⓑ angry
Ⓒ tough
Ⓓ greedy

Skill & Tip Experience Clues

Experience clues rely on your own knowledge or experience to understand an unknown word. Many times, a text mentions something you know about, but it will not directly tell you what the word means. So you need to use logic and reasoning skills based on your experience and common knowledge.

Example

Digital dictionaries are very effective learning tools. They check spelling and word meanings. They also provide synonyms. Even better, they show how words are used in sentences. This helps students learn about the functions of words. Students can learn to use words while making fewer mistakes. They become better writers this way.

Q The word "effective" in the passage is closest in meaning to

Ⓐ impressive
Ⓑ handy
Ⓒ useful
Ⓓ valid

Correct Answer Ⓒ

Drill 7

Soccer has been slow to catch on in the United States. The reason is that most people prefer to watch baseball, basketball, and football. These are American creations. Many Americans think that soccer is a sport for Europeans and South Americans. It is not a part of the USA's identity. They also do not like how the games have low scores.

01-08

Q The phrase "catch on" in the passage is closest in meaning to

Ⓐ become popular
Ⓑ be entertained
Ⓒ become rooted
Ⓓ be confusing

Drill 8

Clouds form when air near the ground is heated by the sun. Hot air rises in the atmosphere because it is less dense than the air around it. Eventually, the rising air cools. The water, at first in vapor form, condenses. It forms visible droplets. At this point, clouds become visible.

01-09

Q The word "dense" in the passage is closest in meaning to

Ⓐ thick
Ⓑ hot
Ⓒ cold
Ⓓ light

Exercises with Short Passages

Exercise 1 Read the following passage and answer the questions.

Time Limit: 30 sec.

Mollusks

01 - 10

Mollusks are an important part of marine life. They have provided humans with sustenance for thousands of years. Mollusks include creatures with shells such as clams, mussels, oysters, and snails. They all have gills that take oxygen from the water. They often live where fresh river water mixes with salt water from the ocean. This water is abundant in food. They feed by opening their shells with a muscle called a "foot" and by passing water through their bodies. They eat nutritious plant matter and tiny animals that live in the water around them. Other types of mollusks include squid and octopuses. These can only live in salt water. Their "foot" has evolved into arms, called tentacles. They are used to grab large prey.

General Comprehension

1 According to the passage, where do mussels live?

Ⓐ Where salt water is cold
Ⓑ Where rivers meet large seas
Ⓒ Where fresh water is warm
Ⓓ Where trees hang over lakes

2 According to the passage, what do gills do?

Ⓐ Acquire oxygen for mollusks
Ⓑ Measure amounts of liquids
Ⓒ Open the shells of mollusks
Ⓓ Help clams find food

Words & Phrases

muscle n tissue that enables a body to move

sustenance n food for nourishment

nutritious adj efficient as food

matter n physical substance; stuff

prey n an animal that is hunted for food

Mastering the Question Type

3 The word "sustenance" in the passage is closest in meaning to

Ⓐ cold
Ⓑ sand
Ⓒ food
Ⓓ salt

4 The word "abundant" in the passage is closest in meaning to

Ⓐ rich
Ⓑ empty
Ⓒ mixed
Ⓓ polluted

Exercise 2 Read the following passage and answer the questions.

Time Limit: 30 sec.

Extreme Sports

01 - 11

Extreme sports are fairly new kinds of sports. They include bungee jumping, certain kinds of bicycle riding, and skateboarding. Young adults often pursue these sports to test their physical ability, braveness, and skill. These sports may feature high speeds or dangerous stunts. They can create a mental rush. This is the feeling a person gets when the brain feels stress. Many people like this feeling. Extreme sports are now an important part of youth culture. Companies have begun to market products such as drinks and clothing at sporting events featuring extreme sports because of their power to attract a young audience.

General Comprehension

1 According to the passage, young adults participate in extreme sports because

Ⓐ they want to test their abilities
Ⓑ they want to be outdoors
Ⓒ they want to have fun
Ⓓ they want to be safe

2 In the passage, the author's description of extreme sports mentions all of the following EXCEPT:

Ⓐ Why companies are associated with them
Ⓑ How people feel when doing them
Ⓒ Some different types of them
Ⓓ The average age of people doing them

Mastering the Question Type

3 The word "pursue" in the passage is closest in meaning to

Ⓐ take part in
Ⓑ make
Ⓒ think about
Ⓓ study

4 The word "market" in the passage is closest in meaning to

Ⓐ manufacture
Ⓑ consider
Ⓒ promote
Ⓓ provide

Words & Phrases

include v to contain; to involve
physical adj of or related to the body; bodily
culture n the activities and interests of people
market v to advertise or sell goods and services
audience n a group of listeners or viewers

Exercise 3 Read the following passage and answer the questions.

Time Limit: 30 sec.

Disasters in Quebec

01 - 12

The year 2003 was brutal for Quebec. The reason was fires. It was the most disastrous fire season in recent times. It was also the most expensive year for natural disasters in that region of Canada. The harshness of the fires was explained by three years of bad weather. Some places had their worst droughts in 100 years. The land was very dry. More than 2,400 forest fires burned vast areas of land. It cost nearly 500 million dollars to fight these fires. Insurance companies paid out 250 million dollars in claims. Three firemen lost their lives. It took a long time to recover from the fires. The year 2003 was the worst in a decade.

General Comprehension

1 According to the passage, what caused a lot of damage in Quebec?

- (A) Storms
- (B) Floods
- (C) Snow
- (D) Fires

2 According to the passage, the year 2003 was remarkable because

- (A) it was the most expensive year for disasters
- (B) insurance companies made money
- (C) three mechanics lost their lives
- (D) it was the worst in five years

Words & Phrases

brutal adj very severe
disastrous adj terrible; awful; damaging
recent adj not long ago
burn v to destroy with fire
loss n something that was destroyed
decade n a period of ten years

Mastering the Question Type

3 The word "harshness" in the passage is closest in meaning to

- (A) ease
- (B) worry
- (C) severity
- (D) discipline

4 The phrase "recover from" in the passage is closest in meaning to

- (A) get better from
- (B) forget about
- (C) move on from
- (D) put out

Exercise 4 Read the following passage and answer the questions.

Time Limit: 30 sec.

The Brain and Computers

01-13

One day, humans will be able to control computers by thinking. People will not need a keyboard or a mouse. Scientists are developing ways to control computers with brainwaves. Korean researchers have made software that measures brain activity. When a person is relaxed, the brain is less active. The computer detects this. It then changes the graphics on a screen. Engineers call this a computer-brain interface. This is a direct link between the brain and a computer. Another researcher at MIT uses monkeys to map brain signals. For a monkey to grab food, its brain sends out electric signals to the arm. The researcher uses these signals to control a robotic arm. The robotic arm grabs the food before the monkey does.

General Comprehension

1 According to the passage, people will control computers in the future

(A) with keys
(B) with their brains
(C) with their eyes
(D) with their hands

2 What is a computer-brain interface?

(A) A way of looking at computers
(B) A screen that has a brain in its center
(C) A connection between the brain and a computer
(D) An electric signal that moves robot arms in a circle

Words & Phrases

brainwaves n electric signals in the brain

researcher n a person who studies something deeply

robotic adj related to robots

graphics n the visual aspect of computers

link n a connection; an association; a bond

map v to locate something in space

Mastering the Question Type

3 The word "detects" in the passage is closest in meaning to

(A) calls
(B) helps
(C) drives
(D) notices

4 The word "grabs" in the passage is closest in meaning to

(A) throws
(B) snatches
(C) attacks
(D) steals

Exercises with Mid-Length Passages

Exercise 1 Read the following passage and answer the questions.

Time Limit: 1 min. 30 sec.

The Wildlife Trade

01 - 14

The illegal wildlife trade involves billions of dollars worldwide each year. It is as serious as the drug and arms trades. It affects a number of species, including rhinos, elephants, tigers, snakes, birds, and turtles. Many are endangered, which means the species might vanish from the Earth.

The animals, or their parts, are often used as trophies, special foods, and exotic medicines. Many animals are losing their natural homes. There are a few reasons this is happening. Jungles are shrinking due to the growth of cities and towns. Wild areas become more accessible. Animals in forest then become easy targets for poachers. The problem is made worse because many police officers do not try to prevent illegal hunting. They do not have enough staff to deal with the issue. The greatest problem is demand. People from around the world still want these animals. They are happy to pay high prices for something special.

As long as people want to buy these products, poachers will hunt. Police must stop poaching. Countries should make greater efforts to preserve jungles. Lastly, cultures must change. People should believe that trading in wildlife is wrong.

1 The word "exotic" in the passage is closest in meaning to

- (A) unusual
- (B) distant
- (C) effective
- (D) expensive

2 The word "accessible" in the passage is closest in meaning to

- (A) understandable
- (B) reachable
- (C) enjoyable
- (D) acceptable

Words & Phrases

illegal adj not allowed by law

affect v to influence

vanish v to disappear

shrink v to get smaller

poacher n a person who hunts illegally

preserve v to keep; to maintain

Summary Note

Harm of the Illegal Wildlife Trade

Problems
- Many species endangered
- Shrinking jungles
- Lax police control
- High demand

Solutions
- Strong police crackdown
- Countries' efforts to protect jungles
- Changing of people's minds

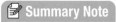

Exercise 2 Read the following passage and answer the questions.

Time Limit: 1 min. 50 sec.

Serengeti Animals

01 - 15

The Serengeti is an enormous plain in Africa. It is found in the countries of Tanzania and Kenya. It is primarily a grassland. It also contains some woodlands and mountains as well as rivers. It has an abundance of wild animals, too.

Most people know the Serengeti because of the vast migrations that take place there. Every year, enormous herds of wildebeests, zebras, and gazelles migrate in search of food and water. Around two million of these animals move from one place to another. But they are not the only grazing animals in the area. There are plenty of giraffes and elephants that live in the region, too.

Predators live there as well. There are numerous lion prides in the Serengeti. Leopards, hyenas, cheetahs, and even wild dogs are other hunters there. Crocodiles can be found in the rivers.

There are more than 500 species of birds living in the Serengeti. There are plenty of reptiles and amphibians. Insects are there in great numbers as well. Overall, the Serengeti has one of the most diverse animal populations in the world. This is especially true considering the number of large animals living there.

1 The word "vast" in the passage is closest in meaning to

Ⓐ huge
Ⓑ continual
Ⓒ risky
Ⓓ apparent

2 The word "diverse" in the passage is closest in meaning to

Ⓐ obvious
Ⓑ dangerous
Ⓒ varied
Ⓓ impressive

Words & Phrases

plain n a large, flat area of land with grasses but few trees

abundance n a large quantity or amount of something

migration n the movement of people or animals in search of food or a new home

predator n an animal that hunts other animals for food

pride n a group of lions

Summary Note

Live in plain in Tanzania and Kenya

Vast migrations of animals each year

Wildebeests, zebras, and gazelles

Serengeti Animals

Very diverse animal population

Many birds, reptiles, amphibians, and insects

Grazing animals as well as predators

Exercise 3 Read the following passage and answer the questions.

Time Limit: 1 min. 20 sec.

Droughts

01 - 16

A drought is a time when a region gets less precipitation than normal. This can be a lack of rain or snow. A drought can last for one or two seasons. It can also last for several years.

Some droughts are expected. For instance, there is a weather phenomenon called El Nino. It occurs every few years. It affects countries all around the Pacific Ocean. In an El Nino year, certain places may suffer from droughts. Other places, such as the American Southwest, have frequent droughts. This region is typically dry. So the people living there do not expect great amounts of rain. However, droughts can also be unexpected. Due to changing weather, some places that normally get plenty of rain may get little or none at times.

The effects of droughts are widespread. People have less water for drinking. Farmers have less water to use for their crops and animals. Lakes and ponds may evaporate. Rivers may become smaller. The ground itself can become very dry. In some instances, wind can blow dry soil away, causing even bigger problems.

1 The word "phenomenon" in the passage is closest in meaning to

- (A) event
- (B) standard
- (C) forecast
- (D) type

2 The word "evaporate" in the passage is closest in meaning to

- (A) expand
- (B) flow
- (C) dry up
- (D) move around

Words & Phrases

precipitation n rain, snow, ice, etc. that falls from the sky

suffer v to endure; to be exposed to

frequent adj common

typically adv usually; normally

unexpected adj not looked for; not predicted

widespread adj extended; spread out

Summary Note

Droughts

Meaning
- Time when a region gets less precipitation than normal

El Nino
- Weather phenomenon
- Can cause droughts around the world

Effects
- Less water for drinking
- Less water for crops and animals
- Lakes and ponds evaporate
- Soil becomes dry

Exercise 4 Read the following passage and answer the questions.

Time Limit: 1 min. 20 sec.

Water Power

01-17

Many civilizations developed by rivers. People used river water for drinking. They transported goods and people on rivers. They were also able to use energy that river water created. This water power, or hydropower, has been developed in many ways over time.

The ancient Greeks employed the power of running water around 2,000 years ago. They built mills by rivers. Running water powered the mills. They would then grind grain to turn it into flour. This type of technology was used for centuries by people in many different cultures. The ancient Egyptians also utilized water power. They used water screws to irrigate their fields. The water screws were much more efficient than having people carry buckets of water to pour in fields.

In recent times, water power has been used to create electricity. The first use of hydroelectric power happened in the United States. It was done in 1880. Since then, dams have been built across rivers around the world. Running water passes through turbines in the dams. These turbines spin and create electricity. The power created is both cheap and clean.

1 The word "employed" in the passage is closest in meaning to

- (A) hired
- (B) experienced
- (C) managed
- (D) used

2 The word "irrigate" in the passage is closest in meaning to

- (A) plant
- (B) water
- (C) harvest
- (D) sow

Words & Phrases

transport (v) to move or carry from one place to another

mill (n) a building where people turn grain into flour

grind (v) to turn into powder

efficient (adj) making good use of time or energy

dam (n) an obstruction across a river or stream

turbine (n) an engine that operates due to running water

Summary Note

Water Power

Ancient Times

- Used by ancient Greeks
- Used water for mills to grind grain
- Egyptians used water screws
- Irrigated fields with them

Recent Times

- Create electricity
- First used hydropower in 1880
- Many dams around the world now
- Create cheap and clean power

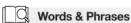

Building Summary Skills

A **Put the following sentences in order to make appropriate summaries based on the mid-length passages you worked on earlier. The first sentence is already provided.**

Exercise 1 The Wildlife Trade

1 The illegal wildlife trade is a big business and puts many animals in danger.
____ The greatest problem is that people continue to ask for animal products.
____ They feel special when they have rare animal parts and are happy to pay for them.
____ The places where they live are getting smaller, which makes them easier to catch.
____ Police cannot stop people from hunting.

Exercise 2 Serengeti Animals

1 There are many wild animals in the Serengeti in Africa.
____ There are also predators such as lions, leopards, hyenas, and cheetahs.
____ Other animals include birds, reptiles, amphibians, and insects.
____ Each year, millions of animals migrate in search of food and water.
____ These animals include wildebeests, zebras, and gazelles.

Exercise 3 Droughts

1 A drought is a time when there is less precipitation than normal.
____ The effects of droughts include less water for people and animals.
____ In other places, droughts are expected to occur.
____ El Nino is a weather phenomenon that causes droughts in some places.

Exercise 4 Water Power

1 People used the power of river water in the past.
____ The ancient Egyptians used water screws to irrigate their fields.
____ People use water power today to make electricity.
____ The ancient Greeks made mills by rivers to grind grain.
____ Dams make power that is cheap and clean.

B **Fill in the blanks with suitable words or phrases to complete the following summaries. Do not look at the previous page until you are finished.**

Exercise 1 The Wildlife Trade

The ______________ wildlife trade is a big business and puts many animals ______________. The places where they live are getting ______________, which makes them ______________ to catch. Police cannot stop people from ______________. The greatest problem is that people continue to ask for ______________. They feel ______________ when they have ______________ animal parts and are happy to pay for them.

Exercise 2 Serengeti Animals

There are many ______________ in the Serengeti in ______________. Each year, millions of animals ______________ in search of ______________. These animals include wildebeests, ______________, and gazelles. There are also ______________ such as lions, ______________, hyenas, and cheetahs. Other animals include birds, ______________, amphibians, and insects.

Exercise 3 Droughts

A drought is a time when there is less ______________ than ______________. It can last for a season or two or ______________. ______________ is a weather ______________ that causes droughts in some places. In other places, droughts are ______________ to occur. The ______________ of droughts include less water for ______________.

Exercise 4 Water Power

People used the power of ______________ in the past. The ______________ made mills by rivers to ______________ grain. The ancient Egyptians used ______________ to irrigate their ______________. People use water power today to make ______________. ______________ make power that is cheap and ______________.

Animal Smuggling

01-18

Recently, airport officials have been shocked by the growth of animal smuggling. They sometimes find live turtles, lizards, frogs, and snakes in passengers' carry-on bags. Smugglers use several tricks to bring animals through airports. They put live snakes into film boxes and birds into tennis ball cans. Police even found an iguana taped to a man's chest once. Not all animals are smuggled alive, however. Many die on the way. Animal body parts are also found. These include antlers, skins, dried organs, hooves, and feet.

2→ Animal smuggling happens because of people's interest in rare things. They believe that owning something rare makes them special. For decoration, people mount animal heads on walls. They buy furs to make rooms more lavish. Some believe that eating animal parts will make them strong. Tigers are highly desirable dead or alive. The fur, the skulls, the gall bladder, and the teeth are all used. No part of a tiger is wasted. Tiger bones are believed to cure arthritis. Tigers are sometimes caught in the wild, but many are not. They are easy to breed in captivity. They can be seen in small zoos and are found as private pets. Captive tigers are sold to people who are willing to pay good money for tiger parts.

3→ In 1975, there was a ban on the trade of rare species. It was endorsed by 136 countries. Animal smuggling is still a major problem though. It is the second-most lucrative business after drug smuggling. It harms individual creatures and wrecks the balance of nature. The diversity of species must be a priority for the next generation.

1 The word "These" in the passage refers to
Ⓐ Live snakes
Ⓑ Police
Ⓒ Not all animals
Ⓓ Animal body parts

2 The word "lavish" in the passage is closest in meaning to
Ⓐ warm
Ⓑ luxurious
Ⓒ desirable
Ⓓ darkish

3 The word "captivity" in the passage is closest in meaning to
Ⓐ confinement
Ⓑ protection
Ⓒ attention
Ⓓ wilderness

4 In paragraph 2, all of the following questions are answered EXCEPT:
Ⓐ What parts of a tiger's body do people use?
Ⓑ Where can many tigers be found?
Ⓒ Why does animal smuggling take place?
Ⓓ How much do some endangered animals cost?

5 In stating that the ban "was endorsed" by 136 countries, the author means that 136 countries
Ⓐ rejected it
Ⓑ praised it
Ⓒ approved it
Ⓓ implemented it

6 According to paragraph 3, what can be inferred about animal smuggling?
Ⓐ It will likely continue.
Ⓑ It is difficult to do.
Ⓒ Most countries support it.
Ⓓ Police participate in it.

The Flying Car

01 - 19

1→ Many people have dreamed about flying in the sky in their own flying cars. They think it would be wonderful to fly at will. They would not need to spend hours in traffic every day. They could also travel long distances very quickly. Since the Wright brothers built their airplane in 1903, several pioneers have worked to invent a flying car. According to car industry experts, the dream of flying cars will soon be reality.

2→ A talented engineer named Paul Moller invented such a car. Moller spent almost forty years and millions of dollars developing his prototype. The car has room for four people. It is designed to take off and land in small spaces and can fly as high as 10,000 meters. It uses four external engines to move up, down, and sideways. The car, unfortunately, is not fuel efficient. It does not get good mileage. Moller's car is guided by computers and satellite systems. In case of a crash, it has airbags and parachutes. He showed that a car could be built to fly.

3→ A flying-car society has many problems to solve. The first concerns safety. If there are no roads, what will stop people from crashing into one another? It is easy for a single car to travel, but what happens when there are thousands? Another issue is cost. At the moment, a single car costs several million dollars. Most people cannot afford to buy one. The third issue is fuel. There needs to be enough fuel to supply these cars. The fuel also needs to be less polluting than the kind being used now. Still, technology is advancing. It is likely that these problems will be solved in the future. Then, dreams of quick and easy flight will come true.

7 The word "pioneers" in the passage is closest in meaning to

Ⓐ diehards
Ⓑ innovators
Ⓒ ancestors
Ⓓ pilots

8 Which of the following can be inferred about flying cars from paragraph 1?

Ⓐ They offer a number of advantages over normal cars.
Ⓑ Many of them are already available for sale.
Ⓒ They are more difficult to drive than regular cars.
Ⓓ They do not have any gears for drivers to use.

9 The word "prototype" in the passage is closest in meaning to

Ⓐ product
Ⓑ model
Ⓒ engine
Ⓓ form

10 According to paragraph 2, which of the following is NOT true of Paul Moller?

Ⓐ He built a car that can fly 10,000 meters high.
Ⓑ His car cost millions of dollars to build.
Ⓒ He drives his flying car in cities.
Ⓓ He is employed as an engineer.

11 In paragraph 3, why does the author mention "safety"?

Ⓐ To discuss the cost of making flying cars safe
Ⓑ To bring up a problem with flying cars
Ⓒ To compare flying cars with airplanes
Ⓓ To prove that flying cars are not dangerous

12 According to paragraph 3, flying cars will exist one day because

Ⓐ technology will solve problems related to them
Ⓑ they will become much cheaper for people to buy
Ⓒ governments are supporting efforts to make them
Ⓓ most car manufacturers are trying to build them

Vocabulary Check-Up

Choose the words with the closest meanings to the highlighted words.

1 It takes a short time to transport goods by plane.

- (A) move
- (B) manufacture
- (C) use
- (D) acquire

2 The war may be disastrous in a couple of months.

- (A) frightened
- (B) fatal
- (C) confused
- (D) encouraging

3 People are creatures of feeling.

- (A) organizations
- (B) necessities
- (C) results
- (D) living beings

4 It is very important for people to know their physical conditions.

- (A) rational
- (B) conscious
- (C) bodily
- (D) mental

5 The doctor is a pioneer in the field of medicine.

- (A) tourist
- (B) innovator
- (C) representative
- (D) assistant

6 He is a frequent visitor at the local museum.

- (A) apparent
- (B) excited
- (C) interested
- (D) regular

7 There are some dangerous predators in the rainforest.

(A) traps
(B) animals
(C) humans
(D) hunters

8 This region gets a lot of precipitation in summer.

(A) wind
(B) rain
(C) sun
(D) clouds

9 Just eating corn does not provide much sustenance.

(A) nutrition
(B) damage
(C) control
(D) guidance

10 It took a lot of time to think about the price issue at the meeting.

(A) humor
(B) behavior
(C) matter
(D) information

UNIT

02 Reference

Overview

Introduction

Reference questions ask you to understand the relationship between the words in the passage. Usually, the relationship is between a pronoun and the word to which the pronoun refers. When you find a referring word or pronoun in the passage, you should find out whether the word is singular or plural and if it is male or female.

Question Types

- The word "X" in the passage refers to
- The phrase "X" in the passage refers to

Useful Tips

- The word to which a pronoun refers often appears before the pronoun in the same sentence.
- Substitute your answer for the highlighted word or phrase in the passage.
- Make sure that your answer is the same number—singular or plural—and case—first, second, or third person—as the highlighted pronoun.

Sample TOEFL iBT Question

Q The word "their" in the passage refers to

Ⓐ countries
Ⓑ the sea
Ⓒ crustaceans
Ⓓ traditional dishes

Crustaceans such as crabs, lobsters, and shrimp live in water and on land. They are easy to catch and to raise. This has allowed humans to use them as food sources. Countries along the sea use crustaceans as part of their traditional dishes. They are nutritious and easy to cook. They are also very tasty.

02-01

Correct Answer

The highlighted word *their* refers to the word *countries*, which is mentioned in the same sentence. So the correct answer is Ⓐ.

Basic Drill

Read the passages and answer the questions.

Skill & Tip Personal Pronouns

Personal pronouns are words which refer to someone—or sometimes something—previously mentioned in the passage. They include *I*, *you*, *he*, *she*, *it*, *we*, *they* and their derived forms (e.g., *me*, *yours*, *his*, *her*, *its*, *them*). On the TOEFL iBT, third-person pronouns such as *it*, *its*, *they*, *their*, and *them* are frequently asked.

Example

An auction is a popular way of buying and selling. It is a useful way to decide the values of things. E-Bay is a good example. On the Internet, buyers bid against one another to buy the items they want. Sellers can sell items at the highest prices that buyers will pay.

Q The word "they" in the passage refers to

Ⓐ the values
Ⓑ things
Ⓒ buyers
Ⓓ the items

Correct Answer Ⓒ

Drill 1

Anne Frank was a victim of World War II. She wrote a diary while hiding in a room from the Nazis. She was there for two years. Her writing shows how miserable life under the Nazis was. After she died, her father published Anne's diary, and it became one of the most widely read books in the world.

02-02

Q The word "it" in the passage refers to

Ⓐ a room
Ⓑ her writing
Ⓒ Anne's diary
Ⓓ the world

Drill 2

In the 1920s, jazz was not well known to white people. Louis Armstrong was a musician who made jazz known to them. At the age of fourteen, Louis learned to play the trumpet. He soon got jobs in nightclubs. His unique voice and brilliant trumpet playing attracted black and white fans. Jazz became famous to all audiences soon after.

02-03

Q The word "them" in the passage refers to

Ⓐ white people
Ⓑ nightclubs
Ⓒ black and white fans
Ⓓ all audiences

Skill & Tip Demonstratives

Demonstratives are pronouns or adjectives that point out which items are being referred to. They include *this, that, these,* and *those. This* and *these* refer to something or someone near to the speaker or writer. *That* and *those* refer to something or someone distant from the speaker or writer. Sometimes *the former* and *the latter* are asked on the TOEFL iBT.

Example

It was a difficult time. The southern states wanted to separate from the Union. President Abraham Lincoln was not happy. This would divide his country in two. He needed to find a way to make the states agree upon the issue of slavery. This was causing problems for the entire country.

Q The word "This" in the passage refers to

Ⓐ President Abraham Lincoln
Ⓑ His country
Ⓒ The issue of slavery
Ⓓ The entire country

Correct Answer Ⓒ

Drill 3

One day, Isaac Newton was sitting under a tree. He was thinking about how objects in the world were related to one another. This was nothing new. Newton often reflected upon these things. He was a physicist. Suddenly, the wind blew. An apple fell from the tree branch above him and hit him on the head. It shocked him into a series of thoughts that soon became the theory of gravity. This would change the world of science.

02-04

Q The word "This" in the passage refers to

Ⓐ The tree branch
Ⓑ The head
Ⓒ A series of thoughts
Ⓓ The theory of gravity

Drill 4

October 29, 1929, was a day when stock prices dropped. Investors panicked. They sold their stocks quickly. This became known as Black Tuesday. It was the first time in thirty years that the American economy had problems. People were afraid of losing money. Even worse, investing banks also lost all their money. Rich people became poor overnight.

02-05

Q The word "This" in the passage refers to

Ⓐ October 29, 1929
Ⓑ A day
Ⓒ America's economy
Ⓓ Money

Skill & Tip Relative Pronouns

Relative pronouns introduce a clause which modifies the noun right before them. The relative pronouns *which*, *that*, and *who* are frequently asked on the TOEFL iBT. *Who* refers to people and *which* to things; *that* refers to both. Sometimes, however, *which* can refer to the entire previous clause.

Example

Scientists have been looking for energy sources to replace oil. They have studied wind, ethanol, and nuclear energy. They have also started to look at coal again. Coal, which is the cheapest energy source, is found in many parts of the world. However, it can be dangerous to mine. It also pollutes the environment.

Q The word "which" in the passage refers to

Ⓐ wind
Ⓑ ethanol
Ⓒ nuclear energy
Ⓓ coal

Correct Answer Ⓓ

Drill 5

One of history's greatest composers was Wolfgang Amadeus Mozart. A child prodigy, he first began to write music when he was five years old. He composed music in many genres. These included operas, concertos, and symphonies. He composed *The Marriage of Figaro*, which is one of his most famous works.

02-06

Q The word "which" in the passage refers to

Ⓐ music
Ⓑ many genres
Ⓒ operas, concertos, and symphonies
Ⓓ *The Marriage of Figaro*

Drill 6

Taxes are a necessary part of society. They help fund schools and build roads. Last year, taxes, which were levied at a rate of twenty-five percent, caused many citizens to complain. These people felt taxes were too high. They wanted to be able to put more money into savings. They believed the government was not efficient.

02-07

Q The word "which" in the passage refers to

Ⓐ schools
Ⓑ roads
Ⓒ taxes
Ⓓ a rate of twenty-five percent

Skill & Tip Pronouns

Indefinite pronouns refer to an unknown or undetermined person, place, or thing. Indefinite pronouns include words with *some*, *any*, *every*, or *no* (e.g., *someone*, *anyone*, *everyone*, and *no one*) as well as *one*, *another*, *some*, *others*, *each*, all, and *none*.

Example

There are many members of an orchestra. All of them have their own parts to play. The first violins often play the basic melody. The cellos and the violas play the harmony. Of course, the bass and the tuba play the low notes. The clarinets and the flutes often play the incidental parts of the music. Together, the musicians make beautiful sounds.

Q The word "All" in the passage refers to

Ⓐ Many members
Ⓑ The first violins
Ⓒ The cellos
Ⓓ The clarinets

Correct Answer Ⓐ

Drill 7

The crisis at Three Mile Island was almost a huge nuclear disaster. This power plant provided electricity for thousands of people in Pennsylvania. One day, a valve failed to close. The core heated up for three days. It nearly exploded. Places around the plant were in great danger. So were local residents. Most of those within twenty miles would have died. It would have affected thousands of people.

02-08

Q The word "Most" in the passage refers to

Ⓐ Three days
Ⓑ Places around the plant
Ⓒ Local residents
Ⓓ Twenty miles

Drill 8

The Wizard of Oz is a famous movie. Its music is great. Millions of people grew up watching this movie on TV every year. Many of them can sing the songs. The most memorable song begins with the very simple phrase "Somewhere over the rainbow." Many Americans can finish the rest of the verse. Even though some cannot sing the remaining words in the verse, it is part of the fabric of culture in the United States.

02-09

Q The word "some" in the passage refers to

Ⓐ millions of people
Ⓑ the songs
Ⓒ many Americans
Ⓓ the remaining words

Exercises with Short Passages

Exercise 1 Read the following passage and answer the questions.

Time Limit: 40 sec.

Johann Sebastian Bach

02-10

1 → Johann Sebastian Bach lived from 1685 to 1750. A German, Bach was a brilliant musician. He could play the organ and the harpsichord. He was also one of the greatest composers of music in history. Bach was very prolific. He wrote hundreds of pieces of music. Some were for choirs. Some were for orchestras. And some were for various instruments, such as the organ.

2 → Bach wrote many religious works. He also wrote secular pieces. In fact, his *Brandenburg* concertos are among his most famous works. After Bach died, many people forgot about his music. Then, in the 1800s, his works were remembered. People began performing them again. Today, Bach is considered a musical genius. Along with Mozart and Beethoven, he is usually considered in the top tier of all composers.

General Comprehension

1 In paragraph 1, the author mentions "the organ and the harpsichord" as examples of

Ⓐ instruments Bach invented
Ⓑ instruments Bach wrote music for
Ⓒ instruments Bach did not care for
Ⓓ instruments Bach could play

2 In paragraph 2, the author's description of Bach mentions which of the following?

Ⓐ The title of a religious work he made
Ⓑ Works of his that are well done
Ⓒ The composers that he helped train
Ⓓ The reason people forgot about his music

Words & Phrases

brilliant adj outstanding
harpsichord n a medieval instrument similar to the piano
choir n a group of singers that sing together
orchestra n a group of musicians that play together
genius n a very intelligent or talented person

Mastering the Question Type

3 The word "some" in the passage refers to

Ⓐ pieces of music
Ⓑ choirs
Ⓒ orchestras
Ⓓ various instruments

4 The word "he" in the passage refers to

Ⓐ Bach
Ⓑ a musical genius
Ⓒ Mozart
Ⓓ Beethoven

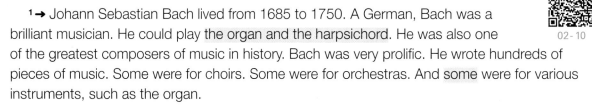

Exercise 2 Read the following passage and answer the questions.

Time Limit: 30 sec.

Hadrian's Wall

02-11

1→ In 43 A.D., the Roman Empire invaded the British Isles. The Romans spent many years there before they controlled the southern parts of the land. However, they could not conquer all of Britain. In addition, barbarians from the north often attacked the Romans. As a result, Emperor Hadrian decided to build a wall to keep them from attacking.

2→ In 122 A.D., construction on the wall began. It would extend from one side of Britain to the other. It was seventy-three miles long. It was ten to twenty feet thick and roughly the same height. The wall, called Hadrian's Wall, divided the country. Up to 10,000 Roman soldiers guarded the wall. It helped prevent invasions from the north during the time the Romans ruled Britain.

General Comprehension

1 According to paragraph 1, why did the Romans build a wall in Britain?

(A) To protect them from barbarians
(B) To help them conquer the land
(C) To keep their cities safe
(D) To use as a place to keep soldiers

2 According to paragraph 2, which of the following is true of Hadrian's Wall?

(A) It took more than ten years to build.
(B) It had walls up to twenty feet thick.
(C) It required 10,000 soldiers to build.
(D) It was finished in the year 122 A.D.

Words & Phrases

conquer v to defeat, often in battle
barbarian n an uncivilized person
extend v to spread; to stretch out
roughly adv about; around

Mastering the Question Type

3 The word "them" in the passage refers to

(A) the British Isles
(B) the southern parts of the land
(C) barbarians
(D) the Romans

4 The word "It" in the passage refers to

(A) One side of Britain
(B) The same height
(C) Hadrian's Wall
(D) The country

Exercise 3 Read the following passage and answer the questions.

Time Limit: 40 sec.

The New Deal

02-12

1→ The New Deal was designed by President Roosevelt in the 1930s. He wanted to help people who were suffering in the Great Depression. Millions of people were poor. The banking system was not reliable. In fact, it was failing. Roosevelt wanted to help the poor. He also wanted to improve the economy. Most of all, he wanted to prevent future problems.

2→ The New Deal included work programs. It gave jobs to people in cities and in the countryside. It also included Social Security. This was a type of insurance that gave poor people money when they were too old to work. If a worker lost his job, the person got unemployment insurance. To make banks safe, the New Deal provided deposit insurance. People received money from the government if the bank lost theirs. These steps put people on their feet again.

General Comprehension

1 According to paragraph 1, what was the New Deal?

Ⓐ A series of government programs to help the economy
Ⓑ A series of taxes to make the government rich
Ⓒ A way to make insurance companies rich
Ⓓ A way to make a business deal with banks

2 According to paragraph 2, the New Deal helped poor people

Ⓐ by giving them insurance money if they lost their jobs
Ⓑ by giving them a chance to buy food stamps
Ⓒ by giving them new types of clothing
Ⓓ by giving them houses to live in

Words & Phrases

reliable adj dependable; trustworthy
economy n the system of buying and selling
include v to contain
unemployment n a time when a person has no work
put someone on his or her feet phr to give someone the ability to support himself or herself

Mastering the Question Type

3 The word "it" in the passage refers to

Ⓐ the Great Depression
Ⓑ the banking system
Ⓒ the poor
Ⓓ the economy

4 The word "This" in the passage refers to

Ⓐ The New Deal
Ⓑ The countryside
Ⓒ Social Security
Ⓓ Money

Exercise 4 Read the following passage and answer the questions.

Time Limit: 30 sec.

Trade Routes

02-13

1➔ People have often traded with individuals in different cultures. Trade helps people obtain the items they both need and desire. In the past, merchants often rode in wagons from one place to another. Most of the time, they took the same routes to get to their destinations. Over time, they established trade routes.

Trade routes were various paths or roads—both on land and water—merchants took. One of the most famous trades routes is the Silk Road. It existed many centuries ago. It started in China and crossed Asia, the Middle East, and parts of Europe. It ended at Rome during the time of the Roman Empire. Trade routes could often be perilous. However, many local rulers protected the areas near them. This let merchants feel safe and want to trade with them.

General Comprehension

1 According to paragraph 1, which of the following is true of merchants in the past?

(A) They were from the same culture.
(B) They became very wealthy.
(C) They created trade routes.
(D) They made the goods they sold.

2 The word "perilous" in the passage is closest in meaning to

(A) long
(B) difficult
(C) dangerous
(D) hidden

Words & Phrases

merchant n a person who buys and sells goods
wagon n a four-wheeled cart used to carry things
destination n the place where a person is going
century n a period of 100 years
protect v to keep safe

Mastering the Question Type

3 The word "they" in the passage refers to

(A) merchants
(B) wagons
(C) their destinations
(D) trade routes

4 The word "It" in the passage refers to

(A) The Silk Road
(B) China
(C) The Middle East
(D) Europe

Exercises with Mid-Length Passages

Exercise 1 Read the following passage and answer the questions.

Time Limit: 1 min. 40 sec.

The Laser

02-14

The laser is one of the major achievements of the twentieth century. It was invented in 1958. It was made possible by theories developed by Albert Einstein. It is used in most sectors of society and is one of the most useful technologies.

Laser light is very different from normal light bulbs. It works by sending out a single color of light in one direction. Light bulbs send out light in a wide spectrum in all directions. The beam from a small laser pointer is much brighter than that of the light bulb. This intense energy has many uses.

Millions of lasers are sold each year. They are used in fiber optics to send information. They are used to record DVDs and CDs. They are found in computer CD/DVD-ROM drives. Lasers are also used for cutting and burning. Doctors use them to correct vision. Industries use them to cut metal. Builders use them to measure and create level surfaces. Police use lasers to clock how fast people drive. Lastly, lasers are used as visual effects in concerts. Lasers have influenced the way people live, work, and play. They remain a promising technology for the future.

1 The word "It" in the passage refers to

Ⓐ The laser
Ⓑ The twentieth century
Ⓒ 1958
Ⓓ Society

2 The word "that" in the passage refers to

Ⓐ a single color
Ⓑ a wide spectrum
Ⓒ the beam
Ⓓ a small laser pointer

Words & Phrases

major adj significant; important
sector n a division of society
spectrum n a range; a distribution
intense adj strong; concentrated
measure v to assess; to calculate
level adj flat

Summary Note

Laser

Invented in 1958

Characteristics of lasers
- A single-colored light
- Brighter than normal light

Used in computers, buildings, medicines, law enforcement, and manufacturing

Exercise 2 Read the following passage and answer the questions.

Time Limit: 1 min. 20 sec.

Billboard Magazine

02-15

Billboard is a famous music magazine. It is highly influential. It collects sales data from music stores and radio stations. It then writes charts of the most popular music sales. It publishes these charts every week.

Billboard magazine appeared in 1894. It was eight pages long and sold for ten cents. At first, it was not about music. It was used to promote local shows and events. The articles now inform music professionals. However, the charts are used by everyone. The *Billboard Hot 100* has been around since 1958. It is the most famous chart. People can find the top 100 songs in the United States. This list provides the news about hit songs, video releases, and music trends.

The company covers many aspects of music. It deals with CD and DVD sales. It also sells Internet music downloads. A few years ago, it started *Billboard Hot Ringtones*. This allows phone users to download any song on the *Billboard* charts. The magazine is aware of trends. It keeps finding ways to modernize itself to remain successful.

1 The word "It" in the passage refers to
- (A) *Billboard* magazine
- (B) Music
- (C) The *Billboard Hot 100*
- (D) The most famous chart

2 The word "This" in the passage refers to
- (A) The company
- (B) *Billboard Hot Ringtones*
- (C) Any song
- (D) The magazine

Words & Phrases

influential adj powerful; important
publish v to print for public reading
cover v to address; to investigate
trend n a fashion or current style
modernize v to become useful in the present time

Summary Note

***Billboard* Magazine**

Introduced in 1894	Used for promotion of local shows and events	Created the *Billboard Hot 100* in 1958	Selling music on CDs, on the Internet, and with *Billboard Hot Ringtones*

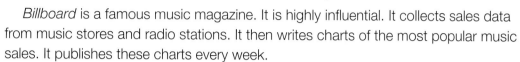

Exercise 3 Read the following passage and answer the questions.

Time Limit: 50 sec.

Amerigo Vespucci

02-16

Most people know that Christopher Columbus discovered America. Yet he believed that he had reached a part of India. Of course, this was not the case. Amerigo Vespucci was the first person from Europe to assert that it was not India. For this reason, America was named after him.

Vespucci was born in Italy in 1454. He spent half of his life as a businessman. In his forties, he moved to Spain. He became the director of a shipping company. He helped Columbus prepare for his second voyage to the New World. This gave Vespucci a chance to go to the New World.

In 1502, Vespucci discovered land. He believed it was a new continent, not a part of Asia. In 1507, a mapmaker suggested calling the new lands "America" in honor of Vespucci. His name was given to both North and South America. He died of malaria in 1512. However, his legacy remains.

1 The word "it" in the first paragraph refers to

Ⓐ America
Ⓑ a part
Ⓒ Europe
Ⓓ India

2 The word "it" in the third paragraph refers to

Ⓐ Vespucci
Ⓑ land
Ⓒ a new continent
Ⓓ Asia

Words & Phrases

assert v to share one's opinion
spend v to pass the time
in one's forties phr between the ages of forty and forty-nine
voyage n a long journey on a ship
continent n a large land mass

Summary Note

Amerigo Vespucci

- Born in Italy but moved to Spain
- Ran a shipping company and sailed to the New World
- Found out that the new land was not India in 1502
- Had the New World named after him in 1507
- Died of malaria in 1512

Exercise 4 Read the following passage and answer the questions.

Time Limit: 1 min. 40 sec.

Canals

02-17

A canal is a manmade waterway that connects two bodies of water. These bodies of water can be oceans, seas, rivers, or lakes. Ships use canals to travel from one body of water to another. Some canals are also used to bring water to farmers' fields. Others drain areas that have too much water.

In the past couple of centuries, many canals have been built. Some have had extensive economic effects on regions. In the early 1800s, the Erie Canal was built. It connected the Atlantic Ocean with the Great Lakes in the American Midwest. It enabled people to move goods quickly by water. In addition, lots of people used the canal to settle new lands.

Later in the 1800s, the Suez Canal was completed. It connected the Mediterranean Sea and the Red Sea. The Red Sea emptied into the Indian Ocean. It allowed ships to travel quickly from Europe to Asia. In the past, they had to travel all the way around Africa. Thanks to the Suez Canal, they could complete their journeys much more quickly. In the early 1900s, the Panama Canal connected the Atlantic and Pacific oceans. It made ocean travel much swifter.

1 The word "It" in the passage refers to

Ⓐ The Erie Canal
Ⓑ The Atlantic Ocean
Ⓒ The American Midwest
Ⓓ Water

2 The word "they" in the passage refers to

Ⓐ the 1800s
Ⓑ the Mediterranean Sea and the Red Sea
Ⓒ ships
Ⓓ their journeys

Words & Phrases

drain v to remove liquid from a place
extensive adj widespread
settle v to move to a place to live there
journey n a trip, often a long one
swift adj fast

Summary Note

Canals

- Connect two waterways
- Used for transportation and watering crops
- Erie Canal connected Atlantic Ocean and Great Lakes
- Suez Canal connected Europe and Asia
- Panama Canal connected Atlantic and Pacific oceans

Building Summary Skills

A **Put the following sentences in order to make appropriate summaries based on the mid-length passages you worked on earlier. The first sentence is already provided.**

Exercise 1 The Laser

1 Albert Einstein's theories made the laser possible.
_____ It is used in computer drives, in factories, in doctors' offices, and in police departments for measuring.
_____ It is also used for visual effects in shows.
_____ Lasers are different from light bulbs because laser light only goes one way with only one color.
_____ The laser has many applications.

Exercise 2 *Billboard* Magazine

1 *Billboard* magazine writes charts about music sales, and it posts the most popular songs in the United States.
_____ Even now, the company continues to modernize, and it sells music downloads.
_____ The magazine started in 1894, but it just advertised shows and events.
_____ It also started a new feature, *Hot Ringtones*, so people's phones can sound like their favorite songs.
_____ Then, it started writing about music.

Exercise 3 Amerigo Vespucci

1 North and South America were named after Amerigo Vespucci because he learned that this land was not India.
_____ Even though Vespucci died in 1512, his name is remembered forever.
_____ A mapmaker suggested calling the New World "America."
_____ This was to honor Vespucci's efforts.
_____ Vespucci moved to Spain to work for a shipping company, and he decided to sail to the New World.

Exercise 4 Canals

1 Canals are manmade waterways connecting two bodies of water.
_____ Then, the Panama Canal connected the Atlantic and Pacific oceans.
_____ Later, the Suez Canal connected Europe and Asia.
_____ Ships often use them to transport goods.
_____ In the 1800s, many people used the Erie Canal.

B **Fill in the blanks with suitable words or phrases to complete the following summaries. Do not look at the previous page until you are finished.**

Exercise 1 The Laser

__________ theories made the laser possible. Lasers are different from __________ because laser light only goes __________ with only __________. The laser has many __________. It is used in __________, in factories, in doctors' offices, and in police departments for __________. It is also used for __________ in shows.

Exercise 2 *Billboard* Magazine

Billboard magazine writes charts about __________, and it posts the __________ songs in the United States. The magazine started in __________, but it just __________ shows and events. Then, it started __________ about music. Even now, the company continues to __________, and it sells __________. It also started a new feature, *Hot Ringtones*, so people's __________ can sound like their favorite songs.

Exercise 3 Amerigo Vespucci

North and South America was __________ after Amerigo Vespucci because he learned that this land was not __________. Vespucci moved to __________ to work for a __________ company, and he decided to sail to the __________. A __________ suggested calling the New World "__________." This was to __________ Vespucci's efforts. Even though Vespucci died in __________, his name is remembered forever.

Exercise 4 Canals

Canals are manmade __________ connecting two bodies of water. __________ often use them to __________. In the __________, many people used the __________. Later, the __________ connected Europe and __________. Then, the __________ connected the Atlantic and __________ oceans.

Mini TOEFL iBT Practice Test

The History of Greek Influence

02-18

Greece is a beautiful country in the south of Europe. It used to be called Hellas in ancient times. Greece is believed to be the birthplace of European civilization. Its culture has had a great influence on Europe and the Middle East.

Greece's past stretches back over thousands of years. Greek culture started in Crete in 3000 B.C. The culture's Golden Age lasted from 600 to 400 B.C. Many famous thinkers, including Socrates and Plato, lived during that time. Greece had great power. It had colonies all over the Mediterranean Sea. These were found in southern France, Spain, North Africa, and Italy.

3→ From 500 to 336 B.C., Greece was made up of around 300 small city-states. Athens and Sparta were two of the most powerful. Their governments were similar, but their ways of life were very different. Sparta was very focused on war but was happy to keep to itself. Athens was focused on art and education but wanted to rule the entire country. Of course, this led to many wars, especially against Sparta. In the end, Sparta won the battles.

4→ After that, Roman armies and Greek armies often fought. In 146 B.C., the Romans conquered Greece. Ironically, this allowed the Greeks to change Roman life. They influenced Roman art and ideas. This mix of cultures eventually became the basis of European culture. When the Romans moved through Europe, they brought Greek culture with them. A thousand years later, Greek ideas were revisited in Europe. This was a time when artists and thinkers studied Greek and Roman ideas. Architecture was one topic. Literature and art were two others. Politics was also studied. The term "democracy" comes from Greek. It meant power to the people. Today, most countries in Europe are democracies. It is a powerful political system thanks to the Greeks.

1 The word "ancient" in the passage is closest in meaning to

Ⓐ friendly
Ⓑ anxious
Ⓒ peaceful
Ⓓ old

2 The word "These" in the passage refers to

Ⓐ Many famous thinkers
Ⓑ Socrates and Plato
Ⓒ Colonies
Ⓓ Southern France, Spain, North Africa, and Italy

3 In paragraph 3, why does the author mention "Athens and Sparta"?

Ⓐ To discuss famous people from them
Ⓑ To describe their governments
Ⓒ To focus on their geographic locations
Ⓓ To name two Greek city-states

4 The word "conquered" in the passage is closest in meaning to

Ⓐ befriended
Ⓑ defeated
Ⓒ copied
Ⓓ attacked

5 According to paragraph 4, what can be inferred about the Romans?

Ⓐ Without them, the Greek influence would not have been as strong today.
Ⓑ The Greeks relied on them for the strength they gave to their country.
Ⓒ The Greeks needed to give them ideas on art.
Ⓓ They had a very powerful military.

6 In paragraph 4, all of the following questions are answered EXCEPT:

Ⓐ What was the time when Greek ideas were revisited called?
Ⓑ What did the Romans take throughout Europe?
Ⓒ What happened to Greece in 146 B.C.?
Ⓓ What language does the term "democracy" come from?

The Euro: A Common Currency

02-19

Euro coins and paper bills

The euro was highly debated in Europe. People asked if many countries should use the same currency. Common money is a symbol of common culture. Many people in Europe did not agree with this idea. They worried about a loss of national identity. They also thought that one country's economy would affect the other ones. For instance, people thought that inflation in Italy might affect the French economy.

2 → In 1999, twelve European countries united under the euro. It benefits citizens and companies. When citizens travel within the euro area, they do not need to change money. They are able to compare prices easily. They also do not need to worry about exchange rates. The united currency helps trade grow. It plays a major role in forming a European single market. In this way, Europeans can compete with the United States and Asian countries.

3 → The euro is managed by the European System of Central Banks (ESCB). The ESCB makes banknotes and coins. All banknotes have the same design regardless of country. Only a country code is printed on one side of the banknotes. Each coin has one common side. The other is a national side. The national sides of the coins are designed by each member country. They use unique national symbols. The designs were chosen through a public survey.

4 → The euro was adopted on January 1, 2002. Belgium, Germany, Greece, Italy, Spain, France, Ireland, Luxembourg, the Netherlands, Austria, Portugal, and Finland all ratified it. England chose not to accept it. Now, the euro is a part of the daily lives of 300 million Europeans. Their unity gives them enough economic power to compete with larger countries.

7 The word "debated" in the passage is closest in meaning to

Ⓐ welcomed
Ⓑ opposed
Ⓒ discussed
Ⓓ persuaded

8 In paragraph 2, the author's description of the euro mentions all of the following EXCEPT:

Ⓐ Some of its benefits
Ⓑ Its value in comparison to the dollar
Ⓒ The number of countries that use it
Ⓓ Its importance to a single European market

9 The word "managed" in the passage is closest in meaning to

Ⓐ produced
Ⓑ controlled
Ⓒ used
Ⓓ designed

10 In paragraph 3, which of the following can be inferred about the euro?

Ⓐ Its value can be changed by the ESCB.
Ⓑ Euro banknotes all mostly look the same.
Ⓒ There are more euro coins than banknotes.
Ⓓ Its value is different throughout Europe.

11 The word "it" in the passage refers to

Ⓐ the euro
Ⓑ Belgium
Ⓒ England
Ⓓ their unity

12 According to paragraph 4, what happened in 2002?

Ⓐ The dollar was replaced by the euro.
Ⓑ Many countries accepted the euro.
Ⓒ Asian countries started trading the euro.
Ⓓ England agreed to use the euro.

Vocabulary Check-Up

Choose the words with the closest meanings to the highlighted words.

1 The flight went swifter than they had expected.

Ⓐ quieter
Ⓑ safer
Ⓒ faster
Ⓓ smoother

2 This merchant deals in imported goods.

Ⓐ vendor
Ⓑ customer
Ⓒ manufacturer
Ⓓ clerk

3 The price of the goods includes shipping and handling.

Ⓐ contains
Ⓑ accepts
Ⓒ mentions
Ⓓ occurs

4 A powerful earthquake caused many buildings to crumble last night.

Ⓐ colorful
Ⓑ vulnerable
Ⓒ exhausted
Ⓓ forceful

5 Humidity is the measuring of moisture in the atmosphere.

Ⓐ concluding
Ⓑ refusing
Ⓒ estimating
Ⓓ decreasing

6 The van travels at a maximum speed of 140 kilometers an hour.

Ⓐ saves
Ⓑ moves
Ⓒ catches
Ⓓ communicates

7 The new edition of this book will be published soon.

(A) expended
(B) separated
(C) printed
(D) operated

8 The country extends from one ocean to another.

(A) moves
(B) stretches
(C) conquers
(D) travels

9 The old movie was creative and unique.

(A) uncommon
(B) regular
(C) fair
(D) complete

10 The country stretches for almost three million square kilometers.

(A) removes
(B) settles
(C) drops
(D) extends

UNIT

03 Factual Information

Overview

Introduction

Factual Information questions ask you to identify specific information that is clearly mentioned in the passage. This is one of the most frequent question types. You need to find the right spot in the passage that has the information about which the question asks within a short time period.

Question Types

- ◆ According to the passage, which of the following is true of X?
- ◆ According to paragraph X, who [when, where, what, how, why] . . . ?
- ◆ The author's description of X mentions which of the following?
- ◆ According to the paragraph, X occurred because
- ◆ Select the TWO answer choices from paragraph 1 that identify X. *To receive credit, you must select TWO answers.*

Useful Tips

- ➤ Read the questions first to know what exactly is being asked.
- ➤ Scan the passage to find out where the relevant specific information is in the passage.
- ➤ Remove the choices that are not relevant to the passage.
- ➤ Do not choose an answer just because it is mentioned in the passage.

Sample TOEFL iBT Question

Q According to the passage, which of the following is true of Tolstoy?

Ⓐ He was in the army for a while.
Ⓑ He was an idealist.
Ⓒ He explained how the poor behaved.
Ⓓ He spent his time helping rich people.

03-01

Leo Tolstoy was a realist. He felt it was his duty to write about the social and political issues of his time. Many of his books do just that. He described how the Russian nobles behaved toward the poor people around them. In many cases, Tolstoy used examples from his own life. He was also a rich noble. He was able to write sharp descriptions of war. He served in the army for some time. In his heart, he wanted to help the poor people of his country and stop war.

Correct Answer

The question is about Tolstoy. You need to find out what specific information is mentioned about him in the passage. Then, remove choices that give information that is not true. So the correct answer is Ⓐ. The passage does not mention the rest of the choices.

Basic Drill

Read the passages and answer the questions. You can use the keywords highlighted in the questions to scan for the answers in the passages.

Skill & Tip

Factual Information questions ask you to identify facts, details, and other information that are explicitly mentioned in the passage. The information is usually found in just one or two sentences of the text. So you can find the correct answer without even reading the entire passage. The correct answer is paraphrased in one of sentences in the passage.

Example

Meteoroids are large bodies that float in space. These bodies are larger than dust but smaller than ten meters across. **When a meteoroid enters the Earth's atmosphere, it heats up. The gas all around it starts to glow.** We see this on the Earth and call it a shooting star. Scientists say that between 1,000 and more than 10,000 tons of meteoroids fall on the Earth every day.

Q According to the passage, which of the following is true of meteoroids?

Ⓐ Meteoroids are the same as space dust.
Ⓑ Meteoroids are too tiny to be seen.
Ⓒ Meteoroids get hot when they hit the Earth's atmosphere.
Ⓓ Meteoroids never fall on the Earth.

Correct Answer Ⓒ

Drill 1

The people of ancient Egypt believed that a dead person moved on to another world. So they wanted to prepare the dead for the afterlife. They tried to use various methods to make dead bodies last for a long time. One way was to make a mummy. The Egyptians dried out the dead body and wrapped it with cloth. This stopped bacteria and fungi from growing.

03-02

Q Why did the ancient Egyptians create mummies?

Ⓐ To prepare the dead for the next world
Ⓑ To show off their wrapping ability
Ⓒ To follow the wills of dead people
Ⓓ To save time and money

Drill 2

Franz Schubert, an Austrian composer, was a musical genius. He was a master of writing short pieces. He began composing when he was only thirteen. Some of his most famous works were written in his teens. He died at the age of thirty-one, but he left more than 600 beautiful pieces. In life, he received little recognition. Schubert remained poor while he was alive.

03-03

Q Which of the following is true of Franz Schubert?

Ⓐ He began composing at the age of thirty-one.
Ⓑ He was good at composing short works.
Ⓒ He wrote more than 600 works in his teens.
Ⓓ He gained popularity during his life.

Drill 3

Galileo Galilei was an Italian astronomer. He was also a physicist and philosopher. He loved to watch the night sky. He was one of the first people to make a telescope. He designed more than sixty of them. The first ones had little power. It was difficult to see through them. He always wanted to make them stronger and clearer. His devices greatly helped people's understanding of the heavens.

03-04

Q According to the passage, Galileo made many telescopes to

Ⓐ give them as gifts
Ⓑ improve them
Ⓒ sell them to customers
Ⓓ help people understand science

Drill 4

Asia is the largest land mass on the Earth. It contains one-third of the world's land. Much of the land is uninhabited. But Asia still holds more than sixty percent of the world's people. It has forty-eight different countries, including China and India. They are the most populous countries in the world. Asia is also the birthplace of the world's five major religions. They are Hinduism, Buddhism, Judaism, Christianity, and Islam.

03-05

Q According to the passage, which of the following is true of Asia?

Ⓐ It is the largest continent on the Earth.
Ⓑ One-third of the world's population lives there.
Ⓒ It takes up sixty percent of the world's land mass.
Ⓓ It is the home of forty-eight different religions.

Drill 5

The modern world began with the Renaissance. It means "rebirth" in French. It started in Italy in the fourteenth century. It was a time of great cultural and intellectual change. Thinkers took old ideas from the Greeks and the Romans and modernized them. This time period changed many people's beliefs. New ideas were expressed through art, literature, and architecture.

03-06

Q According to the passage, what did the Renaissance accomplish?

Ⓐ It made modern society come to an end.
Ⓑ It caused a rebirth of ideas.
Ⓒ It made people move to Italy.
Ⓓ It prevented the chance for intellectual growth.

Exercises with Short Passages

Exercise 1 Read the following passage and answer the questions.

Time Limit: 50 sec.

The *Gemini* Program

03-07

In the 1960s, the American space program was preparing to visit the moon. However, it needed more information before it could send astronauts there. It also needed more experience. So NASA, the American space agency, ran the *Gemini* Program. It lasted from 1965 to 1966. A total of twelve missions went into space. Each mission was crewed by two astronauts. The *Gemini* astronauts did many activities. They did the first spacewalk. Some astronauts stayed in orbit for more than one week. Two *Gemini* capsules even met each other in orbit. They gained plenty of knowledge for the American space program. They also prepared the way for the *Apollo* astronauts. Just a few years later, the astronauts on *Apollo 11* would be the first men on the moon.

General Comprehension

1 The word "It" in the passage refers to

- (A) The American space program
- (B) The moon
- (C) More information
- (D) More experience

2 According to the passage, what can be inferred about *Apollo 11*?

- (A) It used knowledge learned from the *Gemini* program.
- (B) It was in space for more than two weeks.
- (C) It used a more powerful rocket than the *Gemini* missions did.
- (D) It had some astronauts who flew *Gemini* missions on it.

Words & Phrases

astronaut n a person who travels to outer space

agency n a group or organization

mission n a task which a person or group does

crew v to work on a ship, airplane, spaceship, etc.

spacewalk n the act of leaving a spaceship to go out into space

capsule n a small vehicle used for spaceflight

Mastering the Question Type

3 In the passage, the author's description of the *Gemini* program mentions which of the following?

- (A) The names of some of its astronauts
- (B) The lengths of its missions
- (C) The number of missions in it
- (D) The cost of each mission

4 According to the passage, which of the following is true of the *Gemini* program?

- (A) It was the first to send astronauts into space.
- (B) It helped launch some satellites into orbit.
- (C) It took some astronauts close to the moon.
- (D) It acquired knowledge for the *Apollo* program.

Exercise 2 Read the following passage and answer the questions.

Time Limit: 40 sec.

A Robotic Astronaut

03-08

1→ Robots are replacing people in many jobs. They are used in the car industry. However, people often complain that they take needed jobs away from workers. But there is one place where robots are welcome to do work.

2→ A robot astronaut was developed by NASA. It is called Robonaut. Robonauts look like humans. However, they have more flexible arms and hands than humans. They can do some of the more difficult work in space. Robonauts are expected to work with human astronauts in future missions. They need no spacesuits, oxygen, or meals to survive in space. Humans need air to breathe and protection from extreme temperature changes. Most importantly, Robonauts will be sent where astronauts cannot go yet because the risks are too high.

General Comprehension

1 According to paragraph 1, how do people feel about robots?

- (A) They do not like how robots take jobs.
- (B) They do not want Robonauts to hurt astronauts.
- (C) They think robots can provide a lot of assistance.
- (D) They want robots to replace astronauts.

2 The word "extreme" in the passage is closest in meaning to

- (A) various
- (B) distant
- (C) radical
- (D) unreasonable

Words & Phrases

replace v to take the place of

complain v to say one is unhappy

flexible adj able to bend

survive v to continue to live

protection n defense; safety

risk n danger

Mastering the Question Type

3 In paragraph 1, the author's description of robots mentions which of the following?

- (A) Why they are popular
- (B) Where they are used
- (C) Who invented them
- (D) How they are made

4 According to paragraph 2, what is one advantage of Robonauts?

- (A) They do not need food or oxygen to survive in space.
- (B) They do not need extra fuel to keep working in space.
- (C) They resemble humans in appearance.
- (D) They were developed by NASA, which ensures their quality.

Exercise 3 Read the following passage and answer the questions.

Time Limit: 50 sec.

Making Prints

03-09

There were two popular techniques to make prints in the 1600s. They were engraving and etching. Engraving was an older method. It involved cutting lines on to a copper plate with a tool called a burin. It was a steel rod with a sharp end. Little slivers of metal would rise from the plate and had to be carefully removed. Then, the plate would be inked and paper set down on top to make the print. The resulting print had neat lines. Etching was different. First, a copper plate was coated with resin or wax. Then, the artist scratched a picture into the resin with a needle. This exposed the copper only in the scratches. Finally, the plate was given an acid bath, which ate at the metal, causing a more irregular line. The plate would then be inked for the print.

General Comprehension

1 The word "It" in the passage refers to

(A) Etching
(B) Engraving
(C) A copper plate
(D) A burin

2 The phrase "ate at" in the passage is closest in meaning to

(A) dissolved
(B) bent
(C) thinned
(D) corroded

Words & Phrases

method (n) a systematic way of doing things
sliver (n) a thin piece
remove (v) to get rid of
resin (n) a sticky substance found in some plants
expose (v) to uncover

Mastering the Question Type

3 According to the passage, what were two printing techniques in the 1600s?

(A) Inking and pressing
(B) Coating and waxing
(C) Engraving and etching
(D) Etching and scratching

4 Select the TWO answer choices from the passage that identify items used for etching. *To receive credit, you must select TWO answers.*

(A) A steel rod
(B) Wax
(C) Resin
(D) A metal burin

Exercise 4 Read the following passage and answer the questions.

Time Limit: 50 sec.

Stained-Glass Windows

03-10

1→ Stained glass is made of colored glass. The glass is colored when various metallic salts are added to it. For instance, cobalt creates blue glass while gold creates red glass. In the Middle Ages, stained glass was very popular. It was often found in the windows of churches and cathedrals.

2→ In medieval times, most of the population was illiterate. So they were unable to read. As a result, stained-glass windows often featured stories from the Bible. They allowed people to learn about religion without having to read anything. The height of medieval stained-glass windows was in the eleventh and twelfth centuries. The abbey at St. Denis in France had numerous stained-glass windows. They were famous around Europe during that time. Many cathedrals, especially in France and England, featured stained-glass windows of their own. When sunlight shone on them, they created beautiful images.

General Comprehension

1 In paragraph 1, the author uses "gold" as an example of

Ⓐ a valuable metal in medieval times
Ⓑ an element that could be colored blue
Ⓒ something that could give color to glass
Ⓓ a metal that was often found in Europe

2 The word "illiterate" in the passage is closest in meaning to

Ⓐ unpleasant
Ⓑ unknown
Ⓒ uncivilized
Ⓓ uneducated

Words & Phrases

metallic adj being made of metal
cobalt n a type of metallic element
cathedral n a very large church, often in the Catholic Church
feature v to portray; to show; to picture
medieval adj relating to the Middle Ages
image n a picture

Mastering the Question Type

3 According to paragraph 1, which of the following is true of stained glass?

Ⓐ It was often used in windows in churches.
Ⓑ It was developed during the Middle Ages.
Ⓒ It was more expensive to make than regular glass.
Ⓓ It required special skills in order to make.

4 According paragraph 2, stained-glass windows showed pictures of Bible stories because

Ⓐ churches paid money to have the pictures made
Ⓑ they were a type of entertainment for people
Ⓒ glassmakers enjoyed making those images
Ⓓ they could teach people who could not read

Exercises with Mid-Length Passages

Exercise 1 Read the following passage and answer the questions.

Time Limit: 1 min. 50 sec.

Plateaus, Mesas, and Buttes

03-11

The American Southwest includes the states Arizona, New Mexico, Utah, and Colorado. These states are known for their unique geological features. Three of them are plateaus, mesas, and buttes. Because they are fairly similar, people often have difficulty telling them apart.

2→ Plateaus are the largest of the three landforms. They are elevated areas that are relatively flat on top. In addition, they have cliffs on at least one of their sides. Some plateaus can cover areas more than a thousand square miles in size. As for mesas, they are smaller than plateaus. They also used to be a part of a plateau. However, due to water erosion, they have cliffs on all of their sides. Buttes are also similar to mesas. They are smaller though. Another important difference is that buttes are taller than they are wide. Mesas, on the other hand, are wider than they are tall.

3→ In the Southwest, many mesas and buttes can be found near rivers. For instance, the Grand Mesa was shaped by the Colorado and Gunnison rivers. It is more than 500 square miles in size. The Colorado Plateau is more than 130,000 square miles in size. It covers land in four states.

1 According to paragraph 2, which of the following is true of buttes?

Ⓐ They are not as large as mesas.
Ⓑ They have cliffs only on one side.
Ⓒ They have flat tops.
Ⓓ They can be wider than they are tall.

2 In paragraph 3, the author's description of the Grand Mesa mentions which of the following?

Ⓐ The state it is in
Ⓑ Its relative size
Ⓒ Its height
Ⓓ Its general appearance

Words & Phrases

elevated adj being higher than the surrounding area

relatively adv fairly; somewhat

cliff n a steep or vertical overhang of rock

erosion n the natural act of wearing down land by water, wind, or ice

shape v to form

Summary Note

Plateaus, Mesas, and Buttes

Plateaus
- Elevated areas with flat tops; can be large
- Have cliffs on one or more sides

Mesas
- Smaller than plateaus; used to be part of plateaus
- Have cliffs on all sides due to water erosion

Buttes
- Smaller than mesas
- Taller than they are wide

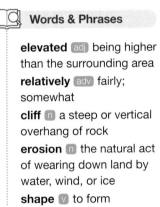

Exercise 2 Read the following passage and answer the questions.

Time Limit: 1 min. 30 sec.

NASA

03-12

Since 1958, NASA has made a number of great gains in science and technology. It is a leader in aerospace research. It has provided humans with new ways to view the Earth and space.

2→ In 1961, President Kennedy announced that America should land a man on the moon and return him safely to the Earth. He wanted to beat the Soviets to the honor. NASA accomplished Kennedy's mandate with *Apollo 11*. It was a famous rocket flight. On July 20, 1969, NASA put men on the moon. The first man to step on the moon's surface was Neil Armstrong. It was a great moment. His first words were, "That's one small step for man, one giant leap for mankind."

3→ In the 1980s, the space shuttle became a new public interest. NASA launched the first space shuttle in 1981. It developed the shuttle to be a reusable craft. Rockets could be used only once. NASA also had many unmanned missions. Robots were used. Spacecraft made flights toward other planets such as Jupiter, Saturn, Uranus, and Neptune. They sent back scientific data and color images.

1 According to paragraph 2, President Kennedy wanted to put a man on the moon because
- (A) NASA was established to explore the moon
- (B) NASA was doing research on space
- (C) he did not want the Soviets to get there first
- (D) he wanted to leave an achievement of lasting memory

2 According to paragraph 3, when was the first space shuttle launched?
- (A) In 1958
- (B) In 1961
- (C) In 1969
- (D) In 1981

Words & Phrases

announce (v) to say to the public

mandate (n) a written order or command

launch (v) to send up into the air

unmanned (adj) without an operator or pilot

Summary Note

NASA

Explores space	Space Race with the Soviets	Neil Armstrong: the first man to set foot on the moon	Recent missions: the space shuttle and unmanned missions to other planets

Exercise 3 Read the following passage and answer the questions.

Time Limit: 2 min.

The Art Thief and His Mother

03-13

A French art thief went to jail in 2002. He stole from over 170 museums across Europe. His entire collection was worth 2.5 billion dollars. The police caught the thief. Unfortunately, the police failed to recover all of the stolen goods. The thief's mother disposed of them in a permanent way.

2→ There were musical instruments, weapons, and vases in his apartment. There were also sixty paintings. The thief, Stephane, and his girlfriend, Anne, stole art and precious objects every weekend. He loved art, but he also enjoyed the thrill of stealing. They often went to museums with relaxed security. She would keep a look out while he cut the paintings from their frames.

3→ The police discovered this and arrested Stephane. Anne ran to his home to tell his mother. The mother was furious that her son was in trouble. She threw all of the items except the paintings into the river. She then cut the sixty paintings up into small pieces and put them in the garbage disposal. These precious paintings from the seventeenth and eighteenth centuries were destroyed forever. The mother did not want the police to find the evidence. She was afraid that she would lose her job because the paintings were kept in her apartment. At her age, she said, she would not be able to find another job. It is a great shame that so much history was lost for a petty reason.

1 According to paragraph 2, how did the couple steal precious objects?

(A) Stephane looked for items while Anne stole them.
(B) Anne watched Stephane, who carried a large backpack.
(C) Stephane talked to the guards while Anne put the objects in a bag.
(D) Anne watched for people while Stephane swiped the objects.

2 According to paragraph 3, the police could not recover many stolen items because

(A) the thief's mother hid them
(B) the thief's mother sold them
(C) the thief's mother gave them away
(D) the thief's mother threw them away

Words & Phrases

keep a look out phr to watch
dispose of phr to throw something away
furious adj very angry
evidence n a clue to a crime; proof
petty adj not important

Summary Note

The Art Thief and His Mother

Stephane: the art thief	Anne: Stephane's girlfriend	Stephane's mother
• Stole $2.5 billion of art and precious objects	• Helped him steal	• Threw all the objects away and destroyed them

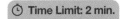

Exercise 4 Read the following passage and answer the questions.

Time Limit: 1 min. 50 sec.

Mammoth Cave

03-14

1→ With more than 579 kilometers of tunnels, Mammoth Cave is the world's longest cave. The word "mammoth" refers to its size. The cave is very famous because of its length and rich history.

2→ Mammoth Cave is a limestone cave. It is hidden under the forests and hills of central Kentucky. The cave is made up of a series of chambers beneath the earth. It has at least five levels. There are many passages and tunnels that are not open to the public. The process of formation of this cave was very slow. It started with the sea. Over millions of years, shells and the bones of animals became thick layers on the sea bottom. The layers became limestone formed in the water. Then, the sea disappeared. Rainwater passed through the rock and slowly dissolved it. It took almost 250 million years for Mammoth Cave to form.

On July 1, 1941, the cave became a national park. This would ensure that the cave was protected against real estate developers. The land is not the only thing that is important. The park is home to thousands of species of plants and animals. It became a World Heritage Site in 1981. Mammoth Cave is a treasure for all the people in the world.

1 According to paragraph 1, what does the word "mammoth" refer to?

Ⓐ An insect that flies around lights
Ⓑ The mammoths buried in the cave
Ⓒ The immensity of the cave
Ⓓ The shape of the cave system

2 According to paragraph 2, what is the layout of the cave?

Ⓐ It has a series of chambers and levels.
Ⓑ There is one large hole in the ground.
Ⓒ It has two rooms side by side.
Ⓓ It is a simple hollow.

Words & Phrases

be made up of phr to consist of
chamber n a large room; a hollow place
layer n a thickness, usually one of several
dissolve v to mix with a liquid and disappear

Summary Note

Mammoth Cave Park

- The longest cave in the world
- Limestone cave
- In Kentucky
- Formed under a sea over 250 million years ago
- Became a national park
- Home to many plants and animals

Building Summary Skills

A **Put the following sentences in order to make appropriate summaries based on the mid-length passages you worked on earlier. The first sentence is already provided.**

Exercise 1 Plateaus, Mesas, and Buttes

1 There are plateaus, mesas, and buttes in the American Southwest.

____ The Grand Mesa is more than 500 square miles in size while the Colorado Plateau is over 130,000 square miles.

____ Plateaus are the largest of the three and have flat tops.

____ Buttes are taller than they are wide.

____ Mesas are formed by water erosion and have cliffs on all sides.

Exercise 2 NASA

1 NASA is an organization that explores space.

____ They were the first human beings to go there.

____ It helps with scientific discoveries.

____ Now, NASA has a space shuttle program and robot missions to other planets.

____ It was responsible for putting Neil Armstrong and other men on the moon.

Exercise 3 The Art Thief and His Mother

1 A French art thief went to jail for stealing 2.5 billion dollars in art.

____ He loved art, but he also loved stealing.

____ His girlfriend, Anne, watched for guards and people while he took precious objects in museums.

____ The mother then threw the big objects in the river and the paintings down the drain.

____ After the police arrested him, Anne told Stephane's mother.

Exercise 4 Mammoth Cave

1 Mammoth Cave is the world's longest cave.

____ In 1941, it became a national park to ensure its preservation.

____ It has many chambers and tunnels though some are not open to the public.

____ It is a typical limestone formation.

____ The cave took 250 million years to form.

B **Fill in the blanks with suitable words or phrases to complete the following summaries. Do not look at the previous page until you are finished.**

Exercise 1 Plateaus, Mesas, and Buttes

There are plateaus, mesas, and __________ in the American Southwest. Plateaus are the __________ of the three and have __________ tops. Mesas are formed by water __________ and have __________ on all sides. __________ are taller than they are wide. The __________ is more than 500 square miles in size while the __________ is over 130,000 square miles.

Exercise 2 NASA

NASA is an __________ that explores __________. It helps with __________. It was __________ for putting Neil Armstrong and other men on the __________. They were the __________ human beings to go there. Now, NASA has a __________ program and __________ to other planets.

Exercise 3 The Art Thief and His Mother

A __________ art thief went to jail for stealing __________ dollars in art. His girlfriend, Anne, watched for __________ and people while he took precious objects in __________. He loved art, but he also loved __________. After the police __________ him, Anne told Stephane's mother. The mother then threw the big objects in the __________ and the paintings down the __________.

Exercise 4 Mammoth Cave

Mammoth Cave is the world's __________ cave. It has many __________ and __________ though some are __________ to the public. The cave took __________ years to form. It is a typical __________ formation. In 1941, it became a __________ to ensure its preservation.

Copyright

03-15

A copyright is a way to control the use of ideas. A person cannot use other people's ideas. It is illegal to print, copy, sell, or distribute someone else's work. A person may not change, translate, record, or perform any part of an author's work. This requires permission. It may also be illegal to copy and paste other people's e-mail messages. Copying without permission equals theft.

2→ Copyright deals with more than ideas. It also deals with the way something is expressed. Copyrights exist in wide areas of creative work. These include written works, designs, and music. They also include paintings, photographs, and TV broadcasts. A copyright may be marked by the symbol © in the work. However, even if there is no symbol, the work is immediately protected by law as soon as the work is created.

3→ The Statute of Anne was the first copyright law. It was passed in England in 1710. Before the statute, the power of creation was held in the hands of select people and guilds. The statute applied to the general public, not just a privileged few. It protected the author of a work, not his guild. It also put a time limit on the copyright. A person had sole rights for twenty-one years.

4→ There is no doubt that copyright plays an important role in creativity. If writers have control over their own work, they feel safe to produce more. For most creators, the work and the legal right to the work are of equal concern. Such legal protection aids economic, cultural, and social development.

1 The word "permission" in the passage is closest in meaning to

(A) protection
(B) prohibition
(C) contribution
(D) approval

2 The word "They" in the passage refers to

(A) Copyrights
(B) Wide areas of creative work
(C) Written works, designs, and music
(D) Paintings, photographs, and TV broadcasts

3 In paragraph 2, why does the author mention the "the symbol ©"?

(A) To show how the history of copyright symbols has changed
(B) To provide an example of how a copyright is indicated
(C) To stress the importance of copyrights and their symbols
(D) To introduce a new way of representing copyrights

4 The word "select" in the passage is closest in meaning to

(A) privileged
(B) elected
(C) needed
(D) talented

5 In paragraph 3, the author's description of copyrights mentions all of the following EXCEPT:

(A) The amount of time a copyright is valid for
(B) The name of the first copyright law
(C) The way copyrights worked in the past
(D) The penalties for violating a copyright

6 In paragraph 4, the author implies that copyrights

(A) are effective
(B) prevent creativity
(C) should be abolished
(D) have become more useful recently

Romanesque Architecture

03-16

Pisa Cathedral in the Romanesque style

1→ The term Romanesque refers to the architectural period in Europe in the eleventh and twelfth centuries. It shared a similarity of forms and materials used by the ancient Romans. Romanesque means "in the manner of the Romans." Before the eleventh century, people in Europe were often busy fighting one another. They rarely had enough to eat. People had no time or energy to build big and fancy buildings. Around 975, Europe society started to calm down. By 1050, kings began to order the building of large stone structures.

The stone vaulted building was a major achievement of Romanesque architects. Curved ceilings replaced wooden roofs. Wood was likely to catch on fire. Vaulted stone posed building problems for builders. They needed to know what shapes worked. They had to learn how to support the weight of the stone.

3→ Builders developed some solutions, which included domes and rounded points. To support heavy stones, they used thick walls and pillars. Windows had to be small to maintain the strength of walls. This resulted in churches with dark interiors. This did not change until the Gothic design was used some centuries later.

4→ Romanesque was the first pan-European building style since Roman times. The spreading of the style can be explained in this way. People at this time traveled for religious purposes. They would see great buildings. Then, people would bring home ideas on how to build them. Romanesque buildings can be seen all over France, England, Italy, Germany, and northern Spain.

7 The word "similarity" in the passage is closest in meaning to

Ⓐ difficulty
Ⓑ difference
Ⓒ sameness
Ⓓ strength

8 In paragraph 1, the author's description of Romanesque architecture mentions which of the following?

Ⓐ The exact year when it ended
Ⓑ The person who created it
Ⓒ The place it was practiced
Ⓓ The names of Romanesque architects

9 The word "achievement" in the passage is closest in meaning to

Ⓐ accomplishment
Ⓑ symbol
Ⓒ performance
Ⓓ monument

10 The word "they" in the passage refers to

Ⓐ builders
Ⓑ some solutions
Ⓒ domes and rounded points
Ⓓ heavy stones

11 According to paragraph 3, what was the result of the thick walls?

Ⓐ The insides of buildings were very dark.
Ⓑ The windows of Romanesque buildings were relatively big.
Ⓒ The inside of a Romanesque church was very bright.
Ⓓ The insides of buildings could be kept warm.

12 In paragraph 4, the author uses "France, England, Italy, Germany, and northern Spain" as examples of

Ⓐ the most popular places in Europe
Ⓑ places that have Romanesque buildings
Ⓒ countries led by kings in the past
Ⓓ areas with many ancient buildings

Vocabulary Check-Up

Choose the words with the closest meanings to the highlighted words.

1 The sign should be immediately removed from public.

Ⓐ kept
Ⓑ hesitated
Ⓒ lasted
Ⓓ taken out

2 People call the thin outer layer of the skin the epidermis.

Ⓐ routine
Ⓑ class
Ⓒ origin
Ⓓ sheet

3 She works at an agency that helps homeless people.

Ⓐ business
Ⓑ school
Ⓒ store
Ⓓ organization

4 The palace is elevated over the other buildings in the area.

Ⓐ considered
Ⓑ promoted
Ⓒ raised
Ⓓ built

5 The books feature stories about heroes and monsters.

Ⓐ portray
Ⓑ sell
Ⓒ remind
Ⓓ create

6 The old man complained about the cold temperature in the theater.

Ⓐ admired
Ⓑ violated
Ⓒ grumbled
Ⓓ praised

7 Buying first-class seats on airplanes is the most expensive method of travel.

(A) means
(B) note
(C) visit
(D) prevention

8 It is useless to argue about such petty matters in the meeting.

(A) important
(B) huge
(C) appropriate
(D) insignificant

9 This cathedral was built several hundred years ago.

(A) castle
(B) church
(C) house
(D) tower

10 The government launched a new business in the small town.

(A) ruined
(B) involved
(C) commenced
(D) consumed

UNIT

04 Negative Factual Information

Overview

Introduction

Negative Factual Information questions ask you to find wrong information that is not mentioned in the passage. Like Factual Information questions, the key is to find the right spot in the passage in which the answer to the question can be found within a short time period. You will probably need more time to answer this type of question than a Factual Information question because you have to scan more of the passage to make sure that your choice is not mentioned.

Question Types

- ◆ According to the passage, which of the following is NOT true of X?
- ◆ The author's description of X mentions all of the following EXCEPT:
- ◆ In paragraph 2, all of the following questions are answered EXCEPT:

Useful Tips

- ➤ Make use of the keywords in the question and the answer choices to spot relevant information in the passage.
- ➤ Do not forget that necessary information may be spread out over one or two paragraphs.
- ➤ Make sure that your answer is NOT mentioned in the passage and does not contradict the passage.

Sample TOEFL iBT Question

Q According to the passage, which of the following is NOT true?

Ⓐ The human body tries to maintain a normal temperature.

Ⓑ Drinking enough water helps the body perspire.

Ⓒ Tight clothing keeps sweat from getting in the air.

Ⓓ Water on the skin dries out easily in high humidity.

04-01

The human body does not like hot weather. It must work hard to maintain a normal temperature. The body needs to sweat to stay cool. Sweating is slowed in a few ways. First, the body may not have enough water, so it is important to drink water. Next, tight clothing prevents sweat from going into the air. Sweat usually takes heat with it and cools the body. Clothes stop air from passing over the skin. Humidity also causes problems. If there is a lot of water in the air, water on the skin does not evaporate easily.

Correct Answer

Check and make sure which choice is not true according to the text. A lot of humidity prevents water on the skin from drying out easily. So the correct answer is Ⓓ.

Basic Drill

Read the passages and answer the questions. You should scan for the information you need to answer the questions and then eliminate obviously wrong answer choices.

Skill & Tip

Negative Factual Information questions ask you to check what information is NOT mentioned in the passage. You should decide which of the four answer choices is not discussed in the passage or does not agree with one or more statements in the passage.

Example

At the end of the nineteenth century, an Australian began using women's names for cyclones. The person wished that they would not have strong winds to damage people and houses. Since 1979, men's names have also been used. There is one interesting thing when people name storms. If a tropical storm causes a lot of damage to people and buildings, its name is never used again in the future. However, if it does not cause much damage, its name is used again. Hurricane Katrina killed thousands of people in the United States. That name will never be used again. Tropical storms are mostly horrible, but they can also be beneficial since strong storms clean dirty air and provide clean air.

Q In the passage, the author's description of tropical storms mentions all of the following EXCEPT:

- (A) How storms can help people
- (B) Why some storm names are not repeated
- (C) How storms are named
- (D) How often storms form

Correct Answer (D)

Drill 1

Atoms are the basic building blocks of the physical world. Yet they are so small that they can only be seen with a powerful microscope. An atom is made up of three parts: protons, neutrons, and electrons. The protons and the neutrons are at the center of the atom. This is called the nucleus. Protons have positive charges. Neutrons have no charge. Electrons, which orbit the nucleus, have negative charges.

04-02

Q According to the passage, which of the following is NOT true of atoms?

- (A) They are made up of three parts.
- (B) They can be seen with a telescope.
- (C) They have electrons that orbit the center.
- (D) They have protons that have positive charges.

Drill 2

Culture is defined as the way groups of people give meaning to their world. Culture achieves this in a systematic way. It affects how people dress, how they act, and even how they think. In one culture, people may look at others in the eye. They may think this is friendly. In another culture, looking someone in the eye is a sign of disrespect. With these belief systems in place, people will regularly behave accordingly.

04-03

Q According to the passage, which of the following is NOT true of culture?

Ⓐ It influences how people find meaning.
Ⓑ It affects how people dress and behave.
Ⓒ It influences people's notions of respect.
Ⓓ It affects nothing in a systematic way.

Drill 3

Charlie Chaplin was the most famous star in silent pictures. He was born in London. He was the director, producer, and writer of his comic films. Of course, he was also an actor. His stardom began in 1914 when he first appeared as "the Little Tramp." His look included a jacket that was too small and pants that were too large. Many people called him the funniest man in the world.

04-04

Q According to the passage, which of the following is NOT true of Charlie Chaplin?

Ⓐ He was good at making comic films.
Ⓑ He produced some silent movies.
Ⓒ He appeared in his movies himself.
Ⓓ He was the funniest composer in the world.

Drill 4

Gravity is the natural force that pulls other objects toward one another. The Earth's gravity keeps people's feet on the ground. Because of this force, people do not float above the ground. It is the result of the great size of the planet. Gravity also holds the solar system together. It makes the moon circle the Earth and the Earth orbit the sun.

04-05

Q In the passage, the author's description of gravity mentions all of the following EXCEPT:

Ⓐ Its nature
Ⓑ Its effect on the Earth
Ⓒ Its effect on flight
Ⓓ Its effect on places other than the Earth

Drill 5

Galaxies are made up of stars, dust, and gas. All of this matter orbits a center of gravity. Earth's galaxy, the Milky Way, is huge. It contains three hundred billion stars. These stars are spread out long distances apart. The distances are so huge that they must be expressed in terms of time and the speed of light. It takes thousands of years for light to travel across our galaxy.

04-06

Q In the passage, all of the following questions are answered EXCEPT:

Ⓐ What are galaxies made up of?
Ⓑ What is the name of the galaxy Earth is in?
Ⓒ How long does it take for light to cross the Milky Way?
Ⓓ How many stars are in the universe?

Exercises with Short Passages

Exercise 1 **Read the following passage and answer the questions.**

Time Limit: 30 sec.

Sea Gypsies

04-07

Small groups of nomads called sea gypsies live on the west coast of Thailand. They have lived there for hundreds of years. Their language, culture, and lifestyle are totally different from the rest of Thai society. Their lives are based on the sea. So these nomads are experts at swimming. They can stay submerged for long periods of time. They also have a great ability to see underwater. They can spot small things underwater without goggles. Their heightened abilities have much to do with their reliance on the ocean. Their eyes have become used to the underwater environment. They also have a great knowledge of marine life. During the great tsunami of 2004, sea gypsies could survive thanks to their understanding of the sea.

General Comprehension

1 The word "reliance" in the passage is closest in meaning to

(A) ignorance
(B) confidence
(C) dependence
(D) residence

2 According to the passage, which of the following is true of the lifestyle of sea gypsies?

(A) It is tightly connected with the ocean.
(B) It is similar to that of mainland people.
(C) It is highly civilized.
(D) It has changed since 2004.

Words & Phrases

nomad n a person who moves from place to place without a fixed home

expert n a master at something; an authority on something

submerged adj being under water

goggles n special glasses worn to protect the eyes from water

heightened adj strengthened; increased; improved

marine adj related to the sea

Mastering the Question Type

3 According to the passage, which of the following is NOT true of sea gypsies?

(A) They are good at diving.
(B) They rarely use goggles.
(C) Their eyesight is better than that of normal people.
(D) They learn to swim at school.

4 In the passage, the author's description of sea gypsies mentions all of the following EXCEPT:

(A) What kind of food they eat
(B) How well they can see underwater
(C) How they survive on the sea
(D) Where they live

Exercise 2 Read the following passage and answer the questions.

Time Limit: 50 sec.

The Red Planet and Percival Lowell

04-08

Astronomers know that there is no life on Mars. The *Viking* robot missions to the Red Planet proved that. The missions were due to one man for the most part. Percival Lowell, a rich American businessman, suggested that Mars contained life. He was fascinated by Mars. He spent twenty-three years studying it. He was so deeply involved in the search for Martian life that he built his own laboratory. It housed a huge telescope. At 7,000 feet above sea level in a dry climate, it was positioned in the perfect site to view Mars. Lowell believed that he saw a network of lines crossing Mars. He also thought that the lines were built by intelligent life. There was additionally a chance that water was on the planet. He drew many maps in his notebooks. His idea attracted the public's attention. People soon believed that life on Mars could exist.

General Comprehension

1 The word "it" in the passage refers to

Ⓐ Martian life
Ⓑ a huge telescope
Ⓒ 7,000 feet above sea level
Ⓓ a dry climate

2 According to the passage, what can be inferred about the *Viking* missions?

Ⓐ They were a kind of telescope.
Ⓑ They were a group of astronauts.
Ⓒ They were involved in exploring Mars.
Ⓓ They were Percival Lowell's observatory.

Words & Phrases

planet n a large body that circles the sun or another star
mission n a trip with a purpose
be involved in phr to give a lot of time, effort, or attention to something
laboratory n a place where scientific research is carried out
climate n the general weather conditions of a particular place
huge adj very large

Mastering the Question Type

3 According to the passage, which of the following is NOT true of Percivall Lowell?

Ⓐ He believed there was no life on Mars.
Ⓑ He established a laboratory to study Mars.
Ⓒ He spent more than twenty years studying Mars.
Ⓓ He sketched the surface of Mars.

4 In the passage, the author's description of Mars mentions all of the following EXCEPT:

Ⓐ The ideas one man had about it
Ⓑ A robot mission that visited it
Ⓒ Another name people call it
Ⓓ The places where water flows on it

Exercise 3 Read the following passage and answer the questions.

Time Limit: 30 sec.

Gone with the Wind

04-09

Gone with the Wind is an American film classic. The story takes place during the American Civil War between the southern and northern states. It is the story of Scarlett O'Hara, a pretty woman who lives on a plantation in the South. She is in love with a man, Ashley. He will not marry her because he is engaged to another woman. Scarlett is angry. It takes war and the threat of his death to realize that she values their friendship. Scarlett hopes to protect her friend from the armies. While doing so, she falls in love with Rhett, a man who teases her but loves her. The movie is a great tale of love in the context of war. History makes the story possible and the characters' situations believable.

General Comprehension

1 The phrase "takes place" in the passage is closest in meaning to

(A) happens
(B) breaks
(C) exists
(D) shoots

2 In the passage, why does the author discuss "Scarlett O'Hara"?

(A) To compare her with Rhett
(B) To describe her actions in a story
(C) To blame her for Ashley's death
(D) To call her a great actress

Words & Phrases

classic n a piece of writing or a film with a high standard and lasting value

plantation n a large farm on which crops are grown

engaged adj having a formal agreement to get married

threat n a warning of harm; a menace

Mastering the Question Type

3 According to the passage, which of the following is NOT true of *Gone with the Wind*?

(A) It is one of the great American films.
(B) The setting is during the Second World War.
(C) It is about a love affair.
(D) It uses historical information.

4 In the passage, all of the following questions are answered EXCEPT:

(A) Who falls in love with Scarlett O'Hara?
(B) When does *Gone with the Wind* take place?
(C) How do people feel about *Gone with the Wind*?
(D) What happens at the end of *Gone with the Wind*?

Exercise 4 Read the following passage and answer the questions.

Time Limit: 30 sec.

Shot Towers

04-10

Gravity has been used for all kinds of mechanical purposes. For one, it was used to make round bullets called shot. Armies used it for hundreds of years. The method involved a shot tower, which was a very tall building. Liquid lead was taken to the top of the tower and poured through a metal grid. This would separate the liquid in a uniform way. As the lead drops fell through, they would form round balls and cool. They would then land in a pool of water to prevent flattening and to ensure the lead was cool. Afterward, the lead balls would be checked for shape and size. They were then ready for guns.

General Comprehension

1 The word "it" in the passage refers to

Ⓐ gravity
Ⓑ shot
Ⓒ a shot tower
Ⓓ a very tall building

2 The word "separate" in the passage is closest in meaning to

Ⓐ shape
Ⓑ pour
Ⓒ stretch
Ⓓ divide

Words & Phrases

purpose n the reason something is made or done
grid n a pattern or structure made from horizontal and vertical lines
liquid n a substance which flows and can be poured, like water
ensure v to make something certain to happen
check v to examine
flatten v to make flat

Mastering the Question Type

3 According to the passage, which of the following is NOT true of the process of making shot?

Ⓐ It involves a tower.
Ⓑ It relies on gravity.
Ⓒ It creates lead.
Ⓓ It needs a grid.

4 In the passage, the author's description of a shot tower mentions all of the following EXCEPT:

Ⓐ Bricks
Ⓑ A grid
Ⓒ Water
Ⓓ Lead

Exercises with Mid-Length Passages

Exercise 1 Read the following passage and answer the questions.

Time Limit: 1 min. 10 sec.

Gypsies

04-11

The Roma are people who live all over Europe, North Africa, and the Americas. They are often called Gypsies. People mistakenly believed that they came from Egypt because they traditionally have dark skin and hair. This misunderstanding explains the origin of the word "Gypsy." In fact, they call themselves Roma. Their people came from northern India to Europe a thousand years ago. Their language, Romany, is an Indo-Aryan language, but they usually speak the language of their home country.

Sadly, they have never had good lives in their home countries. The Roma live with racism all the time. For example, in Hungary, they are often put in separate classrooms in schools. Sometimes they are put in classrooms with students who have learning problems. Consequently, many do not finish school. Less than one percent of Roma have college degrees. This makes them unable to find good work. As a result, many Roma live in poverty. They are plagued by social problems and crime.

1 According to the passage, which of the following is NOT true of the Roma people?

- (A) They came from northern India.
- (B) They all speak Romany.
- (C) They have not been welcomed in Europe.
- (D) They are subject to social problems and crime.

2 Which of the following is NOT mentioned in the passage?

- (A) The customs of the Roma
- (B) The language of the Roma
- (C) The schooling of the Roma
- (D) The work of the Roma

Words & Phrases

mistakenly adv not accurately
traditionally adv historically
misunderstanding n a false belief
consequently adv as a result
be plagued by phr to suffer from

Summary Note

The Roma

Origin of the Roma
- northern India

School Experience
- bad experiences in school & do not go to college

Social Experience
- poverty, unemployment, and social problems

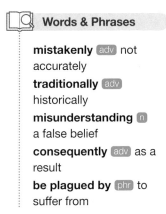

Exercise 2 Read the following passage and answer the questions.

Time Limit: 1 min. 20 sec.

The Planet Mars

04-12

Mars is the fourth planet in the solar system. It is visible from Earth, which has made it a focus of study for centuries. It has some incredible geological features.

2→ Mars is half the size of Earth, but its surface area is about the same as Earth's dry land. The reddish color of its surface comes from the presence of minerals such as iron oxide (rust). The planet is less dense than Earth. It has approximately one-tenth the mass. The northern part of the planet is distinct from the southern part. The north is quite flat due to the amount of lava flows. There is a large, flat volcano called Olympus. It is the highest mountain in the solar system at twenty-six kilometers in height.

3→ The south has the largest canyon system, which is 4,000 kilometers long and seven kilometers deep. Some of it was formed by meteors billions of years ago. It makes the Grand Canyon seem like a small sandbox in comparison. There is one huge crater called the Hellas Impact Basin. It was formed by an asteroid. It is 2,100 kilometers wide.

1 According to paragraph 2, which of the following is NOT true of Mars?

(A) It looks reddish due to minerals.
(B) It is one-tenth of Earth's mass.
(C) It never had any volcanic activity.
(D) Its northern and southern parts look different.

2 In paragraphs 2 and 3, the author's description of Mars mentions all of the following EXCEPT:

(A) The composition of its atmosphere
(B) The topography of its surface
(C) The differences between various areas
(D) The effects of meteors on its surface

Words & Phrases

feature (n) a characteristic; a trait
presence (n) an existence; an appearance
lava (n) hot liquid rock that comes from a volcano
impact (v) to crash
basin (n) a particular region where the surface is lower than in other places

Summary Note

Geological Features of Mars

The Northern Part

- covered by a lava plane
- very flat
- has the highest volcano in the solar system

The Southern Part

- pitted with craters and canyons
- has the largest canyon in the solar system
- has a huge impact crater

Exercise 3 Read the following passage and answer the questions.

Time Limit: 1 min. 50 sec.

Indies

04-13

The independent film industry is on the rise. Indies, as the films are called, are defined by the amount of money they receive from a big Hollywood studio. Fifty percent of their budget is the limit in order to be independent. Part of the reason for the growth is content. Hollywood takes fewer risks than indies. Another reason is the lower cost of technology.

2→ Film viewers know the Hollywood formula. Many movies coming from big studios have the same kinds of stories. The reasons are obvious; they make movies that customers want. And people always want the same sorts of things. However, this is not entirely true. Many viewers are tired of the same stories. They want to see films with refreshing plots and interesting perspectives. They want to see films about unique topics. Indie films have the flexibility to do this.

3→ The costs of cameras and editing equipment are on the decline. These necessary tools for filmmaking were once so expensive that only Hollywood could afford them. High-quality video cameras are now affordable for most people. And now, most editing can be done on home computers. There are many programs for sale. There are even film-editing programs for free on the Internet.

1 According to paragraph 2, which of the following is NOT true of Hollywood films?

Ⓐ They follow a formula.
Ⓑ They come from large studios.
Ⓒ They feature unique stories.
Ⓓ They take fewer risks.

2 In paragraphs 2 and 3, the author's description of factors contributing to the growth of indies mentions all of the following EXCEPT:

Ⓐ Interesting content
Ⓑ Good casting
Ⓒ The ability to change
Ⓓ Cheap equipment

Words & Phrases

on the rise phr increasing
formula n a plan
refreshing adj fresh and pleasing
perspective n a point of view
flexibility n an ability to change

Summary Note

Geological Features of Mars

Hollywood Films
- Follow the same formula
- Have mass appeal

Indie Films
- Refreshing outlook
- Unique topics
- Made possible by the low cost of technology

Exercise 4 Read the following passage and answer the questions.

Time Limit: 1 min. 20 sec.

Thermodynamics

04-14

Thermodynamics is essential to mankind's understanding of science. The term *thermodynamic* came from Lord Kelvin in 1849. It comes from Greek and means "heat power." This theory states four laws, two of which are explained as follows.

2→ When energy moves, people can feel it. The first law states that all energy in a system can be accounted for. When it moves, it has to go somewhere. Energy cannot be created or destroyed. It only moves. An example of this is the difference between a normal light bulb and a fluorescent bulb. Fluorescent bulbs are more efficient because much of the energy is kept in the bulb to create light. In a normal bulb, some of the energy makes light, but much of it is lost in the form of heat.

3→ The second law states that differences in heat will eventually balance out. When ice cubes melt, water warms to the temperature of the room. The air will cool when the river is cool. This degree of equalization is called entropy. All energy differences seek to equalize over time.

1 According to paragraph 2, which of the following is NOT true of energy?

Ⓐ It is capable of movement.
Ⓑ It can be created in some situations.
Ⓒ It can be found in fluorescent light bulbs.
Ⓓ People can feel it whenever it moves.

2 In paragraph 3, all of the following questions are answered EXCEPT:

Ⓐ How are ice cubes able to melt?
Ⓑ What is entropy?
Ⓒ What does the second law of thermodynamics state?
Ⓓ What does energy do over time?

Words & Phrases

account for phr to explain
fluorescent adj glowing from gas
efficient adj bright and glowing
eventually adv sooner or later; in the end
equalize v to become equal; to balance out

Summary Note

Thermodynamics

First Law
- Light / Heat
- No energy is lost

Second Law
- Cold / Hot
- Differences in temperature seek to equalize

Building Summary Skills

A **Put the following sentences in order to make appropriate summaries based on the mid-length passages you worked on earlier. The first sentence is already provided.**

Exercise 1 Gypsies

1 Gypsies originally came from northern India, not from Egypt.
____ Because they do not get well educated, they cannot find good jobs.
____ Some speak Romany, but most speak the language of their home country.
____ Their communities are often poor and have social problems and crime.
____ They have bad experiences in schools, like in Hungary.

Exercise 2 The Planet Mars

1 Mars, Earth's neighboring planet, has some fascinating land features.
____ These were formed billions of years ago.
____ The north is characterized by large lava plains, and it also has the highest volcano in the solar system.
____ The south is characterized by canyons and craters.
____ One crater, the Hellas Impact Basin, is over 2,000 kilometers wide.

Exercise 3 Indies

1 The number of independent films is increasing, but Hollywood is funding films less and less.
____ The costs of cameras and other equipment are decreasing, which gives many people the power to make their own film.
____ This means that movies can be different from the Hollywood formula.
____ These films are flexible enough to address interesting or unpopular topics.
____ Many viewers are tired of the same stories and find indie films refreshing.

Exercise 4 Thermodynamics

1 Thermodynamics describes the relationship between heat and power.
____ The first law states that energy in a system stays in a system.
____ The second law states that different temperatures try to equalize.
____ This means that hot temperatures try to cool down while cold temperatures try to warm up.
____ It only moves and is never lost. Efficient light bulbs do not allow energy to be lost in heat.
____ Efficient light bulbs do not allow energy to be lost in heat.

B **Fill in the blanks with suitable words or phrases to complete the following summaries. Do not look at the previous page until you are finished.**

Exercise 1 Gypsies

__________ originally came from __________, not from Egypt. Some speak __________, but most speak the language of their __________. They have __________ experiences in schools, like in Hungary. Because they do not get well __________, they cannot find good jobs. Their communities are often __________ and have social problems and __________.

Exercise 2 The Planet Mars

Mars, Earth's neighboring planet, has some fascinating __________. The __________ is characterized by large __________, and it also has the highest __________ in the solar system. The __________ is characterized by __________ and craters. These were formed millions of years ago. One crater, the __________, is over __________ wide.

Exercise 3 Indies

The number of __________ is increasing, but __________ is funding films less and less. This means that movies can be __________ from the Hollywood formula. Many viewers are __________ of the same stories and find __________ refreshing. These films are __________ enough to address interesting or unpopular topics. The __________ of cameras and other equipment are __________, which gives many people the power to make their own film.

Exercise 4 Thermodynamics

Thermodynamics describes the relationship between __________. The first law states that __________ in a system __________ in a system. It only moves, __________ to be lost. Efficient __________ do not allow energy to be lost in heat. The second law states that different __________ try to equalize. This means that hot temperatures try to __________ while cold temperatures try to __________.

The Steam Engine

04-15

A drawing of an Industrial steam engine machine

1→ The steam engine was a great advance for mankind. It made modern industry possible. Suddenly, the work of hundreds of men could be replaced by a machine. Work could be accomplished by a new muscle: energy. It relied on the basic principles of thermodynamics. In particular, it relied on Boyle's law. Boyle's Law states that the pressure of a gas is a function of its volume and temperature. When a gas is heated in a balloon, it increases its volume and decreases its pressure. If the volume cannot change, the heat will cause the pressure to increase.

2→ The steam engine took advantage of these facts. Energy, in the form of heat, could be changed into physical power. Energy could move things if controlled in the right way. Captured heat could be used for physical work. First, water was boiled to make steam. In this way, the water behaved like a gas. It would expand when heated. As the steam expanded, it moved into a tube called a cylinder. The bottom of the cylinder, called a piston, moved down as the gas expanded. The piston turned a metal arm which then could be used for all kinds of work.

3→ The steam engine was used in textile mills and in farming and mining. It turned the great wheels of machines used for weaving. It was used to power machinery that separated cotton from the seed or grain from the stalk. The engine was used to pump water out of mines and to lift coal and people up to the surface. Of course, it was also used for the great trains that moved people and goods across continents.

1 The word "advance" in the passage is closest in meaning to

(A) development
(B) procession
(C) complication
(D) usefulness

2 The author discusses "Boyle's Law" in paragraph 1 in order to

(A) prove that it has many different uses
(B) describe how Boyle managed to come up with it
(C) demonstrate its use in different machines
(D) explain the science behind the steam engine

3 According to paragraph 1, what principle is the steam engine based on?

(A) Energy can be used for work.
(B) Water can be boiled.
(C) Man is not strong.
(D) Machines need fuel.

4 The word "it" in the passage refers to

(A) the water
(B) a gas
(C) steam
(D) a tube

5 According to paragraph 2, which of the following is NOT true of the steam engine?

(A) It requires heated water to work.
(B) It has multiple parts.
(C) It can do a variety of work.
(D) It uses coal to heat water.

6 According to paragraph 3, what can be inferred about steam engines?

(A) They were only used in trains.
(B) They were not particularly helpful.
(C) They revolutionized the world.
(D) They have no moving parts.

The History of the Roller Coaster

04-16

A modern roller coaster in Ohio, the United States

1→ The first roller coasters were created in Russia in the seventeenth century. However, they were not like modern ones. They were more like big sleds. People rode down steep ice slides. These sleds required very good navigation skills to slide down safely. There were also many accidents.

2→ At the end of the nineteenth century, American railway companies introduced roller coasters. They set up amusement parks to make money on weekends. This was when people rarely traveled. In 1884, the first real roller coaster appeared. It was a gravity-driven train. Passengers climbed flights of stairs to board the car. Then, the car was pushed from the station to move down a hill and over a few bumps. At the bottom, passengers got out of the car. Then, workers lifted the car to the second station.

3→ During the early twentieth century, there was great progress in roller coasters. Unlike previous coasters, the new ones employed mechanical tracks. The first was built in 1912. This was a great advance. It enabled people to enjoy greater speed and steeper hills but with much more safety than previous ones. Throughout the 1920s, many roller coasters were built, but after World War II, the number of roller coasters significantly decreased.

4→ Disneyland, the first theme park in the United States, opened in 1955. It opened a new era for amusement parks. Disney adopted the first tubular steel roller coaster in 1959. Before this, roller coasters always had been built on wooden frames. The steel track not only offered greater stability but also opened the door for loops and corkscrews.

7 In paragraph 1, the author's description of the first roller coasters mentions which of the following?

Ⓐ The person who made them
Ⓑ The place they were invented
Ⓒ The length they traveled
Ⓓ The name people called it

8 The word "They" in the passage refers to

Ⓐ American railway companies
Ⓑ Roller coasters
Ⓒ Amusement parks
Ⓓ Weekends

9 According to paragraph 2, what can be inferred about roller coasters?

Ⓐ They took a lot of effort to run.
Ⓑ They were not fun to ride.
Ⓒ They were reliant on ice.
Ⓓ They had lots of enthusiasts.

10 The word "employed" in the passage is closest in meaning to

Ⓐ followed
Ⓑ used
Ⓒ left
Ⓓ hired

11 According to paragraph 3, which of the following is NOT true of roller coasters?

Ⓐ Those built in the twentieth century were safe.
Ⓑ Some roller coasters could go up steep hills backward.
Ⓒ Few roller coasters were built after World War II.
Ⓓ One with mechanical tracks was built in the 1900s.

12 In paragraph 4, the author's description of Disneyland mentions all of the following EXCEPT:

Ⓐ The length of its longest roller coaster
Ⓑ The material it made roller coaster tracks with
Ⓒ The year that it first opened
Ⓓ The country it was built in

Vocabulary Check-Up

Choose the words with the closest meanings to the highlighted words.

1 It is good to learn about different cultures by traveling.
- (A) models
- (B) events
- (C) customs
- (D) professions

2 The team equalized the game when it scored a goal.
- (A) evened
- (B) eliminated
- (C) competed
- (D) spread

3 People's gravity is always the same whether they are on a mountaintop or in a valley.
- (A) movement
- (B) figuration
- (C) combination
- (D) heaviness

4 The player accounted for losing too many games recently.
- (A) regretted
- (B) served
- (C) explained
- (D) fixed

5 There are many believable characters in the novel.
- (A) extreme
- (B) realistic
- (C) moderate
- (D) insulting

6 People at the meeting moved on to the subject of pollution.
- (A) proceeded
- (B) decreased
- (C) outlined
- (D) motivated

7 The family's old plantation has been operating for 100 years.

(A) neighbor
(B) society
(C) jungle
(D) farm

8 The country was marked by natural resources.

(A) originated
(B) scheduled
(C) characterized
(D) imagined

9 North America ranges from Newfoundland on the east coast to Alaska on the west coast.

(A) circle
(B) seaside
(C) nature
(D) curve

10 People need a lot of endurance to climb the mountain.

(A) go up
(B) locate
(C) manage
(D) rebound

UNIT

05 Sentence Simplification

Overview

Introduction

Sentence Simplification questions ask you to choose the sentence that best restates the essential meaning of the original sentence in the passage. The correct answer uses different vocabulary and grammar to retell the original sentence in a simpler way. This type of question does not appear in every reading passage. There is also never more than one Sentence Simplification question in a passage.

Question Types

- Which of the following best expresses the essential information in the highlighted sentence? *Incorrect* answer choices change the meaning in important ways or leave out essential information.

Useful Tips

- Figure out what the essential information is in the original sentence.
- Do not focus on minor information such as details and examples.
- Keep in mind that incorrect answers contradict something in the original sentence or leave out important information from it.

Sample TOEFL iBT Question

Q Which of the following best expresses the essential information in the highlighted sentence? *Incorrect* answer choices change the meaning in important ways or leave out essential information.

Ⓐ Poor people have always loved the guitar.

Ⓑ The guitar is nicknamed the poor man's piano.

Ⓒ Various cultures have enjoyed the guitar.

Ⓓ The guitar has been played at cultural events.

The guitar, which is also known as the poor man's piano, has been cherished by many cultures. Spain made the guitar great. This country is responsible for many classical pieces. Brazil is also famous for guitar music. It developed the style of bossa nova. This style blends classical and jazz styles.

05-01

Correct Answer

Choices Ⓐ and Ⓓ change the meaning of the highlighted sentence. Choice Ⓑ focuses on minor details. Choice Ⓒ is the best restatement of the original sentence.

Basic Drill

Read the passages and answer the questions.

Skill & Tip

Sentence Simplification questions ask for the same information stated in a different way. They ask you to choose the sentence that best paraphrases the essential information in the highlighted sentence.

Example

There is great concern about global warming. There is evidence that temperatures are rising. For example, the North Pole has not seen such extreme melting in thousands of years. It was once possible to walk across certain parts of the Arctic Ocean on ice as polar bears do. Now, there are open stretches of water.

Q Which of the following best expresses the essential information in the highlighted sentence?

Ⓐ The North Pole experienced a thousand years of melting.
Ⓑ The North Pole has not melted for thousands of years.
Ⓒ The North Pole has not melted so much in a long time.
Ⓓ The thousands of years of melting were extreme for the North Pole.

Correct Answer Ⓒ

Drill 1

Charles Darwin published *On the Origin of Species*. He wrote that life forms change in response to their environments. His theory of natural selection caused a major change in science. But this challenged religious beliefs. His theory said that life evolved. God was not responsible for the life that exists today.

05-02

Q Which of the following best expresses the essential information in the highlighted sentence?

Ⓐ Darwin thought some environments cause life forms to change.
Ⓑ Darwin wrote that life forms change the environments around them.
Ⓒ According to Darwin, change is the essence of life forms.
Ⓓ Darwin wrote that life forms change spontaneously.

Drill 2

Snowflakes have amazing shapes. No two are exactly the same. Snowflakes are usually flat and six sided. They form when ice grows on a tiny piece of dust. The shapes of snowflakes are determined by the air temperature. Each snowflake falls in the air and passes through different temperatures. This freezes the water in unique shapes. The biggest snowflake was more than twenty-eight centimeters across.

05-03

Q Which of the following best expresses the essential information in the highlighted sentence?

Ⓐ The shapes of snowflakes help predict the temperature.
Ⓑ The temperature determines the sizes of snowflakes.
Ⓒ Snowflakes' shapes depend on the temperature.
Ⓓ The temperature shapes snowflakes.

Drill 3

Meteorologists need data from around the world. They use many methods to collect this data. One is to use satellites. They have changed the study of weather forever. The satellites check the Earth's surface. They look at water vapor and heat. They send back data on weather conditions. By using this data, meteorologists can predict the weather with more accuracy.

05-04

Q Which of the following best expresses the essential information in the highlighted sentence?

Ⓐ The accuracy of data is the most important factor in weather forecasts.
Ⓑ Scientists need more accuracy when predicting the weather.
Ⓒ Weather data enable scientists to forecast the weather well.
Ⓓ Meteorologists cannot predict the weather accurately even with satellite data.

Drill 4

Cells are the basic structural unit in the human body. Each human has around 100 million of them. They are not all the same types though. Cells develop to have specific functions, forming organs, muscles, nerves, skin, and bones. Each body part has a special cell type. However, one type of cell, a stem cell, can grow into any of the other cell types.

05-05

Q Which of the following best expresses the essential information in the highlighted sentence?

Ⓐ Cells form specific functions in certain body parts.
Ⓑ Cells are formed by organs, muscles, and nerves.
Ⓒ Cells take on specific functions to form body parts.
Ⓓ Cells are specifically designed to grow into other cells.

Drill 5

Jeremy Bentham was an English philosopher. Bentham proposed many legal and social reforms which were of great influence. He believed that the church and the state should be separate. He argued for equal rights for women. He was a firm believer in free speech. He also argued for the end of slavery. Bentham believed in health insurance for the rich and the poor, too.

05-06

Q Which of the following best expresses the essential information in the highlighted sentence?

Ⓐ Bentham's legal and social proposals had a great influence.
Ⓑ Bentham influenced many proposals on social and legal reforms.
Ⓒ Bentham proposed many legal and ethical reforms.
Ⓓ Bentham was influenced by social and legal reforms.

Exercises with Short Passages

Exercise 1 Read the following passage and answer the questions.

Time Limit: 30 sec.

Mutant Cells

05-07

Cancer results from the mutation of one cell. The DNA of this cell changes. Only ten percent of this DNA change is hereditary. This means that only ten percent of cancers come from a person's family. Most of the changes are due to the environment. Cancers may be caused by people smoking or living in a polluted area. As people age, they grow more mutated cells. For this reason, cancer occurs more often as people get older. When a cancer cell replicates, it copies the mutant DNA to the new cells it makes. In the end, the cells change so much that they no longer follow the body's normal signals. They start growing, without control, into a tumor.

General Comprehension

1 According to the passage, how do cells change to result in cancer?

Ⓐ The DNA changes in one cell, and then the cell replicates.
Ⓑ The DNA forces cells to change, and then the cells replicate.
Ⓒ The cells change in the environment, and then they repeat.
Ⓓ The cells change to fight against mutated DNA in cells.

2 According to the passage, what is the relationship between age and cancer?

Ⓐ Ten percent of cancers are caused by environmental changes.
Ⓑ Ninety percent of cancers are already present in people's genetic code at birth.
Ⓒ As people get older, they get more mutant cells, which could form cancer.
Ⓓ As people get older, they change their environments, which cause all cancers.

Words & Phrases

mutation n a change from a normal path
hereditary adj coming from one's parents
polluted adj dirty
replicate v to copy oneself
normal adj usual; ordinary; common

Mastering the Question Type

3 Which of the following best expresses the essential information in the first highlighted sentence?

Ⓐ DNA changes result from smoke or living near pollution.
Ⓑ Changes in DNA can be attributed to smoking and pollution.
Ⓒ Smoke causes pollution, which, in turn, forces DNA to change.
Ⓓ Pollution is a type of smoke that causes DNA to change.

4 Which of the following best expresses the essential information in the second highlighted sentence?

Ⓐ Mutant DNA is copied to new cells during the process of replication.
Ⓑ The process of replication makes mutant DNA replication easy.
Ⓒ Cells only copy mutant DNA into new cells during replication.
Ⓓ The cell replicates by copying mutant DNA into some new cells.

Exercise 2 Read the following passage and answer the questions.

Time Limit: 30 sec.

Hail

05-08

Hail is a type of precipitation that falls from the sky. Yet it is neither rain nor snow. It is ice. Hail forms in storm clouds. Basically, a drop of water gets blown around inside a cloud and encounters very cold drops of water. These join together and become a hailstone. A hailstone can become bigger and bigger inside the cloud. At some point, it becomes substantial enough that it falls to the ground. Some hailstones can achieve great speeds, so they can hit and hurt people on the ground. Hailstones can also damage cars, buildings, and other objects. Each year, there are thousands of hailstorms in the United States alone.

General Comprehension

1 According to the passage, what is a hailstone?

(A) A hard rock
(B) A ball of ice
(C) A drop of rain
(D) A type of snowflake

2 The word "substantial" in the passage is closest in meaning to

(A) clear
(B) prepared
(C) obvious
(D) heavy

Words & Phrases

basically adv essentially
encounter v to meet
achieve v to attain; to reach
damage v to hurt; to harm

Mastering the Question Type

3 Which of the following best expresses the essential information in the first highlighted sentence?

(A) Drops of water get blown into a cloud, and then they become cold.
(B) The wind blows a waterdrop in a cloud, where it meets cold waterdrops.
(C) When a cold wind blow, waterdrops in a cloud may become very cold.
(D) Cold waterdrops are responsible for wind blowing water around in clouds.

4 Which of the following best expresses the essential information in the second highlighted sentence?

(A) Hailstones can fall fast enough to injure people they hit.
(B) Hailstones are capable of hurting people on the ground.
(C) At some times, hailstones move at very great speeds.
(D) Only the fastest hailstones can hurt people that they hit.

Exercise 3 Read the following passage and answer the questions.

Time Limit: 45 sec.

Muir Woods

05-09

The logging industry has had great political power for a long time. It uses this power to get at many of America's great forests. In the early part of the century, companies cut down much of the coastal forest of California. Many of the largest trees on the Earth grew there. Great redwoods and sequoias were used for lumber and paper. Most of these forests were reduced. A man called Kent saw what was happening, so he bought the land to preserve it. At first, he thought the trees were saved. Then, a water company wanted to flood the valley for electric power. The company took Kent to court. In order to save the wooded land, Kent donated it to the federal government. It became a national park. It was named Muir Woods after John Muir, a famous naturalist. The valley was the first private donation to become a national park. It set the way for future forest preservation.

General Comprehension

1 According to the passage, the valley was an attractive place for industries because

Ⓐ logging and water companies saw great resources to exploit
Ⓑ logging and water companies saw it as a beautiful place
Ⓒ the lumber could be used to reduce the forests
Ⓓ the beautiful land could be used to attract tourists

2 According to the passage, why was the valley important?

Ⓐ It began a trend of people hiking in forests.
Ⓑ It became an example for future efforts to protect forests.
Ⓒ It was donated by Kent, who was a famous politician.
Ⓓ The trees in it were redwoods and sequoias, which are very big.

Words & Phrases

get at phr to obtain something for one's use
lumber n wood used for building
donate v to give as a gift
set the way for phr to prepare
preservation n the act of saving for the future

Mastering the Question Type

3 Which of the following best expresses the essential information in the first highlighted sentence?

Ⓐ There was a man who called Kent to see how to buy land.
Ⓑ Kent was a man who did not like forests being grown in California.
Ⓒ Kent monitored the situation to buy the land.
Ⓓ Kent bought the land to prevent forest reduction.

4 Which of the following best expresses the essential information in the second highlighted sentence?

Ⓐ The valley was first donated as a private park.
Ⓑ The valley was the first privately donated national park.
Ⓒ The valley was the first park to receive donations.
Ⓓ The valley was the first park to be a national donation.

Exercise 4 Read the following passage and answer the questions.

Time Limit: 30 sec.

The Death Penalty

05-10

The death penalty has been under debate for over a thousand years. This type of justice comes from the Code of Hammurabi. It was comprised of ancient laws, one of which stated, "An eye for an eye; a tooth for a tooth." Some believe that the death penalty is fair. A criminal who commits the worst crime should pay the highest price. The only way to keep society civil is to remove the bad elements. Some see the death penalty as a deterrent. If criminals know they will pay with their lives, they will not commit crimes. Others believe that the death penalty is a sign that a society is very cruel. They believe humans have progressed enough that crude punishment is not needed. There is no right reason for killing.

General Comprehension

1 The phrase "comprised of" in the passage is closest in meaning to

Ⓐ replaced with
Ⓑ reminded of
Ⓒ related to
Ⓓ composed of

2 The word "they" in the passage refers to

Ⓐ criminals
Ⓑ their lives
Ⓒ crimes
Ⓓ others

Words & Phrases

under debate phr controversial
penalty n punishment
criminal n a person who commits a crime
remove v to take out; to get rid of
deterrent n a preventative idea
cruel adj very mean

Mastering the Question Type

3 Which of the following best expresses the essential information in the first highlighted sentence?

Ⓐ Civil society is effective at keeping its bad elements away.
Ⓑ Removing criminals is the sole way to keep society healthy.
Ⓒ The way to organize society is to put bad people in jail.
Ⓓ Civilization is best kept by bad people.

4 Which of the following best expresses the essential information in the second highlighted sentence?

Ⓐ There are some people who think the death penalty is cruel.
Ⓑ Some people believe the death penalty belongs in society.
Ⓒ Some people think a cruel society has the death penalty.
Ⓓ The death penalty needs to belong to a cruel society.

Exercises with Mid-Length Passages

Exercise 1 Read the following passage and answer the questions.

Time Limit: 1 min. 20 sec.

DNA

05-11

DNA is an important means of fighting crime. Detectives use it to catch criminals. They use DNA found at crime scenes in order to determine the actual criminals. This method is one of the most reliable ways to identify criminals.

DNA is a molecule that contains the blueprint for life. It controls how the body develops as it grows. It transfers the genetic traits of parents to their offspring. DNA is found in each of the 100 trillion cells of the human body. Each individual human has a set of DNA that is completely unique.

Investigators often find some traces of DNA at crime scenes or on victims' bodies. There may be a piece of hair, a drop of blood, or even skin. The police can collect these samples to analyze them. With luck, they find a match between the sample and the suspect. Some factors may prevent them from succeeding, however. DNA samples can be contaminated. The sample may be mixed with someone else's, or it may be partially destroyed, by heat, for example.

Words & Phrases

reliable adj dependable; trustworthy
identify v to recognize
transfer v to move from one place to another
trait n a characteristic; a quality; an attribute
offspring n children
suspect n a person thought to have committed a crime
contaminate v to spoil

1 Which of the following best expresses the essential information in the first highlighted sentence? *Incorrect* answer choices change the meaning in important ways or leave out essential information.

Ⓐ DNA is used to figure out who the criminals are.
Ⓑ DNA from criminals is collected and studied.
Ⓒ The criminals use DNA to tip off the investigators.
Ⓓ The crime scene has details of who criminals are.

2 Which of the following best expresses the essential information in the second highlighted sentence? *Incorrect* answer choices change the meaning in important ways or leave out essential information.

Ⓐ The DNA each person has is common.
Ⓑ People's DNA is unique to humans.
Ⓒ Every person has a unique set of DNA.
Ⓓ Basically, the DNA each person has is not unique.

3 Which of the following best expresses the essential information in the third highlighted sentence? *Incorrect* answer choices change the meaning in important ways or leave out essential information.

Ⓐ Someone's DNA is useless if it is exposed to heat or mixed with another person's.
Ⓑ Heat and mixing are two ways to destroy DNA being used in an investigation.
Ⓒ A sample can be exposed to heat or another person's DNA at times.
Ⓓ DNA can be mixed up with someone else's as a way of destroying it.

Summary Note

DNA

- Used to identify criminals
- Transfers genetic traits from parents to children
- Unreliable if it is mixed with another sample or partially destroyed

Exercise 2 Read the following passage and answer the questions.

Time Limit: 1 min.

Tornadoes

05-12

A tornado is a violent, rotating column of air. It reaches from a storm cloud to the ground. The most violent tornadoes are capable of causing a huge amount of damage. They can have wind speeds of 500 kilometers per hour. These twisters are very dangerous to life and property.

Tornadoes are most frequently found in the United States, especially in the spring and summertime. Each year, 800 tornadoes are reported across the country. They result in around eighty deaths and over 1,500 injuries. Paths of damage can be one mile wide and fifty miles long.

There is a region named Tornado Alley. It is a zone that stretches from Ohio to Texas. Violent tornadoes develop more frequently in that place than in anywhere else in the country. The place is unique because cold dry air comes from the Rocky Mountains. It meets warm, moist air from the Gulf of Mexico. These conditions are perfect for tornadoes.

Words & Phrases

rotate v to spin
injury n a casualty
region n an area
unique adj distinctive
moist adj damp

1 Which of the following best expresses the essential information in the first highlighted sentence? *Incorrect* answer choices change the meaning in important ways or leave out essential information.

Ⓐ Only violent tornadoes can cause a lot of damage.
Ⓑ Most violent tornadoes are capable of severe damage.
Ⓒ Very much damage can be caused by most violent tornadoes.
Ⓓ The most powerful tornadoes can cause great destruction.

2 Which of the following best expresses the essential information in the second highlighted sentence? *Incorrect* answer choices change the meaning in important ways or leave out essential information.

Ⓐ The U.S. has most of its tornadoes in the spring and summertime.
Ⓑ The U.S. has the most tornadoes, which usually happen in spring and summer.
Ⓒ The U.S. is frequently affected by tornadoes, especially in spring and summer.
Ⓓ The U.S. has the most tornadoes of all, though only in the spring and summertime.

3 Which of the following best expresses the essential information in the third highlighted sentence? *Incorrect* answer choices change the meaning in important ways or leave out essential information.

Ⓐ Violent tornadoes happen most frequently in the country.
Ⓑ Tornado Alley gets violent tornadoes the most frequently of all the country.
Ⓒ Tornado Alley gets tornadoes, some of which are violent, everywhere within it.
Ⓓ Violent tornadoes occur more frequently in the country than in Tornado Alley.

Summary Note

Tornadoes

- Definition: a violently rotating column of air reaching from a storm cloud to the ground
- Frequency: 800 tornadoes form in the U.S. yearly
- Tornado Alley: from Ohio to Texas

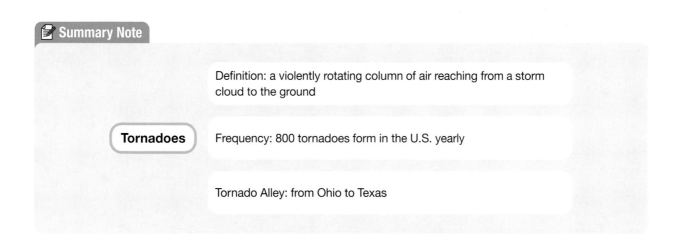

Exercise 3 Read the following passage and answer the questions.

Time Limit: 1 min. 20 sec.

John Muir

05-13

John Muir helped establish one of the greatest national parks in the world. He was born in Scotland in 1838. But he moved to the United States in 1849. He did not graduate from a university. Instead, he got a job as an industrial engineer. Soon after, he decided to explore the wilderness. He walked thousands of miles from Indiana to Florida while enjoying the beauty of nature. Muir had planned to journey to South America. But he was stopped by malaria. He went to California instead.

He arrived in San Francisco in 1868. He soon left for Yosemite, which he had only read about in magazines and newspapers. He was inspired by his first sight of this great place. Muir wrote, "No temple made with hands can compare with Yosemite. Yosemite is the grandest of all special temples of Nature."

In 1903, President Roosevelt visited Yosemite Park with Muir. Muir told the president about the state's poor management of the valley. He emphasized the importance of protecting nature. Muir was able to convince Roosevelt to protect the valley through federal control and management.

Words & Phrases

establish v to create; to designate
wilderness n a place unsettled by man
inspire v to give great thoughts; to impress
emphasize v to repeat what is important
convince v to persuade

1 Which of the following best expresses the essential information in the first highlighted sentence? *Incorrect* answer choices change the meaning in important ways or leave out essential information.

Ⓐ While traveling on foot from Indiana to Florida, Muir enjoyed nature.
Ⓑ Muir walked to enjoy the beauty of nature for thousands of miles.
Ⓒ Muir traveled very long distances in Indiana and throughout Florida.
Ⓓ Muir walked for two thousand miles to enjoy the beauty of nature.

2 Which of the following best expresses the essential information in the second highlighted sentence? *Incorrect* answer choices change the meaning in important ways or leave out essential information.

Ⓐ Muir soon left Yosemite after he read about it.
Ⓑ Muir soon went to Yosemite, about which he had only read.
Ⓒ Muir soon left to see Yosemite and read about it at times.
Ⓓ Muir went to Yosemite but left soon when he read about it.

3 Which of the following best expresses the essential information in the third highlighted sentence? *Incorrect* answer choices change the meaning in important ways or leave out essential information.

Ⓐ Muir was so persuasive that he got Roosevelt to keep the valley safe under federal control.
Ⓑ Muir could only convince Roosevelt to protect the valley through federal control.
Ⓒ Muir persuaded Roosevelt to protect the federal management of the valley.
Ⓓ Muir could convince Roosevelt but only after protection of the valley became federalized.

Summary Note

Born in Scotland in 1838 and moved to the United States

John Muir

Walked long distances from Indiana to Florida and enjoyed the beauty of nature

Insisted that the federal government should protect Yosemite Park

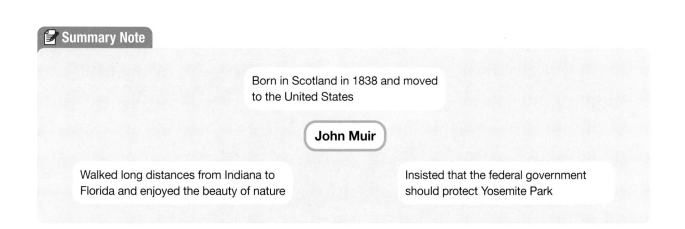

Exercise 4 Read the following passage and answer the questions.

Time Limit: 1 min.

The Code of Hammurabi

05-14

Hammurabi was the sixth king of Babylon. He was born in 1810 B.C. He ruled over his empire from 1792 B.C. until his death in 1750 B.C. He is perhaps best known for creating a set of laws called the Code of Hammurabi.

While the penalties of the law seem cruel to modern people, two aspects of the code were ahead of their time. First, he put the laws in writing. They were not just spoken words. Second, he tried to apply his laws systematically. This was an important step forward in the evolution of civilization. The idea of being innocent until proven guilty comes from the code.

The laws were written on stone tablets and placed in a public place. People could see them, but not many people could read and understand them. The tablets were plundered a number of years later and removed to Elamite Susa. They were rediscovered there in 1901. Now the stone tablets stand in the Louvre Museum in France.

Words & Phrases

aspect n a quality
evolution n development
innocent adj not guilty
tablet n a flat stone
plunder v to rob
remove v to take away

1 Which of the following best expresses the essential information in the first highlighted sentence? *Incorrect* answer choices change the meaning in important ways or leave out essential information.

Ⓐ People know what he did best, which was creating codes and laws.
Ⓑ People know him best because he created the Code of Hammurabi.
Ⓒ People know he made the best laws, called the Code of Hammurabi.
Ⓓ People know what his Code of Hammurabi is and think it was the best.

2 Which of the following best expresses the essential information in the second highlighted sentence? *Incorrect* answer choices change the meaning in important ways or leave out essential information.

Ⓐ Two aspects of the code were advancing while modern people deemed the laws cruel.
Ⓑ While modern people were making cruel penalties, two aspects of the code were used.
Ⓒ Though the penalties seem cruel these days, two aspects were quite advanced.
Ⓓ Since the penalties were cruel, two aspects of the code were advanced by modern people.

3 Which of the following best expresses the essential information in the third highlighted sentence? *Incorrect* answer choices change the meaning in important ways or leave out essential information.

Ⓐ People who saw the rules could read and understand many of them.
Ⓑ Few people could read the codes because they could not see them.
Ⓒ Only people who could see the rules could understand them.
Ⓓ Few could read and comprehend the rules despite their visibility.

Summary Note

The Code of Hammurabi	Hammurabi: the sixth king of Babylon, who lived from 1810 B.C. to 1750 B.C.
	Its importance: A systematic application of the law with the idea of being innocent until proven guilty
	History: Plundered tablets found many years later and are now in Paris

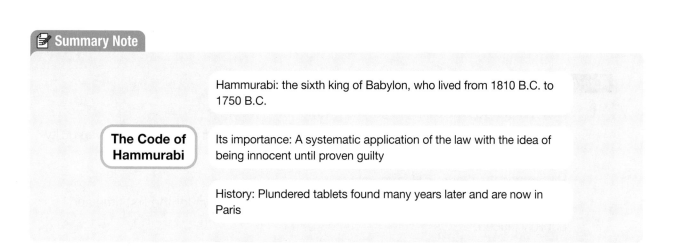

Building Summary Skills

A **Put the following sentences in order to make appropriate summaries based on the mid-length passages you worked on earlier. The first sentence is already provided.**

Exercise 1 DNA

1 DNA is used to catch criminals because it is a very reliable method.
____ If the DNA in the sample matches the DNA of someone they know, police have identified the criminal.
____ All cells contain DNA.
____ DNA can be contaminated though.
____ When investigators find traces of a person, they analyze them.

Exercise 2 Tornadoes

1 Tornadoes are violently rotating columns of air, and they usually occur during spring and summer.
____ They result in around eighty deaths and over 1,500 injuries.
____ They most frequently occur in an area called Tornado Alley.
____ In the U.S., 800 tornadoes are reported each year.
____ It stretches from Ohio to Texas.

Exercise 3 John Muir

1 John Muir, a naturalist, was born in Scotland in 1838.
____ He was fascinated by this great park but was worried about how the state was managing it.
____ After this journey, he went to Yosemite.
____ In his twenties, he decided to explore the American wilderness by walking from Indiana to Florida.
____ He asked the president of the U.S. to protect this beautiful place.

Exercise 4 The Code of Hammurabi

1 Hammurabi was the sixth king of the Babylonian Dynasty.
____ Another importance of this law is that the concept of being innocent until proven guilty comes from the Code of Hammurabi.
____ He created the Code of Hammurabi.
____ These laws became famous because they were written down for the first time and publicly placed.

B **Fill in the blanks with suitable words or phrases to complete the following summaries. Do not look at the previous page until you are finished.**

Exercise 1 DNA

DNA is used to ______________ because it is a very ______________ method. All cells contain ______________. When ______________ find traces of a person, they ______________ them. If the DNA in the sample ______________ the DNA of someone they know, police have ______________ the criminal. DNA can be ______________ though.

Exercise 2 Tornadoes

Tornadoes are violently ______________ columns of air, and they usually occur during ______________. In the U.S., ______________ tornadoes are reported each year. They result in around ______________ deaths and over ______________ injuries. They most frequently occur in an area called ______________. It stretches from ______________ to ______________.

Exercise 3 John Muir

John Muir, a ______________, was born in ______________ in 1838. In his twenties, he decided to explore the ______________ by walking from Indiana to Florida. After this journey, he went to ______________. He was ______________ by this great park but was ______________ by how the state was managing it. He asked the ______________ of the U.S. to ______________ this beautiful place.

Exercise 4 The Code of Hammurabi

______________ was the ______________ king of the ______________. He created the Code of Hammurabi. These ______________ became famous because they were ______________ for the first time and ______________. Another importance of these laws was that the concept of being ______________ until proven ______________ comes from the Code of Hammurabi.

Carnivorous Plants

05-15

Venus fly traps

Carnivorous plants usually grow in places where the soil is barren. These include swamps and bogs. The plants require very humid conditions and lots of sun. But they get their nutrients by eating small animals and insects. These plants have clever ways of trapping their prey. Today, there are around five hundred plants that are known to be carnivorous.

2→ Charles Darwin wrote the first well-known paper on carnivorous plants in 1875. He described five kinds of traps. Pitfall traps catch insects in a rolled leaf that has a pool of bacteria at the bottom. Flypaper traps catch insects by using a sticky liquid. Snap traps catch insects with rapid leaf movements. Bladder traps suck in insects with a bladder that creates a vacuum. Finally, lobster-pot traps use inward-pointing hairs to force insects toward the center of the plant. They cannot go backward.

3→ The changing of carnivorous plants over time is hard to study. There are few fossil records. For the most part, only seeds or pollen exist. However, scientists can learn much from the structure of current traps. Pitfall traps have clearly evolved from rolled leaves. Flypaper traps also show a simple change from sticky nonlethal leaves to the deadly kind. The Venus fly trap is an interesting plant. There are three hairs in the middle of each leaf. An insect must touch two hairs quickly for the leaf to fold shut. Then, the plant can eat it.

Scientists have suggested that all these leaf types are mutations from a simple, hairy leaf. It was able to collect drops of rainwater in which bacteria could breed. Insects landed on the leaf and got caught in the water. They suffocated. The bacteria then began to decay the insect and released nutrients into the plant.

1 The word "barren" in the passage is closest in meaning to

Ⓐ rich
Ⓑ poor
Ⓒ damp
Ⓓ sandy

2 Why does the author mention "Flypaper traps" in paragraph 2?

Ⓐ To challenge common beliefs about plants
Ⓑ To explain what Darwin studied
Ⓒ To provide an example of carnivorous plants
Ⓓ To argue an important point

3 The word "They" in the passage refers to

Ⓐ Bladder traps
Ⓑ Lobster-pot traps
Ⓒ Inward-pointing hairs
Ⓓ Insects

4 According to paragraph 3, what did rolled leaves later evolve into?

Ⓐ Flypaper traps
Ⓑ Venus fly traps
Ⓒ Lobster-pot traps
Ⓓ Pitfall traps

5 Which of the following best expresses the essential information in the highlighted sentence? *Incorrect* answer choices change the meaning in important ways or leave out essential information.

Ⓐ Scientists believe that these leaf types evolved from a hairy leaf.
Ⓑ Scientists do not agree that these leaf types are mutations from a simple, hairy leaf.
Ⓒ Scientists suggest that it is very difficult for hairy leaves every to mutate.
Ⓓ Scientists know all of the types of leaves that have mutated over time.

6 The word "released" in the passage is closest in meaning to

Ⓐ discharged
Ⓑ detached
Ⓒ moved
Ⓓ sticked

Desertification

05-16

1→ The Sahara Desert is growing by around fifty kilometers each year. The entire Earth gets 600 square kilometers more in deserts every year. This process is called desertification. This term started being used in the 1950s.

2→ The idea of desertification was first known in the 1930s. Much of the Great Plains grew very dry as a result of drought and poor farming techniques. It was called the Dust Bowl. Millions were forced to leave their farms and their way of life. Since then, there have been great improvements in farming practices in the Great Plains. These have prevented the Dust Bowl disaster from occurring again. Grazing is another worry. Cows do two things to soil. First, they eat grasses and plants that hold soil in place. Second, their hooves break down the top layer of soil. The result is that good soil can be blown away by the wind. The dirt left behind is not good for growing plants.

Some think that droughts cause this condition. In fact, it is mostly caused by people. It has become one of the most serious global problems. Droughts are normal in dry and semi-dry places. Well-managed lands have the ability to recover from droughts when rain returns. It is man's effect on nature that is the key. A five-year drought was worsened by poor land management in West Africa some years ago. It caused the deaths of more than 100,000 people and twelve million cattle.

Desertification is a common issue in politics. There are still many things that people do not know about it. The process is a very complex form of degradation. More research needs be done to understand it better.

7 In paragraph 1, why does the author mention "The Sahara Desert"?

Ⓐ To call it the world's largest desert
Ⓑ To mention how dangerous it is
Ⓒ To show how it is expanding
Ⓓ To claim it proves desertification

8 The word "they" in the passage refers to

Ⓐ the Great Plains
Ⓑ cows
Ⓒ grasses
Ⓓ plants

9 According to paragraph 2, what has prevented the Dust Bowl from happening again?

Ⓐ Better cattle breeds
Ⓑ Good farming practices
Ⓒ Better irrigation techniques
Ⓓ More rainfall in many regions

10 The word "normal" in the passage is closest in meaning to

Ⓐ ordinary
Ⓑ unusual
Ⓒ frequent
Ⓓ serious

11 Which of the following best expresses the essential information in the highlighted sentence? *Incorrect* answer choices change the meaning in important ways or leave out essential information.

Ⓐ Land only recovers with rain starts to fall.
Ⓑ Rain helps the recovery of all managed land.
Ⓒ Rains support the recovery of well-managed lands.
Ⓓ Droughts prevent land from recovering from poor management.

12 The word "complex" in the passage is closest in meaning to

Ⓐ complicated
Ⓑ chewable
Ⓒ overwhelming
Ⓓ boring

Vocabulary Check-Up

Choose the words with the closest meanings to the highlighted words.

1 His good speech inspired me to become a politician.

Ⓐ behaved
Ⓑ accepted
Ⓒ influenced
Ⓓ acted

2 Japan is moister than Korea due to all the rain it gets.

Ⓐ damper
Ⓑ noisier
Ⓒ drier
Ⓓ lighter

3 He likes to think of himself as a normal person.

Ⓐ harmful
Ⓑ detailed
Ⓒ ordinary
Ⓓ final

4 People usually have many different aspects.

Ⓐ influences
Ⓑ features
Ⓒ professions
Ⓓ pieces

5 The last emperor was so cruel that he killed many innocent people.

Ⓐ personal
Ⓑ talented
Ⓒ mean
Ⓓ gentle

6 Bordeaux, France, is a very famous region for wine.

Ⓐ border
Ⓑ hometown
Ⓒ area
Ⓓ break

7 He hopes to encounter his friends at the movie theater tonight.

Ⓐ challenge
Ⓑ reserve
Ⓒ hire
Ⓓ meet

8 What is the most frequently asked question from your customers?

Ⓐ often
Ⓑ widely
Ⓒ correctly
Ⓓ similarly

9 I work on a rotating system. This week, I work at night.

Ⓐ loading
Ⓑ changing
Ⓒ confusing
Ⓓ counting

10 Europeans plundered a lot of cultural properties from Egypt.

Ⓐ charged
Ⓑ experienced
Ⓒ allowed
Ⓓ robbed

PART Ⅱ

Making Inferences

In this part, the reading comprehension questions include rhetorical purpose, inference, and insert text. The learning objectives of these comprehension questions are to understand the rhetorical function of a statement or paragraph, the logic of the passage, and the strongly implied ideas in the text.

UNIT

06 Rhetorical Purpose

Overview

Introduction

Rhetorical Purpose questions ask you to understand why and how the author uses a particular piece of information in the passage. Because this type of question usually focuses on the logical development of the passage, you need to figure out how a word, a phrase, or information relates to the rest of the passage.

Question Types

- The author discusses "X" in paragraph Y in order to
- Why does the author mention "X"?
- The author uses "X" as an example of

Useful Tips

- Read the question first and then recognize the author's purpose immediately by scanning specific phrases or sentences.
- Focus on the logical links between words and sentences, not on the overall organization of the passage.
- Familiarize yourself with the words or phrases for rhetorical functions such as *to illustrate*, *to criticize*, *to explain*, *to contrast*, *to compare*, and *to note*.

Sample TOEFL iBT Question

Q The author discusses "Digital dictionaries" in the passage in order to

Ⓐ compare them with regular dictionaries
Ⓑ explain some of their functions
Ⓒ write about how they were invented
Ⓓ encourage readers to acquire them

Digital dictionaries are very effective learning tools. They check spellings and word meanings. They also provide synonyms. Even better, they show how words are used in sentences. This helps students learn about the grammar of certain words. Students can learn to use words while making fewer mistakes. They become better writers this way.

06-01

Correct Answer

If you read the passage carefully, you will notice that the author provides several of the functions of digital dictionaries. Therefore, the correct answer is Ⓑ.

Basic Drill

Read the passages and answer the questions.

Skill & Tip

Rhetorical Purpose questions ask you why the author uses particular words and phrases. These words and phrases can be used to argue, define, illustrate, or contrast ideas. So you need to look at the logical links between ideas rather than focusing on the overall organization of the whole passage.

Example

Fireflies are interesting insects. They use their light as a type of signal. They can turn their light on and off in a precise way. The flies do this to find a mate. In some species of flies, females like males that have a long flash. In other species, females prefer males that can flash quickly. Some species of firefly can produce two different colors of light, red and green.

Q In the passage, why does the author mention "a long flash"?

Ⓐ To point out a problem
Ⓑ To explain a mutation
Ⓒ To emphasize a unique characteristic
Ⓓ To describe a preference

Correct Answer Ⓓ

Drill 1

Avalanches are dangerous. When great sheets of ice and snow slide down the mountain, they can destroy everything in their path. Snow that does not stick together is likely to slide. Skiers get hurt and even die. Scientists study snowflakes to learn more about avalanches. They look to see how ice crystals form. Certain shapes make sticky snow. Other shapes can make snow slide.

06-02

Q In the passage, the author uses "Skiers" as an example of

Ⓐ people who often cause avalanches
Ⓑ people who point out where avalanches are
Ⓒ people who can be harmed by avalanches
Ⓓ people who try to avoid avalanches

Drill 2

The Maldives are a group of islands in the Indian Ocean. There are over one thousand small islands in this group. The islands are formed by coral that rests on the tops of underwater volcanoes. The coral often grows in a circular formation. When the coral reaches the surface, an island forms. There is often a section in the middle where there is no coral. This forms a lake in the middle of the island that is fed by sea water.

06-03

Q In the passage, why does the author mention "coral"?

Ⓐ To note that the Maldives were formed millions of years ago
Ⓑ To point out what the Maldives are made from
Ⓒ To explain why the Maldives have different shapes
Ⓓ To describe the different types of it found in the Maldives

Drill 3

An eating disorder is a way of eating that harms a person's health. Some people overeat and gain weight. Others eat too little. Some do something called binge eating. They eat too much at one time to the point where they experience pain. They often feel embarrassed about eating, so they try to do this alone. One aspect of any eating disorder is that people cannot control the way they eat.

06-04

Q The author discusses "binge eating" in the passage in order to

Ⓐ contrast overeating and not eating
Ⓑ explain what overeating and eating too little are
Ⓒ illustrate why people feel embarrassed
Ⓓ compare embarrassing ways of eating alone

Drill 4

Poverty is a major social issue. There are a number of causes. Certain groups of people may be denied basic rights. They are not given work because of their race or religion. A lack of freedom is another. Sometimes a leader prevents people from living and working in the ways they want. He keeps all the money and power for himself. A third cause is war. It can ruin the basic economy of a country. People spend most of their energy surviving rather than improving their lives.

06-05

Q In the passage, the author uses "A lack of freedom" as an example of

Ⓐ a problem in some countries
Ⓑ a reason people are poor
Ⓒ something bad leaders cause
Ⓓ a result of some wars

Drill 5

Cherrapunji in India is the wettest place on the Earth. Sometimes it rains for two months without stopping. Strangely, the water does not stay in one place. The land used to be green with plants, but because of people, this is no longer true. They have destroyed the land. Now, when it rains, the water flows away over the hard ground. The dirt and the plants are washed away.

06-06

Q The author discusses "Cherrapunji" in the passage in order to

Ⓐ describe what the land there used to look like
Ⓑ point out how much it rains there
Ⓒ show what is unusual about the area
Ⓓ explain why it gets so much rainfall

Exercises with Short Passages

Exercise 1 Read the following passage and answer the questions.

Time Limit: 30 sec.

Bugs Have the Answers

06-07

Police must know the exact time and place when a person died. This information can help answer questions about the way the person died. It may have been an accident or a crime. Crime experts can look to insects for these answers. Insects such as moths, mites, and beetles have different life cycles. They also have different eating habits. Some types of mites only eat flesh from dead bodies in the early stages of rot. Other mites feed on flesh at later stages. Beetles typically feed on flesh in late stages and in damp conditions. Moths eat flesh in dry conditions. Experts can look at which insects are present and when they laid their eggs. These can help determine the time and the place a person died.

General Comprehension

1 According to the passage, why do police need to know the time and the place a person died?

Ⓐ To learn how the person died
Ⓑ To tell the family the news
Ⓒ To learn about the insects on the body
Ⓓ To check whether the place was damp or not

2 The word "habits" in the passage is closest in meaning to

Ⓐ skills
Ⓑ behaviors
Ⓒ appearances
Ⓓ tastes

Mastering the Question Type

3 In the passage, why does the author mention "mites"?

Ⓐ To discuss their life cycle
Ⓑ To point out their unique appearance
Ⓒ To state how long they can live
Ⓓ To describe the food that they eat

4 The author discusses "Experts" in the passage in order to

Ⓐ show how they use insects in their investigations
Ⓑ claim that they need to learn much more about insects
Ⓒ point out that many of them have little experience with insects
Ⓓ argue that they do not study insects enough

Words & Phrases

flesh n the soft part of a person's or animal's body between the bones and the skin
rot n decay; decomposition
feed on phr to eat
typically adv normally; usually
damp adj wet; moist
determine v to identify

Exercise 2 Read the following passage and answer the questions.

Time Limit: 30 sec.

Anxiety Disorders

06-08

Anxiety disorders stop people from doing what they want to do. Anxious people actually have physical symptoms of their feelings. Their hearts might beat fast. They may start to sweat. They may even have severe panic attacks. People with this disorder cannot control their worries. They worry about simple things like appointments and cleaning their house. They may even worry that their desks are not well organized. Doctors say people have this disorder if they spend more days worrying than not worrying. They say such people always feel tired or annoyed because of their worries. They cannot sleep or eat sometimes. Basically, worries are at the center of their entire lives.

General Comprehension

1 According to the passage, what is a symptom of anxiety?

Ⓐ A feeling of calm
Ⓑ A rapid heartbeat
Ⓒ A high temperature
Ⓓ A weak voice

2 According to the passage, anxiety disorder is

Ⓐ a type of appointment with a doctor
Ⓑ a time where people only get worried about messes
Ⓒ a condition in which worrying is a regular part of life
Ⓓ the time when people worry the most in their lives

Words & Phrases

anxiety n a feeling of nervousness or worry
disorder n a problem or illness which affects someone's mind or body
severe adj intense; strong
annoyed adj being in a bad mood; fairly upset about something
entire adj total; whole

Mastering the Question Type

3 In the passage, the author uses "severe panic attacks" as an example of

Ⓐ a symptom of anxiety
Ⓑ a reason to visit a doctor
Ⓒ a cause of anxiety
Ⓓ a problem few people have

4 In the passage, why does the author mention "appointments"?

Ⓐ To prove they can help people with anxiety
Ⓑ To explain why some people cancel them
Ⓒ To name something people worry about
Ⓓ To argue that they are often not necessary

Exercise 3 Read the following passage and answer the questions.

Time Limit: 30 sec.

The Strait of Magellan

06-09

At one time, travel from the Atlantic to the Pacific Ocean was dangerous. This was in a time before the Panama Canal. Ships had to go around the bottom of the world. Sometimes they would take the long trip below Africa. They could also take the Drake Passage. This was the stretch of water between the South Pole and South America. The water and the weather were both very dangerous. Huge blocks of ice threatened to wreck ships. Magellan found another way in 1520. The passage was called the Strait of Magellan. It passed between the continent to the north and Tierra del Fuego, an island, to the south. This narrow strip of water was protected by land. It gave ships the safety they needed.

General Comprehension

1 According to the passage, why was it dangerous to travel between the Atlantic and Pacific oceans?

- (A) Ships sometimes got frozen in the ice.
- (B) There were pirates in those waters.
- (C) The water and the weather were not safe.
- (D) Ships could hit land there at any time.

2 According to the passage, the Strait of Magellan is safe because

- (A) it has a lot of room for ships
- (B) it is protected by land on both sides
- (C) large blocks of ice do not flow there
- (D) the South Pole is not far away

Words & Phrases

stretch n a distance
block n a chunk
threaten v to menace; to bully; to intimidate
wreck v to destroy or ruin completely
strip n a thin piece

Mastering the Question Type

3 In the passage, why does the author mention "Africa"?

- (A) To claim that its waters could be dangerous
- (B) To note the location of the Strait of Magellan
- (C) To argue that it was a safe place to sail
- (D) To state that ships sometimes sailed past it

4 In the passage, the author uses "Tierra del Fuego" as an example of

- (A) the most dangerous place for sailors
- (B) a place known for being the end of the world
- (C) an area that had a deep harbor that ships used
- (D) one boundary of the Strait of Magellan

Exercise 4 Read the following passage and answer the questions.

Time Limit: 50 sec.

The Way People Speak

06-10

The way people speak can tell others a lot about their backgrounds. For example, people can guess if someone is from the northern part of the country or the southern. What happens if a child has a southern accent but uses northern words? People might guess that the child's family moved from the north to the south. The child has the accent of his friends but uses some words only spoken by his parents. People's social classes also affect the way they speak. A famous sociolinguist, William Labov, tried to find a link between accent and social class. He went to three different shops in New York. The first was used by upper-class people, the second by the middle class, and the third by the lower class. He found that in general, people in the upper-class shop did not pronounce "R" in the same way as customers in the other shops.

General Comprehension

1 The word "backgrounds" in the passage is closest in meaning to

- (A) families
- (B) settings
- (C) life cycles
- (D) upbringings

2 According to the passage, how do the places where people live affect the way they speak?

- (A) There are links between accents and social classes.
- (B) People want to tell others about their backgrounds.
- (C) People cannot tell the difference between northerners and southerners.
- (D) People use certain words and speak with accents.

Words & Phrases

background (n) history
affect (v) to influence
accent (n) a way of speaking
sociolinguist (n) a person who studies language and society
pronounce (v) to say

Mastering the Question Type

3 In the passage, why does the author mention "People's social classes"?

- (A) To name three different social classes
- (B) To explain why the upper class is different from other classes
- (C) To argue that all of the classes are the same
- (D) To claim it can determine the way they speak

4 The author discusses "William Labov" in the passage in order to

- (A) argue that his results were incorrect
- (B) describe an experiment that he conducted
- (C) name a famous book that he authored
- (D) note that he mostly studied the lower class

Exercises with Mid-Length Passages

Exercise 1 Read the following passage and answer the questions.

Time Limit: 1 min. 40 sec.

Forensic Science

06-11

1→ Forensics is a branch of science used by the legal system. Forensic means "related to the courts." This field helps answer legal questions about the world. A common use of forensics is in fighting crime. Police try to link criminals with crimes. They look for fingerprints and shoeprints in rooms. Police look for evidence in the form of bodily fluids. They can also look at scratch marks on skin and pieces of hair. They can even match bite marks to a suspect.

2→ Police also study how poisons work on the body. Crime experts record how much of a chemical was used. They also guess how much time has passed since its use. They try to see what chemicals were present at a scene. Blood samples can expose the short-term use of a drug or poison. Hair samples can expose long-term use. Hair grows one centimeter per month. This gives experts an idea of when drugs or poisons were used.

These are just a few of the areas that forensics looks at. The field is very broad. Science is very useful to the legal system. It can be used to help answer difficult questions.

Words & Phrases

legal adj related to the law
link v to connect
fluid n a liquid
suspect n a person who is thought to be a criminal
expose v to show or demonstrate

1 In paragraph 1, why does the author mention "Police"?

(A) To discuss how well they do their jobs
(B) To describe their main job duties
(C) To prove that they are not very effective
(D) To name some people who use forensics

2 In paragraph 1, the author uses "fingerprints and shoeprints" as examples of

Ⓐ how police use forensics
Ⓑ how police look for fluids
Ⓒ how police look at hair
Ⓓ how police analyze bite marks

3 The author discusses "Hair samples" in paragraph 2 in order to

Ⓐ compare their usage with that of chemicals
Ⓑ show how they are used in forensics
Ⓒ note the effects of poisons on them
Ⓓ mention how long it takes hair to grow

Summary Note

Forensics: science used by the legal system

Link criminals to crimes

- Fingerprints
- Fluids
- Hair
- Scratch marks
- Teeth marks

How poisons work

- Type of chemical
- Time of use
- Blood
- Hair

Exercise 2 Read the following passage and answer the questions.

Time Limit: 1 min. 50 sec.

Shyness

06-12

1→ Many people feel shy. It is a feeling of wanting to hide when being with others. When people feel shy, they do not wish to be around other people. It often happens when people are in unfamiliar situations or with others they do not know. Sometimes it is an issue of gender. Men and women may feel shy in mixed company. When men are with men or women are with women, they feel less shy.

2→ The cause of shyness is not simple. Sometimes people may become shy because of a bad event in their lives. For example, if a person were hurt by someone she loved, it may make her shy in the future. People can also be naturally shy. In some families, one child is outgoing whereas the other is shy. The family environment is the same for both children. Each child just has a different personality. Scientists even talk of a shyness gene.

3→ Shyness can be a cultural problem. American culture values people who are open and bold. It likes people to be aggressive. So shy people see their feelings as a negative thing. Other cultures do not value people acting differently from others. In these cases, shy people may feel that they fit well into those cultures.

Words & Phrases

gender n the fact of being either male or female
in mixed company phr when men and women are in a place together
outgoing adj friendly and enjoying being with people; extroverted
personality n the mental characteristics of a person
whereas conj in contrast with
aggressive adj behaving in an angry or rude way

1 The author mentions "gender" in paragraph 1 in order to

Ⓐ describe what shyness does to women rather than men
Ⓑ show that shyness may happen in certain company
Ⓒ explain the difference between new situations and old ones
Ⓓ state that shyness only happens to men

2 The author discusses "children" in paragraph 2 in order to

Ⓐ support an impossible idea
Ⓑ explain differences in feelings
Ⓒ describe how shyness does not happen to children
Ⓓ show that people can be born shy

3 In paragraph 3, why does the author mention "American culture"?

Ⓐ To exemplify a culture that does not value shyness
Ⓑ To describe how Americans feel about culture
Ⓒ To show what aggressive people do to shy people
Ⓓ To discuss different ways to be shy around others

Summary Note

Unfamiliar situations

Not wishing to be around others

Shyness

Happens when with members of the opposite sex

Not valued in some cultures

Cause: natural personality

Cause: bad events

Exercise 3 Read the following passage and answer the questions.

Time Limit: 1 min. 30 sec.

Siwa

06-13

Siwa is a famous oasis. It has long been the resting place for armies and traders crossing the African desert. It has been settled for over ten thousand years. It is 560 kilometers west of Cairo, Egypt.

2→ The oasis was also known for its powerful oracle. People would travel hundreds of kilometers to seek his guidance. The temple still stands today, which shows the importance of the place.

3→ Alexander the Great was known to have rested there when he invaded Egypt. It is said that he and his army ran out of water in the desert. The gods sent two crows to guide him to Siwa, which saved his army. Alexander visited the oracle. The oracle told Alexander that he was divine and the rightful ruler of Egypt.

4→ Today, Siwa relies on farming. It is an amazing feat in the middle of the desert. The oasis produces, some argue, the finest dates and olives in the world. Farmers tend to their crops with great care. They ensure that the water flows in and out of their fields in just the right way. They even pollinate their date palm trees by hand.

Words & Phrases

oracle n a person who a god or goddess speaks through
run out of phr no longer to have something
divine adj relating to a god
feat n an accomplishment
tend v to pay attention to
pollinate v to put pollen on a plant to make it grow fruit

1 The author discusses "its powerful oracle" in paragraph 2 in order to

(A) contrast Alexander with the oracle
(B) persuade people to visit the oracle in Siwa
(C) show the cultural importance of Siwa
(D) explain what an oracle usually does

2 The author discusses “Alexander the Great” in paragraph 3 in order to

Ⓐ give an example of the historical importance of Siwa
Ⓑ contrast Alexander with the Egyptian gods
Ⓒ explain how Alexander won a war against Egypt
Ⓓ explain what a rightful ruler is

3 In paragraph 4, the author uses “dates and olives” as examples of

Ⓐ foods planted during Alexander’s time
Ⓑ foods grown at the oasis in Siwa
Ⓒ popular foods in the Middle East
Ⓓ common foods eaten in Egypt

Summary Note

Siwa: A Famous Oasis

- Settled for over 10,000 years
- 560 kilometers west of Cairo
- Relies on farming
- Visited by Alexander the Great
- Had a famous oracle

Exercise 4 Read the following passage and answer the questions.

Time Limit: 1 min. 50 sec.

Mountain Ranges

06-14

1→ A mountain is a type of landform. It rises high above the ground. A mountain range is a group of mountains that are relatively close together. These mountains have the same shapes and features. Around the world, there are hundreds of mountain ranges. Some are fairly short whereas other mountain ranges may extend for thousands of kilometers.

2→ Many mountain ranges are found along fault lines. These are areas where two or more tectonic plates meet. At times, two plates may collide. Generally, one plate goes beneath the other. This causes the second plate to rise higher in the air, thereby forming mountains. This is a slow process that can take millions of years. For instance, the Himalaya Mountains are still increasing in size. They rise a tiny amount each year.

3→ The longest mountain range in the world is the Andes. It is found in South America and runs down almost the entire continent. The Himalaya Mountain Range has the world's highest mountain and many other tall peaks. One of the oldest mountain ranges is the Appalachians in the United States. These mountains have become smaller as they have been eroding for millions of years.

Words & Phrases

landform n a natural feature on a piece of land
relatively adv somewhat
fairly adv quite
rise v to go up
peak n a mountain

1 In paragraph 1, the author uses "the same shapes and features" as examples of

Ⓐ characteristics of mountains in mountain ranges
Ⓑ types of landforms that are found around the world
Ⓒ unique appearances of some of the world's mountains
Ⓓ qualities that landforms must have to be mountains

2 The author discusses "tectonic plates" in paragraph 2 in order to

Ⓐ argue that they can make mountains smaller
Ⓑ prove they are found around the world
Ⓒ state how many of them there are
Ⓓ explain how mountains are formed

3 In paragraph 3, why does the author mention "The Himalaya Mountain Range"?

Ⓐ To state it has many high mountains
Ⓑ To call it the world's oldest mountain range
Ⓒ To compare it with the Appalachians
Ⓓ To name the countries it runs through

Summary Note

Mountain Ranges

- Groups of mountains close together
- Found along fault lines
- Form when tectonic plates collide
- Can take millions of years to form
- Longest mountain range is Andes

Building Summary Skills

A **Put the following sentences in order to make appropriate summaries based on the mid-length passages you worked on earlier. The first sentence is already provided.**

Exercise 1 Forensic Science

1 Forensic science helps collect information that is useful for police work and the law.
____ The field is very broad.
____ Police look for small clues that can identify criminals.
____ Many things are studied for forensic purposes.
____ The clues can come from someone's body (blood, skin, or fingerprints), or they can be chemical (drugs).

Exercise 2 Shyness

1 When people are shy, they wish to avoid others. This often happens in new situations.
____ Things can happen in people lives to make them shy.
____ Sometimes men and women feel shy around one another.
____ Sometimes people are born that way.
____ In some cultures, shyness is not valued, and in other cultures, it is a good quality to have.
____ This often happens in new situations.

Exercise 3 Siwa

1 Siwa is a famous oasis, and it has sheltered people crossing the desert for thousands of years.
____ Alexander the Great stopped in Siwa to consult him while conquering Egypt.
____ A powerful oracle lived there in ancient times.
____ Farmers must be very careful when managing the land and the plants.
____ Siwa has a water source, it depends on farming, and it has some of the best dates and olives in the world.

Exercise 4 Mountain Ranges

1 Mountain ranges are groups of mountains relatively close together.
____ The Andes are the longest mountain range while the Himalayas have the world's highest mountain.
____ Mountain ranges form when two tectonic plates collide.
____ It can take millions of years for mountains to form.
____ There are hundreds of mountain ranges around the world.

B **Fill in the blanks with suitable words or phrases to complete the following summaries. Do not look at the previous page until you are finished.**

Exercise 1 Forensic Science

Forensic science helps collect ______________ that is useful for ______________ and the law. Police look for ______________ that can identify ______________. The clues can come from someone's body (blood, skin, or ______________), or they can be ______________ (drugs). The field is very ______________. Many things are studied for ______________ purposes.

Exercise 2 Shyness

When people are ______________, they wish to ______________ others. This often happens in ______________ situations. Sometimes ______________ feel shy around one another. Things can happen in people lives to make them ______________. Sometimes people are ______________ that way. In some cultures, shyness is not ______________, and in other cultures, it is a ______________ to have.

Exercise 3 Siwa

______________ is a famous oasis, and it has sheltered people crossing the ______________ for thousands of years. A powerful ______________ lived there in ancient times. ______________ stopped in Siwa to consult him while conquering ______________. Siwa has a ______________, it depends on ______________, and it has some of the best ______________ in the world. Farmers must be very careful to manage the land and the plants.

Exercise 4 Mountain Ranges

Mountain ranges are ______________ of mountains relatively ______________ together. There are ______________ of mountain ranges around the world. Mountain ranges ______________ when two ______________ collide. It can take ______________ of years for mountains to form. The ______________ are the longest mountain range while the Himalayas have the world's ______________.

Mini TOEFL iBT Practice Test

06-15

The End of the World

A map of Tierra del Fuego

Tierra del Fuego is the end of the world. In geographical terms, it might just be. It is a small triangle of land that sits at the bottom of South America. The name means "Land of Fire." It was given the name by a famous explorer who saw the natives' fires on the shore. The island is shared by Argentina and Chile. Tierra del Fuego is notable for its unique geography.

However, the land is anything but fire. It rests at the southernmost tip of South America. The average temperature for the year is 5° Celsius. In winter, it gets much colder. Much of the temperature differences are due to altitude. Rivers of ice form on the Andes Mountains to the west. Cold rain and winds chill the flat lands to the north and the east.

3 → It is easy to talk about the land of Tierra del Fuego. The waters that surround it also are unique. They are perhaps the most important in the world. They are home to all kinds of birds. The albatross is the best known. There are also whales, squid, and many fish. For a few days in summer, huge schools of sardines move into this part of the world. Local people can simply walk into the water and catch them with shopping bags. Schools of fish are everywhere. They can be caught without bait. These fish are of huge economic value to the locals and to the world.

4 → Tierra del Fuego is a rare place. In such a small space, it contains varied land features: mountains, forests, and prairies. Two great oceans meet on either side. This group of features makes it home to a huge range of wildlife. The land has very long days in summer and short days in winter. It is a unique place on the Earth.

1 The word "It" in the passage refers to

Ⓐ Tierra del Fuego
Ⓑ The bottom
Ⓒ South America
Ⓓ The name

2 The word "notable" in the passage is closest in meaning to

Ⓐ notorious
Ⓑ remarkable
Ⓒ challenging
Ⓓ supporting

3 The word "altitude" in the passage is closest in meaning to

Ⓐ height
Ⓑ distance
Ⓒ length
Ⓓ shape

4 In paragraph 3, the author uses "huge schools of sardines" as an example of

Ⓐ fish that live in Tierra del Fuego all year
Ⓑ common food that people in Tierra del Fuego eat
Ⓒ fish that go to Tierra del Fuego
Ⓓ the best bait for fishing in Tierra del Fuego

5 According to paragraph 3, why are the waters of Tierra del Fuego unique?

Ⓐ People can catch fish with shopping bags in winter.
Ⓑ Many types of sea life and birds go there.
Ⓒ The water there is great for drinking.
Ⓓ The ice there has various nutritional properties.

6 In paragraph 4, the author's description of Tierra del Fuego mentions all of the following EXCEPT:

Ⓐ The names of some animals there
Ⓑ The oceans that it is located by
Ⓒ What the days there are like
Ⓓ Different types of land there

Family and Money

06-16

The modern world is changing family relationships. The cost of living has had an influence on how American families behave. It may not be the best thing. Several decades ago, the father went to work. His paycheck paid the bills. The mother stayed home. She might have volunteered at a local church or a community program. The children went to school. Sometimes they had weekend jobs when they were teenagers.

2→ In many parts of the United States, things are different. The cost of living is on the rise. The greatest increases in the cost of living are seen in property prices and health care. Basically, one salary is not enough to buy or rent a house and to pay the bills. As a result, both parents must work. This helps the family keep a roof over their heads, and they can go to the doctor when they need to.

When both parents work, it changes the amount of time that their children spend with them. Many parents put their children in daycare. This has the benefit of ensuring their children's care. But it also reduces the amount of time that parents spend with their children in their early years. What is more, daycare is an extra expense. Both parents must therefore work more to pay for it.

4→ During the school year, it is often the case that children come home before their parents do. They are called latchkey kids because they let themselves in the door. Their mothers are not waiting at home to open the door for them. This time alone puts them at risk of problems such as drugs and crime. The children may get in trouble more often because they are not supervised. Rising expenses are changing how families live. While working hard for better lives, they open themselves up to different risks.

7 The word "they" in the passage refers to

Ⓐ American families
Ⓑ the bills
Ⓒ the children
Ⓓ weekend jobs

8 According to paragraph 2, in the United States, both parents often work because

Ⓐ they want to save money
Ⓑ school tuition is rising
Ⓒ they take many trips
Ⓓ bills are too expensive

9 According to paragraph 2, which of the following is NOT true?

Ⓐ The cost of living is increasing.
Ⓑ Two salaries are needed to pay bills.
Ⓒ Doctors are raising their fees.
Ⓓ Property prices are increasing.

10 The word "ensuring" in the passage is closest in meaning to

Ⓐ guaranteeing
Ⓑ making
Ⓒ benefiting
Ⓓ timing

11 In paragraph 4, the author mentions "latchkey kids" in order to

Ⓐ show the consequences of rising costs
Ⓑ describe what latchkey kids do
Ⓒ explain why latchkey kids are important
Ⓓ demonstrate the need for better health care

12 The word "supervised" in the passage is closest in meaning to

Ⓐ commanded
Ⓑ hired
Ⓒ observed
Ⓓ trained

Vocabulary Check-Up

Choose the words with the closest meanings to the highlighted words.

1 The young tend not to vote these days.

Ⓐ are inclined
Ⓑ look after
Ⓒ are prepared
Ⓓ are willing

2 The company is threatened with bankruptcy.

Ⓐ prevented
Ⓑ confused
Ⓒ faced
Ⓓ chased

3 Modern civilization has resulted in a lot of benefits for people.

Ⓐ formats
Ⓑ advantages
Ⓒ defects
Ⓓ contracts

4 Some students study abroad at government expense.

Ⓐ materials
Ⓑ judgments
Ⓒ requirements
Ⓓ payment

5 A lot of students rely on their parents for advice and guidance on the social aspects of college life.

Ⓐ depend on
Ⓑ reply to
Ⓒ mean to
Ⓓ pass by

6 The scientist explored the bottom of the ocean with a lot of technological aids.

Ⓐ surface
Ⓑ ground
Ⓒ opposite
Ⓓ point

7 The rules of the game are relatively easy to understand.

Ⓐ certainly
Ⓑ somewhat
Ⓒ never
Ⓓ apparently

8 Most tree frogs change colors to harmonize with their background.

Ⓐ environment
Ⓑ creation
Ⓒ society
Ⓓ pressure

9 Finally, the rumor about the actress was exposed.

Ⓐ disappeared
Ⓑ disclosed
Ⓒ hidden
Ⓓ discussed

10 No one should be discriminated against according to nationality, gender, or occupation.

Ⓐ religion
Ⓑ personality
Ⓒ faith
Ⓓ sex

UNIT

07 Inference

Overview

Introduction

Inference questions ask you to understand an argument or an idea that is suggested but not explicitly mentioned in the passage. Because the answers to these questions are not directly given in the passage, you should figure out the logical implications of the author's words as well as the surface meaning of those words.

Question Types

- Which of the following can be inferred about X?
- Which of the following can be inferred from paragraph X about Y?
- The author of the passage implies that

Useful Tips

- Think logically to draw a reasonable conclusion from what is implied in the passage.
- Remember that the correct answer does not contradict the main idea of the passage.
- Do not choose an answer just because it is mentioned in the passage.

Sample TOEFL iBT Question

Secondhand smoke is a serious issue in the United States. It causes major health problems. Many people like to smoke in restaurants and bars. Nonsmoking customers can choose to go elsewhere. But employees cannot choose so easily. Servers are exposed to high levels of smoke. Their health is at risk.

07-01

Q Which of the following can be inferred about secondhand smoke?

Ⓐ It has killed a large number of people.

Ⓑ It should be accepted at restaurants.

Ⓒ It is a big problem at some workplaces.

Ⓓ It does not affect many people.

Correct Answer

At first, the passage notes secondhand smoke is a big problem in the United States. Then, it claims that people working in restaurants and bars may suffer from health problems due to secondhand smoke. So you can infer that secondhand smoke in workplaces is a big problem. So the correct answer is Ⓒ.

Basic Drill

Read the passages and answer the questions.

Skill & Tip

Inference questions ask you to identify an idea that is not explicitly stated in the passage. The idea is suggested or implied but never written in the text. In order to make an inference based on some information in the passage, you need to use logical thinking.

Example

The body mass index (BMI) tells people if their weight is healthy. It is a ratio of height to weight. A person with a BMI of less than twenty is not heavy enough. A person with one of twenty-five is healthy. A person with a BMI of thirty or more is overweight. The index is not absolute. It serves only as a rough estimate of people's healthy weight.

Q According to the passage, which of the following can be inferred about the BMI?

Ⓐ It can be used as an absolute measure.
Ⓑ It serves as a general guideline.
Ⓒ It is often incorrect.
Ⓓ It is used by the government.

Correct Answer Ⓑ

Drill 1

In summer, people need to take care of themselves. The heat can make them sick. The most serious sickness is heatstroke. There are a number of signs. One is a very high temperature. A second sign is a change in behavior. Dry skin is another sign. In many cases, the body cannot sweat to cool itself. It is possible to lose consciousness.

07-02

Q According to the passage, which of the following can be inferred about heatstroke?

Ⓐ It can be avoided by staying in a cool place.
Ⓑ It is impossible to avoid in summer.
Ⓒ It only lasts for a short amount of time.
Ⓓ It is a chronic illness.

Drill 2

There is a difference between hard news and soft news. Hard news refers to topics that are serious and timely. These include politics, crime, and war. Soft news refers to topics that are not very serious. Time is not an important factor in telling this kind of news. Soft-news topics include sports and news about famous people.

07-03

Q The author of the passage implies that

Ⓐ hard news is more interesting than soft news
Ⓑ soft news is more interesting than hard news
Ⓒ hard news and soft news serve different purposes
Ⓓ hard news is the most valuable type of news there is

Drill 3

In the United States, states' rights concern how individual states have separate governments from the nation. Each state can decide on important matters for itself. One state may not allow the death penalty while another does. As long as it does not go against the laws of the national government, a state can do what it wants. For now, the nation has not decided on the death penalty. Each state can decide as it wishes.

07-04

Q According to the passage, which of the following can be inferred about states' rights?

Ⓐ States make the death penalty a good punishment.
Ⓑ States are no longer necessary as an element of government.
Ⓒ States' rights may cause debates over many issues.
Ⓓ Each state can make any decision about the country.

Drill 4

Arthritis makes people's joints swell painfully. As people grow older, their bones become less protected from the soft tissue around them. Joints can grow in size and become sore. It happens in many older people and more often in women than men. Nearly one-third of Americans develop some form of this disease. In some cases, a joint may be so painful that doctors must replace it with an artificial one.

07-05

Q Which of the following can be inferred about doctors who treat arthritis?

Ⓐ They are not sure what causes it.
Ⓑ They often have to replace joints.
Ⓒ They only treat women, not men.
Ⓓ They cannot easily treat it.

Drill 5

Reality TV has been very popular in recent times. Viewers like to watch normal people in normal situations. They think that something unusual can be made from daily life. But many people question how real these shows actually are. Sometimes a show puts normal people in unusual situations. They go to strange places. And not all of the events are shown. Editors can pick which scenes to show. This changes how viewers see the event.

07-06

Q The author of the passage implies that reality TV

Ⓐ is somewhat artificial
Ⓑ is great programming
Ⓒ is unusual at times
Ⓓ is going to end soon

Exercises with Short Passages

Exercise 1 Read the following passage and answer the questions.

Time Limit: 40 sec.

Yellow Journalism

07-07

1→ In the 1890s, there were two major newspapers in New York City. They were the *World* and the *Journal*. Both were owned by wealthy men. Joseph Pulitzer owned the *World* and William Randolph Hearst the *Journal*. The *World* had the bigger circulation. In fact, it had the highest circulation in the United States. But the *Journal* competed strongly against it.

2→ To get more readers, both newspapers tried various tactics. They used sensational headlines. Their stories were often not researched well. Instead, they made outlandish claims at times. Their stories were often less than trustworthy. They also used many illustrations. They had cartoons as well. Their methods came to be known as yellow journalism. Today, the term is still used. It mostly refers to tabloids that focus on sensationalism rather than honesty.

General Comprehension

1 In paragraph 1, why does the author mention "Joseph Pulitzer"?

- (A) To compare him with William Randolph Hearst
- (B) To discuss some articles that he wrote
- (C) To name him as the owner of a newspaper
- (D) To state that a famous award was named for him

2 According to paragraph 2, which of the following is NOT true of yellow journalism?

- (A) It features headlines that attract people.
- (B) It results in greater sales for newspapers.
- (C) It includes stories that are not well researched.
- (D) It may utilize many pictures.

Words & Phrases

circulation n the number of issues a newspaper, magazine, etc. regularly prints

tactic n a method or way of accomplishing a goal

sensational adj meaning to create an emotional reaction

outlandish adj strange; beyond reasonable limits

illustration n a picture

tabloid n a newspaper that does not always publish truthful articles

Mastering the Question Type

3 Which of the following can be inferred about the *Journal* from paragraph 1?

- (A) It sold for a higher price than the *World* did.
- (B) It was later purchased by Joseph Pulitzer.
- (C) It hired some reporters from the *World*.
- (D) It was not the leading newspaper in New York City.

4 In paragraph 2, the author implies that yellow journalism

- (A) may have stories that include false statements
- (B) is still popular with many newspapers today
- (C) was only practiced by journalists in New York City
- (D) resulted in journalists making large amounts of money

Exercise 2 Read the following passage and answer the questions.

Time Limit: 30 sec.

Cataracts

07-08

Cataracts are very common. This is when the lens of an eye becomes cloudy. Half of all people over the age of sixty develop cataracts. Eye injury is one possible cause. But the most common cause is the sun's ultraviolet (UV) rays. A study showed that airplane pilots have a high risk of getting cataracts. It is possible that sunlight is not safe when people are high in the sky. Some diseases can also cause cataracts. Of course, old age can cause it, too. Parts of the eye become weak over time. Doctors used to use needles to remove the cloudy parts. Nowadays, they usually replace the entire eye lens with a plastic lens. In most cases, patients can go home on the same day as the surgery.

General Comprehension

1 According to the passage, a result of cataracts is that

- (A) people's eyesight becomes cloudy
- (B) people go blind from them
- (C) people feel like there are needles in their eyes
- (D) people experience great eye pain

2 The word "risk" in the passage is closest in meaning to

- (A) injury
- (B) opportunity
- (C) probability
- (D) appearance

Words & Phrases

injury n hurt

ultraviolet n light beyond the normal range of colors humans can see

remove v to take out; to get rid of

replace v to get rid of something and to put a new thing in its place; to substitute

patient n someone who is receiving medical treatment

Mastering the Question Type

3 The author of the passage implies that sunlight

- (A) is dangerous to people's eyes at all times
- (B) is only dangerous at high altitudes
- (C) helps prevent cloudiness in the eyes
- (D) makes the effects of diseases worse

4 Which of the following can be inferred from the passage about cataracts?

- (A) They are so common that they can be ignored.
- (B) They take a lot of money and time to treat.
- (C) They can develop from various causes.
- (D) They occur only in old people.

Exercise 3 Read the following passage and answer the questions.

Time Limit: 30 sec.

The Bill of Rights

07-09

In 1789, the Constitution was adopted by the American colonies. This created the United States. The Constitution described the various roles of the parts of the government. However, many Americans felt like more was needed. They thought that the rights of the people were not protected enough. So in 1791, the Bill of Rights was ratified. It contains the first ten amendments to the Constitution. It provides a number of important rights. The two most important are freedom of speech and the right to bear arms. Another amendment gives people the right to a swift trial. People have the right to practice their own religion, too. Their private property is protected as well. Without the Bill of Rights, the United States would be a very different place than it is today.

General Comprehension

1 According to the passage, which of the following is true of the Bill of Rights?

Ⓐ It was ratified in 1789.
Ⓑ It has ten amendments.
Ⓒ It was written by the president.
Ⓓ It takes away rights from the people.

2 The word "it" in the passage refers to

Ⓐ their private property
Ⓑ the Bill of Rights
Ⓒ the United States
Ⓓ a very different place

Words & Phrases

adopt v to accept
ratify v to approve formally
amendment n a legal change to a document
bear arms phr to have weapons
private property n a possession owned by a person

Mastering the Question Type

3 The author of the passage implies that the Constitution

Ⓐ was not ratified by every state
Ⓑ is longer than the Bill of Rights
Ⓒ is important to the American government
Ⓓ is frequently changed by the American people

4 Which of the following can be inferred from the passage about the Bill of Rights?

Ⓐ It gives rights to the American people.
Ⓑ It contains all of the amendments to the Constitution.
Ⓒ It was rejected by several American states.
Ⓓ It took a long time for the government to create.

Exercise 4 Read the following passage and answer the questions.

Time Limit: 50 sec.

Horses in Bullfights

07-10

Many horses are hurt in bullfights each year. The bull and the bullfighter are usually the center of attention. The crowd admires the bravery and skill of each. Sometimes the bullfighter is on horseback though. The horse also has skills. It is a highly trained animal that works with the bullfighter. The horse and the rider can move quickly in four directions at the slightest command. This is necessary to avoid the angry bull. The bull does not understand that a man is causing it pain. It only sees the horse. People do not know that the horse is blindfolded and has cotton stuffed in its ears. This prevents it from seeing and hearing the bull. If this were the case, the horse would be terrified. The horse depends on the bullfighter for its life in the ring. Sometimes a bullfighter is not quick enough, and the bull kills the horse.

General Comprehension

1 According to the passage, what is special about horses in bullfights?

(A) They are able to move when they want to.
(B) They are highly trained and help bullfighters.
(C) They do not need commands to avoid bulls.
(D) They have cotton in their ears to protect them.

2 The word "it" in the passage refers to

(A) the slightest command
(B) pain
(C) the horse
(D) the bull

Words & Phrases

admire v to like very much
bravery n brave behavior; the quality of being brave
slight adj very small in degree or quantity
command n an order; instructions
blindfolded adj having one's eyes covered
terrified adj very scared

Mastering the Question Type

3 According to the passage, what can be inferred about how a horse is hurt?

(A) The horse sometimes slips on the ground when the bull charges.
(B) The bullfighter does not give it a command to move in time.
(C) The bullfighter charges the bull with the horse at the wrong time.
(D) The bull cannot see where it is going and accidentally hurts the horse.

4 What can be inferred about bulls in bullfights?

(A) They think horses are causing them pain.
(B) They do not want to fight the bullfighters.
(C) They want to run away from the fight.
(D) They are eager to please the crowd.

Exercises with Mid-Length Passages

Exercise 1 Read the following passage and answer the questions.

Time Limit: 1 min. 50 sec.

Standards in Reporting

07-11

1→ The press is news sources like TV news and newspapers. It keeps people free to choose, to vote, and to think. The press keeps information flowing. For this system to work, there have to be standards. Good reporting can be explained through four ideas: harm, truth, privacy, and balance.

2→ A reporter for a newspaper must think about harm. A writer should be careful about how he might hurt a person's feelings by asking questions. Children, for example, must be treated with care because they are sensitive. When gathering facts, a reporter must think about how a child will be affected. Truth is another concern. A reporter must try to make as few errors as possible in reporting the facts. Facts should be said in a different way from opinions. This helps readers make better decisions.

Privacy is a worry as well. A reporter must balance the public's right to know with a person's right to a private life. Public figures like politicians do not have the same rights as normal people. Balance is also necessary. If possible, both sides of a story should be told. When only one side of a story is told, the reporter may seem to favor a certain person.

Words & Phrases

source n a person or book that provides information
harm n hurt; damage
sensitive adj easily hurt or upset
affect v to influence
normal adj usual; ordinary
favor v to treat better; to prefer

1 In paragraph 1, the author implies that reporting

Ⓐ keeps people free
Ⓑ is the best job to have
Ⓒ requires responsibility
Ⓓ is a tiring job

2 According to paragraph 2, which of the following can be inferred about harming sources?

Ⓐ It is an easy thing to do in difficult situations.
Ⓑ Everybody does it at some point in their lives.
Ⓒ No one has ever done it in the reporting profession.
Ⓓ Reporters prefer to harm their sources if they can.

3 Which of the following can be inferred from paragraph 2 about reporting facts?

Ⓐ It is simple to separate fact from opinion.
Ⓑ It is a challenge to separate fact from opinion.
Ⓒ Reporting the facts help readers make decisions.
Ⓓ Some newspapers do not always report facts.

Summary Note

Standards in Reporting

Truth: Report facts; make no mistakes

Harm: Don't hurt people's feelings

Balance: Report both sides of a story

Privacy: Some people don't want to share their lives

Exercise 2 Read the following passage and answer the questions.

Time Limit: 1 min. 20 sec.

Colorblindness

07-12

1 → Colorblindness mostly affects males. It is wrongly believed that with this condition, a person thinks red and green are the same thing. It is not so simple. In fact, there are several types of colorblindness.

2 → A part of the eye, the retina, helps people see colors. In the retina, there are two types of cells: rods and cones. Rod cells help people see in low light. Cone cells help people see in normal light. Cones come in three types, each with a different sensitivity to types of light. People see different colors when the three cone types work together. Colorblindness happens when one or more types of cones do not work properly. It is possible, though rare, for all three types not to work properly.

3 → Sometimes colorblindness can be the result of an eye injury. However, in most cases, it is genetic. The gene lies on the X chromosome. Because women have two of these, both chromosomes must be affected for the condition. Men have an X and Y chromosome. They only need their one X chromosome to be affected.

Words & Phrases

affect v to influence
retina n the area at the back of the eye
sensitivity n the quality or state of reacting easily
properly adv correctly; appropriately
chromosome n the part of the cell that carries genetic information
rare adj not common

1 According to paragraph 1, what can be inferred about colorblindness?

(A) Relatively few women have this condition.
(B) It happens to men and women equally.
(C) It makes people unable to see the color green.
(D) It is a rare type of condition.

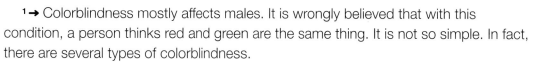

2 According to paragraph 2, which of the following can be inferred about types of colorblindness?

(A) Some types of colorblindness only affect women and not men.
(B) Some types of colorblindness stop people from seeing anything at all.
(C) Some people can only see in either light or dark shades.
(D) Some types of colorblindness only affect men and not women.

3 In paragraph 3, the author implies that colorblindness

(A) is a great challenge to everyone who has it
(B) can have a big effect on a person's quality of life
(C) can cause damage to a person's Y chromosomes
(D) is usually passed on to children from their parents

Summary Note

Can't see all colors

Mostly affects males

Colorblindness

Cone cells in the retina don't work

Mostly a genetic condition

Exercise 3 Read the following passage and answer the questions.

Time Limit: 1 min. 40 sec.

Lincoln in a Divided Land

07-13

1→ Abraham Lincoln helped shape the destiny of the United States. He helped the country through the Civil War. Slavery ended because of the war. But it was not the purpose of the war. The war was about keeping the states united under one government.

2→ In Lincoln's time, many states had not been formed yet. The U.S. government owned a lot of land, but it was not organized into states. This land was called territories. The southern states felt that the territories should have slavery when they became states. This would help them in national politics. The northern states did not want the South to get more political power by having more slave states. Lincoln could see that slavery was dividing the country. He thought the best way to stop this was to end slavery in the entire country.

3→ It is not clear what Lincoln's personal beliefs about race were. It is clear that he believed strongly in a united nation. He believed in the United States. So he decided when he was president that slavery should end. This would change the economic system of the southern states. It would make them more like the North and keep the country united.

Words & Phrases

destiny n the future
civil adj relating to the ordinary people of a country; not military or religious
purpose n a goal; an intention; an objective
political adj relating to politics
race n an ethnic group with distinct physical differences
economic adj relating to the economy

1 According to paragraph 1, what can be inferred about Lincoln's role in the United States?

Ⓐ He made the country what it is today.
Ⓑ He was one of the least important presidents.
Ⓒ He started the Civil War to stop slavery.
Ⓓ He was the first president to start a civil war.

2 According to paragraph 2, which of the following can be inferred about the states' attitudes?

Ⓐ The southern states no longer wanted to have slavery.
Ⓑ The southern states felt the northern states were going to get slaves.
Ⓒ The northern states felt the southern states were getting too much political power.
Ⓓ The northern states did not want to go to war with the southern states.

3 In paragraph 3, the author implies that Lincoln

Ⓐ was a popular president
Ⓑ was from a southern state
Ⓒ believed that slavery was not a moral issue
Ⓓ favored the northern states

Summary Note

Lincoln

Slave states
- were becoming powerful in government

Slavery
- divided politics in the U.S.
- Lincoln wanted to keep the country united

National government
- stop slavery in all states

Exercise 4 Read the following passage and answer the questions.

Time Limit: 1 min. 30 sec.

Bullfighting

07-14

1→ Bullfighting is part of the culture of many Latin countries. Portugal, Spain, and France keep this tradition. Countries in the Americas do, too. Ancient Rome and Greece had competitions that brought man and bull together. Some were more violent than others.

2→ Courage and style are prized in bullfights. This applies to the man and the bull. The bull is seen as a worthy contestant that must be honored. A bull with poor spirit or physical form brings shame to the owner of the bull and the event. If the bullfighter is unskilled, the crowd may cheer for the bull. The bullfighter must show his skill by killing the bull with one blow and standing between the bull's horns.

3→ There have long been concerns about animal cruelty. Many in society feel it is wrong to make an animal suffer. It is even more improper to kill them for entertainment. To keep the tradition, some countries like France and the U.S. have bullfights that are not deadly. The French must grab flowers from the horns of the bull. American bullfighters use Velcro to stick their lances on the bull.

Words & Phrases

tradition n a custom or belief that has existed for a long time
competition n a rivalry; a contest
apply to phr to relate to
contestant n a competitor
cruelty n behavior that deliberately causes pain or suffering
lance n a long spear used by soldiers on horseback

1 In paragraph 1, the author implies that bullfighting

Ⓐ is more popular today than it was in the past
Ⓑ is a tradition dating back to ancient times
Ⓒ sometimes results in the death of a bullfighter
Ⓓ can be a fun event for people to watch

2 According to paragraph 2, which of the following can be inferred about bulls?

Ⓐ They are selected to show strength and spirit.
Ⓑ They become excited when the crowd cheers for them.
Ⓒ They defeat the bullfighter most of the time.
Ⓓ They take part in several bullfights before retiring.

3 According to paragraph 3, what can be inferred about animal cruelty?

Ⓐ It is not taken seriously in the United States.
Ⓑ A lot of people do not care about it.
Ⓒ Some cultures take it seriously.
Ⓓ The French are cruel to animals.

Summary Note

A part of Latin culture

Bullfighting

Courage, skill, and style matter
The bull must be honored

Concerns about animal cruelty

Building Summary Skills

A **Put the following sentences in order to make appropriate summaries based on the mid-length passages you worked on earlier. The first sentence is already provided.**

Exercise 1 Standards in Reporting

1 TV news and newspapers are examples of the press, and they give information that helps people choose, vote, and think.
____ Reporters must be careful not to harm the person they are writing about.
____ There are standards for a good press.
____ A reporter must also consider a person's privacy and try to tell both sides of a story.
____ A reporter must try to report the facts as closely as possible.

Exercise 2 Colorblindness

1 Colorblindness is mostly found in men.
____ When the cones do not work properly, it results in colorblindness.
____ The parts of the eye called cones help people see certain colors of light.
____ Most of the time, this condition is genetic, and it is passed on to children through the X chromosome.
____ Sometimes colorblindness happens because of an injury.

Exercise 3 Lincoln in a Divided Land

1 Abraham Lincoln came to power at a time when the United States was trying to decide on slavery.
____ This issue divided the North and the South.
____ Many southern states wanted new states to have slaves.
____ It would help increase their political power, but northern states did not want this.
____ Lincoln thought it was best to end slavery in the whole country because he believed that the country should be united.

Exercise 4 Bullfighting

1 Bullfighting is an old tradition in some countries.
____ Courage, form, and style are very important in this sport for both man and bull.
____ Some countries have bullfights that do not hurt the bull.
____ Some people think this sport is cruel because it is not fair to make animals suffer.
____ If the bullfighter has poor skills, the crowd will cheer for the bull, so the bullfighter must show his skill by killing the bull quickly.

B **Fill in the blanks with suitable words or phrases to complete the following summaries. Do not look at the previous page until you are finished.**

Exercise 1 Standards in Reporting

TV news and ______________ are examples of the ______________, and they give information that helps people choose, ______________, and think. There are ______________ for a good press. ______________ must be careful not to harm the person they are writing about. A reporter must try to report the ______________ as closely as possible. A reporter must also consider a person's ______________ and try to tell ______________ of a story.

Exercise 2 Colorblindness

Colorblindness is mostly found in ______________. The parts of the eye called ______________ help people see certain ______________. When the cones do not ______________, it results in ______________. Sometimes colorblindness happens because of an ______________. Most of the time, this condition is ______________, and it is passed on to children through the ______________.

Exercise 3 Lincoln in a Divided Land

Abraham Lincoln came to ______________ at a time when the United States was trying to decide on ______________. Many ______________ wanted new states to have slaves. It would help increase their ______________, but ______________ did not want this. This issue ______________ the North and the South. Lincoln thought it was best to ______________ slavery in the whole country because he believed that the country should be ______________.

Exercise 4 Bullfighting

Bullfighting is an old ______________ in some countries. ______________, form, and style are very important in this sport for both ______________. If the bullfighter has ______________ skills, the crowd will cheer for the bull, so the bullfighter must show his skill by killing the bull ______________. Some people think this sport is ______________ because it is not ______________ to make animals suffer. Some countries have bullfights that do not ______________ the bull.

The FDA

07-15

The FDA is the common name for the Food and Drug Administration. It is a government agency that makes consumer goods safe. It regulates food and the food supply. It also controls diet supplements. The FDA is supposed to make sure that drugs and medical devices are safe and effective.

2→ For drugs and medical machines to be approved, they must go through a lengthy process. There are many strict tests. First, anything that humans use must be tested on animals. This may take up to six years. Then, it must be tested with a few people. Testing on fifteen to twenty people can last up to a year and a half. Third, a mid-sized group of 100 to 500 people is used. This often takes two years. Finally, a large group is tested over three years. For every 5,000 drugs discovered, only five enter trials. Of that group, only one passes on to the market.

3→ Food supplements such as ginseng follow a different path. The FDA does not pre-test them as it does for drugs. The agency only controls these products if they are unsafe but are already being sold. Two exceptions are baby and medical food. Because those that use them are not strong, the FDA is more careful with these products.

4→ Labeling is a major focus. A label must show what a product is for. For drugs, labels should show the name of the drug and what it is used for. They should also detail who should take the product and list any side effects. They need to detail directions for pregnant women, children, or old people. They must also include safety information. The FDA's mission is to protect the public from harm. It achieves this through controls and labeling. It has standards for effectiveness in medical products. It also has standards for how information is shared.

1 The word "regulates" in the passage is closest in meaning to

Ⓐ controls
Ⓑ adjusts
Ⓒ forbids
Ⓓ allows

2 According to paragraph 2, how many drugs make it to the market?

Ⓐ Nearly five thousand
Ⓑ One out of five thousand
Ⓒ Five out of five thousand
Ⓓ More than five thousand

3 In paragraph 3, the author uses "Food supplements" as an example of

Ⓐ products the FDA ignores
Ⓑ products the FDA controls
Ⓒ products the FDA buys
Ⓓ products the FDA rejects

4 The word "achieves" in the passage is closest in meaning to

Ⓐ develops
Ⓑ increases
Ⓒ controls
Ⓓ accomplishes

5 Which of the following can be inferred from paragraph 4 about labeling?

Ⓐ It is a necessary way to protect the public.
Ⓑ It does not matter if people read labels or not.
Ⓒ It is only effective when people can find the labels.
Ⓓ It has no use when doctors tell people what to do.

6 In paragraph 4, which of the following is NOT mentioned of labeling?

Ⓐ How large most labels should be
Ⓑ Who needs to have directions on it
Ⓒ What information is on labels
Ⓓ Why it is a major focus

Organ Transplants

07-16

In 1954, doctors did something that had never been done before. They took a kidney from one person. Then, they transplanted it into another person's body. This was the first organ transplant.

An organ transplant requires surgery. During it, an unhealthy organ is replaced with a healthy one. The healthy one comes from another person. This person is called an organ donor. In many cases, the person recently died. But in some cases, such as for kidney transplants, the person may still be alive.

3→ After the first kidney transplant, doctors learned very much about the process. In the 1960s, they would conduct liver, heart, and pancreas transplants. In the 1980s, they did lung and intestinal transplants. Not every transplant was successful. In some cases, the person being operated on died. As doctors became more experienced, the chances of success rose though.

4→ The major problem with organ transplants is that the host's immune system may reject the transplant. Doctors learned that the host and the donor must be a close genetic match. If this does not happen, then the body will reject the transplant. In recent years, various medications have been discovered. They can suppress the body's immune system. As a result, it does not reject the organ. Yet the body is more likely to suffer from infections that its immune system cannot fight.

5→ As of 2022, more than one million organ transplants had been conducted in the United States. More people are also agreeing to be organ donors when they die. That way, parts of their bodies can be used to help others in need. Doctors are experimenting with organs from animals, too. For instance, one person received a pig heart transplant in 2022. The patient died after a couple of months. Yet doctors believe they will be successful in the future.

7 The word "donor" in the passage is closest in meaning to

Ⓐ user
Ⓑ recipient
Ⓒ provider
Ⓓ conductor

8 In paragraph 3, the author uses "lung and intestinal transplants" as examples of

Ⓐ transplants with high failure rates
Ⓑ the most difficult types of transplants
Ⓒ transplants developed in the 1980s
Ⓓ some of the more common types of transplants

9 According to paragraph 3, which of the following is true of organ transplants?

Ⓐ Several different organs can be transplanted now.
Ⓑ They are among the most expensive operations.
Ⓒ More people die from them than survive them.
Ⓓ They can only be conducted by specialists.

10 The word "They" in the passage refers to

Ⓐ Organ transplants
Ⓑ Doctors
Ⓒ The host and the donor
Ⓓ Various medications

11 In paragraph 4, the author's description of the body's immune system mentions which of the following?

Ⓐ What medicines can suppress it
Ⓑ Its importance to organ transplants
Ⓒ The various parts of it
Ⓓ Its relationship with genetics

12 In paragraphs 4 and 5, the author implies that pigs

Ⓐ can live for as long as humans
Ⓑ have hearts that are fairly small in size
Ⓒ are immune to certain kinds of medications
Ⓓ are a close genetic match to humans

Vocabulary Check-Up

Choose the words with the closest meanings to the highlighted words.

1 Every soldier should obey commands in the military.

Ⓐ problems
Ⓑ rules
Ⓒ orders
Ⓓ methods

2 Seatbelts decrease the risk of injuries in car accidents.

Ⓐ wounds
Ⓑ rewards
Ⓒ stress
Ⓓ helps

3 The tactics the company is using are likely to succeed.

Ⓐ employees
Ⓑ products
Ⓒ advertisements
Ⓓ methods

4 Because of his improvement, many people admired him very much.

Ⓐ defended
Ⓑ expected
Ⓒ respected
Ⓓ understood

5 Two more countries will ratify the agreement this week.

Ⓐ reject
Ⓑ approve
Ⓒ consider
Ⓓ research

6 A major purpose for studying abroad is to see more of the world.

Ⓐ result
Ⓑ possibility
Ⓒ production
Ⓓ reason

7 In many Western countries, women by tradition wear white dresses when they get married.

(A) consideration
(B) convention
(C) notification
(D) factor

8 Good listeners are very rare since most people prefer talking.

(A) typical
(B) often
(C) unusual
(D) consistent

9 It is important to season lamb properly with salt and pepper.

(A) correctly
(B) actually
(C) practically
(D) politely

10 There is a very strong connection between smoking and cancer.

(A) division
(B) split
(C) dispute
(D) relation

UNIT

08 Insert Text

Overview

Introduction

Insert Text questions ask you to determine where the best place for a given sentence is in a passage. In this type of question, you will see four black squares appearing in one paragraph. You need to understand the logical stream of the paragraph and focus on any grammatical connections between sentences such as conjunctions, pronouns, demonstratives, and repeated words or phrases.

Question Types

- Look at the four squares [■] that indicate where the following sentence could be added to the passage.

  [a sentence to be inserted into the passage]

  Where would the sentence best fit?

  Click on a square [■] to add the sentence to the passage.

Useful Tips

- Put the sentence in each place next to the squares.
- Pay attention to the logical connection between sentences.
- Be familiar with connecting words, such as *on the other hand*, *for example*, *on the contrary*, *similarly*, *in contrast*, *furthermore*, *therefore*, *in other words*, *as a result*, and *finally*.

Sample TOEFL iBT Question

Q Look at the four squares [■] that indicate where the following sentence could be added to the passage.

Soon after, he succeeded in making the yo-yo the world's most famous toy.

Where would the sentence best fit?

The yo-yo is a popular toy around the world. Filipinos have long used yo-yos to catch animals from trees. **1** Even now, they are considered the best yo-yoers. **2** In 1920, American Donald Duncan saw a Filipino play with a yo-yo. **3** He then entered the yo-yo business. **4**

08-01

Correct Answer

The new sentence is about the actions of American Donald Duncan after he entered the yo-yo business. So **4** is the only place where the new sentence can fit.

Basic Drill

Read the passages and answer the questions.

Skill & Tip

Insert Text questions give you an example sentence and ask where the best place for that sentence in the passage is. You should understand the logical flow of the information in the paragraph. It is helpful to check out pronouns, linking words, demonstratives, and repeated words or phrases.

Example

Bono, a famous rock star, is well known for his other work. He is also a humanitarian. He works to improve the lives of people in poor countries. **1** Bono argues that respect for people's rights should be the first step to helping people. **2** Furthermore, Bono wants to help people help themselves. **3** That means that he wants to remove the structures that keep people poor. It may mean changing the economic rules for a country. It may mean helping people borrow money with a realistic way to pay it back.

Q Look at the three squares [■] that indicate where the following sentence could be added to the passage.

However, human rights are often ignored in these countries.

Where would the sentence best fit?

Correct Answer **1**

Drill 1

Bullying is a mean kind of behavior. It happens when a person scares or hurts someone who is weaker than the person is. **1** With children, this usually happens when there is no adult around. **2** A bully calls victims names and makes fun of how they do things. **3** He may say bad things about the victim to the victim's friends. A bully might even steal the victim's things. Bullying must be stopped at a young age so that children do not develop this behavior.

08-02

Q Look at the three squares [■] that indicate where the following sentence could be added to the passage.

Bullies usually hurt people again and again.

Where would the sentence best fit?

Drill 2

W.B. Yeats was an Irish poet. **1** He wrote about love, Irish myths, magic, and the spirit. **2** Yeats is one of the most important modern poets in English, but he liked to write poetry in traditional forms. **3** He liked to use rhymes and rhythms that older poets used. His poems have a commanding, timeless feeling. Yeats had a way of understanding the human experience. His ideas were so admired that he even had an influence in politics.

08-03

Q Look at the three squares [■] that indicate where the following sentence could be added to the passage.

He was born in 1865.

Where would the sentence best fit?

Drill 3

Human cloning raises some questions. ■1 First, people have to think about what it means to be unique. ■2 Being unique is a crucial human quality. ■3 As a unique individual, a person's sense of self is at the center of everything. If someone were cloned from another person, that individual's idea of identity would change. That might not be for the better. People should also think about relationships. When a person is cloned, that does not just affect one person's life. The lives of the people around that person are also affected.

08-04

Q Look at the three squares [■] that indicate where the following sentence could be added to the passage.

In fact, it is also a necessary quality for all living things.

Where would the sentence best fit?

Drill 4

Common law is an English legal system. It is used in many countries around the world. ■1 Court decisions are based on the results of past cases. ■2 One feature of common law is trial by jury. ■3 A group of people decide on another person's guilt or innocence. Another feature is that no one—not even the president—is above the law. Even the president must follow the law as regular people do.

08-05

Q Look at the three squares [■] that indicate where the following sentence could be added to the passage.

In other words, this law system takes history into account.

Where would the sentence best fit?

Drill 5

There is some debate over the importance of Alexandria in Egypt. It involves whether the city was more important as a center of knowledge or as a center of commerce. Some say that it was more important as a center of knowledge. It had a famous library. At one time, it was the largest in the world. It attracted scholars from many countries. Its contribution to present knowledge is no small feat. ■1 Others say that it was more important for trade. ■2 Much of the grain from Egypt was sold in Alexandria. ■3 The city had great power because of this.

08-06

Q Look at the three squares [■] that indicate where the following sentence could be added to the passage.

It fed hungry nations and made the city rich.

Where would the sentence best fit?

Exercises with Short Passages

Exercise 1 Read the following passage and answer the questions.

Time Limit: 40 sec.

Winston Churchill

08-07

Winston Churchill was a famous leader of Great Britain. He came from a family of politicians and war heroes. As a young boy, he did poorly at school. But when he got older, he became fascinated by military studies. He finished eighth in his class at the Royal Military Academy. He next joined the British Army in India to learn the skills of a soldier. It was a good experience for him. Then, he quit the army and went to South Africa as a reporter. **1** He wanted to cover the war between the Dutch and the British. **2** Churchill insisted on fighting even though he was not a soldier. **3** He was captured by the Dutch. **4** He escaped one month later and crossed hundreds of miles to friendly lands. He returned to England a hero. Churchill ran for Parliament and won a seat. This was the beginning of his famous political career.

General Comprehension

1 According to the passage, which of the following is NOT true of Churchill?

- (A) He was a poor student at school.
- (B) He graduated with honors from a military school.
- (C) He served in the army in India.
- (D) He worked as a reporter in South Africa.

2 According to the passage, Churchill became a hero because

- (A) he escaped from the Dutch enemy
- (B) he helped England win a war
- (C) he ran for Parliament
- (D) he was famous in South Africa

Words & Phrases

be fascinated by phr to be very interested in

military adj relating to soldiers or the armed forces

cover v to report on

insist v to demand

escape v to get away; to run away

run for Parliament phr to try to get elected to Parliament

Mastering the Question Type

3 Look at the four squares [■] that indicate where the following sentence could be added to the passage.

Prison was a difficult experience for him.

Where would the sentence best fit?

Exercise 2 Read the following passage and answer the questions.

Time Limit: 30 sec.

Social Pressure on Women

08-08

There is great social pressure for women to be pretty and successful. This can cause them a lot of stress. They learn from the media that they are supposed to look beautiful like a movie star. They learn that beauty is something that other people decide, not something they can decide for themselves. This conflicts with another message. ■1 Women are supposed to be independent and successful at their careers. ■2 Essentially, they are supposed to be strong, smart, and very good at their work. ■3 Many women between the ages of sixteen and twenty-five feel that this causes a lot of pressure. ■4 They say they do not want to care so much but feel it is impossible not to. By the age of thirty, the stress becomes less. Women learn not to care so much about what other people think.

General Comprehension

1 In the passage, the author uses "the media" as an example of

- (A) a group that few women listen to
- (B) something that puts pressure on women
- (C) a source of news for many women
- (D) the best source of entertainment for women

2 The word "Essentially" in the passage is closest in meaning to

- (A) Finally
- (B) Seriously
- (C) Formally
- (D) Basically

Words & Phrases

media n television, radio, newspapers, and news magazines

be supposed to-V phr to be expected or required to-V

conflict with v to go against

independent adj taking care of oneself

career n one's life's work, especially in business or in a profession

depressed adj very sad

Mastering the Question Type

3 Look at the four squares [■] that indicate where the following sentence could be added to the passage.

In many cases, they can become depressed.

Where would the sentence best fit?

Exercise 3 Read the following passage and answer the questions.

Time Limit: 50 sec.

Ezra Pound

08-09

Ezra Pound was a famous American poet. He grew up in the United States but spent many years in Europe. He was influenced by visual artists and classical Chinese poetry. His poems were complex and delicate. **1** Ezra lived in London for a few years. **2** He met his hero, W.B. Yeats, there. **3** They worked together on writing poetry. **4** Ezra Pound also worked with James Joyce and T.S. Elliot. After World War I, Pound moved to Italy. He loved Italian art. He also thought that Italian society at the time was a good and moral society. It had not been destroyed by capitalism. During World War II, he was arrested by the Americans. They said he was speaking out against the United States. As a result, he went to jail. During those twelve years, he was able to produce some incredible poems that showed his appreciation for life around him.

General Comprehension

1 The word "He" in the passage refers to

Ⓐ W.B. Yeats
Ⓑ Ezra Pound
Ⓒ James Joyce
Ⓓ T.S. Elliot

2 According to the passage, how did imprisonment change Ezra Pound?

Ⓐ He was able to meet James Joyce.
Ⓑ He learned that society was moral and fair.
Ⓒ He was able to speak out against the United States.
Ⓓ He developed an appreciation for life around him.

Words & Phrases

visual adj relating to being seen; seeable
complex adj not simple; complicated
delicate adj made in a fine, sensitive manner
speak out phr to oppose; to protest
incredible adj amazing; unbelievable
appreciation n understanding and liking

Mastering the Question Type

3 Look at the four squares [■] that indicate where the following sentence could be added to the passage.

They influenced each other's work greatly.

Where would the sentence best fit?

Exercise 4 Read the following passage and answer the questions.

Time Limit: 50 sec.

Hooliganism

08-10

Hooligans are people who cause trouble at sporting events. They are fans who like to cause fights. They often damage the area around a sporting event. The term "hooligan" was first used in a London police report in 1898. This violence has a long history. In 532 A.D., thousands of people died in fights that lasted a week. They were started by fans at a race. In modern times, soccer has had the most problems with fan violence. This has been going on in England since the 1950s. [■1] Italy has had a similar problem. [■2] This violence has spread to other countries. [■3] It has made it difficult for nonviolent fans to enjoy sports in a safe way. [■4] The violence also makes it difficult for shops around soccer fields to open safely. Many countries have strict laws to punish fans that cause trouble.

General Comprehension

1 According to the passage, what are hooligans?

(A) Soccer fans who live in England
(B) Sport fans who cause trouble at sports matches
(C) Sport fans who died in fights in 1898
(D) Soccer fans who live in England or Italy

2 According to the passage, for how long has sports violence been going on?

(A) A few years
(B) A few decades
(C) A hundred years
(D) More than a thousand years

Words & Phrases

damage (n) harm; injury; destruction
violence (n) the act of using physical force
last (v) to continue
similar (adj) almost the same
spread (v) to reach more and more people
strict (adj) requiring obedience; not flexible

Mastering the Question Type

3 Look at the four squares [■] that indicate where the following sentence could be added to the passage.

It has almost ruined national sports in some cases.

Where would the sentence best fit?

Exercises with Mid-Length Passages

Exercise 1 Read the following passage and answer the questions.

Time Limit: 1 min. 50 sec.

Betty Freidan

08-11

Betty Friedan argued for women's rights in the United States. Her experiences in her life and education gave her a powerful voice. She was able to change how society views women.

Friedan was born in 1921. She studied psychology at Smith College. She also worked at the college newspaper. Friedan passed on graduate studies at UC Berkley. **A1** Friedan married and had three children. **A2** She started writing for women's housekeeping magazines. **A3** She was bored and unhappy. **A4** Her home life did not challenge her abilities.

In 1957, Friedan questioned Smith graduates to see if they were happy with their lives. She found that many of them were not. **B1** Their lives existed only for the success of their husbands and children. **B2** Friedan wrote about how society was pushing women to live at home. **B3** They were meant to live for their families and not have interesting, challenging careers. **B4** Her book *The Feminine Mystique* became very famous. Twelve years later, she and her husband divorced. Friedan went on to work for a new image for women. She thought that women should take part in society in many more ways than being wives. She said that women should be in equal partnerships with men.

1 Look at the four squares [■] that indicate where the following sentence could be added to the passage.

Instead, she wanted to write about the rights of workers.

Where would the sentence best fit?

2 Look at the four squares [■] that indicate where the following sentence could be added to the passage.

These women had no feeling of their importance.

Where would the sentence best fit?

Words & Phrases

argue v to give reasons to support an opinion; to discuss

psychology n the scientific study of the human mind

pass on v not to make use of an opportunity

push v to force

challenging adj demanding

Summary Note

Betty Friedan

A feminist

Married and had a family

Shaped people's opinions

Changed society's expectations of women

Did not like her lifestyle

Exercise 2 Read the following passage and answer the questions.

⏱ Time Limit: 1 min. 50 sec.

Childhood Obesity

08-12

Being fat is a normal part of many people's childhoods. However, obesity means having too much fat. Children with this problem may stay like this as adults. **A1** It causes health problems that last a long time. **A2** In the United States, about fifteen percent of children are obese. **A3** Some children are more at risk of obesity than others. **A4** A family history of weight problems is one risk. Smoking and a lazy lifestyle are two other risks.

Obesity is not just a personal problem. It is a social problem. An obese person suffers health problems, of course. But when there are too many obese people, society starts paying the costs. Health care costs more, schools have more problems, and people become less productive.

Some of the causes of obesity are social. **B1** Schools do not provide healthy living choices. **B2** Food companies are allowed to advertise and sell junk food in schools. **B3** Even worse, many schools must cut their physical education programs because of budget issues. **B4** At home, children watch too much TV and play too many video games. Parents do not eat well either. They should show what good living habits are. They should not buy too much of the wrong kinds of food. It is important to teach healthy behavior at a young age.

1 Look at the four squares [■] that indicate where the following sentence could be added to the passage.

This number has grown since the 1970s.

Where would the sentence best fit?

2 Look at the four squares [■] that indicate where the following sentence could be added to the passage.

As a result, children do not get enough exercise.

Where would the sentence best fit?

Words & Phrases

normal adj usual; ordinary
at risk phr in danger; at stake
productive adj constructive; fruitful
advertise v to promote a product or service
budget n a plan for money

Summary Note

Obesity in Children

Causes long-lasting health problems	Has social consequences	Some causes are social

Exercise 3 Read the following passage and answer the questions.

Time Limit: 1 min. 40 sec.

The Literary Form of Tragedy

08-13

A tragedy is one of several kinds of plays. The literary form has been part of Western culture for thousands of years.

A1 A tragedy is about a hero who has something bad happen. **A2** This bad event is connected to the hero's actions. **A3** This is normally due to a weakness in the hero's personality called a tragic flaw. **A4** In many cases, the gods are angered by the hero. They make the hero live through a bad event. It is especially cruel, and the hero must suffer. The audience must see this bad event in order to understand the hero's flaw. They must also see his suffering.

At some point, the hero realizes his wrongs. He goes through some kind of learning process. Then, the gods decide to stop his punishment. In the play, a god may come down from the sky to deliver his message. He then frees the hero from his suffering. The audience goes through the changes of emotions from horror to relief. **B1** This is called catharsis. **B2** It means emotional healing. **B3** These simple ideas have lasted for thousands of years. **B4**

1 Look at the four squares [■] that indicate where the following sentence could be added to the passage.

Tragedy has a few key elements.

Where would the sentence best fit?

2 Look at the four squares [■] that indicate where the following sentence could be added to the passage.

Greek poets felt that this was a necessary part of a good tragedy.

Where would the sentence best fit?

Words & Phrases

personality n a person's character and nature
tragic adj extremely sad; miserable
flaw n a weakness; a defect
anger v to make angry
cruel adj very harsh; very painful
relief n feeling better after a bad event; comfort; ease

Summary Note

	A hero has a flaw	
Tragedy	He must suffer to learn about himself	Catharsis
	The gods free him from his suffering	

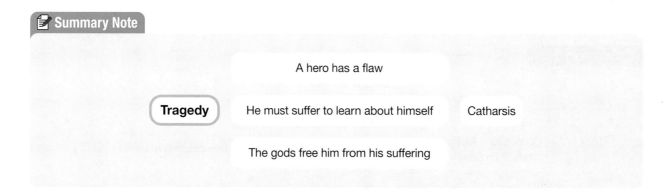

Exercise 4 Read the following passage and answer the questions.

Time Limit: 1 min. 30 sec.

The Paralympics

08-14

The Paralympic Games are held every Olympic year. **A1** The games give athletes the chance to show their skills. **A2** But these athletes are different. **A3** Their bodies are disabled in some way. **A4** The athletes get to use the same fields and stadiums as the athletes in the regular Olympics. The prefix *para* means "beside" in Greek.

To be in the games, athletes must have a disability. There are five types. Some do not have arms or legs. Some have brain damage. They have poor balance. Some athletes are in wheelchairs. Some others are blind. Some have birth defects. The great thing about these games is the attention to their skills. Their disabilities are not the focus.

The sports competition first started in England. It was for English soldiers who came back hurt from World War II. **B1** The first official Paralympic Games were held in 1960. **B2** There were 400 athletes who came. **B3** The most recent summer games had more than 4,000 athletes from over 160 countries. **B4**

1 Look at the four squares [■] that indicate where the following sentence could be added to the passage.

They begin three weeks after the Olympic Games.

Where would the sentence best fit?

2 Look at the four squares [■] that indicate where the following sentence could be added to the passage.

Soon, other countries started sending their people.

Where would the sentence best fit?

Words & Phrases

athlete n a person who plays a sport; a sportsperson

disabled adj not having normal abilities; handicapped

defect n a physical problem; an imperfection

competition n a rivalry, contest, or race

Summary Note

The Paralympic Games

- Held every Olympic year
- Athletes with physical disabilities
- Skill in sport is the focus
- Started in England after WW2
- Many participants

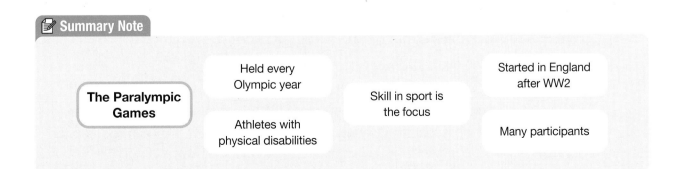

Building Summary Skills

A **Put the following sentences in order to make appropriate summaries based on the mid-length passages you worked on earlier. The first sentence is already provided.**

Exercise 1 Betty Friedan

1 Betty Friedan was a feminist, and she argued for women to be treated fairly in society and in marriage.
____ She asked other female college graduates how they felt.
____ Friedan had a family, but she was not happy with her life as a housewife.
____ She said women should take part in society more actively and be seen as equal to men.
____ Friedan discovered that they felt the same way, so she wrote a book about it.

Exercise 2 Child Obesity

1 Children with obesity might have long-lasting health risks.
____ Obesity also affects society because it affects the cost of health care and creates social problems.
____ There are more children today with this problem than in the 1970s.
____ People can change how schools and companies operate to decrease the risk of obesity, and they should make better food choices and promote good behavior.
____ Some children are more likely to be obese than others.

Exercise 3 The Literary Form of Tragedy

1 A tragedy is a traditional form of theater.
____ The audience experiences a range of emotions while watching the play.
____ It has a hero who, because of his personality, gets put into a bad situation where he must suffer.
____ This emotional change is a key part of tragedy, and this form of drama has lasted for thousands of years.
____ The hero learns from his ways, and the gods stop his punishment.

Exercise 4 The Paralympics

1 The Paralympics give disabled athletes the chance to show their skills.
____ Only certain kinds of disabilities are permitted in the games.
____ The games first started in England after World War II with just a few people.
____ Years later, there are more than 4,000 athletes and 160 countries competing.
____ The important thing is that the disability is not the focus, but excellence in sports is the focus.

B **Fill in the blanks with suitable words or phrases to complete the following summaries. Do not look at the previous page until you are finished.**

Exercise 1 Betty Friedan

Betty Friedan was a __________, and she argued for women to be treated __________ in society and in marriage. Friedan had a family, but she was not __________ with her life as a __________. She asked other female __________ how they felt. Friedan discovered that they felt the same way, so she wrote __________ about it. She said women should take part in society more __________ and be seen as __________ to men.

Exercise 2 Child Obesity

Children with __________ might have long-lasting health risks. There are more children today with this problem than in the __________. Some children are more likely to be __________ than others. Obesity also affects __________ because it affects the cost of __________ and creates social problems. People can change how __________ operate to decrease the risk of obesity, and they should make better __________ and promote good __________.

Exercise 3 The Literary Form of Tragedy

A __________ is a traditional form of __________. It has a hero who, because of his __________, gets put into a __________ situation where he must __________. The hero learns from his ways, and the gods stop his __________. The audience experiences a range of __________ while watching the play. This emotional change is a __________ part of tragedy, and this form of drama has lasted for thousands of years.

Exercise 4 The Paralympics

The Paralympics give __________ athletes the chance to show their __________. Only certain kinds of __________ are permitted in the games. The important thing is that the disability is not the focus, but __________ in sports is the focus. The games first started in __________ after __________ with just a few people. Years later, there are more than __________ athletes and __________ countries competing.

Mini TOEFL iBT Practice Test

William Smith

08-15

1→ William Smith lived in the late 1700s. He was an engineer. He had a simple discovery that led him to a life's work. He wanted to map the geology of England.

Smith came from a farming family in the west of England. His father died when he was young. Smith was raised by his uncle. He had a basic education but taught himself geography from books. He showed an early interest in fossils that he found near where he lived. **1** When Smith grew older, he became an engineer. **2** He worked for coal companies checking the quality of the land. **3** He had to drain water from places and see how easy it was to dig. **4**

Smith had to build a canal for a coal company. He saw as he dug that the earth had different layers. He noticed that each layer had certain kinds of fossils. As he traveled across England, he noticed these same features. Smith believed that the layers of earth in the north of England were connected to those in the south. He understood that these layers told an ancient history of the land. Soon, Smith had traveled all over England. Sometimes he traveled thousands of miles by horse and coach each year to observe the layers of the land.

4→ Smith did his best to share his knowledge with everyone. He made maps that told what kinds of rock, earth, and plants grew in different parts of England. He talked at farmers' meetings and at dinner parties. Smith also wrote several books. Smith was very skilled. Many methods for observing land features are still used today. His maps were very precise and can still be used today. Many geological terms that he created are also used.

1 According to paragraph 1, Smith's goal was to

Ⓐ put the geology of his country on paper
Ⓑ become a famous scientist
Ⓒ help coal companies grow
Ⓓ study the way farmers work

2 The word "those" in the passage refers to

Ⓐ certain kinds
Ⓑ fossils
Ⓒ these same features
Ⓓ the layers of earth

3 The word "ancient" in the passage is closest in meaning to

Ⓐ local
Ⓑ old
Ⓒ early
Ⓓ recent

4 The author discusses Smith's travels in paragraph 3 in order to

Ⓐ complain about his methods
Ⓑ show how much he cared about his work
Ⓒ explain how traveling was necessary
Ⓓ show what traveling was like in the past

5 The word "precise" in the passage is closest in meaning to

Ⓐ strict
Ⓑ careful
Ⓒ complex
Ⓓ accurate

6 Look at the four squares [■] that indicate where the following sentence could be added to the passage.

This work led him to a discovery.

Where would the sentence best fit?

Ancient Egyptian Sports

08-16

A fighting sport scene on the wall of an ancient Egyptian temple

1→ Many of the sports in ancient Egypt are still practiced today. In fact, many of the basic elements of sports, like rules and uniforms, were first used by the Egyptians. The sports had important functions in society. Some were played for fun and fitness. Others were played to make stronger warriors and leaders.

2→ The first group of sports, mostly for fun, included those like rowing, hunting, and the high jump. Hunting and fishing could be enjoyed by kings and regular people. The same was for rowing. Rowing required a lot of strength. Teams of people got into boats and followed the commands of a leader. He would give regular sharp calls to tell them when to row. This technique is still used for rowing teams today. Another popular game was tug-of-war. This was a game in which two teams tried to pull each other over a line. If a team fell forward, they lost. This game is still played in many countries today.

The second group of sports prepared people for the army and the temple. These included boxing, horse riding, running, and archery. **1** They were ways to work on skills for fighting. **2** They were also ways to work on mental and spiritual power. **3** Running a marathon was a good example of this. **4** Hockey was another Egyptian game. There are pictures where people are entombed that show the game. Players held tree branches with a bent end, just like modern hockey sticks. They had to hit a ball made of leather that was brightly colored.

These sports were a part of Egyptian culture. They kept people happy and fit. The basic rules were created thousands of years ago. They are still seen in some form today.

7 According to paragraph 1, what was the purpose of sports? *To receive credit, you must select TWO answers.*

Ⓐ To get people in good shape
Ⓑ To stop people from working too much
Ⓒ To keep people from fighting
Ⓓ To keep people happy

8 The word "regular" in the passage is closest in meaning to

Ⓐ systematic
Ⓑ hopeful
Ⓒ even
Ⓓ common

9 The author discusses "tug-of-war" in paragraph 2 in order to

Ⓐ explain how it was not fashionable
Ⓑ provide an example of an old game played today
Ⓒ state an opinion on ancient Egyptian games
Ⓓ contrast its simplicity with the complexity of other games

10 The word "These" in the passage refers to

Ⓐ Sports
Ⓑ The army and the temple
Ⓒ Boxing, horse riding, running, and archery
Ⓓ Skills for fighting

11 The word "entombed" in the passage is closest in meaning to

Ⓐ hidden
Ⓑ buried
Ⓒ portrayed
Ⓓ killed

12 Look at the four squares [■] that indicate where the following sentence could be added to the passage.

The king would run to show he had the mental strength to guide his country.

Where would the sentence best fit?

Vocabulary Check-Up

Choose the words with the closest meanings to the highlighted words.

1 Drunk driving can lead to tragic results.
- Ⓐ compacted
- Ⓑ miserable
- Ⓒ peaceful
- Ⓓ delighted

2 The bank insists on the store making its payment in full.
- Ⓐ persists in
- Ⓑ approves of
- Ⓒ objects to
- Ⓓ watches

3 There are a lot of defects in the machine.
- Ⓐ interest
- Ⓑ acquisitions
- Ⓒ treatments
- Ⓓ imperfections

4 Chocolate is made by a complex process.
- Ⓐ strange
- Ⓑ careless
- Ⓒ complicated
- Ⓓ simple

5 The company is pushing the sale of its new products on the market.
- Ⓐ spreading
- Ⓑ forcing
- Ⓒ staying
- Ⓓ serving

6 Competition is not evil in itself.
- Ⓐ Rivalry
- Ⓑ Combination
- Ⓒ Harmony
- Ⓓ Settlement

7 When people have no one to love, they may feel lonely and depressed.

Ⓐ joyful
Ⓑ sufficient
Ⓒ sad
Ⓓ excited

8 The bridge connects the land between two small towns.

Ⓐ delivers
Ⓑ links
Ⓒ secedes
Ⓓ divides

9 The school has very strict rules about its dress code.

Ⓐ delicate
Ⓑ firm
Ⓒ vulnerable
Ⓓ soft

10 The view of the sunset was incredible.

Ⓐ proper
Ⓑ restless
Ⓒ flat
Ⓓ unbelievable

PART Ⅲ

Reading to Learn

In this part, the reading comprehension questions include prose summary and fill in a table. The learning objectives of these comprehension questions are to recognize the major ideas and the relative importance of information in a passage and to organize the main ideas and other important information in the appropriate categories.

UNIT

09 Prose Summary

Overview

Introduction

In Prose Summary questions, you will be asked to complete a summary chart by choosing three most important ideas from six choices. In order to solve Prose Summary questions, you should understand the overall theme of the passage and distinguish important ideas from minor ones in the passage.

Question Types

◆ **Directions**: An introductory sentence for a brief summary of the passage is provided below. Complete the summary by selecting the THREE answer choices that express the most important ideas in the passage. Some sentences do not belong in the summary because they express ideas that are not presented in the passage or are minor ideas in the passage. *This question is worth 2 points.*

Drag your answer choices to the spaces where they belong.
To remove an answer choice, click on it. To review the passage, click on **View Text**.

Answer Choices

1 XXXXXXXXXXXXXXXXXXXXXXXXX	4 XXXXXXXXXXXXXXXXXXXXXXXXX
2 XXXXXXXXXXXXXXXXXXXXXXXXX	5 XXXXXXXXXXXXXXXXXXXXXXXXX
3 XXXXXXXXXXXXXXXXXXXXXXXXX	6 XXXXXXXXXXXXXXXXXXXXXXXXX

Useful Tips

- Try to understand the overall structure of the passage.
- Write down the main idea of each paragraph on your scratch paper.
- Distinguish major points from minor details in the passage.
- Incorrect answer choices usually deal with minor points of the passage or are not mentioned in the passage.

Sample TOEFL iBT Question

Recessions

09-01

Every economy goes through cycles. At times, the economy may be good. It may even be booming and be doing very well. Other times, the economy may be doing poorly. During poor economic conditions, a recession may happen.

There are several indicators of a recession. First, a recession is a time of prolonged economic decline. It lasts for at least six months. Some recessions even last a year or two. The unemployment rate goes down, so many people cannot find jobs. In addition, sales at stores decline. This causes many stores to go bankrupt and to close. Manufacturing also declines, so factories produce fewer products. Every country goes through recessions at times. Recently in the United States, one recession lasted from 2007 to 2009. It happened when many financial institutions collapsed.

Q **Directions**: An introductory sentence for a brief summary of the passage is provided below. Complete the summary by selecting the THREE answer choices that express the most important ideas in the passage. Some sentences do not belong in the summary because they express ideas that are not presented in the passage or are minor ideas in the passage. *This question is worth 2 points.*

A recession is a time of poor economic conditions.

-
-
-

Answer Choices

[1] One recession happened in the United States in 2007.

[2] It is hard for people to find jobs during a recession.

[3]] The economy declines for several months during a recession.

[4] There have been many recessions in the history of the United States.

[5] A boom period is the opposite of a recession.

[6] Stores sell few goods, and factories do not make them in a recession.

Correct Answer

Choices [2], [3], and [6] are the correct answers because they represent main points in the passage. Choices [1] and [5] are minor points, so they are incorrect. Choice [4] contains information not mentioned in the passage, so it is incorrect, too.

Basic Drill

Read the passages and answer the questions.

Skill & Tip

Prose Summary questions ask you to complete a summary chart with the most important ideas from the passage. The topic sentence is given for the summary. It is important that minor ideas or ideas that are not mentioned in the passage be avoided.

Example

If there is not enough rain, farmers must bring water to their plants in other ways. In the short term, this is a good thing, but in the long term, it could be dangerous for the land. In most cases, this water contains small amounts of salt. Normally, this is not a bad thing. But over time, salt starts to build up in the soil. Eventually, there is so much salt that the soil is no good for farming. Farmers need to be careful about how water flows through the earth to control the salt level.

Q **Directions**: An introductory sentence for a brief summary of the passage is provided. Complete the summary by selecting the TWO answer choices that express the most important ideas in the passage.

Watering crops has some effects.

•

•

1 It is good for plants.

2 It can cause a buildup of salt.

3 It is good for the land in the long term.

Correct Answer 1, 2

Drill 1

Scarcity means not to have enough of something. If people need something that is scarce, they have to decide what to do. For example, when gasoline is scarce, the price goes up. People must decide if they are going to pay the higher price. In some cases, people may not want to pay the higher price. They could look for a lower price elsewhere. But they may have to travel far. They could also just learn to live without it. In the case of gasoline, people may drive less often. They may also ride their bikes or share rides with others.

09-02

Q **Directions**: Complete the summary by selecting the TWO answer choices that express the most important ideas in the passage.

When necessary things are scarce, people have to make decisions.

•

•

1 The price of gasoline goes up.

2 People must make choices about rising prices.

3 People may pay more or go elsewhere.

Drill 2

The philosophy of law is called jurisprudence. This means "knowledge of law." People who study this try to understand the reasons for certain laws, how they are organized, and how they are used. It is important to know how laws affect society. Students of law can look at laws that are currently in use. In addition to the benefits, there may be some results that were not expected. Students can also study the ideas of new laws. Since crimes change, there is always a need for new laws.

09-03

Q **Directions**: Complete the summary by selecting the TWO answer choices that express the most important ideas in the passage.

Jurisprudence means the philosophy of law.

-
-

1 The study of jurisprudence is used in developing new laws.

2 Certain laws have benefits and disadvantages in society.

3 People study current laws to see how they affect society.

Drill 3

The number of dollar bills in use must be controlled. If the government prints too much money, prices will rise. At first, that does not seem logical. But more money means that people have more to spend. In this situation, it is easy to raise prices because people can afford it. There is also another effect. If the economy doubles the number of bills, then it cuts the actual value of all the bills in half. In that situation, employers have to pay workers twice as much for them to get the same value. These new costs force prices to rise.

09-04

Q **Directions**: Complete the summary by selecting the TWO answer choices that express the most important ideas in the passage.

The amount of money in use affects the economy.

-
-

1 Too much money results in the value of money decreasing.

2 Prices rise because people have more money.

3 Printing too much money has many effects.

Exercises with Short Passages

Exercise 1 Read the following passage and answer the questions.

Time Limit: 30 sec.

The Liability of Drunk Driving

09-05

Drunk driving is a major factor in traffic accidents. When a drunk driver has an accident, a number of things happen. If the driver hurts someone or property gets damaged, the victim can sue the driver. The reason is that the driver must be responsible for his acts. In legal terms, "liable" means responsible. But liability does not stop at the driver. In the United States, a victim of an accident can also sue the bar where the driver got his alcohol. The victim can even sue the bartender. It is believed that because the bar "helped" the driver get drunk, the bar is also at fault for the accident. This means that these places must be very careful. They should not allow people to get drunk.

General Comprehension

1 The word "liability" in the passage is closest in meaning to

Ⓐ caution
Ⓑ credibility
Ⓒ responsibility
Ⓓ recklessness

2 According to the passage, why can a bartender be sued in a drunk driving accident?

Ⓐ He is responsible for the person drinking.
Ⓑ He wanted to get the person drunk.
Ⓒ He had no control over the drinker.
Ⓓ He knows how to make drinks.

Words & Phrases

property n a possession; a belonging; an asset
victim n a person who is hurt
sue v to start a legal case against someone; to take someone to court
bartender n a person who serves alcohol at a bar
be at fault phr to be responsible for; to be to blame

Mastering the Question Type

3 **Directions**: An introductory sentence for a brief summary of the passage is provided below. Complete the summary by selecting the TWO answer choices that express the most important ideas in the passage.

Drunk driving carries a lot of consequences, especially when there is an accident.

•
•

1 The bar and the bartender can be named in a lawsuit and must be careful.

2 The driver can be sued by the victim of an accident.

3 The victim of an accident may become very upset.

4 The family of the victim can sue the drunk driver.

Exercise 2 Read the following passage and answer the questions.

Time Limit: 50 sec.

Advantages of Crop Rotation

09-06

Crop rotation was a great advance for society during the Middle Ages. Special farming techniques made it easier than before to grow food. This allowed populations to grow. The idea was simple. Each kind of plant takes different nutrients from the soil. It also attracts specific kinds of insects. So if a farmer grows the same plant in the same place all the time, eventually, the soil will not have what it needs to grow. What does grow will be eaten by insects.

People in the Middle Ages learned that if they grew different plants in the same spot every season, the second plant would replace what the first plant took from the soil. If they grew a plant that cows liked to eat, then their manure would add nutrients to the soil. This was a new discovery. So every season, people grew a different crop. The soil became better for growing, and there was more food.

General Comprehension

1 According to the passage, what is crop rotation?

(A) A method of farming plants
(B) A way of moving animals around
(C) A means of keeping animals
(D) A way of growing corn

2 According to the passage, what effect does growing the same plant repeatedly have?

(A) It takes different nutrients from the soil.
(B) It attracts insects which eat the plants.
(C) It attracts insects and ruins the soil.
(D) It makes the soil better for growing.

Words & Phrases

rotation n the act of taking turns to do a particular job
advance n progress; development
nutrient n a substance that helps plants and animals grow
specific adj particular
replace v to put back what was removed, taken, or used
manure n animal waste

Mastering the Question Type

3 **Directions**: An introductory sentence for a brief summary of the passage is provided below. Complete the summary by selecting the TWO answer choices that express the most important ideas in the passage.

Crop rotation was an effective farming method.

•
•

1 Old methods made it difficult to grow strong plants.
2 Old methods ruined the soil in the Middle Ages.
3 New methods replaced nutrients in the soil.
4 New methods allowed animals to eat.

Exercise 3 Read the following passage and answer the questions.

Time Limit: 50 sec.

Sleep Disorders

09-07

There are three major kinds of sleep disorders: a person cannot sleep, a person must always sleep, or a person's breathing affects sleep. The first kind, insomnia, means that a person cannot sleep well. An individual may have a hard time falling asleep or keep waking up. During the day, the person may feel sleepy or stressed and may have a hard time concentrating. The second kind, narcolepsy, is called the sleeping sickness. In this case, a person cannot control when he or she falls asleep, even during the day. In fact, if a person gets excited, his or her body tries to fall asleep. When a person wakes up, that individual cannot move or talk. The third kind is sleep apnea. It is a breathing problem while sleeping. Usually, a person's throat starts to close. This may happen because of alcohol or because a person is too heavy. The muscles do not have enough control. Other times, the brain does not send the signal to breathe. Then, the person wakes up.

General Comprehension

1 According to the passage, insomnia happens

(A) when a person cannot sleep well if at all
(B) when a person has to sleep all the time
(C) when a person keeps sleeping in the day
(D) when a person wakes up in the afternoon

2 According to the passage, what is the difference between narcolepsy and sleep apnea?

(A) Alcohol is used to treat apnea but not narcolepsy.
(B) Apnea is like narcolepsy but more severe.
(C) Apnea involves breathing, but narcolepsy does not.
(D) Apnea and narcolepsy only happen during the daytime.

Words & Phrases

disorder (n) a problem or disease that affects a person

have a hard time V-ing (phr) have difficulty V-ing

concentrate (v) to focus on

muscle (n) body tissues which are used to make movements

Mastering the Question Type

3 **Directions**: An introductory sentence for a brief summary of the passage is provided below. Complete the summary by selecting the TWO answer choices that express the most important ideas in the passage.

There are three types of sleeping disorders.

•

•

1 Sleep apnea relates breathing to waking up.

2 Sleep apnea relates alcohol to waking up.

3 Insomnia and narcolepsy describe the ability to control falling asleep.

4 Insomnia and narcolepsy do not involve the use of medication.

Exercise 4 Read the following passage and answer the questions.

Time Limit: 50 sec.

Game Theory

09-08

Economists study the use of choice. They call it game theory. The results depend on the choices of all the people involved. Sometimes people have to make decisions that are selfish. The decision will make people's lives better but will not help the people around them. It may even hurt them. Other times, people make decisions that are the best for everyone but are not the best for themselves. For example, imagine that there is garbage all over a town. The town does not look nice. Tourists do not want to visit. The shop owners agree that the best thing for the town is to go out and to clean it up. If one shop owner cleans it up, everyone benefits. However, that owner is using his own time. He is not getting paid for his work, and no one is helping him.

General Comprehension

1 According to the passage, what does game theory describe?

(A) What selfish decisions are
(B) How people use choices
(C) Why tourists visit places
(D) How to pay people for doing work

2 The word "selfish" is closest in meaning to

(A) greedy
(B) alone
(C) bold
(D) aggressive

Words & Phrases

depend on phr to rely on
involve v to include
selfish adj thinking about oneself rather than others
hurt v to cause pain
benefit n an advantage

Mastering the Question Type

3 **Directions**: An introductory sentence for a brief summary of the passage is provided below. Complete the summary by selecting the TWO answer choices that express the most important ideas in the passage.

This passage describes game theory.

•
•

1 Game theory is important due to its usefulness.
2 Game theory is based on the use of choice.
3 People tend to make selfish decisions.
4 People make decisions for their benefit or for others' benefit.

Exercises with Mid-Length Passages

Exercise 1 Read the following passage and answer the questions.

Time Limit: 1 min. 50 sec.

Miranda Rights

09-09

According to American law, a person has the right to silence if police ask him about a crime. He also has the right to a lawyer if he goes to jail for a crime. The reason for these rights is simple: Police cannot force a person to say anything that will make him guilty. An arrested person must know this.

The Miranda Rights are something that police say when a person is arrested. They say, "You have the right to remain silent. If you give up that right, anything you say can and will be used against you in a court of law. You have the right to a lawyer during questioning. If you cannot afford a lawyer, one will be given at no cost. During questioning, you may decide not to answer if you choose." The police make sure the person understands this. They may have to say the Miranda Rights in the person's own language.

Criminals have been set free because the police did not do a good job of reading them their rights. It is important in any society for accused individuals to know the law and also to know their rights. This is a way to make sure that a society is fair for everyone.

Q **Directions**: An introductory sentence for a brief summary of the passage is provided below. Complete the summary by selecting the THREE answer choices that express the most important ideas in the passage.

The right to silence is an important right.

-
-
-

Words & Phrases

according to prep in the words of
crime n an illegal act
force v to require
guilty adj having broken a law; being at fault
afford v to have enough money
fair adj having justice

Answer Choices

1. Police cannot force a person to say something against his will.
2. A person can be set free if that individual's rights have been abused.
3. Anything a person says can be used against that person in a court of law.
4. Criminals have to be set free if the police do not do their job.
5. Police read people their Miranda Rights when they are arrested.
6. Criminals are set free if they do not know the law.

Summary Note

Miranda Rights

Right to silence

Right to a lawyer

Inform a person of his rights

Set free if the rights were not made clear

Exercise 2 Read the following passage and answer the questions.

Time Limit: 1 min. 50 sec.

How to Cultivate Tea

09-10

Tea is a drink prized by many cultures. It has a long history. It used to be grown only in the southern part of China and northern India. Today, it is grown all over the world.

A tea bush takes around four years to start producing good leaves for tea. The tea plant usually grows between five and fifteen meters high in the wild. For farming, it is usually kept to two meters high. This small size ensures that the plant often grows new leaves. The season for picking tea leaves lasts from March to November.

Tea bushes like lots of water. Ideally, it should rain at night. This allows the plant to drink and to be ready for the sun the next day. The days should be long and warm with lots of sunshine. The sun and the water give the plant what it needs to keep growing new leaves.

The best tea leaves are picked by hand. Most of the time, the top two leaves, which are the most delicate, are picked. The small size of the bush makes it easy to pick the leaves from all sides. The tea leaves are then carried in baskets to the next stage in the process.

Q **Directions**: An introductory sentence for a brief summary of the passage is provided below. Complete the summary by selecting the THREE answer choices that express the most important ideas in the passage.

There are a few considerations involved in growing tea.

-
-
-

Words & Phrases

prize v to value; to esteem
in the wild phr not farmed
ensure v to make sure
ideally adv in the best situation
delicate adj fragile

Answer Choices

1. Four-year-old tea plants are kept small to produce lots of hand-picked leaves.
2. Rain should fall at night instead of the day to feed the plant.
3. Tea leaves are carried in baskets to the next stage of the process.
4. The tea plant produces the most leaves from March to November in warm, wet climates.
5. Tea bushes like a lot of water and sunshine.
6. The two top leaves are very delicate and must be picked by hand.

Summary Note

Growth season: March to November

Top delicate leaves picked by hand

Tea Cultivation

Warm, wet climates

Kept to two meters in height

Exercise 3 **Read the following passage and answer the questions.**

Time Limit: 2 min.

Vitamins

09-11

Vitamins help the body build itself. There are thirteen kinds of vitamins that the body needs. Four can be taken into the body through fat. The other nine are taken in by water. They allow the right chemical reactions to happen. They allow the body to use the food it takes in. This is especially important when children are growing. Adults also need vitamins to stay in good health.

Children need vitamins to build good bones and tissue. If children lack vitamin D, their bones may become soft. This may cause the leg bones to curve. Adults need vitamins for their nervous systems to work. They can get a number of illnesses without vitamins. They may have poor eyesight and bad heartbeats. They may feel weak all the time.

People learned over a hundred years ago that diets were the cause of good health because of vitamins. A poor diet was also the cause of some diseases. British sailors had a disease called scurvy. They had spots on their skin, and their mouths would bleed. This happened because they did not get enough vitamin C. A doctor discovered this cause and made sure that lemons and limes were put on all British ships.

Q **Directions**: An introductory sentence for a brief summary of the passage is provided below. Complete the summary by selecting the THREE answer choices that express the most important ideas in the passage.

Vitamins are necessary for the body.

-
-
-

Words & Phrases

reaction n a response; an answer
tissue n a group of cells that form different parts of animals and plants
lack v to be without something needed
curve v to bend
spot n a mark that looks different from its background

Answer Choices

1. Adults and children need vitamins to help their bodies in many ways.
2. Spots on the skin and sore mouths are indications of a lack of vitamins.
3. Scurvy used to affect British sailors until doctors put lemons and limes on ships.
4. The quality of a diet is linked to vitamin intake and health.
5. The right chemical reactions happen when the body is treated well.
6. There are thirteen different kinds of vitamins needed by the body.

Summary Note

Four: fat soluble — **13 Essential Vitamins** — Nine: water soluble

Allow the right chemical reactions to happen

Adults and children need them for their health

A proper diet is needed for vitamins

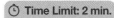

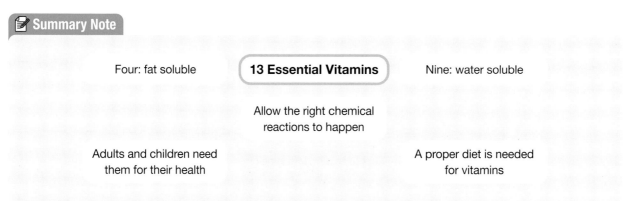

Exercise 4 Read the following passage and answer the questions.

Time Limit: 2 min.

Pennsylvania's Coal

09-12

Coal is a huge source of energy. Countries have spent lots of money getting the coal they have. The eastern United States has a tradition of mining coal. Pennsylvania is one such place. It is the source of so much coal, but it is also the home of a great mining disaster.

There are two ways to get at coal in the ground. The first way is to dig a hole below the surface of the Earth. Miners make tunnels that can be miles long. The second way is called open mining. Miners will remove the surface of the earth over a huge area until they reach what they want.

Centralia, Pennsylvania has very high-quality coal. It burns hotter than most other kinds of coal. Many open mines are in that town. Sadly, the town garbage dump was near an old open mine pit. In 1962, the garbage caught fire. It set the open mine on fire, too. The fire started burning underground, where it was impossible to put out. The fine quality of the coal made the disaster even worse. The fire has been burning underground for over sixty years. No one knows how to stop it. Experts believe it will burn for 250 years.

Q **Directions**: An introductory sentence for a brief summary of the passage is provided below. Complete the summary by selecting the THREE answer choices that express the most important ideas in the passage.

Pennsylvania has a great mining tradition and a sad history.

-
-
-

Answer Choices

1. The town garbage dump was near an old open mine.
2. The coal near a town caught fire and has been burning for decades.
3. The town of Centralia has many open mines.
4. Pennsylvania uses open mining to get coal from the ground.
5. No one knows how to make the fire burn for 250 years.
6. There is high-quality coal in Pennsylvania.

Words & Phrases

source (n) a supply
get at (phr) to reach
mine (v) to take minerals from beneath the Earth's surface
surface (n) the top part of something
remove (v) to take away; to get rid of
put out (v) to extinguish a fire

Summary Note

Pennsylvania Coal

A huge source of energy

Open pit mining

Fire in a town's garbage dump

Coal mine may burn for 250 years

Building Summary Skills

A **Put the following sentences in order to make appropriate summaries based on the mid-length passages you worked on earlier. The first sentence is already provided.**

Exercise 1 Miranda Rights

1 Miranda Rights remind people that they have the right to silence and a lawyer if police question them about a crime.

____ Criminals have been set free because the police failed to give them this warning.

____ The reason is that people do not have to say anything that will make them guilty of a crime.

____ All people—even criminals—must know their rights.

Exercise 2 How to Cultivate Tea

1 Tea is drunk all over the world.

____ The best tea is picked by hand.

____ The tea plant takes four years to mature and is kept small to ensure lots of leaves and easy picking.

____ It grows well in climates that are warm and wet.

____ The delicate top leaves are picked and carried in baskets to the next stage of processing.

Exercise 3 Vitamins

1 Vitamins are necessary for the body to build itself and to stay healthy.

____ Some diseases occur if people do not eat well.

____ Some are taken in through fat and others through water.

____ People have learned that their diets are the key to getting enough vitamins.

____ Children need vitamins to grow strong bones and organs, and adults need them for strong nervous systems.

Exercise 4 Pennsylvania's Coal

1 Pennsylvania has provided a lot of coal, which is an important fuel.

____ There are many coal mines there.

____ One of the coal mines caught fire and started burning underground.

____ Open mining was used in a town called Centralia, where there is high-quality coal.

____ It is impossible to put out the fire, and it may burn for 250 years.

B **Fill in the blanks with suitable words or phrases to complete the following summaries. Do not look at the previous page until you are finished.**

Exercise 1 Miranda Rights

__________ remind people that they have the right to __________ and a __________ if police question them about a crime. The reason is that people do not have to __________ anything that will make them __________ of a crime. Criminals have been __________ because police failed to give them this __________. All people—even __________—must know their rights.

Exercise 2 How to Cultivate Tea

__________ is drunk all over the world. The tea plant takes __________ years to mature and is kept __________ to ensure lots of leaves and easy __________. It grows well in climates that are __________ and __________. The best tea is picked __________. The delicate __________ are picked and carried in baskets to the next stage of processing.

Exercise 3 Vitamins

Vitamins are __________ for the body to build itself and to stay __________. Some are taken in through __________ and others through __________. Children need vitamins to grow strong __________ and organs, and adults need them for strong __________. People have learned that their __________ are the key to getting enough vitamins. Some __________ occur if people do not eat well.

Exercise 4 Pennsylvania's Coal

Pennsylvania has provided a lot of __________, which is an important __________. There are many __________ there. Open mining was used in a town called __________, where there is high-quality coal. One of the coal mines caught __________ and started burning __________. It is impossible to __________ the fire, and it may burn for __________ years.

Organic Farming

09-13

The idea behind organic farming is to use no chemicals. Farmers must use natural means to make plants grow strong and to protect them from insects. It is believed that without chemicals, plants will make better food for humans. But the idea is bigger than that. Organic farming respects all plants and animals in the environment. This kind of farming should improve nature's health.

2→ Fertilizers are chemicals that give plants strength. If a farmer grows the same plant over and over in the same place, the soil will lose its ability to feed the plant. The farmer must add fertilizer to help the soil. Organic farmers do not add fertilizer. They instead rotate crops or use animal manure and plant compost to make the soil rich again. Compost is made from plant material that has broken down into soil. It has all the food a plant needs to grow.

Pesticides are also avoided. These are chemicals that kill pests like insects. Organic farmers have other ways to deal with pests because pesticides kill good animals and insects that protect plants. Foxes and snakes eat mice. Some insects like ladybugs eat bad insects. And, of course, there are weeds. These are plants that farmers do not want because they steal growing space from good plants. To stop weeds, organic farmers may scrape the soil several times. Eventually, the weeds die.

4→ Organic farming usually needs a lot of human labor to do the job of chemicals. This is one reason that organic food costs more. But when considering the health of the Earth, its plants, and its animals, perhaps it is worth it. In the end, a healthy planet means that people will be healthy, too.

1 The word "rotate" in the passage is closest in meaning to

Ⓐ spin
Ⓑ stir
Ⓒ clean
Ⓓ change

2 The author mentions "plant compost" in paragraph 2 as an example of

Ⓐ a way to add nutrients back to the soil
Ⓑ a type of pesticide
Ⓒ a kind of fertilizer
Ⓓ a way to avoid labor

3 The word "they" in the passage refers to

Ⓐ some insects like ladybugs
Ⓑ bad insects
Ⓒ weeds
Ⓓ farmers

4 According to paragraph 4, what replaces the chemical treatment of crops?

Ⓐ Topsoil
Ⓑ Weed killer
Ⓒ Animal feed
Ⓓ Human labor

5 **Directions**: An introductory sentence for a brief summary of the passage is provided below. Complete the summary by selecting the THREE answer choices that express the most important ideas in the passage. Some answer choices do not belong in the summary because they express ideas that are not in the passage or are minor ideas in the passage. *This question is worth 2 points.*

Organic farming uses natural means to grow plants.

•
•
•

Answer Choices

1 It relies on crop rotation, manure, and plant compost to keep the soil rich.

2 Organic food costs more, but it is worth the expense.

3 This type of farming keeps plants and people healthy.

4 It avoids the use of pesticides, which kill good animals as well as bad ones.

5 It has been used for thousands of years and has been very successful.

6 It is the only farming technique that works all over the world.

The WTO

09-14

The WTO building in Geneva, Switzerland

The World Trade Organization (WTO) has more than 160 member countries. They look to improve trade. Trade means the buying and selling of goods. The WTO provides a place where these countries can talk about what they need. The goal of the WTO is to make trade grow by removing legal barriers between countries.

2→ The WTO helps trade in several ways. First, it asks countries to treat one another equally. They should not give special trade deals to one country and not to another. These countries should also not try to stop foreign products from any one country. The idea is that goods and services should be able to cross borders easily. A second way to improve trade is to lower tariffs. These are special taxes for things bought and sold. A third way to strengthen trade is to make sure that the rules stay the same. In order for people to invest their money, they need to feel secure about the future. A fourth way is to allow greater competition between countries. The central belief is that competition makes for stronger economies. The last way to improve trade is to help countries that are poor. They need help coming up to the level of modern countries. They can be helped by allowing them extra time to get their systems in order. They can be given priority in making deals with other countries.

Free and easy trade is the WTO's goal. It supports rich countries and helps poor countries get ahead. It is one way of improving the lives of more people in the world. It asks countries to make laws that help this process. Every year, more countries apply to be in the WTO. They see membership as a good thing.

6 The word "barriers" in the passage is closest in meaning to

Ⓐ bans
Ⓑ disputes
Ⓒ obstacles
Ⓓ documents

7 In paragraph 2, the author discusses how the WTO helps trade in order to

Ⓐ illustrate how it improves international trade
Ⓑ complain about the actions of the WTO
Ⓒ distinguish between the WTO and banks
Ⓓ promote discussion about the WTO

8 According to paragraph 2, which of the following is NOT true of the WTO?

Ⓐ It wants to improve trade by lowering taxes.
Ⓑ It tries to make trade better.
Ⓒ It does not give poor countries priority.
Ⓓ It believes competition is important.

9 In stating that the WTO helps poor countries "get ahead," the author means that competition helps poor countries

Ⓐ make more decisions
Ⓑ improve their situations
Ⓒ feed the poor
Ⓓ elect leaders

10 **Directions**: An introductory sentence for a brief summary of the passage is provided below. Complete the summary by selecting the THREE answer choices that express the most important ideas in the passage. Some answer choices do not belong in the summary because they express ideas that are not in the passage or are minor ideas in the passage. *This question is worth 2 points.*

The WTO provides ways for countries to improve trade.

-
-
-

Answer Choices

1 Countries should try to rise to the level of the richest country.

2 Countries should allow goods and services to cross borders easily.

3 Countries should lower tariffs and make investors feel secure.

4 Countries should allow time to organize political protests.

5 Countries should be fair to one another and help poor members.

6 Countries should never stop themselves from raising taxes.

Vocabulary Check-Up

Choose the words with the closest meanings to the highlighted words.

1 Parents should be very careful with their babies' delicate skin.

Ⓐ sufficient
Ⓑ pretty
Ⓒ sweat
Ⓓ fragile

2 The water source in this country is not infinite.

Ⓐ supply
Ⓑ prevention
Ⓒ negligence
Ⓓ demand

3 Governments can manage to import specific items.

Ⓐ normal
Ⓑ particular
Ⓒ various
Ⓓ common

4 Allergies are the body's natural reaction to foreign substances.

Ⓐ introduction
Ⓑ comparison
Ⓒ opinion
Ⓓ response

5 People should remove their bicycles from the hallway.

Ⓐ add
Ⓑ depart
Ⓒ take away
Ⓓ file

6 The company can save money on insurance benefits starting next year.

Ⓐ advantages
Ⓑ alarms
Ⓒ faults
Ⓓ decisions

7 People must concentrate on improving the environment.

Ⓐ overcome
Ⓑ focus
Ⓒ express
Ⓓ complete

8 Many people are likely to prize possessions such as expensive cars and big houses.

Ⓐ compare
Ⓑ sorrow
Ⓒ ignore
Ⓓ value

9 Firefighters are good at putting out fires.

Ⓐ extinguishing
Ⓑ observing
Ⓒ recording
Ⓓ firing

10 What is a major product in Canada?

Ⓐ insignificant
Ⓑ boring
Ⓒ primary
Ⓓ inferior

UNIT

10 Fill in a Table

Overview

Introduction

Fill in a Table questions ask you to recognize and organize major ideas and important supporting information from across the passage. Then, you should classify them into the appropriate categories. Passages used for this type of question usually have particular types of organization such as compare/contrast, cause/effect, or problem/solution. A five-answer table is worth 3 points, and a seven-answer table is worth 4 points.

Question Types

◆ **Directions**: Complete the table below to summarize the information about X discussed in the passage. Match the appropriate statements to the categories with which they are associated. TWO of the answer choices will NOT be used. *This question is worth 3 points.*

Drag your answer choices to the spaces where they belong.
To remove an answer choice, click on it. To review the passage, click on **View Text**.

Answer Choices	
1 XXXXXXXXXXXXXXXXXXXXXXXXX	**Category 1**
2 XXXXXXXXXXXXXXXXXXXXXXXXX	•
3 XXXXXXXXXXXXXXXXXXXXXXXXX	•
4 XXXXXXXXXXXXXXXXXXXXXXXXX	•
5 XXXXXXXXXXXXXXXXXXXXXXXXX	
6 XXXXXXXXXXXXXXXXXXXXXXXXX	**Category 2**
7 XXXXXXXXXXXXXXXXXXXXXXXXX	•
	•

Useful Tips

- Look at the categories of information in the table first.
- Using your scratch paper, make an outline of the passage according to these categories.
- Distinguish between major and minor information in the passage.
- Wrong answers usually include information that is not mentioned in the passage or that is not directly relevant to the categories in the table.

Sample TOEFL iBT Question

Civil Law and Common Law

10-01

There are two major kinds of law: civil law and common law. Civil law comes from the Romans while common law comes from England.

Civil law developed over more than 1,000 years. It started with the Twelve Tables in 449 B.C. It continued developing in the sixth century A.D. with Justinian the Great. Today, it influences law systems around the world. It is based mainly on laws the government passes. There were laws for Roman citizens, laws for foreigners, and natural laws. Natural laws were based on common sense. Civil law included concepts such as checks and balances, term limits, and the separation of powers.

Common law began in the Middle Ages during the reign of King John of England. The founding document is the Magna Carta, which was signed in 1215. The main aspect of common law is that it is based on the decisions of judges in previous court cases. These judges create precedents. Later judges look for precedents when making rulings. In most cases, they rule the same way as past judges. Common law spread to places ruled by the British Empire, such as the United States.

Q **Directions**: Complete the table below to summarize the information about civil and common law. Match the appropriate statements to the type of law with which they are associated. TWO of the answer choices will NOT be used. *This question is worth 3 points.*

Answer Choices

1 Relies upon a written constitution

2 Includes laws that are based on common sense

3 Was developed in England

4 Has stopped being used by many countries today

5 Is based on laws created by governments

6 Focuses on precedents set by judges

7 Formed over the course of many centuries

Civil Law

•

•

•

Common Law

•

•

Correct Answer

According to the passage, choices 2, 5 and 7 represent civil law, and choices 3 and 6 refer to common law. Choices 1 and 4 include information that is not mentioned in the passage.

Basic Drill

Read the passages and answer the questions.

Skill & Tip

Fill in a Table questions ask you to identify and organize the major ideas of the passage into table categories. They are similar to Prose Summary questions in that they ask for important information.

Example

People's bodies have an internal clock. They have regular patterns of feeling hungry, sleeping, and waking. The cells in people's bodies also repair themselves according to the clock. The clock is located in two places. First, cells in the liver affect when people eat. Second, a small group of cells in the brain controls the body clock. They respond to sunlight so that people's bodies are on a similar schedule as the sun. If people travel around the world by plane, their bodies adjust themselves to the local time. Of course, this takes a few days, so their bodies experience jet lag.

Q **Directions**: Complete the table below by matching TWO of the five answer choices with the functions of the liver and the brain.

Answer Choices

1 People travel around the world.

2 The sun affects people.

3 People's bodies adjust to local time.

4 People experience hunger.

5 People can avoid jet lag.

Liver

-

Brain

-

Correct Answer **Liver: 4, Brain: 2**

Drill 1

An earthquake happens when the surface plates of the Earth move. Sometimes the plates rub together. These are called interplate quakes. When there is a sudden slip between the plates, energy is released in the form of shock waves. Both plates shake like a guitar string when it is picked. Earthquakes can also happen when a crack in the middle of a plate forms. These are called intraplate quakes. They often surprise scientists because they happen in places that they do not ever expect earthquakes.

10-02

Q **Directions**: Complete the table below by matching TWO of the five answer choices with the kinds of earthquakes.

Answer Choices

1 Both plates shake like guitar strings.

2 Two plates rub together and slip.

3 A plate cracks in the middle.

4 A surface plate moves.

5 Energy is released in waves.

Interplate Quakes

-

Intraplate Quakes

-

Drill 2

The word *nebula* used to refer to anything that was not a planet or a comet. This meant that galaxies and clusters of stars were kinds of nebulas. However, today, the term refers to clouds of dust and gas in space. In fact, the word nebula means "cloud" in Latin. One kind of nebula is made of gas. When the hot gas cools, it lets out light. Usually, these nebulas are red. Another kind is made of dust. They reflect the light of stars nearby. Another kind of dust nebula blocks the light of something shining behind it.

10-03

Q **Directions**: Complete the table below by matching THREE of the five answer choices describing the types of nebulas.

Answer Choices

1. It is a group of planets.
2. Starlight reflects off its particles.
3. It is anything that is not a comet.
4. Red light usually escapes as gases cool.
5. It can block light.

Gaseous Nebula

-

Dust Nebula

-
-

Drill 3

The Erie Canal was a water highway that connected the Hudson River in New York to the Great Lakes. Before the canal, travel and trade in the region were difficult. People and goods had to move across land in carts. They sometimes used rivers, but they depended very much on the weather. Travel and trade were slow, expensive, and dangerous. After the canal was built, things got better. First, it cut costs and time in moving goods. This increased trade. Crops that grew in the west could be sold in Europe. Second, people were able to move west and increase the size of the United States more easily.

10-04

Q **Directions**: Complete the table below by matching THREE of the five answer choices contrasting the times before and after the Erie Canal was built.

Answer Choices

1. The U.S. was wealthy.
2. Travel was slow, costly, and perilous.
3. It became easier for Indians to move westward.
4. People were able to move west to explore more easily.
5. It was cheaper to move goods.

Before

-

After

-
-

Exercises with Short Passages

Exercise 1 Read the following passage and answer the questions.

Time Limit: 50 sec.

Black Holes

10-05

Black holes are difficult to see. They neither give off nor reflect light because gravity pulls everything in. The only way physicists know a black hole exists is by seeing things falling into it. As it enters, an object will be squeezed and give off heat and light. This radiation can be seen. Sometimes stars that die form black holes. Only large stars can become black holes. A star collapses into its center, where it becomes very small but still has gravity. This is the heart of a black hole.

Sometimes a black hole is formed by a large cloud of gas. It shrinks because of the gravity that is created between the gas molecules. The Hubble Telescope took a picture of this kind of black hole. Scientists think that such a black hole is right at the center of our own galaxy.

General Comprehension

1 The word "radiation" in the passage is closest in meaning to

Ⓐ gas
Ⓑ energy
Ⓒ liquid
Ⓓ dust

2 According to the passage, what is the defining characteristic of a black hole?

Ⓐ Light
Ⓑ Gas
Ⓒ Mass
Ⓓ Gravity

Words & Phrases

give off phr to produce something and to send it out; to emit

reflect v to throw back light, heat, sound, etc. from a surface

squeeze v to compress

collapse v to fall inward and to become smaller

gravity n the force that attracts objects in space toward one another

shrink v to get smaller

Mastering the Question Type

3 **Directions**: Complete the table below by matching THREE of the five answer choices with the ways black holes are formed.

Answer Choices

1 Only large stars can form black holes.
2 The center of the hole becomes black.
3 A large cloud of gas gets very small.
4 The death of a star creates a black hole.
5 The center of a galaxy collapses.

First Way of Formation

•
•

Second Way of Formation

•

Exercise 2 Read the following passage and answer the questions.

Time Limit: 50 sec.

Sumerian Civilization

10-06

The Sumerians made many advances. They first improved agriculture. They later established a military. The Sumerians are thought to have invented the wheel. It was first used for pottery, which was essential for storing crops. Then, it was used for grinding grain. Last, it was used for farming and military vehicles. The Sumerians were the first to use writing and math. The Sumerians used them even before the Egyptians. These helped them organize their society. These systems were used to keep track of food storage and trade. The military used them to keep track of men, weapons, and supplies. They were the first to study the stars and the sun in a serious way. Their studies helped them tell time so that they could decide when to plant crops. A way of reading the stars also helped them plan when to attack their enemies. They believed that the stars could predict their success or failure.

General Comprehension

1 The word "advances" in the passage is closest in meaning to

(A) merits
(B) innovations
(C) approaches
(D) inventions

2 According to the passage, the Sumerians believed the stars could tell

(A) how to keep track of men
(B) how to grind grain
(C) how to store food for winter
(D) how to proceed with a battle

Words & Phrases

pottery n the skill of making pots and dishes out of clay
grind v to smash
keep track of phr to monitor
storage n the keeping of food
predict v to say that something will happen in the future

Mastering the Question Type

3 **Directions**: Complete the table below by matching THREE of the five answer choices with the ways that Sumerian advances supported agriculture and the military.

Answer Choices

1 They were the first to invent the wheel.
2 The Sumerians were the first to use writing.
3 The stars told when it was time to plant crops.
4 The wheel was used for carts used in battle.
5 Writing helped the Sumerians keep track of food storage.

Agriculture
-
-

Military
-

Exercise 3 Read the following passage and answer the questions.

Time Limit: 50 sec.

Termite Colonies

10-07

Termites live in large groups called colonies. There can be millions of these insects living together. A colony survives thanks to cooperation between different kinds of termites. Each nest has at least one king and one queen. Their role is to produce more termites, not to direct the life of the colony. A termite queen can lay thousands of eggs each day. Its body can grow up to ten centimeters with eggs. The eggs grow into young termites called nymphs. Worker termites are blind. They are in charge of looking for food, feeding soldiers and young termites, and taking care of the nest. Soldier termites defend the nest. Their heads grow a protective covering. However, their jaws are so large that they must be fed by worker termites. With this type of organization, a colony is able to achieve more than a single individual ever could.

General Comprehension

1 The word "cooperation" in the passage is closest in meaning to

Ⓐ corroboration
Ⓑ cohabitation
Ⓒ conflation
Ⓓ collaboration

2 The word "they" in the passage refers to

Ⓐ soldier termites
Ⓑ their heads
Ⓒ their jaws
Ⓓ worker termites

Words & Phrases

colony (n) a group of plants or animals that live together or grow in the same place

cooperation (n) working together

be in charge of (phr) be responsible for

Mastering the Question Type

3 **Directions**: Complete the table below by matching FOUR of the five answer choices with the kinds of termites and their roles.

Answer Choices

1 They have large jaws.
2 They lay eggs.
3 They cannot see.
4 They look for food.
5 They have large bodies

Queens
•

Soldiers
•

Workers
•
•

Exercise 4 Read the following passage and answer the questions.

Time Limit: 50 sec.

The Theory of Continental Drift

10-08

Continental drift is an old theory of geology. It is older than the theory of plate tectonics. Early scientists saw that the different land masses had shapes that fit together. They also noticed that their geologies were similar. Africa and South America had many similarities. The same types of fossils were found in both places. Even today, there is a type of earthworm that is found in both places. Scientists learned that at one time all the land was stuck together. The great land mass was named Pangaea. The land moved apart over time. The problem was to explain how the land masses moved apart. Scientists could not understand how whole continents could move through the rock on the sea floor. Eventually, they learned that even the sea floor spreads in certain places. This gave rise to the idea of floating plates and plate tectonics.

General Comprehension

1 The phrase "gave rise to" in the passage is closest in meaning to

Ⓐ caused
Ⓑ lifted
Ⓒ spread
Ⓓ moved

2 According to the passage, what was a problem with the theory of continental drift?

Ⓐ Scientists found fossils of earthworms in South America.
Ⓑ Scientists did not know why continents stopped moving.
Ⓒ Scientists could not explain how continents could move through rock.
Ⓓ Scientists believed that the land was stuck together in places.

Words & Phrases

drift n a slow, steady movement from one place to another

theory n a formal idea or set of ideas that is intended to explain something

stuck adj fixed in one place

eventually adv in the end

float v to move slowly on the water or in the air

Mastering the Question Type

3 **Directions**: Complete the table below by matching FOUR of the five answer choices that contrast continental drift with plate tectonics.

Answer Choices

1 Continents do not move.
2 Continents have some similar geology.
3 The sea floor has spread zones.
4 Plates float over the Earth's core.
5 Continents have shapes that seem to fit together.

Continental Drift

-
-

Plate Tectonics

-
-

Exercises with Mid-Length Passages

Exercise 1 Read the following passage and answer the questions.

Time Limit: 1 min. 40 sec.

Humans' Perception of the Universe

10-09

Man has been watching the night sky for thousands of years. It has held people's imagination and also served in their search for knowledge.

Humans' ancient ancestors first noticed that the stars moved across the sky but kept the same patterns. They grouped the stars into familiar shapes. These shapes guided people in their travels and told them when to plant his crops. These shapes also were the focus of stories and beliefs. For hundreds of years, people believed that the Earth and humans were the center of the universe. In 1543, Nicolaus Copernicus proved that this was wrong. In fact, the Earth travels around the sun. It opened the way for a deeper understanding of the universe. Galileo Galilei later used telescopes to learn more about the sun and the planets.

Finally, the idea of gravity made the universe come together. This was thanks to Isaac Newton. Gravity makes a small object move toward a larger one. It explains how the solar system was formed. It explains how the planets move around the sun. It explains how comets move the way they do through our solar system. Humans' understanding of gravity helps people explore space.

Q **Directions**: Complete the table below by matching FIVE of the seven answer choices with the impact of Copernicus and Newton.

Answer Choices

1. Gravity explains why small objects move toward larger ones.
2. The generation of the solar system can be explained.
3. The Earth orbits the sun.
4. Telescopes were used to observe objects in the sky.
5. Humans are not at the center of the universe.
6. Humans had many beliefs and stories about the universe.
7. Comets move through the solar system because of gravity.

Copernicus

-
-

Newton

-
-
-

Words & Phrases

search (n) an attempt to find someone or something

perception (n) understanding

gravity (n) the force that pulls two objects together

comet (n) a bright object with a long tail that travels around the sun

explore (v) to travel around a place to learn about it

Summary Note

Patterns of stars in the night sky

Newton: Gravity explains movement

Humans' Perception of the Universe

Copernicus and Galileo: the Earth moves around the sun

Exercise 2 Read the following passage and answer the questions.

Time Limit: 1 min. 50 sec.

Lewis and Clark and the Louisiana Purchase

10-10

President Thomas Jefferson bought the land west of the Mississippi from Napoleon Bonaparte, the ruler of France, in 1803. This created several challenges for the young country at the time, but the advantages were great.

Many people did not like the purchase then. Some thought that buying the land from the French was not necessary. Instead, it could be taken because the French had no military power in North America. Some did not believe the president had the power to buy land. Others felt that buying this land would upset their Spanish neighbors. Yet others still worried that new states would take power away from the old states.

Despite the concerns, the purchase doubled the country's land in 1803. At first, however, President Jefferson and the rest of the people in the United States knew almost nothing about this new land. They did not know what resources could be used. They were to learn that it had abundant resources. Vast amounts of land could be used for farming. There were minerals in the earth to be mined. Most importantly, there were great rivers that would help the economy grow. The president sent a team, headed by Lewis and Clark, to explore the land. They traveled over eight thousand miles in twenty-eight months. The team made many maps and took many notes. This information was used to plan the future of the United States.

Q **Directions**: Complete the table below by matching FIVE of the seven answer choices with the pros and cons of the Louisiana Purchase.

Answer Choices

1. Spain was a power to fear.
2. There was a supply of mineral resources.
3. The exploration team had many maps.
4. There was a vast amount of land to explore.
5. There was no need to buy from the French.
6. New states would shift the balance of power.
7. There were rivers to support the economy.

Pros

-
-

Cons

-
-
-

Words & Phrases

purchase n a thing that is bought
challenge n a difficulty
upset v to make someone unhappy
double v to make something twice its size

Summary Note

Louisiana Purchase

Political Opposition
- Relations with other countries
- Change balance of power within the U.S.

Lack of Information
- Geography and resources
- Indigenous people

Exercise 3 Read the following passage and answer the questions.

Time Limit: 1 min. 40 sec.

The Opossum

10-11

Marsupials are mammals that have a pouch. The female keeps its babies in the pouch until they are old enough to live outside the pouch. The only marsupial in North America is the opossum.

The opossum is about the size of a large cat. Its fur is gray, and it has a pink nose, feet, and tail. It has large black eyes for seeing at night, which is when it moves around the most. Even though it has fifty very sharp teeth, it is a very gentle animal. It tries to avoid any kind of fight.

The opossum is very adaptable. It can live in many places, including in trees and underground. It eats all kinds of food, including both plants and animals. It eats insects, mice, small snakes, grass, leaves, and berries.

The opossum has a variety of defenses. It is mostly immune to snake venom. It usually does not get rabies, a nasty disease, because of the temperature of its blood. Its best-known defense is to play dead. Because most animals do not eat dead things, it is a good defense. The opossum turns on its back and shows its teeth. It then produces a bad smell near its tail. Usually, the other animal goes away.

Q **Directions**: Complete the table below by matching FIVE of the seven answer choices with the adaptability and defenses of the opossum.

Answer Choices

1. It has a variety of homes.
2. Snake venom does not usually affect it.
3. Its blood temperature prevents rabies.
4. It is as large as a cat.
5. It avoids fights.
6. It can eat many different things.
7. It sometimes plays dead.

Adaptability

•
•

Defenses

•
•
•

Words & Phrases

mammal n an animal that gives birth to live babies and feeds its young milk
pouch n a pocket
adaptable adj able to change in order to deal with new situations
immune adj unable to catch a particular disease
rabies n a deadly viral disease that makes one crazy

Summary Note

The Opossum

Adaptability

- Omnivorous
- Homes in varied places

Defenses

- Defenses against rabies and snake venom
- Plays dead

Exercise 4 Read the following passage and answer the questions.

Time Limit: 1 min. 30 sec.

The Mariana Trench

10-12

Trenches are long holes. They form when one tectonic plate slides under another. There are twenty-two great trenches under the ocean. Three are in the Atlantic Ocean, and one is in the Indian Ocean. Eighteen are in the Pacific Ocean. The greatest is called the Mariana Trench. It is located in the Pacific Ocean not far from Japan.

The Mariana Trench is the deepest place on the Earth. It is 542 kilometers long and sixty-nine kilometers wide. It is 11,033 meters deep. The tallest mountain on the Earth still would not reach the surface of the ocean if it were inside. There would still be two kilometers of water above it.

The bottom is very different from near the surface. Down below, the pressure is one thousand times that of the surface. A person could not survive without a submarine. It is impossible to believe that anything could live in those conditions. But in fact, fish and shrimp live at the bottom of the trench.

The water at the bottom is not heated by the sun. It does not freeze because of cracks that cut into the Earth's crust. Heat comes out at 300 degrees Celsius. At the surface, the water is comparatively clear. Down below, the water is filled with the remains of tiny skeletons and skins of animals that once lived as well as bacteria. This forms a thick mixture.

Q **Directions**: Complete the table below by matching FIVE of the seven answer choices that describe the water in the trench.

Answer Choices

1. Animal particles change textures.
2. Water is heated by the sun.
3. There are two kilometers of water above the bottom.
4. Animals are not capable of withstanding the pressure in the water.
5. The water is clearer.
6. The pressure is enormous.
7. Water does not freeze.

Water at the Bottom

-
-
-

Water at the Surface

-
-

Words & Phrases

submarine n a type of ship that can travel both above and below the water

comparatively adv relatively

skeletons n bones

remains n pieces of a dead animal

Summary Note

The Mariana Trench

Geography

- Deepest place on the Earth
- Near Japan

Water Quality

- Does not freeze
- A thick mixture
- Great pressure

Building Summary Skills

A **Put the following sentences in order to make appropriate summaries based on the mid-length passages you worked on earlier. The first sentence is already provided.**

Exercise 1 Humans' Perception of the Universe

1 Humans have tried to understand the night sky for a long time and have created many stories about it.
___ Newton came up with the idea of gravity.
___ For years, it was believed that humans were the center of the universe.
___ Copernicus and Galileo provided information to the contrary.
___ This helped explain the motion of all the objects in the universe.

Exercise 2 Lewis and Clark and the Louisiana Purchase

1 The Louisiana Purchase was a great addition to the United States, but it posed a few challenges.
___ Some were concerned about relations with other countries, and others were concerned about how it would affect political power in the U.S.
___ Politically, many people did not like the idea.
___ After buying the land, information about the people, the resources, and the rivers was needed to make use of it.

Exercise 3 The Opossum

1 The opossum is the only marsupial in North America.
___ It has a number of defenses.
___ It is adaptable in that it is an omnivore and can find a home in lots of places.
___ It is mostly immune to rabies and snake venom, and it can also play dead.
___ It is mostly nocturnal and, despite having many teeth, is very gentle.

Exercise 4 The Mariana Trench

1 The Mariana Trench is a long hole at the bottom of the sea.
___ The water has unique qualities: It does not freeze because of heat vents in the Earth, and the water is a thick mixture of bacteria and animal particles.
___ It is the deepest place on the Earth.
___ The pressure is huge at the bottom, but animals still manage to live there.

B **Fill in the blanks with suitable words or phrases to complete the following summaries. Do not look at the previous page until you are finished.**

Exercise 1 Man's Perception of the Universe

Humans have tried to understand the ______________ for a long time and have created many ______________ about it. For years, it was believed that humans were the ______________ of the universe. ______________ and ______________ provided information to the contrary. ______________ came up with the idea of ______________. This helped explain the ______________ of all the objects in the universe.

Exercise 2 Lewis and Clark and the Louisiana Purchase

The ______________ was a great addition to the United States, but it posed a few ______________. Politically, many people did not ______________ the idea. Some were concerned about ______________ with other countries, and others were concerned about how it would affect ______________ power in the U.S. After ______________ the land, information about the people, the ______________, and the rivers was needed to ______________ it.

Exercise 3 The Opossum

The opossum is the only ______________ in ______________. It is mostly ______________ and, despite having many teeth, is very ______________. It is adaptable in that it is an ______________ and can find a home in lots of places. It has a number of ______________. It is mostly ______________ to rabies and snake venom, and it can also ______________.

Exercise 4 The Mariana Trench

The Mariana Trench is a long ______________ at the ______________ of the sea. It is the ______________ place on the Earth. The pressure is huge at the bottom, but ______________ still manage to live there. The water has unique ______________: it does not ______________ because of ______________ in the Earth, and the water is a thick mixture of ______________ and animal particles.

The Solar System

10-13

The solar system is made up of the objects that move around the sun in a regular path. Things were not always this way. The sun and the objects that encircle it started out in very different forms.

2→ It is believed that the solar system began as a large cloud of gas and dust. The cloud had a round shape and spun slowly. The spinning caused the gas and the dust to flatten into a large disc. The mass of gas and dust at the center became the sun. The gas and the dust were pulled together by gravity so that nuclear reactions started. The rest of the dust and the gas outside this moved so slowly that it started to cling together in places. Eventually, enough material stuck together to form planets.

3→ There are many different objects in the solar system. Of course, there are planets. Each one is unique. Some planets are made of rock or metal elements. Mercury, Venus, Earth, and Mars are like that. Other planets are more like gas and ice. Jupiter, Saturn, and the others are those types of planets. The planets have large numbers of moons.

4→ The solar system has a major asteroid belt. An asteroid is basically a rock. The largest can be hundreds of kilometers across. Huge numbers of these rocks circle the sun between Mars and Jupiter. Sometimes asteroids crash into each other and move toward Earth. When they pass near the planet, they heat up and burn. They are seen as shooting stars.

Lastly, there are comets, which are made of ice and gas. They also go around the sun but do not follow normal paths. When they are near the sun, they start to melt and form tails. Far from the sun, where space is cold, comets remain frozen solid.

1 The word "encircle" in the passage is closest in meaning to

Ⓐ hide
Ⓑ divide
Ⓒ follow
Ⓓ surround

2 The word "cling" in the passage is closest in meaning to

Ⓐ stick
Ⓑ throw
Ⓒ move
Ⓓ drag

3 According to paragraph 2, which of the following is NOT true of the formation of the solar system?

Ⓐ Gravity had an important role in its creation.
Ⓑ It was created from gas and dust.
Ⓒ Nuclear reactions helped create the sun.
Ⓓ The formation took a short time to occur.

4 In paragraph 3, the author uses "Mercury, Venus, Earth, and Mars" as examples of

Ⓐ planets close to the sun
Ⓑ planets that are small
Ⓒ planets without moons
Ⓓ planets made of rock

5 According to paragraph 4, what happens when an asteroid burns near the planet?

Ⓐ It becomes dust.
Ⓑ It crashes into other asteroids.
Ⓒ It looks like a shooting star.
Ⓓ It hits the Earth's surface.

6 **Directions**: Complete the table below by matching FIVE of the seven answer choices that describe the features of the solar system. TWO of the answer choices will NOT be used. *This question is worth 3 points.*

Answer Choices

1 They have metal elements.
2 They avoid the Earth.
3 They can have moons.
4 They may be hundreds of kilometers across.
5 They have gaseous elements.
6 They have tails.
7 They are made of rock.

Planets

•
•
•

Asteroids

•
•

Plate Tectonic Theory

10-14

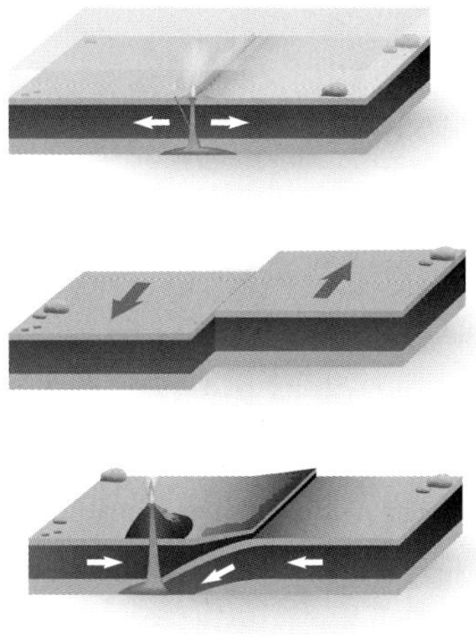

Three types of plate boundaries

Plate tectonics is a theory in the field of geology. It explains how the surface of the Earth moves. It states that the surface of the Earth is made of floating plates that move.

2→ The Earth is made of several different layers. The top layer is solid but broken into about ten different plates. They are about one hundred kilometers thick. These plates float on top of the layer below, which is liquid. The heat of the lower layer forces the plates to move. As the plates move, they create volcanoes, mountains, and trenches in the ocean along their edges.

Plates can move in three different ways. They can move apart. This is called a divergent boundary. There are a few such places at the ocean floor. When plates move this way, the liquid in the Earth's core moves up to fill in the space, called a rift. The rock closest to the rift is younger than the rock further away from it. Rifts usually spread about two centimeters per year. A transform boundary happens when two plates move side to side. This happens a lot in California. The Pacific Plate rubs against the North American Plate for nearly 1,300 kilometers. They shift about 0.6 centimeters per year. This has formed the San Andreas Fault, which is responsible for many earthquakes. Convergent boundaries form when two plates move toward each other. Usually, one plate goes below the other. When this happens, the top plate rises. Mountains can form this way. The Himalaya Mountains were formed this way. It is one of the youngest mountain ranges in the world. The plate underneath India continues to move into the plate under Tibet. These great mountains rise about five millimeters each year.

7 In paragraph 2, why does the author mention "volcanoes, mountains, and trenches in the ocean"?

Ⓐ To name different types of natural disasters
Ⓑ To state what the movements of plates form
Ⓒ To compare their effects with one another
Ⓓ To show where they are the most common

8 According to paragraph 2, what is the nature of the top layer of the Earth?

Ⓐ It is very hot at the center.
Ⓑ It is fragmented into about ten different plates.
Ⓒ It is heated by forces at the center of the Earth.
Ⓓ It moves when the seasons change.

9 The word "divergent" in the passage is closest in meaning to

Ⓐ separating
Ⓑ moving
Ⓒ squeezing
Ⓓ shaking

10 The word "it" in the passage refers to

Ⓐ the Earth's core
Ⓑ the space
Ⓒ the rift
Ⓓ the rock

11 The word "shift" in the passage is closest in meaning to

Ⓐ jump
Ⓑ break
Ⓒ move
Ⓓ shake

12 **Directions**: Complete the table below by matching FIVE of the seven answer choices below that describe different types of plate boundaries. TWO of the answer choices will NOT be used. *This question is worth 3 points.*

Answer Choices

1. The liquid core fills the space.
2. They move toward each other.
3. They move side to side.
4. The San Andreas Fault forms.
5. They formed the youngest mountains in the world.
6. They move apart.
7. This happens at the ocean floor.

Convergent Boundaries

•

•

Transform Boundaries

•

•

Divergent Boundaries

•

Vocabulary Check-Up

Choose the words with the closest meanings to the highlighted words.

1 This kind of sand is made by grinding glass.

Ⓐ setting
Ⓑ mixing
Ⓒ smashing
Ⓓ shaving

2 The quality of the environment plays a huge role in people's health.

Ⓐ material
Ⓑ junk
Ⓒ interest
Ⓓ part

3 The director is in charge of the export division.

Ⓐ keeps out of
Ⓑ gets rid of
Ⓒ is responsible for
Ⓓ comes around

4 The young child has a great imagination.

Ⓐ disgrace
Ⓑ mind
Ⓒ relationship
Ⓓ journey

5 Almost every geologist agrees with the theory of continental drift.

Ⓐ trouble
Ⓑ beginning
Ⓒ habit
Ⓓ slow movement

6 Happiness is not achieved according to one's performance.

Ⓐ failed
Ⓑ intended
Ⓒ accomplished
Ⓓ determined

7 The new device squeezes the package under its bar.

(A) spreads
(B) blows
(C) succeeds
(D) compresses

8 There are many packaging boxes, bags, and pouches.

(A) sticks
(B) pockets
(C) pieces
(D) covers

9 The big pictures were stuck everywhere on the walls.

(A) attached
(B) loose
(C) relaxed
(D) completed

10 The accountant should keep track of the company's expenses.

(A) forget
(B) leave
(C) calculate
(D) monitor

Actual Test

Actual Test

CONTINUE

Reading Section Directions

This section measures your ability to understand academic passages in English. You will have **36 minutes** to read and answer questions about **2 passages**. A clock at the top of the screen will show you how much time is remaining.

Most questions are worth 1 point but the last question for each passage is worth more than 1 point. The directions for the last question indicate how many points you may receive.

Some passages include a word or phrase that is underlined in blue. Click on the word or phrase to see a definition or an explanation.

When you want to move to the next question, click on **Next**. You may skip questions and go back to them later. If you want to return to previous questions, click on **Back**. You can click on **Review** at any time, and the review screen will show you which questions you have answered and which you have not answered. From this review screen, you may go directly to any question you have already seen in the Reading section.

Click on **Continue** to go on.

Ancient Cave Painting

11-01

Prehistoric rock paintings of Tassili N'Ajjer, Algeria

Prehistoric cave paintings were made since the Upper Paleolithic Era from 40,000 to 10,000 B.C. Yet they were not discovered until 1879. At first, people believed that they were hoaxes. But their authenticity was accepted as cave art was found in other sites around the globe. Modern techniques of carbon dating have confirmed their ancient origins. Other impressive work has been located on the walls of caves in France, Italy, Africa, Australia, and Southeast Asia.

The 1879 find was the work of the Magdalenian people. They were named after the nearby town of Magdalena, Spain. They lived from about 18,000 to 10,000 B.C. Magdalenian art is distinctive. It is characterized by recurring themes and styles. The most popular subjects were animals. Popular ones were **bison**, deer, horses, and the woolly mammoth, which is now extinct. Realistic human subjects were rare. They were limited to abstractions of human shapes. But recognizable human hands, which an artist might have included as a type of signature, can be seen.

Cave paintings remained hidden as long as they did because of two factors. First, artists chose to do their work deep inside caves. In those places, the stone walls were protected from the weather. These locales were often inaccessible to modern searchers for signs of ancient civilizations. Second, once cave art is detected and announced to a curious public, excavations are made. They expose the work to both people and the elements, from which it had been protected for thousands of years. In that way, a treasure trove of paintings identified in France during World War I disappeared within six months of becoming open to the public. Air conditioning can preserve some sites for viewing. But most are closed to tourists. Scholars must apply for access. Then, they are permitted to study the artwork for only short periods.

Despite cave art's relative inaccessibility, scientists have managed to infer much about the methods and the materials used by ancient artisans. The earliest works were finger drawings in soft clay on the surface of rock. These depicted animals' claw marks. Artists then adopted engraving methods. They used stone tools to carve figures into rock walls. Using their own skill as well as specialized tools, artists could alter the tone, the color, and the depth of a scene. The last technique to evolve was wall painting. Few colors were available as Paleolithic people were limited to what they found in nature. They made their colors from various minerals and trees. For example, red was extracted from oxidized iron and white from mica. From burned wood, they obtained carbon to make a black pigment.

Even with primitive resources, the artists showed ingenuity in mixing and applying colors. Nearly 200 color-producing mineral fragments have been found in barnacle shells, in which pigments were mixed. One artist used a human skull to mix his colors. Cave water containing calcium was used as a mixing agent. Animal and vegetable oils bound the pigments. Though no paint brushes have survived, the finished works show telltale brush marks. Paint was sometimes sprayed onto surfaces covered by prepared **stencils**. Blowpipes served as paint sprayers.

Painting was a profession. It was too difficult and expensive to be practiced by casual amateurs, who had to spend all their time hunting and focusing on means of survival. One difficulty was illuminating the dark cave walls. Scientists theorize that ancient painters worked with torches fueled by animal fat. Another problem was the inaccessibility of some wall surfaces. Some scenes could only have been painted lying down in narrow openings. Others were so high from the floor as to have required scaffolding.

The locales chosen for painting offer anthropologists vital clues about the lifestyles of the Upper Paleolithic people. Despite often being called cavemen, they did not live inside caves. Cave walls served as their canvasses for the simple reason that open-air work quickly disappeared. So caves sheltered and preserved the art. They wanted the art to last. They desired this both for their own entertainment and for the cultural function it served. Art was the medium through which prehistoric civilizations passed on their history and honored their traditions and ancestry.

Glossary

bison: a buffalo; a large mammal similar to a cow

stencil: a thin sheet of material with a design or image cut out of it

1 The word "hoaxes" in the passage is closest in meaning to

- (A) fakes
- (B) exceptions
- (C) mirages
- (D) copies

2 According to paragraph 2, which of the following is NOT true of Magdalenian art?

- (A) It is found as far east as Southeast Asia.
- (B) Most of its themes involve animals.
- (C) Artists signed their work with paintings of their hands.
- (D) It is named after the inhabitants of a town in Spain.

Ancient Cave Painting

Prehistoric cave paintings were made since the Upper Paleolithic Era from 40,000 to 10,000 B.C. Yet they were not discovered until 1879. At first, people believed that they were hoaxes. But their authenticity was accepted as cave art was found in other sites around the globe. Modern techniques of carbon dating have confirmed their ancient origins. Other impressive work has been located on the walls of caves in France, Italy, Africa, Australia, and Southeast Asia.

2→ The 1879 find was the work of the Magdalenian people. They were named after the nearby town of Magdalena, Spain. They lived from about 18,000 to 10,000 B.C. Magdalenian art is distinctive. It is characterized by recurring themes and styles. The most popular subjects were animals. Popular ones were **bison**, deer, horses, and the woolly mammoth, which is now extinct. Realistic human subjects were rare. They were limited to abstractions of human shapes. But recognizable human hands, which an artist might have included as a type of signature, can be seen.

Glossary

bison: a buffalo; a large mammal similar to a cow

3 The word "excavations" in the passage is closest in meaning to

Ⓐ journeys
Ⓑ sightings
Ⓒ drawings
Ⓓ diggings

4 In paragraph 3, why does the author mention cave paintings found in France?

Ⓐ To show that they are found all over the world
Ⓑ To illustrate how cave art can disappear
Ⓒ To indicate that some cave art is considered valuable
Ⓓ To give an example of cave paintings that are still preserved

5 According to paragraph 3, which of the following can be inferred about the site of cave paintings found in France during World War I?

Ⓐ It was destroyed by bombing during the war.
Ⓑ It was first discovered in 1879.
Ⓒ It was destroyed by exposure to weather and people.
Ⓓ It is still visited by scholars today.

6 According to paragraph 4, few colors were used in cave paintings because

Ⓐ prehistoric people preferred to paint in black and white
Ⓑ only some colors could be seen in dark caves
Ⓒ artists had no need to use many different colors
Ⓓ prehistoric people made paint from natural objects

3→ Cave paintings remained hidden as long as they did because of two factors. First, artists chose to do their work deep inside caves. In those places, the stone walls were protected from the weather. These locales were often inaccessible to modern searchers for signs of ancient civilizations. Second, once cave art is detected and announced to a curious public, excavations are made. They expose the work to both people and the elements, from which it had been protected for thousands of years. In that way, a treasure trove of paintings identified in France during World War I disappeared within six months of becoming open to the public. Air conditioning can preserve some sites for viewing. But most are closed to tourists. Scholars must apply for access. Then, they are permitted to study the artwork for only short periods.

4→ Despite cave art's relative inaccessibility, scientists have managed to infer much about the methods and the materials used by ancient artisans. The earliest works were finger drawings in soft clay on the surface of rock. These depicted animals' claw marks. Artists then adopted engraving methods. They used stone tools to carve figures into rock walls. Using their own skill as well as specialized tools, artists could alter the tone, the color, and the depth of a scene. The last technique to evolve was wall painting. Few colors were available as Paleolithic people were limited to what they found in nature. They made their colors from various minerals and trees. For example, red was extracted from oxidized iron and white from mica. From burned wood, they obtained carbon to make a black pigment.

7 The word "ingenuity" in the passage is closest in meaning to

Ⓐ boldness
Ⓑ timidity
Ⓒ cleverness
Ⓓ reluctance

8 Which of the sentences below best expresses the essential information highlighted sentence? *Incorrect* choices change the meaning in important ways or leave out essential information.

Ⓐ Cave painting was a form of entertainment practiced by all.
Ⓑ Cave painting was done mainly by women because the men were occupied with hunting.
Ⓒ Only a few people had the skill and means to devote their lives to painting.
Ⓓ Cave painters gathered materials during their hunting expeditions.

Even with primitive resources, the artists showed ingenuity in mixing and applying colors. Nearly 200 color-producing mineral fragments have been found in barnacle shells, in which pigments were mixed. One artist used a human skull to mix his colors. Cave water containing calcium was used as a mixing agent. Animal and vegetable oils bound the pigments. Though no paint brushes have survived, the finished works show telltale brush marks. Paint was sometimes sprayed onto surfaces covered by prepared **stencils**. Blowpipes served as paint sprayers.

Painting was a profession. It was too difficult and expensive to be practiced by casual amateurs, who had to spend all their time hunting and focusing on means of survival. One difficulty was illuminating the dark cave walls. Scientists theorize that ancient painters worked with torches fueled by animal fat. Another problem was the inaccessibility of some wall surfaces. Some scenes could only have been painted lying down in narrow openings. Others were so high from the floor as to have required scaffolding.

The locales chosen for painting offer anthropologists vital clues about the lifestyles of the Upper Paleolithic people. Despite often being called cavemen, they did not live inside caves. Cave walls served as their canvasses for the simple reason that open-air work quickly disappeared. So caves sheltered and preserved the art. They wanted the art to last. They desired this both for their own entertainment and for the cultural function it served. Art was the medium through which prehistoric civilizations passed on their history and honored their traditions and ancestry.

Glossary

stencil: a thin sheet of material with a design or image cut out of it

9 Look at the four squares [■] that indicate where the following sentence can be added to the passage.

The first to be spotted were in a cave located in Spain.

Where would the sentence best fit?

Click on a square [■] to add the sentence to the passage.

Prehistoric cave paintings were made since the Upper Paleolithic Era from 40,000 to 10,000 B.C. [1] Yet they were not discovered until 1879. [2] At first, people believed that they were hoaxes. [3] But their authenticity was accepted as cave art was found in other sites around the globe. [4] Modern techniques of carbon dating have confirmed their ancient origins. Other impressive work has been located on the walls of caves in France, Italy, Africa, Australia, and Southeast Asia.

10 **Directions**: An introductory sentence for a brief summary of the passage is provided below. Complete the summary by selecting the THREE answer choices that express the most important ideas in the passage. Some answer choices do not belong in the summary because they express ideas that are not in the passage or are minor ideas in the passage. *This question is worth 2 points.*

Drag your answer choices to the spaces where they belong.
To remove an answer choice, click on it. To review the passage, click **View Text**.

This passage is about the history of ancient cave painting.

•
•
•

Answer Choices

1 Cave paintings have been studied by scholars ever since 1879.

2 The authenticity of cave paintings was not established until the late nineteenth century.

3 Cave art is viewable today because of the protection offered by its location deep inside caves.

4 A frequent subject for cave painters was the human body.

5 Cave painters only used black pigments since they had no way to make colors.

6 Cave painting served as a means to communicate history and traditions.

The History of Time Zones

11-02

Time zones are necessary because of the rotation of the Earth as it revolves around the sun. The Earth spins around once every twenty-four hours. So it continuously moves each place on the planet toward the sun in the morning and away at night. As one traces the globe in a westerly direction, the sun reaches the overhead point—noon—at different times at each location. So one city's noon is not the same as that of a city just a hundred miles to the east, where the sun has already passed overhead.

This was not a problem in the preindustrial age. That was the time before technology allowed rapid communication across long distances. Timekeeping was a local phenomenon. Each town would set its clocks so that noon was when the sun reached its zenith in that particular place. A person who traveled to another city would have to change his pocket watch to reflect the new local time.

In the nineteenth century, railroads were laid. The telegraph also became widespread. For the first time, people could traverse many miles each day. They could also conduct cross-country business by telegram. The old system of irregular timekeeping made commerce and communication difficult and confusing. Uniform train schedules were impossible as each stop observed a different local time. Each railroad company used its own standard time. This was usually the time at its corporate headquarters or at an important stop. Some train stations had separate clocks for each railroad using that station. So a traveler stopping in a major city might see six clocks on the wall of the train platform. Each would display a different time. Efficient operation of railroads demanded that the time be standardized.

In 1878, a solution was proposed by a Canadian railway engineer, Sir Sandford Fleming. He suggested that the globe be marked by time zones. They would be separated by the Earth's lines of longitude. Each zone should be fifteen degrees wide. The Earth's 360 degrees would therefore be sectioned into twenty-four zones of fifteen degrees each. By this system, the rotation of the planet would move each zone fifteen degrees, or one twenty-fourth of the globe, in one hour.

American railroads began using Fleming's system in 1883. But efficient use worldwide required that a beginning line of longitude be designated as a base line for measuring a day. In 1884, an international gathering, the International Prime Meridian Conference, met for that purpose in Washington, D.C. It chose the longitude line passing through Greenwich, England as the Prime Meridian, or the line of zero longitude. The time at this longitude is known as Greenwich Mean Time, or GMT. Each longitude line runs from the North Pole to the South Pole and is perpendicular to the equator. The longitude lines are straight in theory. But in practice, many have been bent to accommodate the needs of local populations.

Not all countries adopted the system right away. Most of the United States did not do so until 1895. It was not mandated by Congress with the Standard Time Act until 1918. Even today, some countries depart from its uniformity. Israel begins its day at 6:00 PM instead of at 12:00 AM. While China should have five time zones, its government has chosen to have just one for the whole country. Some other countries employ half-hour time zones. Another common manipulation of time zones is Daylight Saving Time. It is called Summer Time in some countries. Those countries move their clocks ahead one hour in the spring. They maintain that system until fall. This provides an extra hour of daylight at the end of the day. The main purpose is energy conservation. If darkness arrives an hour later, that equates to one less hour that people are awake to consume electricity. Another benefit is to lengthen the time that people can be outside during warmer months.

GMT is based on the rate of the Earth's rotation, which is not constant. So it is subject to slight inaccuracies over time. Accordingly, in 1972, GMT was synchronized with super-accurate atomic clocks, which incorporate "leap seconds" that account for variations in planetary rotation. This new system is called Coordinated Universal Time, or UTC.

Glossary

preindustrial age: the time in human history before machines were introduced during the Industrial Revolution

line of longitude: an imaginary line that runs from the North Pole to the South Pole and that shows an east-west position on the Earth

REVIEW HELP BACK NEXT

11 According to paragraph 1, time zones became necessary when

Ⓐ humans began to use written language
Ⓑ technology permitted long-distance travel and communication
Ⓒ longitude lines were created by mapmakers
Ⓓ people began to travel long distances to different continents

12 The word "phenomenon" in the passage is closest in meaning to

Ⓐ abnormality
Ⓑ event
Ⓒ technology
Ⓓ destination

13 In paragraph 3, why does the author mention "six clocks on the wall of the train platform"?

Ⓐ To show that clocks how inaccurate clocks were in the past
Ⓑ To explain why time zones were not needed for early rail travel
Ⓒ To argue that each major city needed six time zones
Ⓓ To illustrate the need for the standardization of time

The History of Time Zones

1→ Time zones are necessary because of the rotation of the Earth as it revolves around the sun. The Earth spins around once every twenty-four hours. So it continuously moves each place on the planet toward the sun in the morning and away at night. As one traces the globe in a westerly direction, the sun reaches the overhead point—noon—at different times at each location. So one city's noon is not the same as that of a city just a hundred miles to the east, where the sun has already passed overhead.

This was not a problem in the **preindustrial age**. That was the time before technology allowed rapid communication across long distances. Timekeeping was a local phenomenon. Each town would set its clocks so that noon was when the sun reached its zenith in that particular place. A person who traveled to another city would have to change his pocket watch to reflect the new local time.

3→ In the nineteenth century, railroads were laid. The telegraph also became widespread. For the first time, people could traverse many miles each day. They could also conduct cross-country business by telegram. The old system of irregular timekeeping made commerce and communication difficult and confusing. Uniform train schedules were impossible as each stop observed a different local time. Each railroad company used its own standard time. This was usually the time at its corporate headquarters or at an important stop. Some train stations had separate clocks for each railroad using that station. So a traveler stopping in a major city might see six clocks on the wall of the train platform. Each would display a different time. Efficient operation of railroads demanded that the time be standardized.

Glossary

preindustrial age: the time in human history before machines were introduced during the Industrial Revolution

14 The word "sectioned" in the passage is closest in meaning to

- (A) divided
- (B) drawn
- (C) collected
- (D) multiplied

15 According to paragraph 5, Fleming's system could not be used worldwide until

- (A) time was more accurately kept by atomic clocks
- (B) railroad schedules were standardized
- (C) Congress passed the Standard Time Act in 1918
- (D) countries chose a line of zero longitude as a base line

16 In paragraph 5, the author's description of the International Prime Meridian Conference mentions all of the following EXCEPT:

- (A) The year that it took place
- (B) The decisions that it made
- (C) The people who participated
- (D) The place where it was held

Glossary

line of longitude: an imaginary line that runs from the North Pole to the South Pole and that shows an east-west position on the Earth

In 1878, a solution was proposed by a Canadian railway engineer, Sir Sandford Fleming. He suggested that the globe be marked by time zones. They would be separated by the Earth's lines of longitude. Each zone should be fifteen degrees wide. The Earth's 360 degrees would therefore be sectioned into twenty-four zones of fifteen degrees each. By this system, the rotation of the planet would move each zone fifteen degrees, or one twenty-fourth of the globe, in one hour.

5➔ American railroads began using Fleming's system in 1883. But efficient use worldwide required that a beginning **line of longitude** be designated as a base line for measuring a day. In 1884, an international gathering, the International Prime Meridian Conference, met for that purpose in Washington, D.C. It chose the longitude line passing through Greenwich, England as the Prime Meridian, or the line of zero longitude. The time at this longitude is known as Greenwich Mean Time, or GMT. Each longitude line runs from the North Pole to the South Pole and is perpendicular to the equator. The longitude lines are straight in theory. But in practice, many have been bent to accommodate the needs of local populations.

17 According to paragraph 6, which of the following can be inferred about time zones?

Ⓐ They were not needed around the United States in the nineteenth century.
Ⓑ They are not needed now that atomic clocks have been invented.
Ⓒ The Internet has decreased their importance.
Ⓓ A person who flies to different places may get confused by changing times.

18 The word "it" in the passage refers to

Ⓐ GMT
Ⓑ the rate
Ⓒ the Earth's rotation
Ⓓ time

19 Look at the four squares [■] that indicate where the following sentence can be added to the passage.

This means that the sun can sometimes set at 2:00 PM in certain places.

Where would the sentence best fit?

Click on a square [■] to add the sentence to the passage.

6➔ Not all countries adopted the system right away. Most of the United States did not do so until 1895. It was not mandated by Congress with the Standard Time Act until 1918. Even today, some countries depart from its uniformity. **1** Israel begins its day at 6:00 PM instead of at 12:00 AM. **2** While China should have five time zones, its government has chosen to have just one for the whole country. **3** Some other countries employ half-hour time zones. **4** Another common manipulation of time zones is Daylight Saving Time. It is called Summer Time in some countries. Those countries move their clocks ahead one hour in the spring. They maintain that system until fall. This provides an extra hour of daylight at the end of the day. The main purpose is energy conservation. If darkness arrives an hour later, that equates to one less hour that people are awake to consume electricity. Another benefit is to lengthen the time that people can be outside during warmer months.

GMT is based on the rate of the Earth's rotation, which is not constant. So it is subject to slight inaccuracies over time. Accordingly, in 1972, GMT was synchronized with super-accurate atomic clocks, which incorporate "leap seconds" that account for variations in planetary rotation. This new system is called Coordinated Universal Time, or UTC.

20 **Directions**: Fill in the table below by matching the appropriate statement to whether it refers to the problems or solutions related to time zones. *This question is worth 3 points.*

Drag your answer choices to the spaces where they belong.
To remove an answer choice, click on it. To review the passage, click **View Text**.

Answer Choices

1 The Earth revolves around the sun every twenty-four hours.

2 A base line of zero longitude passes through Greenwich, England.

3 The rotation of the Earth causes variations in local time.

4 Each country in the world has one time zone.

5 Local time differences complicated travel and communications.

6 The globe is divided into various time zones.

7 Atomic clocks correct for variations in the Earth's rotation.

Problem

-
-

Solution

-
-
-

Appendix

Mastering Word List

This part provides lists of important vocabulary words in each unit. They are essential words for understanding any academic texts. Many of the words are listed with their derivative forms so that students can expand their vocabulary in an effective way. These lists can be used as homework assignments.

UNIT 01 Vocabulary

Step A

- ☐ affect
- ☐ brainwave
- ☐ brutal
- ☐ disastrous
- ☐ drought
- ☐ fresh
- ☐ illegal
- ☐ link
- ☐ muscle
- ☐ nutritious
- ☐ physical
- ☐ prey
- ☐ researcher
- ☐ shrink
- ☐ signal
- ☐ vanish
- ☐ wildlife

Step B

- ☐ *n.* access
- ☐ *v.* access
- ☐ *adj.* accessible
- ☐ *adv.* accessibly

- ☐ *n.* affordability
- ☐ *v.* afford
- ☐ *adj.* affordable
- ☐ *adv.* affordably

- ☐ *n.* attraction
- ☐ *v.* attract
- ☐ *adj.* attractive
- ☐ *adv.* attractively

- ☐ *n.* condensation
- ☐ *v.* condense
- ☐ *adj.* condensed

- ☐ *n.* decoration
- ☐ *v.* decorate
- ☐ *adj.* decorative
- ☐ *adv.* decoratively

- ☐ *n.* density
- ☐ *v.* densify
- ☐ *adj.* dense
- ☐ *adv.* densely

- ☐ *n.* detection
- ☐ *v.* detect
- ☐ *adj.* detective
- ☐ *adv.* detectively

- ☐ *n.* electricity
- ☐ *v.* electrify
- ☐ *adj.* electric
- ☐ *adv.* electrically

- ☐ *n.* endangerment
- ☐ *v.* endanger
- ☐ *adj.* endangered

- ☐ *n.* evolution
- ☐ *v.* evolve
- ☐ *adj.* evolutionary
- ☐ *adv.* evolutionarily

- ☐ *n.* extremity
- ☐ *adj.* extreme
- ☐ *adv.* extremely

- ☐ *n.* identity
- ☐ *v.* identify
- ☐ *adj.* identifiable
- ☐ *adv.* identifiably

- ☐ *n.* improvement
- ☐ *v.* improve
- ☐ *adj.* improving
- ☐ *adv.* improvingly

- ☐ *n.* innovation
- ☐ *v.* innovate
- ☐ *adj.* innovative
- ☐ *adv.* innovatively

- ☐ *n.* invention
- ☐ *v.* invent
- ☐ *adj.* inventive
- ☐ *adv.* inventively

- ☐ *n.* migration
- ☐ *v.* migrate
- ☐ *adj.* migratable

- ☐ *n.* pollution
- ☐ *v.* pollute
- ☐ *adj.* polluted

- ☐ *n.* preservation
- ☐ *v.* preserve
- ☐ *adj.* preservative

- ☐ *n.* sufferance
- ☐ *v.* suffer
- ☐ *adj.* sufferable
- ☐ *adv.* sufferably

- ☐ *n.* sustenance
- ☐ *v.* sustain
- ☐ *adj.* sustainable

- ☐ *n.* transportation
- ☐ *v.* transport
- ☐ *adj.* transportable

UNIT 02 Reference

Step A

- ☐ aware of
- ☐ brilliant
- ☐ continent
- ☐ decide
- ☐ dish
- ☐ economy
- ☐ entire
- ☐ famous
- ☐ genius
- ☐ intense
- ☐ miserable
- ☐ modernize
- ☐ panic
- ☐ publish
- ☐ release
- ☐ secular
- ☐ series
- ☐ traditional
- ☐ trend
- ☐ value

Step B

- ☐ *n.* achievement
- ☐ *v.* achieve
- ☐ *adj.* achievable

- ☐ *n.* assertion
- ☐ *v.* assert
- ☐ *adj.* assertive
- ☐ *adv.* assertively

- ☐ *n.* civilization
- ☐ *v.* civilize
- ☐ *adj.* civilized

- ☐ *n.* comparison
- ☐ *v.* compare
- ☐ *adj.* comparative
- ☐ *adv.* comparatively

- ☐ *n.* complaint
- ☐ *v.* complain
- ☐ *adj.* complaining
- ☐ *adv.* complainingly

- ☐ *n.* competition
- ☐ *v.* compete
- ☐ *adj.* competitive
- ☐ *adv.* competitively

- ☐ *n.* consideration
- ☐ *v.* consider
- ☐ *adj.* considerable
- ☐ *adv.* considerably

- ☐ *n.* depression
- ☐ *v.* depress
- ☐ *adj.* depressing
- ☐ *adv.* depressingly

- ☐ *n.* education
- ☐ *v.* educate
- ☐ *adj.* educative

- ☐ *n.* extension
- ☐ *v.* extend
- ☐ *adj.* extensive
- ☐ *adv.* extensively

- ☐ *n.* inflation
- ☐ *v.* inflate
- ☐ *adj.* inflated

- ☐ *n.* influence
- ☐ *v.* influence
- ☐ *adj.* influential
- ☐ *adv.* influentially

- ☐ *n.* invasion
- ☐ *v.* invade

- ☐ *n.* measurement
- ☐ *v.* measure
- ☐ *adj.* measurable
- ☐ *adv.* measurably

- ☐ *n.* provision
- ☐ *v.* provide
- ☐ *adj.* providable

- ☐ *n.* reflection
- ☐ *v.* reflect
- ☐ *adj.* reflective
- ☐ *adv.* reflectively

- ☐ *n.* reliability
- ☐ *v.* rely
- ☐ *adj.* reliable
- ☐ *adv.* reliably

- ☐ *n.* variable
- ☐ *v.* vary
- ☐ *adj.* various
- ☐ *adv.* variously

- ☐ *n.* vision
- ☐ *v.* visualize
- ☐ *adj.* visual
- ☐ *adv.* visually

- ☐ *n.* voyage
- ☐ *v.* voyage

UNIT 03 Factual Information

Step A

- ☐ behave
- ☐ design
- ☐ evidence
- ☐ expose
- ☐ flexible
- ☐ float
- ☐ gain
- ☐ glow
- ☐ knowledge
- ☐ launch
- ☐ mandate
- ☐ method
- ☐ permanent
- ☐ privileged

Step B

- ☐ *n.* announcement
- ☐ *v.* announce
- ☐ *adj.* announcing
- ☐ *adv.* announcingly

- ☐ *n.* breath
- ☐ *v.* breathe
- ☐ *adj.* breathing
- ☐ *adv.* breathingly

- ☐ *n.* carefulness
- ☐ *v.* care
- ☐ *adj.* careful
- ☐ *adv.* carefully

- ☐ *n.* collection
- ☐ *v.* collect
- ☐ *adj.* collective
- ☐ *adv.* collectively

- ☐ *n.* composition
- ☐ *v.* compose
- ☐ *adj.* compositional
- ☐ *adv.* compositionally

- ☐ *n.* distribution
- ☐ *v.* distribute
- ☐ *adj.* distributive
- ☐ *adv.* distributively

- ☐ *n.* elevation
- ☐ *v.* elevate
- ☐ *adj.* elevated

- ☐ *n.* exploration
- ☐ *v.* explore
- ☐ *adj.* explorative
- ☐ *adv.* exploratively

- ☐ *n.* metal
- ☐ *v.* metal
- ☐ *adj.* metallic

- ☐ *n.* orbit
- ☐ *v.* orbit
- ☐ *adj.* orbital
- ☐ *adv.* orbitally

- ☐ *n.* performance
- ☐ *v.* perform
- ☐ *adj.* performative
- ☐ *adv.* performatively

- ☐ *n.* population
- ☐ *v.* populate
- ☐ *adj.* populous
- ☐ *adv.* populously

- ☐ *n.* protection
- ☐ *v.* protect
- ☐ *adj.* protective
- ☐ *adv.* protectively

- ☐ *n.* public
- ☐ *v.* publicize
- ☐ *adj.* public
- ☐ *adv.* publicly

- ☐ *n.* recovery
- ☐ *v.* recover
- ☐ *adj.* recoverable
- ☐ *adv.* recoverably

- ☐ *n.* reference
- ☐ *v.* refer
- ☐ *adj.* referential
- ☐ *adv.* referentially

- ☐ *n.* risk
- ☐ *v.* risk
- ☐ *adj.* risky

- ☐ *n.* solution
- ☐ *v.* solve
- ☐ *adj.* soluble
- ☐ *adv.* solubly

- ☐ *n.* translation
- ☐ *v.* translate
- ☐ *adj.* translatable

UNIT 04 Negative Factual Information

Step A

- ☐ basin
- ☐ climate
- ☐ consequently
- ☐ efficient
- ☐ ensure
- ☐ essential
- ☐ eventually
- ☐ expert
- ☐ feature
- ☐ formula
- ☐ laboratory
- ☐ liquid
- ☐ marine
- ☐ nomad
- ☐ perspective
- ☐ planet
- ☐ plantation
- ☐ presence
- ☐ purpose
- ☐ submerged

Step B

- ☐ *n.* accomplishment
- ☐ *v.* accomplish
- ☐ *adj.* accomplished

- ☐ *n.* amusement
- ☐ *v.* amuse
- ☐ *adj.* amusing / amused
- ☐ *adv.* amusingly / amusedly

- ☐ *n.* approximation
- ☐ *v.* approximate
- ☐ *adj.* approximate
- ☐ *adv.* approximately

- ☐ *n.* behavior
- ☐ *v.* behave
- ☐ *adj.* behavioral
- ☐ *adv.* behaviorally

- ☐ *n.* decrease
- ☐ *v.* decrease
- ☐ *adj.* decreasing
- ☐ *adv.* decreasingly

- ☐ *n.* destruction
- ☐ *v.* destroy
- ☐ *adj.* destructive
- ☐ *adv.* destructively

- ☐ *n.* equipment
- ☐ *v.* equip
- ☐ *adj.* equipped

- ☐ *n.* engagement
- ☐ *v.* engage
- ☐ *adj.* engaged

- ☐ *n.* equality
- ☐ *v.* equalize
- ☐ *adj.* equal
- ☐ *adv.* equally

- ☐ *n.* expansion
- ☐ *v.* expand
- ☐ *adj.* expansive
- ☐ *adv.* expansively

- ☐ *n.* flatness
- ☐ *v.* flatten
- ☐ *adj.* flattening

- ☐ *n.* flexibility
- ☐ *v.* flex
- ☐ *adj.* flexible
- ☐ *adv.* flexibly

- ☐ *n.* fluorescence
- ☐ *v.* fluoresce
- ☐ *adj.* fluorescent
- ☐ *adv.* fluorescently

- ☐ *n.* height
- ☐ *v.* heighten
- ☐ *adj.* high
- ☐ *adv.* high

- ☐ *n.* involvement
- ☐ *v.* involve
- ☐ *adj.* involved

- ☐ *n.* liquid
- ☐ *v.* liquidize
- ☐ *adj.* liquid
- ☐ *adv.* liquidly

- ☐ *n.* mistake
- ☐ *v.* mistake
- ☐ *adj.* mistaken
- ☐ *adv.* mistakenly

- ☐ *n.* normality
- ☐ *v.* normalize
- ☐ *adj.* normal
- ☐ *adv.* normally

- ☐ *n.* perfection
- ☐ *v.* perfect
- ☐ *adj.* perfect
- ☐ *adv.* perfectly

- ☐ *n.* threat
- ☐ *v.* threaten
- ☐ *adj.* threatening
- ☐ *adv.* threateningly

UNIT 05 Sentence Simplification

Step A

- ☐ achieve
- ☐ aspect
- ☐ barren
- ☐ carnivorous
- ☐ criminal
- ☐ cruel
- ☐ damage
- ☐ decay
- ☐ encounter
- ☐ environment
- ☐ graduate
- ☐ hereditary
- ☐ lumber
- ☐ offspring
- ☐ plunder
- ☐ replicate
- ☐ tablet
- ☐ trait
- ☐ tumor
- ☐ unique

Step B

- ☐ *n.* contamination
- ☐ *v.* contaminate
- ☐ *adj.* contaminative
- ☐ *adv.* contaminatively

- ☐ *n.* conviction
- ☐ *v.* convince
- ☐ *adj.* convincing
- ☐ *adv.* convincingly

- ☐ *n.* deterrence
- ☐ *v.* deter
- ☐ *adj.* deterrent
- ☐ *adv.* deterrently

- ☐ *n.* donation
- ☐ *v.* donate
- ☐ *adj.* donative
- ☐ *adv.* donatively

- ☐ *n.* emphasis
- ☐ *v.* emphasize
- ☐ *adj.* emphatic
- ☐ *adv.* emphatically

- ☐ *n.* establishment
- ☐ *v.* establish
- ☐ *adj.* established

- ☐ *n.* injury
- ☐ *v.* injure
- ☐ *adj.* injurious
- ☐ *adv.* injuriously

- ☐ *n.* inspiration
- ☐ *v.* inspire
- ☐ *adj.* inspirational
- ☐ *adv.* inspirationally

- ☐ *n.* legality
- ☐ *v.* legalize
- ☐ *adj.* legal
- ☐ *adv.* legally

- ☐ *n.* moisture
- ☐ *v.* moisten
- ☐ *adj.* moist
- ☐ *adv.* moistly

- ☐ *n.* mutation
- ☐ *v.* mutate
- ☐ *adj.* mutational
- ☐ *adv.* mutationally

- ☐ *n.* prediction
- ☐ *v.* predict
- ☐ *adj.* predictable
- ☐ *adv.* predictably

- ☐ *n.* reduction
- ☐ *v.* reduce
- ☐ *adj.* reducible
- ☐ *adv.* reducibly

- ☐ *n.* reformation
- ☐ *v.* reform
- ☐ *adj.* reformative
- ☐ *adv.* reformatively

- ☐ *n.* response
- ☐ *v.* respond
- ☐ *adj.* responsive
- ☐ *adv.* responsively

- ☐ *n.* rotation
- ☐ *v.* rotate
- ☐ *adj.* rotational
- ☐ *adv.* rotationally

- ☐ *n.* selection
- ☐ *v.* select
- ☐ *adj.* selective
- ☐ *adv.* selectively

- ☐ *n.* suffocation
- ☐ *v.* suffocate
- ☐ *adj.* suffocating / suffocative
- ☐ *adv.* suffocatingly

- ☐ *n.* suspicion
- ☐ *v.* suspect
- ☐ *adj.* suspicious
- ☐ *adv.* suspiciously

- ☐ *n.* transfer
- ☐ *v.* transfer
- ☐ *adj.* transferable
- ☐ *adv.* transferably

UNIT 06 Rhetorical Purpose

Step A

- ☐ aggressive
- ☐ altitude
- ☐ anxiety
- ☐ avalanche
- ☐ beat
- ☐ chemical
- ☐ damp
- ☐ decade
- ☐ disorder
- ☐ entire
- ☐ feat
- ☐ flesh
- ☐ fluid
- ☐ forensics
- ☐ gender

- ☐ geographical
- ☐ oracle
- ☐ outgoing
- ☐ personality
- ☐ pollinate
- ☐ ruin
- ☐ sociolinguist
- ☐ stretch
- ☐ tend
- ☐ threaten
- ☐ varied
- ☐ whereas
- ☐ wreck

Step B

- ☐ *n.* annoyance
- ☐ *v.* annoy
- ☐ *adj.* annoying / annoyed
- ☐ *adv.* annoyingly

- ☐ *n.* argument
- ☐ *v.* argue
- ☐ *adj.* arguable
- ☐ *adv.* arguably

- ☐ *n.* collision
- ☐ *v.* collide
- ☐ *adj.* collisional
- ☐ *adv.* collisionally

- ☐ *n.* determination
- ☐ *v.* determine
- ☐ *adj.* determinative
- ☐ *adv.* determinatively

- ☐ *n.* divination
- ☐ *v.* divine
- ☐ *adj.* divine / divinatory
- ☐ *adv.* divinely

- ☐ *n.* embarrassment
- ☐ *v.* embarrass
- ☐ *adj.* embarrassing
- ☐ *adv.* embarrassingly

- ☐ *n.* erosion
- ☐ *v.* erode
- ☐ *adj.* erodible

- ☐ *n.* guidance
- ☐ *v.* guide
- ☐ *adj.* guidable

- ☐ *n.* invasion
- ☐ *v.* invade
- ☐ *adj.* invasive
- ☐ *adv.* invasively

- ☐ *n.* precision
- ☐ *adj.* precise
- ☐ *adv.* precisely

- ☐ *n.* pronunciation
- ☐ *v.* pronounce
- ☐ *adj.* pronounceable

- ☐ *n.* supervision
- ☐ *v.* supervise
- ☐ *adj.* supervisory

- ☐ *n.* type
- ☐ *v.* typify
- ☐ *adj.* typical
- ☐ *adv.* typically

UNIT 07 Inference

Step A

- ☐ absolute
- ☐ arthritis
- ☐ blindfolded
- ☐ cataract
- ☐ chromosome
- ☐ civil
- ☐ command
- ☐ cruelty
- ☐ customer
- ☐ destiny
- ☐ gain
- ☐ journalism
- ☐ lance
- ☐ liver
- ☐ political
- ☐ properly
- ☐ retina
- ☐ slight
- ☐ supplement
- ☐ ultraviolet

Step B

- ☐ *n.* administration
- ☐ *v.* administrate
- ☐ *adj.* administrative
- ☐ *adv.* administratively

- ☐ *n.* admiration
- ☐ *v.* admire
- ☐ *adj.* admirable
- ☐ *adv.* admirably

- ☐ *n.* application
- ☐ *v.* apply
- ☐ *adj.* applicative
- ☐ *adv.* applicatively

- ☐ *n.* approval
- ☐ *v.* approve
- ☐ *adj.* approving
- ☐ *adv.* approvingly

- ☐ *n.* avoidance
- ☐ *v.* avoid
- ☐ *adj.* avoidable
- ☐ *adv.* avoidably

- ☐ *n.* circulation
- ☐ *v.* circulate
- ☐ *adj.* circulative

- ☐ *n.* consumption
- ☐ *v.* consume
- ☐ *adj.* consumable
- ☐ *adv.* consumably

- ☐ *n.* contest
- ☐ *v.* contest
- ☐ *adj.* contestable
- ☐ *adv.* contestably

- ☐ *n.* economy
- ☐ *v.* economize
- ☐ *adj.* economic / economical
- ☐ *adv.* economically

- ☐ *n.* entertainment
- ☐ *v.* entertain
- ☐ *adj.* entertaining
- ☐ *adv.* entertainingly

- ☐ *n.* experiment
- ☐ *v.* experiment
- ☐ *adj.* experimental
- ☐ *adv.* experimentally

- ☐ *n.* favor
- ☐ *v.* favor
- ☐ *adj.* favorable
- ☐ *adv.* favorably

- ☐ *n.* honesty
- ☐ *adj.* honest
- ☐ *adv.* honestly

- ☐ *n.* medication
- ☐ *v.* medicate
- ☐ *adj.* medicated

- ☐ *n.* owner
- ☐ *v.* own
- ☐ *adj.* ownable

- ☐ *n.* pregnancy
- ☐ *adj.* pregnant
- ☐ *adv.* pregnantly

- ☐ *n.* ratification
- ☐ *v.* ratify

- ☐ *n.* sensitivity
- ☐ *v.* sensitize
- ☐ *adj.* sensitive
- ☐ *adv.* sensitively

- ☐ *n.* regulation
- ☐ *v.* regulate
- ☐ *adj.* regulative / regulatory
- ☐ *adv.* regulatively / regulatorily

- ☐ *n.* replacement
- ☐ *v.* replace
- ☐ *adj.* replaceable
- ☐ *adv.* replaceably

UNIT 08 Insert Text

Step A

- ☐ archery
- ☐ athlete
- ☐ budget
- ☐ bully
- ☐ capitalism
- ☐ challenging
- ☐ clone
- ☐ complex
- ☐ conflict
- ☐ defect
- ☐ delicate
- ☐ drain
- ☐ element
- ☐ emotional
- ☐ entomb
- ☐ flaw
- ☐ heal
- ☐ humanitarian
- ☐ geology
- ☐ incredible
- ☐ independent
- ☐ jury
- ☐ leather
- ☐ media
- ☐ mental
- ☐ military
- ☐ mystique
- ☐ myth
- ☐ obese
- ☐ prefix
- ☐ quit
- ☐ respect
- ☐ rule
- ☐ similar
- ☐ spread
- ☐ stress
- ☐ strict
- ☐ warrior

Step B

- ☐ *n.* advertisement
- ☐ *v.* advertise
- ☐ *adj.* advertising
- ☐ *adv.* advertisingly

- ☐ *n.* anger
- ☐ *v.* anger
- ☐ *adj.* angry
- ☐ *adv.* angrily

- ☐ *n.* conflict
- ☐ *v.* conflict
- ☐ *adj.* conflictive

- ☐ *n.* delivery
- ☐ *v.* deliver
- ☐ *adj.* deliverable

- ☐ *n.* escape
- ☐ *v.* escape
- ☐ *adj.* escaping / escaped
- ☐ *adv.* escapingly

- ☐ *n.* femininity
- ☐ *v.* feminize
- ☐ *adj.* feminine
- ☐ *adv.* femininely

- ☐ *n.* insistence
- ☐ *v.* insist
- ☐ *adj.* insistent
- ☐ *adv.* insistently

- ☐ *n.* production
- ☐ *v.* produce
- ☐ *adj.* productive
- ☐ *adv.* productively

- ☐ *n.* profession
- ☐ *v.* professionalize
- ☐ *adj.* professional
- ☐ *adv.* professionally

- ☐ *n.* relief
- ☐ *v.* relieve
- ☐ *adj.* relievable
- ☐ *adv.* relievably

- ☐ *n.* tragedy
- ☐ *adj.* tragic
- ☐ *adv.* tragically

- ☐ *n.* uniformity
- ☐ *v.* uniform
- ☐ *adj.* uniform
- ☐ *adv.* uniformly

UNIT 09 Prose Summary

Step A

- ☐ advance
- ☐ allow
- ☐ afford
- ☐ arrest
- ☐ compost
- ☐ curve
- ☐ delicate
- ☐ drunk

- ☐ dump
- ☐ economist
- ☐ fair
- ☐ force
- ☐ ideally
- ☐ insomnia
- ☐ jurisprudence
- ☐ labor
- ☐ lack
- ☐ liability
- ☐ logical
- ☐ major
- ☐ manure
- ☐ mining
- ☐ minor
- ☐ narcolepsy
- ☐ nutrient
- ☐ organic
- ☐ pesticide
- ☐ property
- ☐ remove
- ☐ scurvy
- ☐ secure
- ☐ selfish
- ☐ share
- ☐ solid
- ☐ spot
- ☐ sue
- ☐ surface
- ☐ theory
- ☐ throat
- ☐ tissue
- ☐ victim
- ☐ weed

Step B

- ☐ *n.* blood
- ☐ *v.* bleed
- ☐ *adj.* bleeding
- ☐ *adv.* bleedingly

- ☐ *n.* concentration
- ☐ *v.* concentrate
- ☐ *adj.* concentrative
- ☐ *adv.* concentratively

- ☐ *n.* decision
- ☐ *v.* decide
- ☐ *adj.* decisive
- ☐ *adv.* decisively

- ☐ *n.* fertility / fertilization
- ☐ *v.* fertilize
- ☐ *adj.* fertile
- ☐ *adv.* fertilely

- ☐ *n.* guilt
- ☐ *v.* guilt
- ☐ *adj.* guilty
- ☐ *adv.* guiltily

- ☐ *n.* reaction
- ☐ *v.* react
- ☐ *adj.* reactive
- ☐ *adv.* reactively

- ☐ *n.* reliance
- ☐ *v.* rely
- ☐ *adj.* reliable
- ☐ *adv.* reliably

- ☐ *n.* removal
- ☐ *v.* remove
- ☐ *adj.* removable
- ☐ *adv.* removably

- ☐ *n.* specification
- ☐ *v.* specify
- ☐ *adj.* specific
- ☐ *adv.* specifically

UNIT 10 Fill in a Table

Step A

- ☐ abundant
- ☐ asteroid
- ☐ canal
- ☐ cling
- ☐ cluster
- ☐ comet
- ☐ common
- ☐ comparatively
- ☐ core
- ☐ crust
- ☐ dangerous
- ☐ double
- ☐ drift
- ☐ encircle
- ☐ float
- ☐ give off
- ☐ gravity
- ☐ grind
- ☐ jet lag
- ☐ mammal
- ☐ marsupial
- ☐ nebula
- ☐ nuclear
- ☐ opossum
- ☐ physicist
- ☐ pottery
- ☐ pouch
- ☐ precedent
- ☐ quake
- ☐ rabies
- ☐ remains
- ☐ shift
- ☐ skeleton
- ☐ solar
- ☐ spin
- ☐ squeeze
- ☐ submarine
- ☐ termite
- ☐ trench
- ☐ upset

Step B

- ☐ *n.* collapse
- ☐ *v.* collapse
- ☐ *adj.* collapsible
- ☐ *adv.* collapsibly

- ☐ *n.* colony
- ☐ *v.* colonize
- ☐ *adj.* colonial
- ☐ *adv.* colonially

- ☐ *n.* convergence
- ☐ *v.* converge
- ☐ *adj.* convergent
- ☐ *adv.* convergently

- ☐ *n.* cooperation
- ☐ *v.* cooperate
- ☐ *adj.* cooperative
- ☐ *adv.* cooperatively

- ☐ *n.* divergence
- ☐ *v.* diverge

☐ *adj.* divergent
☐ *adv.* divergently

☐ *n.* immunization
☐ *v.* immunize
☐ *adj.* immune

☐ *n.* influence
☐ *v.* influence
☐ *adj.* influential
☐ *adv.* influentially

☐ *n.* internalization
☐ *v.* internalize
☐ *adj.* internal
☐ *adv.* internally

☐ *n.* location
☐ *v.* locate
☐ *adj.* locatable

☐ *n.* neighbor / neighborhood
☐ *v.* neighbor
☐ *adj.* neighboring
☐ *adv.* neighborly

☐ *n.* perception
☐ *v.* perceive
☐ *adj.* perceptive
☐ *adv.* perceptively

☐ *n.* purchase
☐ *v.* purchase
☐ *adj.* purchasable

☐ *n.* radiation
☐ *v.* radiate
☐ *adj.* radiate
☐ *adv.* radiately

☐ *n.* storage
☐ *v.* store
☐ *adj.* storable
☐ *adv.* storably

MEMO

MEMO

MEMO

How to
Master Skills for the

Second Edition

TOEFL® iBT

READING

Basic

Answers and Translations

DARAKWON

PART I Basic Comprehension

UNIT 01 Vocabulary

Basic Drill p.14

Drill 1 Ⓐ

해석

위장이란 적으로부터 몸을 숨기는 것이다. 일부 동물들이 적으로부터 자신을 보호하기 위해 위장을 한다. 먹이를 잡기 위해 위장을 하기도 한다. 개구리, 나비, 그리고 뱀이 이러한 동물의 예이다. 이들은 색깔이나 모양을 바꿔서 주변 환경과 섞인다. 위장을 통해 풀, 나뭇잎, 혹은 돌처럼 보일 수가 있다. 이로써 야생에서의 생존 가능성이 높아진다.

Drill 2 Ⓑ

해석

몇몇 야생 동물들은 동면을 하는데, 동면은 겨울 동안 잠을 자는 것이다. 이들은 늦은 가을에 동굴로 들어가 봄이 될 때까지 밖으로 나오지 않는다. 동물들은 동면에 들어가기 전에 먹이를 먹어 지방을 비축한다. 이러한 지방 때문에 겨울을 보낼 수 있다. 봄에 밖으로 나오면 동물들은 매우 말라 있다. 또한 몹시 배고파 한다. 동면 덕분에 많은 야생 동물들이 먹이가 없는 추운 겨울에도 생존할 수 있다.

Drill 3 Ⓐ

해석

조사관들이 지난 주에 동물원을 방문했다. 원숭이들이 어떻게 지내는지 확인하려고 했다. 동물원 안의 일부 원숭이들은 비만이었다. 이쑤시개처럼 삐쩍 마른 원숭이들도 있었다. 조사관들은 왜 차이가 발생했는지 알고 싶었다. 아마도 몇몇 원숭이들이 다른 원숭이들의 먹이를 훔쳤을 것이다.

Drill 4 Ⓓ

해석

대부분의 TV에는 리모컨이 포함되어 있다. 리모컨은 적외선 기술을 이용한다. TV 화면에서 나오는 빛은 눈에 보이는 반면, 적외선은 감지할 수가 없다. 리모컨은 적외선을 이용해서 TV에 명령을 보낸다. TV에는 이러한 빛의 섬광을 읽을 수 있는 특수한 수신 장치가 있어야 한다. 시청자들은 리모컨으로 채널을 바꾸고 메뉴를 살펴볼 수 있다.

Drill 5 Ⓑ

해석

미국의 북동부에 가장 다양한 형태의 강수가 내린다. 이 지역에서는 비, 진눈깨비, 그리고 눈이 내린다. 어떤 해에는 너무 많이 내려서 농작물에 피해를 입히기도 한다. 이 때문에 많은 농부들은 경비를 지불하기 위해 은행에서 대출을 받는다. 이는 또한 건물에도 피해를 끼칠 수 있다.

Drill 6 Ⓒ

해석

울버린은 강인한 동물이다. 힘이 세고 날씨가 추운 지역에서도 생존할 수 있다. 또한 덩치가 큰 동물도 붙잡을 수 있다. 울버린은 캐나다 및 미국의 숲에서 서식한다. 울버린은 먹이를 사냥할 때 하루에 100마일까지 이동할 수 있다. 울버린은 곰의 먹이를 빼앗을 정도로 힘이 세고 공격적이다.

Drill 7 Ⓐ

해석

축구는 미국에서 큰 인기를 얻지 못하고 있다. 그 이유는 대부분 사람들이 야구, 농구, 그리고 미식 축구 경기를 보는 것을 더 좋아하기 때문이다. 이들은 미국에서 생긴 것들이다. 많은 미국인들이 축구는 유럽 사람이나 남미 사람들을 위한 스포츠라고 생각한다. 미국적인 특성을 나타내는 것이 아니다. 미국인들은 또한 축구에서 점수가 잘 나지 않는 점도 좋아하지 않는다.

Drill 8 Ⓐ

해석

지면 가까이에 있는 공기가 태양에 의해 가열되면 구름이 형성된다. 대기에서 뜨거운 공기는 위로 올라가는데, 그 이유는 뜨거운 공기의 밀도가 주변 공기보다 낮기 때문이다. 결국 상승하는 공기는 차가워진다. 처음에는 수증기 상태였던 물이 응결된다. 이로써 눈에 보이는 물방울이 만들어진다. 이 시점에 이르면 구름이 보이게 된다.

Exercises with Short Passages

Exercise 1 1 Ⓑ 2 Ⓐ 3 Ⓒ 4 Ⓐ p.18

해석

연체동물

연체동물은 해양 생물의 중요한 일부이다. 이들은 수천 년 동안 인간에게 영양분을 제공해 주었다. 연체동물에는 대합, 홍합, 굴, 그리고 골뱅이와 같이 껍질이 있는 생물들이 포함된다. 이들은 모두 아가미를 가지고 있어서 아가미로 물속의 산소를 받아들인다. 이들은 종종 민물과 바다의 염수가 만나는 곳에서 서식한다. 이러한 물에는 먹이가 풍부하다. 연체동물은 "발"이라고 불리는 근육으로 껍질을 열어 몸에 물을 통과시킴으로써 먹이를 얻는다. 이들은 영양분이 풍부한 식물이나 주변 물속에 있는 작은 동물들을 먹는다. 또 다른 형태의 연체동물로는 오징어와 문어가 있다. 이들은 바닷물에서만 살 수 있다. 이들의 "발"은 촉수라고 불리는 팔로 진화했다. 이를 이용하여 커다란 먹이를 붙잡을 수 있다.

Exercise 2 1 Ⓐ 2 Ⓓ 3 Ⓐ 4 Ⓒ p.19

해석

익스트림 스포츠

익스트림 스포츠는 상당히 새로운 종류의 스포츠이다. 여기에는 번지 점프, 특수한 자전거 타기, 그리고 스케이트보딩 등이 포함된다. 젊은이들은 종종 자신들의 신체적인 능력, 용맹함, 그리고 기술을 시험하기 위해 이러한 스포츠를 하려고 한다. 이러한 스포츠의 특징은 빠른 속도와 위험한 묘기일 것이다. 이는 정신적인 쾌감을 가져다 줄 수 있다. 정신적인 쾌감이란 뇌가 스트레스를 느낄 때 사람들이 갖게 되는 느낌이다. 많은 사람들은 이러한 느낌을 좋아한다. 익스트림 스포츠는 젊은 사람들의 문화의 중요한 부분이다. 기업들은 젊은 관객들을 끌어들이는 힘 때문에 익스트림 스포츠 행사에 음료나 의류와 같은 제품을 마케팅하기 시작했다.

Exercise 3 1 Ⓓ 2 Ⓐ 3 Ⓒ 4 Ⓐ p.20

해석

퀘벡의 재앙

2003년은 퀘벡에 끔찍한 해였다. 그 이유는 화재 때문이었다. 근래에 가장 끔찍한 화재가 발생한 기간이었다. 또한 캐나다의 해당 지역에서 자연 재해로 가장 큰 피해 비용이 발생했던 해이기도 했다. 참담했던 화재는 3년간의 악천후 때문에 발생했다. 일부 지역에서는 100년 동안 가장 심했던 가뭄이 발생했다. 땅은 크게 메말라 있었다. 2,400건이 넘는 산불로 광활한 지역이 불에 탔다. 화재 진압에 사용된 비용이 5억 달러에 달했다. 보험 회사는 보험료로 2억 5천만 달러를 지불했다. 세 명의 소방관이 목숨을 잃었다. 화재 피해를 복구하기까지 오랜 시간이 걸렸다. 2003년은 10년 중 최악의 해였다.

Exercise 4 1 Ⓑ 2 Ⓒ 3 Ⓓ 4 Ⓑ p.21

해석

뇌와 컴퓨터

언젠가는 생각만으로 인간이 컴퓨터를 제어할 수 있게 될 것이다. 키보드나 마우스가 필요 없을 것이다. 과학자들은 뇌파로 컴퓨터를 제어할 수 있는 방법을 개발 중이다. 한국의 연구자들이 뇌의 활동을 측정하는 소프트웨어를 만들었다. 사람은 이완 상태가 되면 뇌의 활동이 적어진다. 컴퓨터가 이를 감지한다. 그런 다음에는 화면의 그래픽이 변한다. 엔지니어들은 이것을 컴퓨터-뇌 인터페이스라고 부른다. 이것은 뇌와 컴퓨터 간의 직접적인 연결 방식이다. MIT의 또 다른 연구자는 원숭이를 이용해 뇌 신호 지도를 그리고 있다. 원숭이가 먹이를 잡으려고 하면 원숭이 뇌는 팔로 전기 신호를 보낸다. 이 연구자는 이러한 신호를 이용해서 로봇 팔을 제어한다. 로봇 팔은 원숭이보다 먼저 먹이를 잡는다.

Exercises with Mid-Length Passages

Exercise 1 1 Ⓐ 2 Ⓑ p.22

해석

야생 동물 거래

전 세계적으로 불법적인 야생 동물 거래액은 매년 수십억 달러에 달한다. 마약이나 무기 밀매만큼 심각한 수준이다. 이는 코뿔소, 코끼리, 호랑이, 뱀, 조류, 그리고 거북이를 포함하여 수많은 종에 영향을 끼치고 있다. 많은 종이 멸종 위기에 처해져 있는데, 이 말은 이들 종이 지구에서 사라질 수도 있음을 의미한다.

동물이나 동물의 신체 부위는 종종 트로피, 특별한 음식, 그리고 특이한 약품으로 사용된다. 수많은 동물들이 자신의 자연 서식지를 잃고 있다. 이러한 일이 일어나는 몇 가지 이유가 있다. 도시 및 마을의 성장으로 정글이 줄어들고 있다. 야생 지역도 접근하기가 쉬워지고 있다. 숲속에 사는 동물들은 밀렵꾼들의 손쉬운 목표가 된다. 많은 경찰들이 불법 사냥을 막기 위한 노력을 하지 않기 때문에 문제는 더욱 심각해지고 있다. 문제를 해결하기 위한 경찰 병력도 충분하지 않다. 가장 큰 문제는 수요에 있다. 전 세계의 사람들이 여전히 이러한 동물들을 원한다. 특별한 것을 위해 기꺼이 높은 비용을 지불하고자 한다.

사람들이 이러한 상품을 구입하고자 하는 한 밀렵꾼들은 사냥을 계속할 것이다. 경찰은 밀렵을 막아야 한다. 국가는 정글을 보전하기 위해 더 많이 노력해야 한다. 마지막으로 문화가 변해야 한다. 사람들은 야생 동물 거래가 잘못된 것이라는 믿음을 가져야 할 것이다.

Exercise 2 1 Ⓐ 2 Ⓒ p.23

해석

세렌게티의 동물들

세렌게티는 아프리카에 있는 거대한 평원이다. 탄자니아와 케냐에서 찾아볼 수 있다. 이곳은 대부분이 초원 지대이다. 숲과 산, 그리고 강도 포함되어 있다. 또한 많은 야생 동물들이 이곳에서 산다.

대부분의 사람들은 그곳에서 이루어지는 대규모의 이동 때문에 세렌게티를 알고 있다. 매년 수많은 영양, 얼룩말, 그리고 가젤의 무리들이 먹이와 물을 찾아 이동을 한다. 약 2백만 마리의 동물들이 한 곳에서 다른 곳으로 이동을 한다. 하지만 이 지역에서 풀을 뜯어 먹는 동물은 이들만이 아니다. 많은 수의 기린과 코끼리들도 이곳에서 살고 있다.

포식자들 또한 이곳에서 살고 있다. 세렌게티에는 다수의 사자 무리들이 살고 있다. 표범, 하이에나, 치타, 그리고 들개들도 이곳에서 사냥을 한다. 강에서는 악어를 찾아볼 수도 있다.

세렌게티에는 500종 이상의 조류들이 서식한다. 파충류와 양서류들도 많다. 수많은 곤충들도 이곳에서 살고 있다. 종합하면, 세렌게티는 지구에서 가장 다양한 동물들이 서식하는 지역 중 하나이다. 이러한 점은 그곳에서 살고 있는 커다란 동물들을 수를 고려할 때 특히 사실이다.

Exercise 3 1 Ⓐ 2 Ⓒ p.24

해석

가뭄

가뭄은 어떤 지역의 강수량이 평상시보다 적은 시기이다. 비나 눈이 적게 올 수 있다. 가뭄은 한두 계절 동안 지속될 수 있다. 또한 몇 년 동안 지속될 수도 있다.

일부 가뭄들은 예상이 가능하다. 예를 들어 엘리뇨와 같은 기상 현상이 있다. 이는 몇 년에 한 번씩 발생한다. 엘리뇨는 태평양 주변의 모든 국가에 영향을 미친다. 엘니뇨가 발생한 해에는 특정 지역에서 가뭄이 나타날 수 있다. 한편 미국의 남서부와 같은 지역들은 종종 가뭄을 겪는다. 이러한 지역은 전형적으로 건조한 곳이다. 따라서 이곳에서 사는 사람들은 많은 비를 예상하지 않는다. 하지만 예상이 불가능한 가뭄도 있다. 날씨 변화 때문에 보통 비가 많이 내리는 지역에서 때때로 비가 거의 내리지 않거나 전혀 내리지 않을 수도 있다.

가뭄의 영향은 광범위하다. 사람들이 마실 물이 줄어든다. 농부들의 경우, 작물과 동물에게 줄 물이 줄어든다. 호수와 연못이 증발할 수도 있다. 강물이 줄어들 수도 있다. 땅 자체가 매우 건조해질 수도 있다. 일부 경우, 바람이 건조한 토양을 날려보낼 수도 있는데, 이로 인해 더 큰 문제가 발생한다.

Exercise 4 1 Ⓓ 2 Ⓑ p.25

해석

수력

많은 문명들이 강가에서 발전했다. 사람들은 강물을 음용수로 사용했다. 강으로 물품과 사람들을 수송했다. 또한 강물이 만들어 내는 에너지를 이용할 수 있었다. 이러한 물의 힘, 즉 수력은 오랜 시간에 걸쳐 여러 가지 방식으로 이용되었다.

고대 그리스인들은 약 2,000년 전에 흐르는 물의 힘을 이용했다. 강가에 방앗간을 세웠다. 흐르는 물이 방앗간에 동력을 제공해 주었다. 그러면 곡식을 갈아서 가루를 만들 수가 있었다. 이러한 유형의 기술은 다양한 문화권에서 수 세기 동안 이용되었다. 고대 이집트인들 또한 수력을 이용했다. 나선 양수기를 이용해 농경지에 물을 공급했다. 나선 양수기는 사람들이 양동이로 물을 날라서 농경지에 쏟아 붓는 방식보다 훨씬 더 효과적인 것이었다.

최근에는 수력이 전기 생산을 위해 사용되고 있다. 최초의 수력 발전은 미국에서 이루어졌다. 1880년의 일이었다. 그 후 전 세계적으로 강에 댐이 건설되었다. 흐르는 물이 댐의 터빈을 통과한다. 이러한 터빈은 회전을 하면서 전기를 생산한다. 이때 만들어지는 전기는 저렴하면서도 깨끗하다.

Building Summary Skills

p.26

A

Exercise 1 The Wildlife Trade

1 The illegal wildlife trade is a big business and puts many animals in danger.

4 The greatest problem is that people continue to ask for animal products.

5 They feel special when they have rare animal parts and are happy to pay for them.

2 The places where they live are getting smaller, which makes them easier to catch.

3 Police cannot stop people from hunting.

Exercise 2 Serengeti Animals

1 There are many wild animals in the Serengeti in Africa.

4 There are also predators such as lions, leopards, hyenas, and cheetahs.

5 Other animals include birds, reptiles, amphibians, and insects.

2 Each year, millions of animals migrate in search of food and water.

3 These animals include wildebeests, zebras, and gazelles.

Exercise 3 Droughts

1 A drought is a time when there is less precipitation than normal.

4 The effects of droughts include less water for people and animals.

3 In other places, droughts are expected to occur.

2 El Nino is a weather phenomenon that causes droughts in some places.

Exercise 4 Water Power

1 People used the power of river water in the past.

3 The ancient Egyptians used water screws to irrigate their fields.

4 People use water power today to make electricity.

2 The ancient Greeks made mills by rivers to grind grain.

5 Dams make power that is cheap and clean.

B

Exercise 1 The Wildlife Trade

The illegal wildlife trade is a big business and puts many animals in danger. The places where they live are getting smaller, which makes them easier to catch. Police cannot stop people from hunting. The greatest problem is that people continue to ask for animal products. They feel special when they have rare animal parts and are happy to pay for them.

Exercise 2 Serengeti Animals

There are many wild animals in the Serengeti in Africa. Each year, millions of animals migrate in search of food and water. These animals include wildebeests, zebras, and gazelles. There are also predators such as lions, leopards, hyenas, and cheetahs. Other animals include birds, reptiles, amphibians, and insects.

Exercise 3 Droughts

A drought is a time when there is less precipitation than normal. It can last for a season or two or several years. El Nino is a weather phenomenon that causes droughts in some places. In other places, droughts are expected to occur. The effects of droughts include less water for people and animals.

Exercise 4 Water Power

People used the power of river water in the past. The ancient Greeks made mills by rivers to grind grain. The ancient Egyptians used water screws to irrigate their fields. People use water power today to make electricity. Dams make power that is cheap and clean.

Mini TOEFL iBT Practice Test

p.28

1 Ⓓ 2 Ⓑ 3 Ⓐ 4 Ⓓ 5 Ⓒ 6 Ⓐ

7 Ⓑ 8 Ⓐ 9 Ⓑ 10 Ⓒ 11 Ⓑ 12 Ⓐ

해석

[1-6]

동물 밀수

최근 동물 밀수의 증가로 공항 직원들이 충격을 받고 있다. 때로는 승객의 기내용 가방에서 살아 있는 거북, 도마뱀, 개구리, 그리고 뱀이 발견되기도 한다. 밀수꾼들은 동물이 공항을 통과할 수 있도록 여러 가지 속임수를 사용한다. 살아 있는 뱀을 필름통에 넣고, 새는 테니스공통에 넣는다. 경찰은 한 남자의 가슴에 테이프로 붙여진 이구아나를 발견한 적도 있다. 하지만 동물들이 모두 산 채로 밀수되는 것은 아니다. 다수는 이동 중에 죽는다. 동물의 신체 부위가 발견되기도 한다. 여기에는 뿔, 가죽, 말린 장기, 발굽, 그리고 발이 포함된다.

동물 밀수는 희귀한 것에 대한 사람들의 관심 때문에 일어난다. 희귀한 것을 소유하면 자신이 특별해진다고 믿는다. 장식용으로 벽에 동물의 머리를 걸어 놓는다. 방을 보다 고급스럽게 만들기 위해 모피를 산다. 동물의 신체 부위를 먹으면 몸이 튼튼해질 것이라고 믿는 사람들도 있다. 호랑이는 산 것이건 죽은 것이건 매우 인기가 높다. 모피, 두개골, 쓸개, 그리고 이빨 모두 사용된다. 단 한 부분도 버려지지 않는다. 호랑이 뼈는 관절염을 치료해 준다고 알려져 있다. 호랑이는 야생에서 포획되지만, 그렇지 않은 경우도 많다. 사육 상태에서 번식하기가 쉽다. 작은 동물원에서도 볼 수 있고, 개인의 애완 동물인 경우도 있다. 사육 상태의 호랑이는 높은 비용으로 호랑이의 신체 부위를 사고자 하는 사람들에게 팔린다.

1975년에 희귀종 거래가 금지되었다. 136개국이 이를 지지했다. 하지만 동물 밀수는 여전히 큰 문제이다. 마약 밀수 다음으로 수익성이 높은 사업이다. 이는 개별적인 동물들에게 해를 끼치고 자연의 균형도 파괴한다. 다음 세대를 위해 종의 다양성은 최우선 목표가 되어야 한다.

[7-12]

하늘을 나는 자동차

많은 사람들이 자신의 차로 하늘을 날아다니는 꿈을 꾼다. 생각대로 하늘을 날아다니는 것은 멋진 일이라고 생각한다. 매일 교통 정체로 몇 시간을 허비하지 않아도 될 것이다. 먼 거리를 매우 빠르게 이동할 수도 있을 것이다. 1903년 라이트 형제가 비행기를 발명한 이후로 몇몇 선구자들이 하늘을 나는 자동차를 발명하기 위해 노력해 왔다. 자동차업계 전문가들의 말에 따르면, 하늘을 나는 자동차에 대한 꿈은 머지 않아 실현될 것이다.

폴 몰러라고 하는 유능한 엔지니어가 그러한 차를 발명했다. 몰러는 거의 40년 동안 수백만 달러를 쓰면서 시제품을 개발했다. 이 차는 4인승이다. 좁은 공간에서도 이착륙할 수 있게 설계되었고, 10,000미터 상공까지 날 수 있다. 4기통 외연 기관을 이용해 상하 좌우로 움직일 수 있다. 안타깝게도 연료 효율은 좋지가 않다. 연비가 나쁜 편이다. 몰러의 차는 컴퓨터와 인공 위성 시스템의 안내를 받는다. 충돌에 대비해 에어백과 낙하산이 갖추어져 있다. 그는 하늘을 나는 자동차의 제작이 가능하다는 점을 보여 주었다.

하늘을 나는 자동차는 해결해야 할 많은 문제들을 안고 있다. 첫 번째는 안전과 관련된 것이다. 도로가 없는 경우 어떻게 서로 충돌하는 것을 막을 것인가? 한 대의 차가 이동하는 것은 쉽지만, 수천 대의 차가 있으면 어떻게 될 것인가? 또 다른 문제는 비용이다. 현재로서는 차 한 대의 가격이 수백만 달러에 이른다. 대부분의 사람들은 이를 구입할 여력이 없다. 세 번째 문제는 연료이다. 이러한 차들에 공급할 수 있는 연료가 충분해야 한다. 또한 현재 사용되는 연료보다 오염 물질을 덜 배출하는 연료이어야 한다. 하지만 기술은 발전 중이다. 미래에는 이러한 문제들이 해결될 가능성이 크다. 그러게 되면 빠르고 쉽게 하늘을 날아다니는 꿈이 실현될 것이다.

Vocabulary Check-Up p.32

1 Ⓐ 2 Ⓑ 3 Ⓓ 4 Ⓒ 5 Ⓑ
6 Ⓓ 7 Ⓓ 8 Ⓑ 9 Ⓐ 10 Ⓒ

UNIT 02 Reference

Basic Drill p.36

Drill 1 Ⓒ

해석

안네 프랑크는 2차 세계 대전의 희생자였다. 그녀는 나치를 피해 방에 숨어 있는 동안 일기를 썼다. 2년 동안 그곳에 있었다. 그녀의 일기는 나치 하의 삶의 얼마나 비참했는지를 보여 준다. 그녀가 사망한 뒤 그녀의 아버지가 안네의 일기를 출판했는데, 이는 세계에서 가장 널리 읽히는 책 중의 하나가 되었다.

Drill 2 Ⓐ

해석

1920년대에 재즈는 백인들에게 잘 알려져 있지 않았다. 루이 암스트롱은 그들에게 재즈를 알린 음악가였다. 루이는 14세 때 트럼펫을 연주하는 법을 배웠다. 그는 곧 나이트클럽에서 일자리를 얻었다. 그의 독특한 음색과 뛰어난 트럼펫 연주는 흑인과 백인 팬들을 끌어모았다. 얼마 지나지 않아 재즈는 모든 관객들에게 잘 알려지게 되었다.

Drill 3 Ⓓ

해석

어느 날 아이작 뉴턴이 나무 아래 앉아 있었다. 세상의 모든 물체가 어떻게 서로 연결되어 있는지에 대해 생각하고 있었다. 이것은 전혀 새로운 일이 아니었다. 뉴턴은 종종 이런 것들에 대해 고민을 했다. 그는 물리학자였다. 갑자기 바람이 불었다. 위쪽에 있던 나뭇가지에서 사과가 그의 머리 위로 떨어졌다. 이로 인해 그는 불현듯 여러 가지 생각을 하게 되었는데, 이는 곧 중력 이론이 되었다. 이로써 과학계가 바뀌게 되었다.

Drill 4 Ⓐ

해석

1929년 10월 29일은 주가가 폭락한 날이었다. 투자자들은 아연실색했다. 그들은 재빨리 주식을 팔아 치웠다. 이 날은 검은 화요일로 알려지게 되었다. 30년 동안 미국 경제에 문제가 생긴 것은 이때가 처음이었다. 사람들은 돈을 잃는 것을 두려워했다. 설상가상으로 투자 은행들이 모든 돈을 잃었다. 부자들은 하룻밤 사이에 가난해졌다.

Drill 5 Ⓓ

해석

역사상 가장 위대한 작곡가 중 한 명은 볼프강 아마데우스 모짜르트였다. 신동이었던 그는 5살 때부터 작곡을 하기 시작했다. 그는 다양한 장르의 음악을 작곡했다. 여기에는 오페라, 협주곡, 그리고 교향곡이 포함되었다. 그는 *피가로의 결혼*도 작곡했는데, 이 곡은 그의 작품 중에서 가장 유명한 작품 중 하나이다.

Drill 6 Ⓒ

해석

세금은 사회에 필요한 부분이다. 학교에 재정 지원을 하고, 도로를 건설하기도 한다. 작년 세금은 25%의 세율로 징수되었는데, 많은 사람들이 이에 대해 불만을 가졌다. 이러한 사람들은 세금이 너무 높다고 생각했다. 그들은 더 많은 돈을 저축하고 싶어했다. 그들은 정부가 효율적이지 못하다고 믿었다.

Drill 7 Ⓒ

해석

스리마일섬에서의 위기가 거대한 핵 재앙으로 이어질 뻔 했다. 이 발전소는 펜실베이니아에 있는 수천 명의 사람들에게 전력을 공급해 주었다. 어느 날 밸브 하나가 닫히지 않았다. 노심이 3일 동안 가열되었다. 거의 폭발할 뻔 했다. 발전소 주변 지역이 엄청난 위험에 처했다. 지역 주민들도 마찬가지였다. 반경 20마일 이내의 사람들 중 대부분이 사망할 수 있었다. 수천 명의 사람들이 영향을 받을 수 있었다.

Drill 8 Ⓒ

해석

*오즈의 마법사*는 유명한 영화이다. 음악도 훌륭하다. 수백만 명의 사람들이 해마다 TV로 이 영화를 보면서 자랐다. 그들 중 많은 이들이 노래도 부를 줄 안다. 가장 외우기 쉬운 곡은 "썸웨어 오버 더 레인보우"라는 매우 간단한 가사로 시작한다. 많은 미국인들이 이 곡의 나머지 부분을 끝까지 부를 수 있다. 이 곡의 나머지 부분을 부르지 못하는 사람들도 있지만, 이 곡은 미국 문화의 일부이다.

Exercises with Short Passages

Exercise 1 1 Ⓓ 2 Ⓑ 3 Ⓐ 4 Ⓐ p.40

해석

요한 세바스찬 바흐

요한 세바스찬 바흐는 1685년부터 1750년까지 살았다. 독일인인 바흐는 뛰어난 음악가였다. 오르간과 하프시코드를 연주할 수 있었다. 또한 역사상 가장 위대한 작곡가 중 한 명이었다. 바흐는 매우 많은 작품을 남겼다. 그는 수백 편의 곡의 작곡했다. 일부는 합창곡이었다. 일부는 관현악곡이었다. 그리고 일부는, 예컨대 오르간과 같은, 다양한 악기들을 위한 곡이었다.

바흐는 종교적인 작품들도 많이 작곡했다. 또한 세속적인 곡들도 작곡했다. 실제로 그의 *브란덴부르크* 협주곡은 그의 가장 유명한 작품 중 하나이다. 바흐가 사망한 뒤 많은 사람들이 그의 음악을 잊었다. 그 후 1800년대에 그의 작품들이 기억되었다. 사람들은 그의 작품을 다시 연주하기 시작했다. 오늘날 바흐는 천재 음악가로 여겨지고 있다. 일반적으로 그는 모든 작곡가들 중에서, 모짜르트와 베토벤과 함께, 최정상의 자리에 위치한다고 생각된다.

Exercise 2 1 Ⓐ 2 Ⓑ 3 Ⓒ 4 Ⓒ p.41

해석

하드리아누스의 방벽

기원후 43년, 로마 제국이 영국 제도를 침공했다. 로마인들은 그곳에서 여러 해를 보낸 후 섬의 남쪽 지역을 장악할 수 있었다. 하지만 영국 전체를 정복할 수는 없었다. 또한 북부의 야만인들이 로마인들을 종종 공격했다. 그 결과 하드리아누스 황제는 그들의 침입을 막기 위해 장벽을 세우기로 결심했다.

기원후 122년에 방벽 공사가 시작되었다. 방벽은 영국의 한쪽 끝에서 다른 끝까지 뻗어 있었다. 길이는 73마일이었다. 두께는 10에서 20피트 사이였고, 높이도 대략적으로 그와 같았다. 하드리아누스의 방벽이라고 불린 이 방벽은 영국을 갈라놓았다. 최대 10,000명의 로마 군인들이 방벽을 지켰다. 이는 로마가 영국을 통치하던 당시 북쪽 사람들의 침입을 예방하는데 도움이 되었다.

Exercise 3 1 Ⓐ 2 Ⓐ 3 Ⓑ 4 Ⓒ p.42

해석

뉴딜 정책

뉴딜 정책은 1930년대에 루즈벨트 대통령에 의해 만들어졌다. 그는 대공황 시대에 고통을 받고 있던 사람들을 돕고자 했다. 수백만 명의 사람들이 가난했다. 은행 시스템은 신뢰할 수 없었다. 실제로 무너지고 있었다. 루즈벨트는 가난한 사람들을 돕고자 했다. 또한 경제도 발전시키려고 했다. 무엇보다 미래의 문제들을 예방하고자 했다.

뉴딜 정책에는 직업 프로그램이 포함되어 있었다. 이로써 도시 및 시골 사람들에게 일자리가 생겼다. 또한 사회 보장 제도도 포함되어 있었다. 이는 가난한 사람들이 나이가 너무 많아서 일을 할 수 없을 때 그들에게 돈을 지급하는 일종의 보험이었다. 노동자가 일자리를 잃는 경우 이들은 실업 수당을 받았다. 은행을 안전하게 만들기 위해 뉴딜 정책으로 예금 보험이 제공되었다. 은행이 사람들의 돈을 잃는 경우, 사람들은 정부로부터 돈을 받았다. 이런 조치들로 인해 사람들은 다시 일어설 수 있었다.

Exercise 4 1 Ⓒ 2 Ⓒ 3 Ⓐ 4 Ⓐ p.43

해석

무역로

사람들은 종종 다른 문화권의 사람들과 무역을 해 왔다. 무역은 사람들이 필요로하면서도 원하는 물건을 얻을 수 있게 해 준다. 과거에는 상인들이 종종 짐마차를 타고 이곳 저곳을 돌아다녔다. 대부분의 경우 이들은 동일한 길을 이용해서 목적지에 도착했다. 시간이 지남에 따라 그로 인해 무역로가 만들어졌다.

무역로는 상인들이 이용했던 – 육상과 해상 모두의 – 다양한 길 혹은 도로였다. 가장 유명한 무역로 중 하나는 실크 로드이다. 이는 수 세기 전에 존재했다. 중국에서 시작되어 아시아, 중동, 그리고 유럽의 일부를 가로질렀다. 로마 제국 당시에는 로마에서 끝이 났다. 무역로는 종종 위험할 수 있었다. 하지만 인근의 많은 통치자들이 주변 지역을 보호해 주었다. 이로써 상인들은 안심을 하고 그들과 무역을 하고자 했다.

Exercises with Mid-Length Passages

Exercise 1 1 Ⓐ 2 Ⓒ p.44

해석

레이저

레이저는 20세기의 주요 업적 중 하나이다. 레이저는 1958년에 발명되었다. 이는 알버트 아인슈타인이 만든 이론 덕분에 가능했다. 레이저는 사회의 대부분의 영역에서 사용되며, 가장 유용한 기술 중 하나이다.

레이저 광선은 일반적인 전구와 크게 다르다. 레이저 광선은 한 방향으로 한 가지 색깔의 빛만 내보냄으로써 작동한다. 전구는 모든 방향으로 넓은 스펙트럼의 빛을 내보낸다. 작은 레이저 포인터에서 나오는 광선이 전구의 광선보다 훨씬 더 밝다. 이 강렬한 에너지는 용도가 다양하다.

해마다 수백만 대의 레이저가 판매된다. 정보를 보내기 위한 섬유광학에서 사용된다. DVD와 CD로 기록을 할 때에도 사용된다. 컴퓨터의 CD/DVD-ROM 드라이브에서도 찾아볼 수 있다. 레이저는 또한 절단이나 연소 작업에서도 사용된다. 의사들은 시력 교정을 위해 레이저를 사용한다. 기업들은 레이저를 이용해 금속을 자른다. 건축업체는 레이저를 이용해 측정을 해서 평탄화 작업을 한다. 경찰은 레이저로 차량 속도를 측정한다. 마지막으로, 레이저는 공연에서 시각 효과를 나타내기 위해 사용된다. 레이저는 사람들이 생활하고, 일하고, 그리고 즐기는 방식에 영향을 끼쳤다. 레이저는 앞으로도 유망한 테크놀로지이다.

Exercise 2 1 Ⓒ 2 Ⓑ p.45

해석

빌보드

*빌보드*는 유명한 음악 잡지이다. 영향력이 매우 크다. 음반 매장과 라디오 방송국으로부터 판매 데이터를 수집한다. 그런 다음에 가장 인기 있는 음악의 판매 차트를 작성한다. 이러한 차트는 매주 발표된다.

*빌보드*는 1894년 창간되었다. 분량은 8페이지였고 가격은 10센트였다. 처음에는 음악 잡지가 아니었다. 지역 공연 및 행사를 홍보하기 위한 것이었다. 현재 기사들은 음악 전문가들에게 정보를 제공해 준다. 하지만 차트는 모든 사람들이 참고한다. *빌보드 핫 100*은 1958년 이래로 계속 존재해 왔다. 이것이 가장 유명한 차트이다. 미국에서 가장 인기 있는 100곡을 알 수 있다. 이 리스트는 히트곡, 뮤직 비디오 출시, 그리고 음악 트렌드에 관한 뉴스를 전해 준다.

이 잡지사는 음악의 다양한 면들을 다룬다. CD 및 DVD 판매량도 다룬다. 또한 인터넷에서 다운로드가 가능한 음악도 판매한다. 몇 년 전 *빌보드 핫 링톤즈*가 시작되었다. 이로써 전화 사용자들이 *빌보드* 차트에 있는 어떤 노래도 다운로드를 할 수가 있다. 이 잡지는 유행을 알고 있다. 유행에 뒤쳐지지 않고 성공을 이어가기 위해 계속해서 방법을 찾고 있다.

Exercise 3 1 Ⓐ 2 Ⓑ p.46

해석

아메리고 베스푸치

대부분의 사람들은 크리스토퍼 콜럼버스가 아메리카를 발견했다고 알고 있다. 하지만 그는 자신이 인도의 한 지역에 도착했다고 믿었다. 물론 이것은 사실이 아니었다. 그곳이 인도가 아니라고 주장한 최초의 유럽 사람은 아메리고 베스푸치였다. 이러한 이유 때문에 그의 이름을 따서 아메리카라는 이름이 지어졌다.

베스푸치는 1454년 이탈리아에서 태어났다. 그는 반평생을 사업가로 살았다. 40대에 스페인으로 넘어 갔다. 그는 선박 회사의 이사가 되었다. 그는 콜럼버스가 두 번째 신세계 항해를 준비하는 것을 도왔다. 이로 인해 베스푸치는 신세계에 방문할 기회를 얻게 되었다.

1502년에 베스푸치가 육지를 발견했다. 그는 그것이 아시아의 일부가 아니라 새로운 대륙이라고 믿었다. 1507년에 한 지도제작자가 베스푸치를 기념하여 새로 발견된 땅을 "아메리카"라고 부르자는 제안을 했다. 그의 이름은 북아메리카와 남아메리카 모두에 적용되었다. 그는 1512년에 말라리아로 사망했다. 하지만 그의 유산은 남아 있다.

Exercise 4 1 Ⓐ 2 Ⓒ p.47

해석

운하

운하는 두 개의 수역을 연결하는 인공 수로이다. 이러한 수역에는 대양, 바다, 강, 혹은 호수가 해당될 수 있다. 선박들은 운하를 이용해서 한 수역에서 다른 수역으로 이동할 수 있다. 또한 일부 운하들은 농경지에 물을 대기 위한 목적으로 사용된다. 물이 너무 많은 지역에서는 운하가 물을 빼내는 경우도 있다.

지난 두 세기 동안 많은 운하들이 건설되었다. 일부는 지역적으로 막대한 경제적 영향력을 끼쳐 왔다. 1800년대 초에 이리 운하가 건설되었다. 이는 대서양과 미 중서부 지역의 오대호를 연결시켰다. 이로써 사람들은 물자를 수로로 빠르게 운송할 수 있었다. 또한 많은 사람들이 이 운하를 이용하여 새로운 지역에 정착할 수 있었다.

1800년대 후반에는 수에즈 운하가 완공되었다. 이는 지중해와 홍해를 연결시켰다. 홍해는 인도양으로 흘러 들었다. 이로써 선박들이 유럽에서 아시아로 빠르게 항해할 수 있었다. 과거에는 아프리카 주변을 돌아가야 했다. 수에즈 운하 덕분에 선박들은 훨씬 더 빠르게 운항을 마칠 수 있었다. 1900년대 초에는 파나마 운하가 대서양과 태평양을 연결시켰다. 이로써 대양 항행의 속도가 훨씬 빨라졌다.

Building Summary Skills

p.48

A

Exercise 1 The Laser

1 Albert Einstein's theories made the laser possible.

4 It is used in computer drives, in factories, in doctors' offices, and in police departments for measuring.

5 It is also used for visual effects in shows.

2 Lasers are different from light bulbs because laser light only goes one way with only one color.

3 The laser has many applications.

Exercise 2 *Billboard* Magazine

1 *Billboard* magazine writes charts about music sales, and it posts the most popular songs in the United States.

4 Even now, the company continues to modernize, and it sells music downloads.

2 The magazine started in 1894, but it just advertised shows and events.

5 It also started a new feature, *Hot Ringtones*, so people's phones can sound like their favorite songs.

3 Then, it started writing about music.

Exercise 3 Amerigo Vespucci

1 North and South America were named after Amerigo Vespucci because he learned that this land was not India.

5 Even though Vespucci died in 1512, his name is remembered forever.

3 A mapmaker suggested calling the New World "America."

4 This was to honor Vespucci's efforts.

2 Vespucci moved to Spain to work for a shipping company, and he decided to sail to the New World.

Exercise 4 Canals

1 Canals are manmade waterways connecting two bodies of water.

5 Then, the Panama Canal connected the Atlantic and Pacific oceans.

4 Later, the Suez Canal connected Europe and Asia.

2 Ships often use them to transport goods.

3 In the 1800s, many people used the Erie Canal.

B

Exercise 1 The Laser

Albert Einstein's theories made the laser possible. Lasers are different from light bulbs because laser light only goes one way with only one color. The laser has many applications. It is used in computer drives, in factories, in doctors' offices, and in police departments for measuring. It is also used for visual effects in shows.

Exercise 2 *Billboard* Magazine

Billboard magazine writes charts about music sales, and it posts the most popular songs in the United States. The magazine started in 1894, but it just advertised shows and events. Then, it started writing about music. Even now, the company continues to modernize, and it sells music downloads. It also started a new feature, *Hot Ringtones*, so people's phones can sound like their favorite songs.

Exercise 3 Amerigo Vespucci

North and South America was named after Amerigo Vespucci because he learned that this land was not India. Vespucci moved to Spain to work for a shipping company, and he decided to sail to the New World. A mapmaker suggested calling the New World "America." This was to honor Vespucci's efforts. Even though Vespucci died in 1512, his name is remembered forever.

Exercise 4 Canals

Canals are manmade waterways connecting two bodies of water. Ships often use them to transport goods. In the 1800s, many people used the Erie Canal. Later, the Suez Canal connected Europe and Asia. Then, the Panama Canal connected the Atlantic and Pacific oceans.

Mini TOEFL iBT Practice Test

p.50

1 Ⓓ	2 Ⓒ	3 Ⓓ	4 Ⓑ	5 Ⓐ
6 Ⓐ				
7 Ⓒ	8 Ⓑ	9 Ⓑ	10 Ⓑ	11 Ⓐ
12 Ⓑ				

해석

[1-6]

그리스의 영향

그리스는 유럽 남쪽에 있는 아름다운 나라이다. 고대에는 헬라스라고 불렸다. 그리스는 유럽 문명의 탄생지로 생각된다. 이곳 문명은 유럽 및 중동 지역에 막대한 영향을 끼쳤다.

그리스의 과거는 수천 년 전으로 거슬러 올라간다. 그리스 문화는 기원전 3000년에 크레타섬에서 시작되었다. 그리스 문화의 황금기는 기원전 600년에서 400년까지였다. 소크라테스와 플라톤을 포함하여 많은 유명한 사상가들이 이 시대에 살았다. 그리스는 막강한 힘을 가지고 있었다. 지중해 전역에 식민지가 있었다. 이는 프랑스 남부, 스페인, 북아프리카, 그리고 이탈리아에서 찾아볼 수 있었다.

기원전 500년부터 336년까지 그리스는 300여개의 소규모 도시 국가로 이루어져 있었다. 그중에서 아테네와 스파르타가 가장 강력했다. 이들의 정부 형태는 비슷했으나 생활 방식은 크게 달랐다. 스파르타는 전쟁에 역점을 두었지만 스스로를 지키는 것으로 만족해 했다. 아테네는 예술과 교육에 역점을 두었지만 국가 전체를 통치하고 싶어했다. 물론 이 때문에, 특히 스파르타를 상대로, 수많은 전쟁이 일어났다. 결국 스파르타가 전투에서 승리했다.

그 후 로마군과 그리스군이 자주 전투를 벌였다. 기원전 146년, 로마인들이 그리스를 정복했다. 모순적이게도 그리스인들이 로마의 삶을 변화시켰다. 그리스인들은 로마의 예술과 사상에 영향을 미쳤다. 이러한 문화의 결합은 결국 유럽 문화의 기초가 되었다. 로마인들은 유럽 전역을 돌아다닐 때 그리스 문화를 가지고 다녔다. 천 년 후, 그리스 사상은 유럽에서 다시 관심의 대상이 되었다. 이때는 예술가들과 사상가들이 그리스와 로마 사상을 연구하던 시기였다. 건축도 한 가지 주제였다. 문학과 미술도 마찬가지였다. 정치 역시 연구의 대상이었다. "민주주의"라는 용어도 그리스에서 비롯된 것이다. 민주주의는 국민에게 권력이 있다는 것을 의미했다. 오늘날 유럽의 대다수 국가들이 민주주의 국가이다. 민주주의는 그리스인들 덕분에 만들어진 강력한 정치 시스템이다.

[7-12]

유로화: 공동 통화

유로화는 유럽에서 뜨거운 논쟁의 대상이었다. 많은 국가들이 동일한 통화를 사용해야 하는지에 대한 질문이 제기되었다. 공동 화폐는 공통된 문화의 상징이다. 유럽 내 많은 사람들이 이러한 아이디어에 동의하지 않았다. 그들은 국가 정체성을 잃는 것에 대해 우려했다. 또한 한 국가의 경제가 다른 국가의 경제에 영향을 끼치게 될 것이라고 생각했다. 예컨대 이탈리아에서의 인플레이션이 프랑스에 영향을 미칠 수도 있다고 생각했다.

1999년, 유럽 12개국이 유로화로 통합되었다. 유로화는 유럽 시민들과 기업에 도움을 준다. 시민들은 유로화 지역에서 여행을 할 때 환전을 할 필요가 없다. 물가도 쉽게 비교할 수 있다. 또한 환율에 대해서도 걱정할 필요가 없다. 단일 통화 덕분에 기업 거래도 활발해진다. 유로화는 유럽을 단일 시장으로 만드는데 중요한 역할을 한다. 이러한 방식으로, 유럽인들은 미국 및 아시아 국가들과 경쟁을 할 수 있다.

유로화는 유럽 중앙 은행 시스템(ESCB)에 의해 관리된다. ESCB가 지폐와 동전을 발행한다. 모든 지폐에는 국가에 상관없이 동일한 디자인이 적용된다. 지폐의 한쪽 면에는 국가 코드만 인쇄되어 있다. 동전은 한쪽 면이 공통이다. 나머지 면은 국가별로 다르다. 국가별로 다른 동전의 면은 각 회원국에 의해 디자인된다. 독특한 국가 상징물들이 이용된다. 디자인은 여론 조사를 통해 선정된다.

유로화는 2002년 1월 1일에 채택되었다. 벨기에, 독일, 그리스, 이탈리아, 프랑스, 아일랜드, 룩셈부르크, 네덜란드, 오스트리아, 포르투갈, 그리고 핀란드 모두 이를 승인했다. 영국은 승인하지 않기로 결정했다. 현재 유로화는 3억 유럽인들에게 일상 생활의 일부이다. 통합 덕분에 그들은 보다 큰 국가들과 경쟁할 수 있을 정도의 충분한 경제력을 갖추게 되었다.

Vocabulary Check-Up p.54

1 Ⓒ	2 Ⓐ	3 Ⓐ	4 Ⓓ	5 Ⓒ
6 Ⓑ	7 Ⓒ	8 Ⓑ	9 Ⓐ	10 Ⓓ

UNIT 03 Factual Information

Basic Drill p.58

Drill 1 Ⓐ

해석

고대 이집트인들은 사람이 죽으면 다른 세상으로 가게 된다고 믿었다. 그래서 죽은 사람이 사후 세계에 대한 준비가 되어 있기를 바랐다. 시신이 오랫동안 보존되도록 만들기 위해 여러 가지 방법이 사용되었다. 한 가지 방법은 미이라를 만드는 것이었다. 이집트인들은 시신을 건조시킨 뒤 천으로 감쌌다. 이렇게 하면 박테리아나 곰팡이가 자랄 수 없었다.

Drill 2 Ⓑ

해석

오스트리아의 작곡가인 프란츠 슈베르트는 천재 음악가였다. 그는 소품 작곡의 대가였다. 불과 13세의 나이에 작곡을 시작했다. 그의 가장 유명한 작품 중 일부는 그가 십대였을 때 쓰여졌다. 그는 31세의 나이에 사망했지만, 600곡이 넘는 아름다운 곡들을 남겼다. 그는 살아 있을 당시 거의 인정을 받지 못했다. 슈베르트는 생전에 가난을 면치 못했다.

Drill 3 Ⓑ

해석

갈릴레오 갈릴레이는 이탈리아의 천문학자였다. 또한 물리학자이자 철학자이기도 했다. 그는 밤하늘을 관찰하는 것을 좋아했다. 그는 최초로 망원경을 만든 사람 중 한 명이었다. 그는 60개 이상의 망원경을 설계했다. 최초의 망원경들은 배율이 매우 낮았다. 망원경을 통해 보는 것이 어려웠다. 그는 항상 배율이 높고 화질이 선명한 망원경을 만들고 싶어했다. 그의 장치들은 우리가 천체를 이해하는데 막대한 도움을 주었다.

Drill 4 Ⓐ

해석

아시아는 지구에서 가장 큰 대륙이다. 전 세계 육지의 3분의 1을 포함하고 있다. 아시아의 많은 지역에는 사람이 살지 않는다. 하지만 아시아에는 전 세계 인구의 60% 이상이 거주하고 있다. 중국과 인도를 포함하여 48개국이 존재한다. 이 나라들은 세계에서 가장 인구가 많은 나라들이다. 아시아는 또한 세계 5대 종교의 발상지이기도 하다. 바로 힌두교, 불교, 유대교, 기독교, 그리고 이슬람교이다.

Drill 5 Ⓑ

해석

근대 사회는 르네상스와 함께 시작되었다. 르네상스라는 말은 프랑스어로 "재탄생"을 의미한다. 르네상스는 14세기 이탈리아에서 시작되었다. 이때는 거대한 문화적 및 지적 변화의 시기였다. 사상가들이 그리스와 로마의 옛 아이디어를 받아들여서 이를 근대화시켰다. 이 시대는 많은 사람들의 믿음을 바꾸어 놓았다. 새로운 사상들이 예술, 문학, 그리고 건축을 통해 표현되었다.

Exercises with Short Passages

Exercise 1 1 Ⓐ 2 Ⓐ 3 Ⓒ 4 Ⓓ p.60

해석

***제미니* 프로그램**

1960년대 미국의 우주 프로그램은 달 착륙을 준비하기 위한 것이었다. 하지만 그곳으로 우주비행사를 보내기에 앞서 보다 많은 정보가 필요했다. 또한 더 많은 경험도 필요했다. 따라서 미 항공 우주국인 NASA는 *제미니* 프로그램을 가동했다. 이는 1965년부터 1966년까지 계속되었다. 총 12대의 우주선이 우주로 발사되었다. 각각의 우주선에는 2명의 우주비행사가 탑승을 했다. *제미니* 프로그램의 우주비행사들은 많은 활동을 했다. 최초로 우주 유영을 했다. 일부 우주비행사들은 1주일 이상 궤도를 따라 돌았다. 두 대의 *제미니* 캡슐이 궤도를 돌다 서로 만나기도 했다. 그들은 미국의 우주 프로그램에 필요한 많은 지식을 얻었다. 또한 *아폴로* 우주비행사들을 위한 길도 닦아 주었다. 불과 몇 년 뒤, *아폴로 11호*의 우주비행사들은 달에 도착한 최초의 인류가 되었다.

Exercise 2 1 Ⓐ 2 Ⓒ 3 Ⓑ 4 Ⓐ p.61

해석

로봇 우주비행사

로봇은 여러 작업에서 인간을 대신하고 있다. 이들은 자동차 산업에서 사용된다. 하지만 사람들은 로봇이 노동자들에게 필요한 일자리를 빼앗아간다고 불평한다. 하지만 로봇이 일하는 것이 환영을 받는 분야가 하나 있다.

로봇 우주비행사는 NASA에서 개발되었다. 이는 로보놋으로 불린다. 로보놋은 인간처럼 생겼다. 하지만 인간보다 유연한 팔과 손을 가지고 있다. 이들은 우주에서 보다 어려운 임무를 수행할 수 있다. 로보놋은 차후 우주 탐사 활동에서 인간 우주비행사들과 함께 일하게 될 것으로 예상된다. 이들은 우주에서 살아남기 위해 우주복, 산소, 식량 등을 필요로 하지 않는다. 인간에게는 호흡할 수 있는 공기와 급격한 온도 변화에 대비하기 위한 보호 장치가 필요하다. 가장 중요한 것은, 너무 위험해서 우주비행사가 갈 수 있는 곳에 로보놋을 보낼 것이라는 점이다.

Exercise 3 1 Ⓓ 2 Ⓓ 3 Ⓒ 4 Ⓑ, Ⓒ p.62

해석

판화

1600년대에 인기 있었던 판화 기법은 두 가지였다. 식각과 에칭이었다. 식각이 더 오래된 방법이었다. 식각은 조각칼이라는 도구로 동판에 선을 새기는 것이었다. 이는 끝이 날카로운 강철 막대였다. 동판에서 작고 가는 금속 조각이 올라오게 되는데, 이는 조심스럽게 제거되어야 했다. 그런 다음에는 동판에 잉크를 칠한 후 그 위에 종이를 올려 놓고 판화를 찍었다. 그 결과 깔끔한 선들이 찍혀 나왔다. 에칭은 이와 달랐다. 우선 동판에 수지나 왁스를 바른다. 그런 다음 판화가가 바늘로 수지에 그림을 새겨 넣었다. 이렇게 하면 긁힌 부분의 동만 노출이 되었다. 마지막으로 동판을 산에 담그면 산이 금속에 스며들어 보다 불규칙한 선이 나타났다. 그런 다음 동판에 잉크를 칠해서 판화를 찍었다.

Exercise 4 1 Ⓒ 2 Ⓓ 3 Ⓐ 4 Ⓓ p.63

해석

스테인드글라스 창문

스테인드글라스는 색이 칠해진 유리로 만들어진다. 유리 위에 다양한 금속염을 바름으로써 유리에 색이 칠해진다. 예를 들어 코발트는 파란색 유리를 만들고, 금은 붉은색 유리를 만든다. 중세 시대에는 스테인드글라스의 인기가 매우 높았다. 이는 교회 및 대성당의 창문에서 종종 찾아볼 수 있었다.

중세 시대에는 대부분의 사람들이 문맹이었다. 따라서 글을 읽을 수 없었다. 그 결과, 스테인드글라스 창문은 종종 성경 속 이야기들을 보여 주었다. 이로 인해 사람들은 글을 전혀 모르더라도 종교에 대해 알 수 있었다. 중세 시대 스테인드글라스 창문의 전성기는 11세기와 12세기였다. 프랑스 생 드니의 수도원에는 많은 스테인드글라스 창문이 있었다. 이는 당시 유럽 전역에서 유명했다. 많은 성당들, 특히 프랑스와 영국의 성당에는 고유한 스타일의 스테인드글라스 창문이 있었다. 여기에 햇빛이 비춰지면 아름다운 이미지들이 나타났다.

Exercises with Mid-Length Passages

Exercise 1 1 Ⓐ 2 Ⓑ p.64

해석

고원, 메사, 그리고 뷰트

미국의 남서부 지역에는 애리조나주, 뉴멕시코주, 유타주, 그리고 콜로라도주가 포함된다. 이러한 주들은 독특한 지질학적 특성들로 유명하다. 그중 세 가지가 고원, 메사, 그리고 뷰트이다. 이들은 상당히 유사하기 때문에 사람들이 종종 이들을 구분하는데 어려움을 겪는다.

고원이 세 가지 지형 중에서 가장 크다. 이들은 융기된 지역으로, 비교적 꼭대기가 평평한 편이다. 또한 최소한 한 면에 절벽이 있다. 일부 고원들은 넓이가 천 평방 마일 이상인 지역에 걸쳐 있을 수 있다. 메사에 대해 말하자면, 이들은 고원보다 작다. 또한 한때 고원의 일부였다. 하지만 물에 의한 침식 작용 때문에 모든 면에 절벽이 있다. 뷰트 또한 메사와 유사하다. 하지만 이들이 더 작다. 또 다른 중요한 차이점은 뷰트의 경우 높이가 폭보다 크다는 점이다. 반면 메사의 경우 높이보다 폭이 더 크다.

남서부 지역에서는 강 근처에서 많은 메사와 뷰트들을 찾아볼 수 있다. 예를 들어 그랜드 메사는 콜라라도강과 거니슨강에 의해 만들어졌다. 그 크기는 500 평방마일 이상이다. 콜로라도 고원은 크기가 130,000평방마일을 넘는다. 이곳은 네 개의 주에 걸쳐 있다.

Exercise 2 1 Ⓒ 2 Ⓓ p.65

해석

나사(NASA)

1958년 이후로 나사는 과학과 기술 분야에서 많은 성과를 거두었다. 나사는 항공 연구 분야의 선두 주자이다. 나사는 인류에게 지구와 우주를 바라보는 새로운 방법을 제시해 주었다.

1961년 케네디 대통령은 미국이 인간을 달에 착륙시킨 뒤 지구로 안전하게 돌아오도록 만들어야 한다고 발표했다. 그는 소련을 물리치고 그러한 명예를 얻고자 했다. 나사는 *아폴로 11호*로 케네디의 명령을 수행했다. 이는 유명한 로켓이었다. 1969년 7월 20일, 나사는 달에 인간을 착륙시켰다. 달 표면을 처음 밟은 사람은 닐 암스트롱이었다. 위대한 순간이었다. 그의 첫마디는 "한 사람에게는 작은 한 걸음이지만 인류에게는 거대한 도약입니다."였다.

1980년대에는 우주 왕복선이 대중의 새로운 관심사가 되었다. 나사는 1981년에 최초의 우주 왕복선을 발사했다. 나사는 재사용이 가능한 우주선을 개발했다. 로켓은 단 한 번만 사용이 가능했다. 나사는 또한 많은 무인 우주 탐사 계획을 세웠다. 로봇이 사용되었다. 우주선은 목성, 토성, 천왕성, 그리고 해왕성과 같은 행성들을 향해 비행했다. 이들은 과학적 데이터와 컬러 이미지들을 보내 주었다.

Exercise 3 1 Ⓓ 2 Ⓓ p.66

해석

미술품 도둑과 그의 어머니

2002년에 프랑스인인 한 미술품 도둑이 수감되었다. 그는 유럽 전역의 170개 이상의 박물관에서 미술품을 훔쳤다. 그가 훔친 미술품의 가격은 총 25억 달러에 이르렀다. 경찰이 도둑을 붙잡았다. 불행하게도 그가 훔친 모든 작품을 되찾지는 못했다. 도둑의 어머니가 영구적인 방법으로 처분했기 때문이었다.

그의 아파트에는 악기, 무기, 그리고 꽃병이 있었다. 또한 60점의 회화 작품도 있었다. 도둑인 스테판과 그의 여자 친구 앤은 주말마다 미술품 및 값진 물건들을 훔쳤다. 그는 미술품을 좋아했지만, 훔칠 때의 스릴 역시 좋아했다. 그들은 종종 보안이 허술한 박물관을 찾았다. 그가 액자에서 그림을 잘라내는 동안 여자 친구는 망을 보곤 했다.

경찰이 이를 발견하고 스테판을 체포했다. 앤은 그의 집으로 달려가 그의 어머니에게 이야기했다. 어머니는 자신의 아들이 곤경에 처했다는 말을 듣고 격노했다. 그래서 그림은 제외하고 물건들을 모두 강에 던져 버렸다. 그리고 나서 60점의 그림은 잘게 조각 내어 쓰레기 수거함에 버렸다. 17세기와 18세기에 그려진 값진 회화 작품들이 영원히 사라져 버렸다. 어머니는 경찰이 증거를 찾지 못하기를 바랐다. 그녀는 그림들이 자신의 아파트에 있었다는 이유로 일자리를 잃게 될까 두려웠다. 자신의 나이로는 다른 일자리를 찾지 못할 것이라고 그녀는 말했다. 사소한 이유 때문에 역사의 상당 부분이 사라져 버렸다는 점은 대단히 안타까운 일이다.

Exercise 4 1 Ⓒ 2 Ⓐ p.67

해석

매머드 동굴

동굴 길이가 579킬로미터가 넘는 매머드 동굴은 세계에서 가장 긴 동굴이다. "매머드"라는 말은 동굴의 크기를 가리킨다. 이 동굴은 그 길이와 다채로운 역사 때문에 매우 유명하다.

매머드 동굴은 석회 동굴이다. 켄터키 중심의 숲과 언덕 아래에 가려져 있다. 이 동굴은 땅속에서 연결되어 있는 여러 개의 방으로 이루어져 있다. 최소 다섯 개의 층이 존재한다. 일반인들에게 개방되지 않은 통로와 터널들도 많다. 이 동굴은 매우 느리게 만들어졌다. 처음에는 바다에서 시작되었다. 수백만 년에 걸쳐 조개 껍질과 동물들의 뼈로 이루어진 층이 해저에 두껍게 쌓였다. 이 층은 물속에서 석회석이 되었다. 이후에 바다가 사라졌다. 빗물이 바위를 통과하면서 서서히 바위를 용해시켰다. 매머드 동굴이 만들어지기까지 거의 2억 5천만 년이 걸렸다.

1941년 7월 1일, 동굴은 국립 공원으로 지정되었다. 이로써 동굴은 부동산 개발업자들로부터 확실히 보호받을 수 있었다. 중요한 것은 땅만이 아니다. 이 공원은 수천 종의 동식물들의 보금자리이다. 1981년에는 세계 문화 유산으로 지정되었다. 매머드 동굴은 전 세계 모든 사람들의 재산이다.

Building Summary Skills

p.68

A

Exercise 1 Plateaus, Mesas, and Buttes

1 There are plateaus, mesas, and buttes in the American Southwest.

5 The Grand Mesa is more than 500 square miles in size while the Colorado Plateau is over 130,000 square miles.

2 Plateaus are the largest of the three and have flat tops.

4 Buttes are taller than they are wide.

3 Mesas are formed by water erosion and have cliffs on all sides.

Exercise 2 NASA

1 NASA is an organization that explores space.

4 They were the first human beings to go there.

2 It helps with scientific discoveries.

5 Now, NASA has a space shuttle program and robot missions to other planets.

3 It was responsible for putting Neil Armstrong and other men on the moon.

Exercise 3 The Art Thief and His Mother

1 A French art thief went to jail for stealing 2.5 billion dollars in art.

3 He loved art, but he also loved stealing.

2 His girlfriend, Anne, watched for guards and people while he took precious objects in museums.

5 The mother then threw the big objects in the river and the paintings down the drain.

4 After the police arrested him, Anne told Stephane's mother.

Exercise 4 Mammoth Cave

1 Mammoth Cave is the world's longest cave.

5 In 1941, it became a national park to ensure its preservation.

2 It has many chambers and tunnels though some are not open to the public.

4 It is a typical limestone formation.

3 The cave took 250 million years to form.

B

Exercise 1 Plateaus, Mesas, and Buttes

There are plateaus, mesas, and buttes in the American Southwest. Plateaus are the largest of the three and have flat tops. Mesas are formed by water erosion and have cliffs on all sides. Buttes are taller than they are wide. The Grand Mesa is more than 500 square miles in size while the Colorado Plateau is over 130,000 square miles.

Exercise 2 NASA

NASA is an organization that explores space. It helps with scientific discoveries. It was responsible for putting Neil Armstrong and other men on the moon. They were the first human beings to go there. Now, NASA has a space shuttle program and robot missions to other planets.

Exercise 3 The Art Thief and His Mother

A French art thief went to jail for stealing 2.5 billion dollars in art. His girlfriend, Anne, watched for guards and people while he took precious objects in museums. He loved art, but he also loved stealing. After the police arrested him, Anne told Stephane's mother. The mother then threw the big objects in the river and the paintings down the drain.

Exercise 4 Mammoth Cave

Mammoth Cave is the world's longest cave. It has many chambers and tunnels though some are not open to the public. The cave took 250 million years to form. It is a typical limestone formation. In 1941, it became a national park to ensure its preservation.

Mini TOEFL iBT Practice Test

p.70

1 Ⓓ 2 Ⓑ 3 Ⓑ 4 Ⓐ 5 Ⓓ
6 Ⓐ

7 Ⓒ 8 Ⓒ 9 Ⓐ 10 Ⓐ 11 Ⓐ
12 Ⓑ

해석

[1-6]

저작권

저작권은 아이디어 사용을 규제하는 방법이다. 다른 사람의 아이디어를 사용해서는 안 된다. 다른 누군가의 저작물을 인쇄, 복사, 판매, 혹은 배포하는 것은 불법이다. 작가의 작품 일부를 변경, 번역, 녹음, 혹은 각색해서도 안 된다. 이는 허락을 필요로 한다. 또한 다른 사람의 이메일을 복사해서 붙여 쓰는 것도 불법일 수 있다. 허락 없는 복사는 절도와 같다.

저작권은 아이디어 이외의 것들과도 관련이 있다. 어떤 것이 표현되는 방식과도 관련이 있다. 저작권은 다양한 창작물에도 존재한다. 여기에는 글, 디자인, 그리고 음악이 포함된다. 또한 그림, 사진, 그리고 TV 방송도 포함된다. 저작권은 저작물에 ©라는 기호를 넣어 표시될 수 있다. 하지만 아무런 표시가 없더라도 저작물은 만들어지는 순간부터 그 즉시 법으로 보호를 받는다.

앤여왕법은 최초의 저작권법이었다. 이 법은 1710년 영국에서 통과되었다. 그 전에는 창작의 권한이 특권층 및 길드의 손에 놓여 있었다. 이 법은 소수의 특권층뿐만 아니라 일반 대중들에게도 적용되었다. 이 법은 길드가 아니라 작품의 저자를 보호했다. 또한 저작권에 시간적 제한을 두었다. 21년 동안만 독점권을 가질 수 있었다.

저작권이 창작에 있어서 중요한 역할을 한다는 점에는 의심의 여지가 없다. 자신의 작품에 대한 권리를 가지면 작가들은 안심하고 더 많은 작품을 만들어 낸다. 대부분의 창작자들에게 저작물과 저작물에 대한 법적 권리는 동일한 관심사이다. 그러한 법적 보호 장치는 경제적, 문화적, 그리고 사회적 발전에 도움을 준다.

[7-12]

로마네스크 건축

로마네스크라는 용어는 11세기와 12세기 유럽의 건축학적 시기를 가리킨다. 이때에는 고대 로마인들이 사용했던 것과 비슷한 형태와 자재들이 사용되었다. 로마네스크는 "로마인들의 방식으로"라는 의미이다. 11세기 이전 유럽 사람들은 종종 서로 싸우느라 바빴다. 먹을 것도 거의 없었다. 크고 멋진 건물을 짓는데 쓸 시간이나 에너지는 없었다. 975년 무렵에 유럽 사회가 진정되기 시작했다. 1050년, 왕들은 거대한 석조 건물을 지으라는 명령을 내리기 시작했다.

로마네스크 건축가들의 주요 업적은 아치형 석조 건물이었다. 곡선 형태의 천장이 목재 지붕을 대체했다. 목재는 불이 붙기 쉬웠다. 아치형 석조 건물을 만드는 일은 건축가들에게 문제였다. 어떤 형태가 적합한지 알아야 했다. 석재의 무게를 어떻게 지탱해야 할 것인지도 알아내야 했다.

건축가들은 돔 형태나 끝이 둥근 형태를 포함하여 몇 가지 해결책을 생각해냈다. 무거운 석재를 지탱하기 위해서 두꺼운 벽과 기둥을 사용했다. 벽의 무게를 감당하기 위해서는 창문이 작아야 했다. 그 결과 내부가 어두컴컴한 교회들이 지어졌다. 이러한 형태는 몇 세기 후 고딕 양식이 나타날 때까지 변하지 않았다.

로마네스크는 로마 시대 이후 최초의 범유럽적 건물 양식이었다. 이 양식이 확산된 과정은 다음과 같이 설명될 수 있다. 당시 사람들은 종교적 이유 때문에 여행을 했다. 이들은 거대한 건축물을 보았다. 그런 다음 이러한 건물을 짓는 법에 대한 아이디어를 가지고 고향으로 돌아왔다. 로마네스크 양식의 건물은 프랑스, 영국, 이탈리아, 독일, 그리고 스페인 북부 전역에서 찾아볼 수 있다.

Vocabulary Check-Up

p.74

1 Ⓓ 2 Ⓓ 3 Ⓓ 4 Ⓒ 5 Ⓐ
6 Ⓒ 7 Ⓐ 8 Ⓓ 9 Ⓑ 10 Ⓒ

UNIT 04 Negative Factual Information

Basic Drill

p.78

Drill 1 Ⓑ

해석

원자는 물리적인 세계를 이루는 기본적인 구성 요소이다. 하지만 너무나 작기 때문에 고배율 현미경으로만 볼 수 있다. 원자는 세 부분, 즉 양성자, 중성자, 그리고 전자로 이루어져 있다. 양성자와 중성자는 원자의 중심에 있다. 이 부분을 핵이라고 한다. 양성자는 양전하를 띤다. 중성자는 전하를 띠지 않는다. 전자는 핵 주위를 돌며 음전하를 띤다.

Drill 2 Ⓓ

해석

문화는 사람들이 자신의 세계에 의미를 부여하는 방식으로 정의된다. 문화는 체계적인 방식으로 그렇게 한다. 문화는 우리가 옷을 입고, 행동하고, 그리고 심지어 사고하는 방식에도 영향을 미친다. 어떤 문화에서 사람들이 서로의 눈을 바라볼 수 있다. 이는 친근한 행동으로 생각될 수 있다. 다른 문화에서는 누군가의 눈을 바라보는 것이 무례한 일로 간주된다. 이러한 믿음 체계가 자리 잡히면 사람들은 지속적으로 적절한 행동을 취하게 될 것이다.

Drill 3 Ⓓ

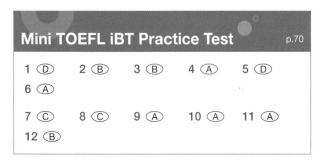

해석

찰리 채플린은 무성 영화에서 가장 유명한 스타였다. 그는 런던에서 태어났다. 그는 감독이자 제작자였고, 자신의 코미디 영화의 시나리오 작가이기도 했다. 물론 배우이기도 했다. 그의 스타덤은 그가 "리틀 트램프"에 처음 출연했던 1914년에 시작되었다. 그는 너무 작은 재킷과 너무 큰 바지를 입고 있었다. 많은 사람들이 그를 세상에서 가장 웃긴 사람이라고 불렀다.

Drill 4 Ⓒ

해석

중력은 다른 물체들을 자기 쪽으로 끌어당기는 자연적인 힘이다. 지구의 중력 때문에 사람들이 땅에 발을 붙이고 있을 수 있다. 이 힘 때문에 사람들은 지구 위를 떠다니지 않는다. 이는 지구의 막대한 크기 때문이다. 중력은 또한 태양계를 잡아 두는 역할도 한다. 중력으로 인해 달이 지구 주위를 돌고 지구는 태양 주위를 도는 것이다.

Drill 5 Ⓓ

해석

은하는 항성, 먼지, 그리고 기체로 이루어져 있다. 이러한 물질은 모두 중력의 중심 주위를 돈다. 지구가 있는 은하인 은하수는 거대하다. 이곳에는 3천억 개의 항성들이 있다. 이 항성들은 서로 멀리 떨어져 있다. 그 거리가 엄청나기 때문에 빛의 속도나 시간의 개념으로 거리를 표현해야 한다. 빛이 우리 은하를 가로지르는데 수천 년이 걸린다.

Exercises with Short Passages

Exercise 1 1 Ⓒ 2 Ⓐ 3 Ⓓ 4 Ⓐ p.80

해석

바다 집시

태국의 서쪽 해안에는 바다 집시라고 불리는 소규모의 유목민들이 살고 있다. 이들은 수백 년 동안 그곳에서 살았다. 그들의 언어, 문화, 그리고 생활 방식은 태국의 나머지 지방들과 완전히 다르다. 그들의 삶은 바다에 기반해 있다. 그래서 이들 유목민은 수영에 능숙하다. 오랫동안 잠수를 할 수도 있다. 또한 물속에서 보는 능력이 뛰어나다. 물안경 없이도 물속에서 작은 것들을 찾아낼 수 있다. 이들의 뛰어난 능력은 바다에 대한 의존도과 밀접한 관련이 있다. 이들의 눈은 물속 환경에 적응해 왔다. 이들은 또한 바다에서의 생활에 대한 지식이 풍부하다. 2004년 끔찍한 쓰나미가 발생한 때에도 바다 집시들은 바다에 대한 지식 덕분에 살아남을 수 있었다.

Exercise 2 1 Ⓑ 2 Ⓒ 3 Ⓐ 4 Ⓓ p.81

해석

붉은 행성과 퍼시벌 로웰

천문학자들은 화성에 생명체가 없다는 것을 알고 있다. *바이킹* 로봇의 붉은 행성 탐사로 그러한 점이 밝혀졌다. 이 탐사는 주로 한 사람 때문에 진행되었다. 미국의 부유한 사업가였던 퍼시벌 로웰이 화성에 생명체가 산다고 주장했다. 그는 화성에 매료되어 있었다. 23년 동안 화성을 연구하며 지냈다. 화성의 생명체에 대한 연구에 너무 깊이 빠져서 자신이 직접 연구소를 세우기도 했다. 여기에는 거대한 망원경이 있었다. 건조한 지역의 해발 7,000피트 높이에 설치된 이 망원경은 화성을 관찰하기 위한 최적의 장소에 위치해 있었다. 로웰은 자신이 화성을 가로지르는 선들을 보았다고 생각했다. 또한 이 선들은 지적 생명체에 의해 만들어졌다고 생각했다. 뿐만 아니라 화성에 물이 존재할 가능성도 있었다. 그는 노트에 많은 지도를 그렸다. 그의 아이디어는 대중들의 주의를 끌었다. 곧 사람들은 화성에 생명체가 존재할 수도 있을 것이라고 생각했다.

Exercise 3 1 Ⓐ 2 Ⓑ 3 Ⓑ 4 Ⓓ p.82

해석

바람과 함께 사라지다

*바람과 함께 사라지다*는 미국 영화의 고전이다. 남부와 북부 주들 사이에서 남북 전쟁이 일어났을 때가 그 배경이다. 영화는 남부의 농장에 사는 귀여운 여인인 스칼렛 오하라의 이야기이다. 그녀는 애슐리라고 하는 남자와 사랑에 빠진다. 하지만 애슐리는 다른 여자와 약혼한 상태이기 때문에 스칼렛과 결혼을 하지 않으려고 한다. 스칼렛은 분노한다. 전쟁과 그의 목숨이 위협받는 상황을 겪고 나서야 그녀는 자신이 우정을 소중히 여긴다는 점을 깨닫는다. 스칼렛은 군대로부터 친구를 보호하고 싶어한다. 그렇게 하는 과정에서 그녀는 자신을 놀리면서도 자신을 사랑한 레트와 사랑에 빠진다. 이 영화는 전쟁이라는 맥락 속에서 사랑을 이야기하는 훌륭한 영화이다. 역사 때문에 줄거리 및 인물들이 처한 상황이 현실적으로 느껴진다.

Exercise 4 1 Ⓑ 2 Ⓓ 3 Ⓒ 4 Ⓐ p.83

해석

탄환 재조탑

중력은 온갖 종류의 역학적인 목적으로 이용되어 왔다. 한 가지 예를 들면 중력은 탄환이라고 불리는 동그란 총알을 만드는데 이용되었다. 군대에서 수백 년 동안 이를 이용했다. 이 방법에서는 높이가 매우 높은 건물인 탄환 제조탑이 사용되었다. 액체 상태의 납을 탑 꼭대기로 가져가서 이를 금속 격자 틀에 붓는다. 이렇게 하면 액체가 균일하게 나뉜다. 납이 떨어지면 동그란 공 형태가 만들어지면서 식는다. 그런 다음에는 형태가 납작해지지 않도록, 그리고 납이 확실히 식도록 이들을 물웅덩이에 넣는다. 그 후에는 공 모양인 납의 형태와 크기를 점검한다. 그러면 총에서 쓸 준비가 끝난다.

Exercises with Mid-Length Passages

Exercise 1 1 Ⓑ 2 Ⓐ p.84

해석

집시

로마는 유럽, 북아프리카, 그리고 아메리카 전역에서 사는 사람들이다. 이들은 종종 집시라고 불린다. 사람들은 그들의 피부와 머리카락이 오래전부터 어두웠기 때문에 이들이 이집트에서 왔다고 잘못 알고 있었다. 이러한 오해 때문에 "집시"라는 말이 생겨났다. 실제로 그들은 자기 자신을 로마라고 부른다. 이 민족은 천 년 전 인도의 북부 지방에서 유럽으로 건너왔다. 그들의 언어인 로마니어는 인도아리아어이지만, 그들은 보통 거주지 국가의 언어를 사용한다.

안타깝게도 이들은 거주지 국가에서 단 한 번도 풍요로운 삶을 살지 못했다. 로마들은 항상 인종 차별을 겪는다. 예를 들어, 헝가리의 경우, 로마들은 학교에서 종종 별도의 교실에 배정된다. 때때로 학습 장애가 있는 학생들과 같은 교실에 배정되기도 한다. 그 결과 많은 학생들이 학교를 마치지 못한다. 로마들 중 대학 학위를 가진 사람은 1%가 되지 않는다. 이로 인해 좋은 직장을 찾을 수가 없다. 그 결과 많은 로마들이 가난하게 산다. 그들은 사회적 문제와 범죄에 시달리고 있다.

Exercise 2 1 Ⓒ 2 Ⓐ p.85

해석

화성

화성은 태양계에서 네 번째 행성이다. 지구에서 볼 수 있기 때문에 수 세기 동안 연구의 대상이었다. 화성에는 몇 가지 놀라운 지질학적 특징이 존재한다.

화성의 크기는 지구의 반 정도이지만, 표면적은 지구의 육지와 거의 비슷한 크기이다. 표면의 붉은 빛깔은 산화철(녹)과 같은 광물질이 존재하기 때문에 나타난다. 화성은 지구보다 밀도가 낮다. 질량은 지구의 10분의 1정도이다. 화성의 북쪽 부분은 남쪽 부분과 확연히 다르다. 북쪽은 화산유암 때문에 꽤 평평하다. 여기에는 올림푸스라고 불리는 크고 평평한 화산이 있다. 이 화산은 높이가 26킬로미터로 태양계에서 가장 높은 산이다.

남쪽에는 가장 큰 협곡이 있는데, 길이가 4,000킬로미터이고 깊이는 7킬로미터이다. 이 가운데 일부는 수십억 년 전 운석에 의해 만들어졌다. 이에 비하면 그랜드 캐년은 작은 모래 놀이통처럼 보인다. 여기에는 헬라스 분지라고 불리는 거대한 분화구가 있다. 이는 소행성에 의해 만들어졌다. 폭은 2,100킬로미터이다.

Exercise 3 1 Ⓒ 2 Ⓑ p.86

해석

인디 영화

독립 영화 산업이 성장하는 중이다. 독립 영화를 이르는 말인 인디 영화는 대형 할리우드 제작사로부터 받는 금액에 의해 정의된다. 독립 영화가 되기 위해서는 예산의 50% 이하로만 받아야 한다. 성장세의 이유 중 일부는 컨텐츠에 있다. 할리우드는 인디 영화에 비해 위험을 무릅쓰지 않는다. 또 다른 이유로는 기술 비용이 더 적게 든다는 점을 들 수 있다.

영화 관객들은 할리우드의 공식을 알고 있다. 대형 제작사에서 만든 많은 영화들은 똑같은 줄거리를 가지고 있다. 이유는 간단하다. 고객이 바라는 영화를 만들기 때문이다. 그리고 사람들은 언제나 같은 유형을 원한다. 하지만 반드시 그런 것만은 아니다. 많은 관객들이 똑같은 줄거리에 식상해 하고 있다. 이들은 신선한 줄거리와 흥미로운 관점을 지닌 영화를 보고 싶어한다. 독특한 주제를 다룬 영화를 보고 싶어한다. 인디 영화는 그럴 수 있는 유연성을 가지고 있다.

카메라 및 편집 장비의 비용도 낮아지고 있다. 영화 제작에 필요한 이런 장비들은 한때 너무나 비싸서 할리우드만이 이를 감당할 수 있었다. 요즘에는 대부분의 사람들도 구입이 가능한 고화질 비디오 카메라들이 나와 있다. 그리고 현재 대부분의 편집 작업은 가정용 컴퓨터로도 할 수 있다. 많은 프로그램들이 판매 중이다. 심지어 인터넷에는 무료인 영화 편집 프로그램도 있다.

Exercise 4 1 Ⓑ 2 Ⓐ p.87

해석

열역학

열역학은 인류가 과학을 이해하는데 필수적인 것이다. *열역학*이라는 용어는 1849년 켈빈경이 처음 사용했다. 이는 그리스어에서 나온 것으로 "열의 힘"이라는 뜻을 나타낸다. 이 이론에는 네 가지 법칙이 있는데, 그중 두 가지는 다음과 같이 설명될 수 있다.

에너지가 이동하면 사람들은 그것을 느낄 수 있다. 첫 번째 법칙에 따르면 어떤 시스템 안의 모든 에너지는 설명이 가능하다. 에너지가 이동하면 에너지는 어딘가로 가야만 한다. 에너지는 생성되거나 파괴될 수 없다. 단지 이동할 뿐이다. 이에 대한 한 가지 예는 일반적인 백열등과 형광등 사이에서 찾을 수 있다. 형광등은 에너지의 상당 부분이 빛을 내는 전구 안에 갇혀 있기 때문에 보다 효율적이다. 일반적인 백열등의 경우, 에너지의 일부는 빛을 만들어 내지만, 그중 상당 부분은 열의 형태로 소실된다.

두 번째 법칙에 따르면 열의 차이는 결국 균형을 이루게 된다. 얼음 조각이 녹으면 녹은 물은 따뜻해져서 실내 온도와 같아진다. 강물이 차가우면 공기도 차가워질 것이다. 이러한 평등화의 정도를 엔트로피라고 부른다. 모든 에너지 차이는 시간이 지남에 따라 평형을 이루려고 한다.

Building Summary Skills

p.88

A

Exercise 1 Gypsies

1 Gypsies originally came from northern India, not from Egypt.

4 Because they do not get well educated, they cannot find good jobs.

2 Some speak Romany, but most speak the language of their home country.

5 Their communities are often poor and have social problems and crime.

3 They have bad experiences in schools, like in Hungary.

Exercise 2 The Planet Mars

1 Mars, Earth's neighboring planet, has some fascinating land features.

4 These were formed millions of years ago.

2 The north is characterized by large lava plains, and it also has the highest volcano in the solar system.

3 The south is characterized by canyons and craters.

5 One crater, the Hellas Impact Basin, is over 2,000 kilometers wide.

Exercise 3 Indies

1 The number of independent films is increasing, but Hollywood is funding films less and less.

5 The costs of cameras and other equipment are decreasing, which gives many people the power to make their own film.

2 This means that movies can be different from the Hollywood formula.

4 These films are flexible enough to address interesting or unpopular topics.

3 Many viewers are tired of the same stories and find indie films refreshing.

Exercise 4 **Thermodynamics**

1 Thermodynamics describes the relationship between heat and power.

2 The first law states that energy in a system stays in a system.

5 The second law states that different temperatures try to equalize.

6 This means that hot temperatures try to cool down while cold temperatures try to warm up.

3 It only moves and is never lost. Efficient light bulbs do not allow energy to be lost in heat.

4 Efficient light bulbs do not allow energy to be lost in heat.

B

Exercise 1 **Gypsies**

Gypsies originally came from northern India, not from Egypt. Some speak Romany, but most speak the language of their home country. They have bad experiences in schools, like in Hungary. Because they do not get well educated, they cannot find good jobs. Their communities are often poor and have social problems and crime.

Exercise 2 **The Planet Mars**

Mars, Earth's neighboring planet, has some fascinating land features. The north is characterized by large lava plains, and it also has the highest volcano in the solar system. The south is characterized by canyons and craters. These were formed millions of years ago. One crater, the Hellas Impact Basin, is over 2,000 kilometers wide.

Exercise 3 **Indies**

The number of independent films is increasing, but Hollywood is funding films less and less. This means that movies can be different from the Hollywood formula. Many viewers are tired of the same stories and find indie films refreshing. These films are flexible enough to address interesting or unpopular topics. The costs of cameras and other equipment are decreasing, which gives many people the power to make their own film.

Exercise 4 **Thermodynamics**

Thermodynamics describes the relationship between heat and power. The first law states that energy in a system stays in a system. It only moves, never to be lost. Efficient light bulbs do not allow energy to be lost in heat. The second law states that different temperatures try to equalize. This means that hot temperatures try to cool down while cold temperatures try to warm up.

Mini TOEFL iBT Practice Test p.90

1 Ⓐ 2 Ⓓ 3 Ⓐ 4 Ⓒ 5 Ⓓ 6 Ⓒ

7 Ⓑ 8 Ⓐ 9 Ⓐ 10 Ⓑ 11 Ⓑ 12 Ⓐ

해석

[1-6]

증기 기관

증기 기관은 인류에게 있어서 커다란 발전이었다. 이로 인해 근대 산업이 발전했다. 어느 날 갑자기 수백 명의 사람들이 하던 일이 한 대의 기계로 가능해졌다. 일은 새로운 근육, 즉 에너지에 의해 행해질 수 있었다. 일은 열역학의 기본 법칙에 의해서 이루어졌다. 특히 보일의 법칙에 의해 이루어졌다. 보일의 법칙에 따르면 기체의 압력은 기체의 부피와 온도에 의해 결정된다. 풍선 안의 기체를 데우면 부피가 증가하고 압력은 낮아진다. 만약 부피가 변할 수 없는 경우에는 열 때문에 압력이 증가할 것이다.

증기 기관은 이러한 사실을 이용했다. 열 형태의 에너지는 물리적인 힘으로 바뀔 수 있었다. 에너지는, 적절한 방법으로 제어하는 경우, 물건을 이동시킬 수 있었다. 수집된 열은 물리적인 일을 하는데 사용될 수 있었다. 먼저, 물을 끓여 증기를 만들었다. 이러한 방식으로 물은 기체처럼 활동했다. 가열이 되면 팽창했다. 증기가 팽창하면 증기는 실린더라는 관 속으로 들어갔다. 기체가 팽창하면서 피스톤이라는 실린더 바닥이 아래로 내려갔다. 피스톤이 금속 팔을 회전시킴으로써 금속 팔은 온갖 종류의 일에 사용될 수 있었다.

증기 기관은 직물 공장 및 농업과 광업 분야에서 사용되었다. 증기 기관은 방직기의 거대한 바퀴를 회전시켰다. 목화씨에서 목화를 분리하거나 줄기에서 낟알을 분리하는 기계에 동력을 공급하기 위해 사용되었다. 광산에서 물을 퍼내고 석탄과 사람들을 지상으로 들어올릴 때에도 사용되었다. 물론 대륙을 가로질러 사람과 상품을 운반했던 대형 기차에서도 사용되었다.

[7-12]

롤러코스터의 역사

최초의 롤러코스터는 17세기 러시아에서 만들어졌다. 하지만 현재의 롤러코스터와는 달랐다. 커다란 썰매와 더 비슷했다. 사람들은 롤러코스터를 타고 가파른 얼음 미끄럼틀을 내려갔다. 이러한 썰매를 안전하게 몰기 위해서는 매우 뛰어난 조종 기술이 필요했다. 또한 사고도 많았다.

19세기 말에 미국의 철도 회사들이 롤러코스터를 선보였다. 이들은 주말에도 돈을 벌기 위해 놀이 공원을 만들었다. 주말에는 사람들이 거의 이동을 하지 않았다. 1884년에 진정한 롤러코스터가 최초로 등장했다. 중력에 의해 움직이는 기차였다. 승객들은 계단을 올라가 차량에 탑승했다. 그 후에는 차량이 정거장에서 밀려나 아래로 내려가기도 하고 몇개의 언덕을 넘기도 했다. 맨 아랫부분에 도달하면 승객들이 차량에서 내렸다. 그러면 직원들이 차량을 들어올려서 두 번째 정거장으로 옮겨 놓았다.

20세기 초반에 롤러코스터는 크게 발전했다. 이전의 롤러코스터들과 달리 새로운 롤러코스터에는 기계로 작동되는 트랙이 사용되었다. 최초의 트랙은 1912년에 만들어졌다. 엄청난 발전이었다. 이로써 사람들은 더 빠른 속도와 더 가파른 경사를 즐길 수 있었고, 안전성도 이전보다 훨씬 높아졌다. 1920년대에 걸쳐 많은 롤러코스터들이 만들어졌지만, 2차 세계 대전 후 롤러코스터의 수는 크게 감소했다.

미국 최초의 테마 파크인 디즈니랜드가 1955년에 문을 열었다. 디즈니랜드는 놀이 공원의 새 시대를 열었다. 디즈니는 1959년에 최초의 튜브형 강철 롤러코스터를 도입했다. 그 전에는 롤러코스터가 항상 목재 프레임 위에 만들어졌다. 강철 트랙은 보다 높은 안정성을 보장해 주었을 뿐만 아니라, 고리형 및 나선형 롤러코스터의 등장을 가능하게 만들었다.

Vocabulary Check-Up

p.94

1 Ⓒ 2 Ⓐ 3 Ⓓ 4 Ⓒ 5 Ⓑ
6 Ⓐ 7 Ⓓ 8 Ⓒ 9 Ⓑ 10 Ⓐ

UNIT 05 Sentence Simplification

Basic Drill

p.98

Drill 1 Ⓐ

해석

찰스 다윈은 *종의 기원*을 발표했다. 그는 생명체가 환경에 따라 변화한다고 썼다. 그의 자연 선택설은 과학계에 커다란 변화를 일으켰다. 하지만 이는 종교적인 신념에 도전하는 것이었다. 그의 이론에 따르면 생명체는 진화한 것이었다. 신이 오늘날 존재하는 생명체를 창조한 것이 아니었다.

Drill 2 Ⓒ

해석

눈 결정은 놀라운 형태를 가지고 있다. 어떤 두 개의 눈 결정도 정확하게 같지는 않다. 눈 결정은 보통 평평하고 납작하며 6면으로 되어 있다. 눈 결정은 매우 작은 먼지에 얼음이 생길 때 만들어진다. 눈 결정의 형태는 기온에 의해 결정된다. 눈 결정은 하늘에서 떨어지면서 각기 다른 온도층을 통과한다. 이로 인해 눈 결정은 독특한 형태로 얼어붙는다. 가장 큰 눈 결정은 지름이 28센티미터 이상이었다.

Drill 3 Ⓒ

해석

기상학자는 전 세계에서 온 데이터를 필요로 한다. 이러한 데이터를 수집하기 위해 여러 가지 방법이 사용된다. 한 가지 방법은 위성을 이용하는 것이다. 위성은 기상학을 완전히 바꾸어 놓았다. 위성이 지표면을 확인한다. 수증기와 열기를 조사한다. 기상 상황에 관한 데이터를 보낸다. 이러한 데이터를 이용함으로써 기상학자들은 보다 정확하게 날씨를 예측할 수 있다.

Drill 4 Ⓒ

해석

세포는 인체의 기본적인 구조 단위이다. 인간의 몸에는 각각 1억개 정도의 세포가 들어 있다. 하지만 모두가 동일한 형태는 아니다. 세포는 발달해서 특별한 기능을 담당하며, 이로써 기관, 근육, 신경, 피부, 그리고 뼈가 만들어진다. 신체의 각 부위에는 특별한 형태의 세포가 존재한다. 하지만 한 가지 형태의 세포, 즉 줄기 세포는 다른 어떤 형태의 세포로도 자랄 수 있다.

Drill 5 Ⓐ

해석

제레미 벤담은 영국의 철학자였다. 벤담은 다수의 법률 개혁안과 사회 개혁안을 제시했는데, 이들의 영향력은 매우 컸다. 그는 교회와 국가가 분리되어야 한다고 믿었다. 여성도 동등한 권리를 가져야 한다고 주장했다. 그는 언론의 자유에 대한 신봉자였다. 또한 노예 제도의 폐지를 주장했다. 그는 부자 및 가난한 사람들을 위한 건강 보험이 필요하다고도 주장했다.

Exercises with Short Passages

Exercise 1 1 Ⓐ 2 Ⓒ 3 Ⓑ 4 Ⓐ p.100

해석

돌연변이 세포

암은 세포의 돌연변이로부터 발생한다. 세포의 DNA가 변한다. 변화된 DNA 중 10%만이 유전된다. 이는 암의 10%만이 가족력 때문에 생긴다는 점을 의미한다. 대부분의 변화는 환경 탓이다. 암은 흡연을 하거나 오염된 지역에 거주하기 때문에 생길 수 있다. 나이가 들면서 돌연변이 세포는 점점 많아진다. 이러한 이유로 암은 노년기에 보다 빈번하게 발생한다. 암세포가 복제를 하면 복제되는 새로운 세포에 돌연변이 DNA가 복제된다. 결국에는 세포에 너무 많은 변화가 일어나서 세포가 더 이상 신체의 신호를 따를 수 없게 된다. 이들이 자라서 통제 불가능한 상태가 되면 종양이 된다.

Exercise 2 1 Ⓑ 2 Ⓓ 3 Ⓑ 4 Ⓐ p.101

해석

우박

우박은 하늘에서 떨어지는 강우의 한 형태이다. 하지만 비도 아니고 눈도 아니다. 얼음이다. 우박은 폭풍우에서 만들어진다. 기본적으로 구름 안에서 물방울이 흩날리면서 매우 차가운 물방울들과 만나게 된다. 이들이 서로 합쳐지면 우박덩어리가 된다. 우박덩어리는 구름 안에서 점점 더 커질 수 있다. 어느 시점에 이르면 지면으로 떨어질 정도로 충분히 무거워진다. 일부 우박덩어리는 막대한 속도에 도달할 수 있기 때문에 지상에 있는 사람에게 떨어져 사람을 다치게 할 수도 있다. 우박덩어리는 또한 자동차, 건물, 그리고 기타 물체에 피해를 줄 수도 있다. 매년 미국에서만 우박을 동반한 수천 개의 폭풍이 발생한다.

Exercise 3 1 Ⓐ 2 Ⓑ 3 Ⓓ 4 Ⓑ p.102

해석

뮤어 우즈

벌목 산업은 오랫동안 막대한 정치적 영향력을 끼쳤다. 벌목 산업은 이러한 영향력을 이용해서 미국의 거대한 여러 삼림 지대에 접근했다. 20세기 초, 기업들은 캘리포니아 해안 삼림 지대의 많은 나무들을 벌목했다. 지구에서 가장 큰 나무들 중 다수가 그곳에서 자라고 있었다. 거대한 미국 삼나무와 세쿼이어들이 목재와 종이 생산에 사용되었다. 이들 숲 대부분이 크기가 줄어들었다. 켄트라고 하는 한 남자가 무슨 일이 일어나고 있는지를 파악하고 이를 보존하기 위해 땅을 사들였다. 처음에 그는 자신이 나무들을 구했다고 생각했다. 이후 한 수도 회사가 계곡을 범람시켜 전력을 생산하려고 했다. 이 회사는 켄트를 법정에 세웠다. 켄트는 산림 지대를 구하기 위해 그곳을 연방 정부에 기부했다. 이곳은 국립 공원이 되었다. 유명한 동식물 연구자인 존 뮤어의 이름을 따서 뮤어 우즈라는 이름이 붙여졌다. 이 계곡은 개인의 기부에 의해 만들어진 최초의 국립 공원이 되었다. 이로써 추후 산림 보존을 위한 길이 열렸다.

Exercise 4 1 Ⓓ 2 Ⓐ 3 Ⓑ 4 Ⓒ p.103

해석

사형 제도

사형 제도는 수천 년 동안 논쟁의 대상이었다. 이러한 정의는 함무라비 법전에서 비롯되었다. 이는 고대의 법들로 이루어진 것으로, 그중 하나에는 "눈에는 눈, 이에는 이"라고 쓰여 있었다. 어떤 이들은 사형 제도가 공정한 것이라고 생각한다. 최악의 범죄를 저지른 범죄자는 최고의 대가를 치러야 할 것이다. 사회 질서를 유지할 수 있는 유일한 방법은 나쁜 요소들을 제거하는 것이다. 어떤 이들은 사형 제도가 억지의 기능을 한다고 생각한다. 만약 범죄자들이 그 대가로서 목숨을 내놓아야 한다는 점을 안다면 그들은 범죄를 저지르지 않을 것이다. 사형 제도는 사회가 매우 잔인하다는 점을 드러내는 징후라고 생각하는 사람들도 있다. 이들은 인류가 참형이 더 이상 필요하지 않을 정도로 발전했다고 믿는다. 살인에는 정당한 이유가 있을 수 없다.

Exercises with Mid-Length Passages

Exercise 1 1 Ⓐ 2 Ⓒ 3 Ⓐ p.104

해석

DNA

DNA는 범죄와의 싸움에서 중요한 수단이다. 형사들은 DNA를 이용해 범인을 잡는다. 범죄 현장에서 발견된 DNA를 이용해서 진짜 살인범을 찾아낸다. 이 방법은 범인을 밝혀내는 가장 믿을 수 있는 방법 중 하나이다.

DNA는 생명체에 대한 청사진을 담고 있는 분자이다. 신체가 성장할 때 신체가 어떻게 발달할지를 제어한다. 이는 부모의 유전적 특징을 자식에게 전달한다. DNA는 인체 내 100조개의 모든 세포에 들어 있다. 인간 개개인은 완전히 고유한 DNA 조합을 가지고 있다.

조사관들은 종종 범죄 현장이나 희생자의 신체에서 DNA 흔적을 찾아낸다. 이는 한 가닥의 체모, 한 방울의 혈액, 혹은 피부 조직일 수도 있다. 경찰은 이러한 샘플을 수집해서 분석할 수 있다. 운이 좋은 경우에는 샘플과 용의자 사이에 일치하는 점이 발견된다. 하지만 일부 요인들로 인해 실패하는 경우도 있다. DNA 샘플은 오염될 수 있다. 샘플이 다른 사람의 것과 섞일 수도 있고, 열 등에 의해서 샘플이 부분적으로 손상될 수도 있다.

Exercise 2 1 Ⓓ 2 Ⓑ 3 Ⓑ p.106

해석

토네이도

토네이도는 강력하고 회전하는 공기 기둥이다. 폭풍 구름에서 지상으로 이어져 있다. 가장 강력한 토네이도는 막대한 피해를 입힐 수 한다. 풍속이 시속 500킬로미터에 이를 수도 있다. 이 회오리바람은 인명과 재산에 큰 피해를 입힐 수 있다.

토네이도는 미국에서, 특히 봄과 여름에 가장 흔히 발생한다. 매년 전국적으로 800개의의 토네이도가 보고된다. 그 결과 약 80명이 사망하고 1,500명이 부상을 입는다. 피해 경로는 폭이 1.6킬로미터, 길이가 80킬로미터에 이를 수도 있다.

토네이도 앨리라는 이름의 지역이 있다. 오하이오에서 텍사스에 걸쳐 있는 지역이다. 이 지역에서는 미국의 어느 지역에서보다도 토네이도가 더 자주 발생한다. 이곳은 로키산맥의 차갑고 건조한 공기가 불어온다는 점에서 독특하다. 이 공기는 멕시코만의 따뜻하고 습한 공기와 만난다. 이는 토네이도가 발상하기에 완벽한 조건이다.

Exercise 3 1 Ⓐ 2 Ⓑ 3 Ⓐ p.108

해석

존 뮤어

존 뮤어는 세계에서 가장 큰 국립 공원 중 하나가 세워지는데 일조했다. 그는 1838년 스코틀랜드에서 출생했다. 하지만 1849년에 미국으로 이주했다. 대학을 졸업하지는 않았다. 대신 기술자로서 일자리를 구했다. 얼마 지나지 않아 그는 황무지를 탐험하기로 결심했다. 자연의 아름다움을 만끽하면서 인디애나에서부터 플로리다까지 수천 마일을 걸었다. 뮤어는 남아메리카 여행도 계획했다. 하지만 말라리아 때문에 중단해야 했다. 대신 그는 캘리포니아로 갔다.

그는 1868년에 샌프란시스코에 도착했다. 그는 곧 요세미티를 향해 출발했는데, 그는 잡지와 신문을 통해 그곳에 관한 기사만 읽어 보았을 뿐이었다. 그는 이 멋진 장소를 처음 보고 감명을 받았다. 뮤어는 "손으로 만든 어떤 사원도 요세미티와 비교할 수 없을 것이다. 요세미티는 자연이 만든 모든 특별한 사원 중에서 가장 장엄한 곳이다."라고 썼다.

1903년에 루즈벨트 대통령이 뮤어와 함께 요세미티 공원을 방문했다. 뮤어는 대통령에게 주 당국이 공원을 제대로 관리하지 못한다고 이야기했다. 그는 자연 보존의 중요성을 역설했다. 뮤어는 연방 정부의 통제와 관리를 통해 공원을 보호해야 한다는 점을 루즈벨트 대통령에게 설득시킬 수 있었다.

Exercise 4 1 Ⓑ 2 Ⓒ 3 Ⓓ p.110

해석

함무라비 법전

함무라비는 바빌론의 6대 왕이었다. 그는 기원전 1810년에 태어났다. 기원전 1792년부터 기원전 1750년에 자신이 사망할 때까지 제국을 통치했다. 그는 함무라비 법전이라고 불리는 일련의 법을 제정한 것으로 가장 잘 알려져 있을 것이다.

법전의 형벌이 현대인들에게는 잔인해 보이지만 법전의 두 가지 측면은 시대를 앞선 것이었다. 첫째, 그는 법을 글로 남겼다. 단순히 말을 한 것이 아니었다. 둘째, 그는 법을 체계적으로 적용하고자 했다. 이는 문명의 진화에 있어서 중요한 진전이었다. 무죄 추정의 원리도 이 법전에서 비롯된 것이다.

법은 석판에 쓰여져 공공 장소에 비치되었다. 사람들은 이를 볼 수 있었지만 읽고 이해할 수 있는 사람들은 많지 않았다. 수년 후 석판은 약탈을 당해서 엘라

마이트 수사로 보내졌다. 그곳에서 1901년에 재발견되었다. 현재 이 석판은 프랑스의 루브르 박물관에 세워져 있다.

Building Summary Skills

p.112

A

Exercise 1 DNA

1 DNA is used to catch criminals because it is a very reliable method.

4 If the DNA in the sample matches the DNA of someone they know, police have identified the criminal.

2 All cells contain DNA.

5 DNA can be contaminated though.

3 When investigators find traces of a person, they analyze them.

Exercise 2 Tornadoes

1 Tornadoes are violently rotating columns of air, and they usually occur during spring and summer.

3 They result in around eighty deaths and over 1,500 injuries.

4 They most frequently occur in an area called Tornado Alley.

2 In the U.S., 800 tornadoes are reported each year.

5 It stretches from Ohio to Texas.

Exercise 3 John Muir

1 John Muir, a naturalist, was born in Scotland in 1838.

4 He was fascinated by this great park but was worried about how the state was managing it.

3 After this journey, he went to Yosemite.

2 In his twenties, he decided to explore the American wilderness by walking from Indiana to Florida.

5 He asked the president of the U.S. to protect this beautiful place.

Exercise 4 The Code of Hammurabi

1 Hammurabi was the sixth king of the Babylonian Dynasty.

4 Another importance of this law is that the concept of being innocent until proven guilty comes from the Code of Hammurabi.

2 He created the Code of Hammurabi.

3 These laws became famous because they were written down for the first time and publicly placed.

B

Exercise 1 DNA

DNA is used to catch criminals because it is a very reliable method. All cells contain DNA. When investigators find traces of a person, they analyze them. If the DNA in the sample matches the DNA of someone they know, police have identified the criminal. DNA can be contaminated though.

Exercise 2 Tornadoes

Tornadoes are violently rotating columns of air, and they usually occur during spring and summer. In the U.S., 800 tornadoes are reported each year. They result in around eighty deaths and over 1,500 injuries. They most frequently occur in an area called Tornado Alley. It stretches from Ohio to Texas.

Exercise 3 John Muir

John Muir, a naturalist, was born in Scotland in 1838. In his twenties, he decided to explore the American wilderness by walking from Indiana to Florida. After this journey, he went to Yosemite. He was fascinated by this great park but was worried by how the state was managing it. He asked the president of the U.S. to protect this beautiful place.

Exercise 4 The Code of Hammurabi

Hammurabi was the sixth king of the Babylonian Dynasty. He created the Code of Hammurabi. These laws became famous because they were written down for the first time and publicly placed. Another importance of these laws was that the concept of being innocent until proven guilty comes from the Code of Hammurabi.

Mini TOEFL iBT Practice Test

p.114

1 Ⓑ 2 Ⓒ 3 Ⓓ 4 Ⓓ 5 Ⓐ
6 Ⓐ

7 Ⓒ 8 Ⓑ 9 Ⓑ 10 Ⓐ 11 Ⓒ
12 Ⓐ

해석

[1-6]

식충 식물

식충 식물은 대부분 토양이 척박한 장소에서 자란다. 여기에는 늪과 습지가 포함된다. 이 식물은 매우 높은 습도와 다량의 햇빛을 필요로 한다. 하지만 양분은 작은 동물과 곤충을 잡아먹음으로써 얻는다. 이러한 식물들은 보다 영리한 방법으로 먹이를 붙잡는다. 오늘날 약 500개의 식물들이 식충 식물로 알려져 있다.

찰스 다윈은 1875년에 최초로 식충 식물에 관한 유명한 논문을 썼다. 그는 다섯 종류의 덫을 설명했다. 함정형 덫은 잎을 말아서 곤충을 잡는데, 바닥 부분에는 박테리아들이 모여 있다. 파리채형 덫은 끈적끈적한 액체를 사용해서 곤충을 잡는다. 스냅형 덫은 잎을 재빨리 움직여 곤충을 잡는다. 기포형 덫은 진공 상태인 기포 안으로 곤충을 끌어들인다. 마지막으로 통발형 덫은 안쪽을 향하고 있는 털을 이용해 곤충들을 식물의 중심부로 밀어넣는다. 곤충들은 뒤로 빠져나갈 수가 없다.

시간에 따른 식충 식물의 변화는 연구하기가 어렵다. 화석 기록도 거의 존재하지 않는다. 대부분 씨나 꽃가루만 남아 있을 뿐이다. 그러나 과학자들은 현재의 덫의 구조에서 많은 것을 알아낼 수 있다. 함정형 덫은 분명히 말린 잎으로부터 진화했을 것이다. 파리채형 덫 또한 끈적하고 치명적이지 않은 잎이 치명적인 유형으로 변화된 것이라는 점을 보여 준다. 파리지옥은 흥미로운 식물이다. 각 잎의 가운데에 세 가닥의 털이 있다. 어떤 곤충이 두 개의 털을 빠르게 건드려야만 잎이 닫힌다. 그런 다음에 식물이 곤충을 잡아먹는다.

과학자들은 이러한 모든 잎 형태가 털이 많은 단순한 잎에서 비롯된 돌연변이일 것이라고 주장한다. 잎에 빗방울이 모일 수 있었고, 이곳에서 박테리아가 번식할 수 있었다. 곤충이 잎에 내려앉으면 물에 갇혔다. 이들은 질식하게 되었다. 그러면 박테리아가 곤충을 부패시켜서 식물에게 양분을 제공해 주었다.

[7-12]

사막화

사하라 사막은 매년 약 10킬로미터씩 커지고 있다. 지구에서 매년 사막의 넓이는 600평방킬로미터씩 늘어나고 있다. 이러한 과정을 사막화라고 부른다. 이러한 용어는 1950년대부터 사용되기 시작했다.

사막화의 개념은 1930년대에 처음 알려졌다. 대평원 지대의 상당 부분이 가뭄과 잘못된 농법으로 인해 매우 건조해졌다. 이는 더스트 볼이라고 불렸다. 수백만 명이 농장을 떠나 다른 방식의 삶을 택해야 했다. 그 이후로 대평원에서의 농법이 크게 개선되었다. 이로써 더스트 볼이라는 재해가 다시 일어나는 일을 막을 수 있었다. 방목은 또 다른 문제였다. 소는 토양에 두 가지 영향을 미친다. 첫째, 토양을 제자리에 있게 만드는 풀과 식물을 먹는다. 둘째, 발굽이 토양의 상층부를 망가뜨린다. 그 결과 양질의 토양이 바람에 날아가 버릴 수 있다. 남겨진 흙은 식물이 자라기에 좋은 흙이 아니다.

어떤 사람들은 가뭄이 이러한 현상을 일으킨다고 생각한다. 실제로는 거의 사람에 의해 일어난다. 이는 전 지구적으로 가장 심각한 문제 중 하나가 되었다. 건조 지역 및 반건조 지역에서 가뭄은 흔한 일이다. 잘 관리된 땅은 비가 다시 내리면 가뭄에서 회복할 수 있는 역량을 갖추고 있다. 중요한 것은 사람이 자연에 미치는 영향이다. 5년 간의 가뭄이 몇 년 전 서아프리카에서의 잘못된 토양 관리에 의해 악화되었다. 이로 인해 10만 명 이상이 목숨을 잃었고 1,200만 마리의 소가 죽었다.

사막화는 정치에서도 흔히 등장하는 문제이다. 이와 관련해서 사람들이 모르고 있는 것들이 아직도 많다. 이 과정은 매우 복잡한 악화의 한 형태이다. 이를 더 잘 이해하기 위해서는 보다 많은 연구가 이루어져야 한다.

Vocabulary Check-Up

p.118

1 Ⓒ	2 Ⓐ	3 Ⓒ	4 Ⓑ	5 Ⓒ
6 Ⓒ	7 Ⓓ	8 Ⓐ	9 Ⓑ	10 Ⓓ

PART II Making Inferences

UNIT 06 Rhetorical Purpose

Basic Drill

p.124

Drill 1 Ⓒ

해석

눈사태는 위험하다. 거대한 눈덩이 및 얼음 덩어리가 산을 미끄러져 내려오면 그 경로에 있는 모든 것들이 파괴될 수 있다. 서로 뭉쳐지지 않는 눈은 미끄러져 내려오기가 쉽다. 스키를 타는 사람들이 부상을 입거나 심지어 사망을 하기도 한다. 과학자들은 눈사태에 관해 더 많은 것들을 알아내기 위해 눈송이를 연구한다. 얼음 결정이 어떻게 형성되는지 관찰한다. 어떤 모양은 눈이 서로 달라붙게 만든다. 눈을 미끄럽게 만드는 모양도 있다.

Drill 2 Ⓑ

해석

몰디브는 인도양에 있는 군도이다. 이 군도에는 천 개 이상의 작은 섬들이 있다. 이 섬들은 해저 화산의 꼭대기에 붙어 있는 산호에 의해 만들어진다. 산호는 종종 원형으로 자란다. 산호가 해수면에 도달하면 섬이 형성된다. 종종 가운데 부분에 산호가 없는 영역이 존재하는 경우가 있다. 이로써 섬의 한가운데에 바닷물이 수원인 호수가 만들어지기도 한다.

Drill 3 Ⓐ

해석

섭식 장애는 개인의 건강을 해치는 식습관 중 하나이다. 어떤 사람들은 과식을 해서 살이 찐다. 거의 식사를 하지 않는 사람들도 있다. 폭식이라는 것을 하는 사람들도 있다. 이들은 고통을 느끼는 순간에 이를 때까지 한 번에 너무나 많은 음식을 먹는다. 이들은 종종 먹는 일이 창피하다고 느끼기 때문에 혼자서 이러한 행동을 한다. 모든 섭식 장애의 한 가지 측면은 자신의 식습관을 통제할 수 없다는 점이다.

Drill 4 Ⓑ

해석

가난은 중요한 사회 문제이다. 많은 원인이 존재한다. 특정 집단의 사람들은 기본적인 권리를 부정당할 수도 있다. 인종이나 종교 때문에 일자리를 구하지 못한다. 자유의 부재는 또 다른 이유이다. 때때로 사람들이 원하는 방식으로 생활하고 일하는 것을 지도자가 막기도 한다. 그 혼자서 모든 돈과 권력을 가진다. 세 번째 이유는 전쟁이다. 전쟁은 한 국가의 경제 기반을 파괴시킬 수 있다. 사람들은 대부분의 에너지를 삶의 질을 향상시키기보다 생존을 위해 사용한다.

Drill 5 Ⓒ

해석

인도의 체라푼지는 지구에서 가장 습한 지역이다. 때로는 두 달 동안 비가 멈추지 않고 내리기도 한다. 이상하게도 물은 한곳에 머물러 있지 않는다. 이 지역은 한때 식물들로 푸르렀지만, 사람들 때문에 더 이상 그렇지가 않다. 사람들이 이 지역을 파괴했다. 지금은 비가 내리면 빗물이 단단한 땅 위에서 흘러가 버린다. 흙과 식물들이 쓸려 내려간다.

Exercises with Short Passages

Exercise 1 1 Ⓐ 2 Ⓑ 3 Ⓓ 4 Ⓐ p.126

해석

곤충에 답이 있다

경찰은 사망자가 사망한 정확한 시각과 장소를 알아야 한다. 이러한 정보는 사망자가 사망한 방식에 대한 질문에 답을 가져다 줄 수 있다. 이는 사고일 수도, 혹은 범죄일 수도 있다. 범죄 전문가들은 이러한 답을 찾기 위해 곤충을 조사할 수도 있다. 나방, 진드기, 그리고 딱정벌레와 같은 곤충들은 서로 다른 생애 주기를 갖는다. 또한 식습관도 서로 다르다. 일부 진드기들은 부패가 진행되는 초기 단계에만 사체의 살을 먹는다. 보다 나중에 살을 먹는 진드기들도 있다. 딱정벌레는 전형적으로 이후 단계에서, 그리고 습한 상황에서만 살을 먹는다. 나방은 건조한 상황에서 살을 먹는다. 전문가들은 어떤 곤충이 존재하는지와 이들이 언제 알을 낳았는지를 조사할 수 있다. 이는 사망 시각과 사망 장소를 밝혀내는데 도움이 될 수 있다.

Exercise 2 1 Ⓑ 2 Ⓒ 3 Ⓐ 4 Ⓒ p.127

해석

불안 장애

불안 장애가 있는 사람은 하고 싶은 일을 하지 못한다. 실제로 불안한 사람은 감정으로 인한 신체적 증상을 겪을 수 있다. 심장 박동이 빨라질 수도 있다. 땀이 나기 시작할 수도 있다. 심지어는 심한 공황 발작이 나타날 수도 있다. 이러한 장애가 있는 사람들은 불안감을 통제하지 못한다. 약속이나 집안 청소와 같은 간단한 일에 대해서도 불안해 한다. 책상이 정리되어 있지 않다는 이유로도 불안해 할 수 있다. 의사들은 불안하지 않은 시간보다 불안한 시간이 더 많은 경우에 사람들이 이러한 질환을 겪는다고 말한다. 의사들은 그러한 사람들이 불안 때문에 항상 피곤함을 느끼거나 짜증을 낸다고 말한다. 때로는 잠을 못 자거나 식사를 못할 수도 있다. 기본적으로 삶의 중심에 불안이 존재한다.

Exercise 3 1 Ⓒ 2 Ⓑ 3 Ⓓ 4 Ⓓ p.128

해석

마젤란 해협

한때는 대서양에서 태평양으로 가는 여정이 위험했다. 이는 파나마 운하가 없던 때의 일이었다. 선박들은 세상의 가장 아랫부분을 돌아서 가야 했다. 때로는 아프리카 아래로 긴 여행을 해야 했다. 또는 드레이크 해협 택할 수도 있었다. 이곳은 남극과 남아메리카 사이에 있는 해역이었다. 물살과 날씨 모두 매우 위험했다. 커다란 얼음 덩어리 때문에 선박이 난파될 위험성이 있었다. 마젤란이 1520년에 또 다른 길을 찾아냈다. 이 항로는 마젤란 해협이라고 불렸다. 이 해협은 북쪽의 대륙과 남쪽의 섬 티에라 델 푸에고 사이를 통과했다. 이 좁은 해협은 육지에 의해 보호를 받았다. 선박에 필요한 안전성이 주어졌다.

Exercise 4 1 Ⓓ 2 Ⓓ 3 Ⓓ 4 Ⓑ p.129

해석

말하는 방식

사람들이 말하는 방식을 통해서 그들의 배경에 대해 많은 것을 알 수 있다. 예를 들어 어떤 사람이 남부 지역 출신인지 혹은 북부 지역 출신인지 추측할 수 있다. 만약 어떤 아이가 남부 지방의 억양을 나타내면서 북부 지방의 단어를 쓴다면 어떻게 될 것인가? 그 아이의 가족이 북부에서 남부로 이주했을 것이라고 짐작할 수 있을 것이다. 아이는 친구들과 같은 억양을 나타내지만 부모들만 사용하는 단어를 사용한다. 사회 계급 또한 말하는 방식에 영향을 미친다. 유명한 사회언어학자인 윌리엄 라보프는 억양과 사회 계급 사이의 연관성을 찾으려고 노력했다. 그는 뉴욕에 있는 세 곳의 가게를 방문했다. 첫 번째 가게는 상류층이, 두 번째는 중류층이, 그리고 세 번째는 하류층이 이용하는 가게였다. 그는 상류층 가게의 고객들이 다른 가게의 고객들과는 달리 일반적으로 "R"을 발음하지 않는다는 사실을 알아냈다.

Exercises with Mid-Length Passages

Exercise 1 1 Ⓓ 2 Ⓐ 3 Ⓑ p.130

해석

법의학

법의학은 법률 시스템에서 사용되는 과학 분야이다. 포렌식(forensic)이라는 단어는 "법정과 관련된"이라는 뜻을 나타낸다. 이 분야는 세상에 대한 법적 질문에 답을 제공해 준다. 법의학이 일반적으로 사용되는 곳은 범죄 수사 분야이다. 경찰은 범죄자와 범죄 간의 연관성을 찾으려고 노력한다. 현장에서 지문 및 발자국을 찾는다. 경찰은 체액 형태의 증거를 찾는다. 또한 피부에 있는 할퀸 상처와 머리카락을 조사할 수도 있다. 심지어 깨문 자국이 용의자의 것인지 확인할 수도 있다.

경찰은 또한 독이 인체에 어떤 영향을 미치는지 연구한다. 범죄 전문가들은 얼마나 많은 양의 화학 물질이 사용되었는지 기록한다. 또한 그 물질이 사용된 후 시간이 얼마나 지났는지도 추정한다. 이들은 현장에 어떤 화학 물질이 있었는지를 알아내려고 노력한다. 혈액 샘플로 마약이나 독극물의 단기간 복용 여부를 알 수도 있다. 머리카락 샘플로는 장기간 복용 여부를 알 수 있다. 머리카락은 한 달에 1센티미터씩 자란다. 이는 전문가들에게 마약 혹은 독극물이 언제 사용되었는지에 대한 단서를 제공해 준다.

이들은 법의학이 살펴보는 몇 가지 부분에 불과하다. 이 분야는 매우 광범위하다. 과학은 법률 시스템에서 매우 유용하다. 이는 어려운 문제에 대한 답을 찾기 위해 사용될 수 있다.

Exercise 2 1 Ⓑ 2 Ⓓ 3 Ⓐ p.132

해석

수줍음

많은 사람들이 수줍음을 탄다. 이는 다른 사람들과 함께 있을 때 숨고 싶어하는 느낌이다. 사람들은 수줍음을 느낄 때 다른 사람들과 함께 있고 싶어하지 않는다. 익숙하지 않은 상황에 처하거나 모르는 사람들과 함께 있을 때에 종종 그렇게 된다. 때로는 성별 이슈인 경우도 있다. 남성과 여성이 섞여 있을 때 수줍음을 느낄 수가 있다. 남성끼리 혹은 여성끼리 있는 경우에는 수줍음을 덜 느끼게 된다.

수줍음의 원인은 간단하지 않다. 때로는 삶에서 겪은 좋지 않은 일 때문에 수줍음이 생길 수도 있다. 예를 들어 사랑하는 사람에게 상처를 받은 경우, 이후에 수줍음이 나타날 수 있다. 또한 천성적으로 수줍음을 탈 수도 있다. 몇몇 가정에서 한 아이는 외향적인 반면 다른 아이는 수줍음을 타기도 한다. 두 아이 모두에게 가정 환경은 동일하다. 각각의 아이는 서로 다른 성격을 갖는다. 과학자들은 심지어 수줍음과 관련된 유전자에 대해 이야기를 하기도 한다.

수줍음은 문화적인 문제일 수도 있다. 미국 문화에서는 솔직하고 당찬 사람을 높이 평가한다. 적극적인 사람이 선호된다. 그래서 수줍은 성격의 사람들은 자신의 감정을 부정적으로 생각한다. 다른 사람들과 다르게 행동하는 사람들을 높이 평가하지 않는 문화도 있다. 이 경우 수줍은 성격의 사람들은 자신이 그러한 문화에 잘 맞는다고 생각할 수 있다.

Exercise 3 1 Ⓒ 2 Ⓐ 3 Ⓑ p.134

해석

시와

시와는 유명한 오아시스이다. 이곳은 아프리카 사막을 건너는 군대와 상인들의 휴식처였다. 1만 년 이상 사람들이 이곳에 정착해서 살아 왔다. 이곳은 이집트의 카이로에서 서쪽으로 560킬로미터 떨어진 곳에 있다.

이 오아시스는 또한 강력한 신관으로도 유명했다. 사람들은 그의 가르침을 얻기 위해 수백 마일의 거리를 이동했다. 사원은 오늘날에도 존재하는데, 이러한 점은 이곳의 중요성을 나타낸다.

이집트 침공 당시 알렉산더 대왕이 이곳에서 휴식을 취한 것으로 알려져 있다. 그와 그의 군대는 사막에서 물을 다 써 버렸다고 전해진다. 신들이 두 마리의 까마귀를 보내 그를 시와로 인도했고, 이로써 군대를 구할 수 있었다. 알렉산더가 신관을 방문했다. 신관은 알렉산더에게 그가 신성한 존재이며 이집트의 정당한 통치자라고 말했다.

오늘날 시와는 농업에 의존하고 있다. 사막 한 가운데서 일어나기에는 놀라운 일이다. 어떤 사람들은 이 오아시스에서 세계 최고의 대추야자와 올리브가 생산된다고 주장한다. 농부들이 세심하게 작물들을 돌본다. 적절한 방식으로 물이 밭으로 흘러 들고 나가게 만든다. 심지어 손으로 대추야자 나무를 수분시키기도 한다.

Exercise 4 1 Ⓐ 2 Ⓓ 3 Ⓐ p.136

해석

산맥

산은 지형의 일종이다. 지상으로 높이 솟아 있다. 산맥은 비교적 가까이에 있는 산들로 이루어진 그룹이다. 이러한 산들은 동일한 형태와 특징을 지닌다. 전 세계적으로 수백 개의 산맥이 존재한다. 일부는 상당히 작은 반면, 일부 산맥들은 수천 킬로미터까지 뻗어 있을 수 있다.

많은 산맥들이 단층을 따라 형성되어 있다. 단층은 두 개 이상의 지각판이 만나는 곳이다. 때때로 두 개의 판이 충돌할 수 있다. 보통은 하나의 판이 다른 판 아래로 들어가게 된다. 이로써 두 번째 판이 더 높이 솟아오르게 되는데, 이로 인해 산이 만들어진다. 이는 수백 만년에 걸쳐 일어날 수 있는 느린 과정이다. 예를 들어 히말라야의 산들은 여전히 크기가 증가하고 있다. 매년 조금씩 높이가 높아지고 있다.

세계에서 가장 긴 산맥은 안데스산맥이다. 남아메리카에 있으며, 거의 남아메리카 대륙 전체에 뻗어 있다. 히말라야산맥에는 세계에서 가장 높은 산과 기타 높은 봉우리들이 있다. 가장 오래된 산맥 중 하나는 미국에 있는 애팔래치아산맥이다. 이곳 산들은 수백 만년 동안의 침식 작용에 의해 크기가 작아지고 있다.

Building Summary Skills

p.138

A

Exercise 1 Forensic Science

1 Forensic science helps collect information that is useful for police work and the law.

4 The field is very broad.

2 Police look for small clues that can identify criminals.

5 Many things are studied for forensic purposes.

3 The clues can come from someone's body (blood, skin, or fingerprints), or they can be chemical (drugs).

Exercise 2 Shyness

1 When people are shy, they wish to avoid others. This often happens in new situations.

4 Things can happen in people lives to make them shy.

3 Sometimes men and women feel shy around one another.

5 Sometimes people are born that way.

6 In some cultures, shyness is not valued, and in other cultures, it is a good quality to have.

2 This often happens in new situations.

Exercise 3 Siwa

1 Siwa is a famous oasis, and it has sheltered people crossing the desert for thousands of years.

3 Alexander the Great stopped in Siwa to consult him while conquering Egypt.

2 A powerful oracle lived there in ancient times.

5 Farmers must be very careful when managing the land and the plants.

4 Siwa has a water source, it depends on farming, and it has some of the best dates and olives in the world.

Exercise 4 Mountain Ranges

1 Mountain ranges are groups of mountains relatively close together.

5 The Andes are the longest mountain range while the Himalayas have the world's highest mountain.

3 Mountain ranges form when two tectonic plates collide.

4 It can take millions of years for mountains to form.

2 There are hundreds of mountain ranges around the world.

B

Exercise 1 **Forensic Science**

Forensic science helps collect information that is useful for police work and the law. Police look for small clues that can identify criminals. The clues can come from someone's body (blood, skin, or fingerprints), or they can be chemical (drugs). The field is very broad. Many things are studied for forensic purposes.

Exercise 2 **Shyness**

When people are shy, they wish to avoid others. This often happens in new situations. Sometimes men and women feel shy around one another. Things can happen in people lives to make them shy. Sometimes people are born that way. In some cultures, shyness is not valued, and in other cultures, it is a good quality to have.

Exercise 3 **Siwa**

Siwa is a famous oasis, and it has sheltered people crossing the desert for thousands of years. A powerful oracle lived there in ancient times. Alexander the Great stopped in Siwa to consult him while conquering Egypt. Siwa has a water source, it depends on farming, and it has some of the best dates and olives in the world. Farmers must be very careful to manage the land and the plants.

Exercise 4 **Mountain Ranges**

Mountain ranges are groups of mountains relatively close together. There are hundreds of mountain ranges around the world. Mountain ranges form when two tectonic plates collide. It can take millions of years for mountains to form. The Andes are the longest mountain range while the Himalayas have the world's highest mountain.

Mini TOEFL iBT Practice Test p.140

1 Ⓐ 2 Ⓑ 3 Ⓐ 4 Ⓒ 5 Ⓑ
6 Ⓐ

7 Ⓒ 8 Ⓓ 9 Ⓒ 10 Ⓐ 11 Ⓐ
12 Ⓒ

해석

[1-6]

세상의 끝

티에라 델 푸에고는 세상의 끝이다. 지리학적인 관점에서 그렇다. 이곳은 남아메리카의 가장 아래쪽에 위치한 자그마한 삼각형 모양의 땅이다. 그 이름은 "불의 땅"이라는 의미이다. 한 유명한 탐험가가 원주민들이 해변에 지른 불을 보고 그러한 이름을 붙였다. 이 섬은 아르헨티나와 칠레가 공유하고 있다. 티에라 델 푸에고는 독특한 지형으로 유명하다.

하지만 이 섬은 불과 아무런 상관이 없다. 이곳은 남아메리카의 남단에 위치해 있다. 연중 평균 기온은 5℃다. 겨울에는 훨씬 더 추워진다. 기온 차이는 대부분 고도에 의한 것이다. 안데스산맥 서쪽에 얼음 강이 만들어진다. 차가운 비와 바람 때문에 북쪽과 동쪽의 평지가 차가워진다.

티에라 델 푸에고의 땅에 대해 말하기는 쉽다. 땅을 둘러싸고 있는 해역 또한 독특하다. 이곳은 아마도 세계에서 가장 중요한 해역일 것이다. 이곳은 온갖 종류의 새들의 보금자리이다. 알바트로스가 가장 잘 알려져 있다. 또한 고래, 오징어, 그리고 많은 어류들도 서식한다. 여름의 며칠 동안에는 엄청난 무리의 정어리가 이 지역으로 이동해 온다. 현지 주민들은 물에 걸어 들어가기만 하면 쇼핑백으로 물고기를 잡을 수 있다. 사방에 물고기 떼가 있다. 미끼가 없어도 물고기를 잡을 수 있다. 지역 경제 및 세계 경제에서 이 물고기들의 경제적 가치는 막대하다.

티에라 델 푸에고는 희귀한 장소이다. 그처럼 좁은 장소에 산맥, 산림 지대, 그리고 평원과 같은 다양한 지형들이 포함되어 있다. 양쪽에서는 두 대양이 만난다. 이러한 특징 덕분에 이곳은 매우 다양한 야생 생물들의 서식지가 된다. 이곳 여름에는 낮이 매우 길고 겨울에는 낮이 짧다. 지구에서 유일무이한 곳이다.

[7-12]

가족과 돈

현대 사회는 가족 관계를 변화시키고 있다. 생활비는 미국 가정의 생활 방식에 영향을 끼쳐 왔다. 이는 최선이 아닐 수도 있다. 몇 십 년 전에는 아버지가 일을 하러 갔다. 아버지의 월급으로 생활비를 지불했다. 어머니는 집에 머물렀다. 근처 교회나 지역 프로그램에서 자원봉사 활동을 했을 수도 있다. 아이들은 학교에 다녔다. 십대인 경우에는 주말에 아르바이트를 할 때도 있었다.

미국의 여러 부분에서 상황이 달라졌다. 생활비가 증가하고 있다. 생활비가 가장 많이 증가한 영역은 부동산 가격과 의료비이다. 기본적으로 한 사람의 급여로 주택을 구입하거나 집세를 내고 생활비를 감당하기에는 충분하지 않다. 그 결과 부모 두 사람이 다 일을 해야 한다. 이렇게 해야 가족이 거처할 곳을 마련할 수 있고 필요한 경우 진료를 받으러 갈 수도 있다.

부모 모두 일을 하는 경우에는 부모가 자녀와 함께 하는 시간에 변화가 생긴다. 많은 부모들이 자녀를 위탁 시설에 맡긴다. 이렇게 하면 아이들을 확실히 돌볼 수 있다는 장점이 있다. 하지만 어린 시기에 아이들이 부모와 함께 보내는 시간도 줄어든다. 더욱이 아이를 위탁하면 추가 비용이 든다. 따라서 이를 감당하기 위해서는 부모 둘 다 더 많이 일해야 한다.

학창 시절에 아이들이 부모보다 일찍 귀가하게 되는 경우도 흔하다. 아이들이 스스로 문을 열고 집에 들어가야 하기 때문에 이들은 열쇠 아동이라고 불린다. 이들의 어머니는 집에서 기다리고 있다가 아이들에게 문을 열어 주지 않는다. 이처럼 혼자 지내는 시간 때문에 아이들이 마약이나 범죄와 같은 문제들을 겪을 위험성이 커진다. 감독을 받지 않기 때문에 아이들은 보다 자주 곤경에 처할 수 있다. 생활비 상승은 가족의 생활 방식을 변화시킨다. 보다 나은 삶을 위해 열심히 일하는 동안 사람들은 여러 가지 위험에 스스로를 노출시키고 있다.

Vocabulary Check-Up p.144

1 Ⓐ 2 Ⓒ 3 Ⓑ 4 Ⓓ 5 Ⓐ
6 Ⓑ 7 Ⓑ 8 Ⓐ 9 Ⓑ 10 Ⓓ

UNIT

07 Inference

Basic Drill ········· p.148

Drill 1 Ⓐ

해석

여름에는 건강을 잘 챙겨야 한다. 더위 때문에 병이 날 수도 있다. 가장 심각한 병은 열사병이다. 여러 가지 증상이 있다. 하나는 심한 고열이다. 두 번째 증상은 행동의 변화이다. 건조한 피부도 또 다른 증상이다. 많은 경우, 신체에서 땀이 나지 않아 몸이 식지 않는다. 의식을 잃어 버릴 수도 있다.

Drill 2 Ⓒ

해석

하드 뉴스와 소프트 뉴스 사이에는 차이점이 있다. 하드 뉴스는 심각한 주제 및 현안을 다루는 뉴스이다. 여기에는 정치, 범죄, 그리고 전쟁이 포함된다. 소프트 뉴스는 그다지 심각하지 않은 주제를 다루는 뉴스이다. 이러한 뉴스를 전달하는 경우 시기는 중요한 요인이 아니다. 소프트 뉴스의 주제에는 스포츠 및 유명 인사에 관한 소식이 포함된다.

Drill 3 Ⓒ

해석

미국에서 주의 권리는 각각의 주가 어떻게 국가로부터 분리된 정부를 갖는지와 관련이 있다. 각 주는 중요한 사안에 대해 스스로 결정을 내릴 수 있다. 어떤 주는 사형 제도를 허용하지 않는 반면 이를 허용하는 주도 있다. 중앙 정부의 법을 위반하지 않는 한 주는 원하는 것을 할 수 있다. 현재로서는 국가가 사형 제도에 대한 결정을 내리지 않았다. 각 주는 원하는 대로 결정을 내릴 수 있다.

Drill 4 Ⓑ

해석

관절염에 걸리면 관절이 붓고 통증이 생긴다. 나이가 들수록 뼈가 주위 연조직의 보호를 받지 못하게 된다. 관절이 붓고 아플 수 있다. 관절염은 노년층에서 더 많이 발생하며 남성보다 여성의 경우에 더 자주 발생한다. 미국인 가운데 거의 3분의 1이 이 질병을 앓고 있다. 어떤 경우에는 관절의 통증이 너무 심해서 의사가 이를 인공 관절로 대체해야만 한다.

Drill 5 Ⓐ

해석

리얼리티 TV가 최근에 인기를 얻고 있다. 시청자들은 일상적인 상황에 놓인 평범한 사람들을 보는 것을 좋아한다. 사람들은 일상 생활에서 특별한 일이 이루어질 수 있다고 생각한다. 하지만 많은 사람들은 이러한 쇼가 실제로 얼마나 현실적인 것인지에 대해 의문을 제기한다. 때로는 쇼에서 평범한 사람들을 특별한 상황에 처하도록 만든다. 이들은 낯선 장소에 가게 된다. 그리고 일어나는 모든 일들이 보여지는 것은 아니다. 편집자들이 방영될 장면을 고를 수 있다. 이는 시청자들이 사건을 바라보는 방식을 바꾸어 놓는다.

Exercises with Short Passages

Exercise 1 1 Ⓒ 2 Ⓑ 3 Ⓓ 4 Ⓐ p.150

해석

황색 저널리즘

1890년대 뉴욕시에는 두 곳의 주요 신문사가 있었다. 바로 *월드*와 *저널*이었다. 두 곳 모두 부자들이 소유하고 있었다. 조셉 퓰리처가 *월드*를 소유했고, 윌리엄 랜돌프 허스트가 *저널*을 소유했다. *월드*의 발행부수가 더 높았다. 실제로 미국에서 가장 높은 발행부수였다. 하지만 *저널*과 치열한 경쟁을 벌이고 있었다.

더 많은 독자들을 모으기 위해 두 신문사 모두 다양한 전략을 사용했다. 선정적인 제목을 사용했다. 사건들은 종종 제대로 조사되지 않았다. 대신 황당한 주장을 하는 경우가 많았다. 기사는 결코 신뢰할 수 없는 것이었다. 그들은 또한 많은 삽화를 사용했다. 만화도 실었다. 이들의 방식은 황색 저널리즘이라고 알려지게 되었다. 오늘날 이 용어는 여전히 사용되고 있다. 사실 보다 선정성에 초점을 맞춘 타블로이드 신문들을 주로 가리킨다.

Exercise 2 1 Ⓐ 2 Ⓒ 3 Ⓐ 4 Ⓒ p.151

해석

백내장

백내장은 매우 흔하다. 백내장에 걸리면 수정체가 뿌옇게 된다. 60세 이상의 전체 인구 중 절반이 백내장에 걸린다. 안구 손상이 한 가지 원인일 수 있다. 하지만 가장 흔한 원인은 태양의 자외선이다. 한 연구에 따르면 비행기 조종사들은 백내장에 걸릴 위험이 크다. 고도가 높은 곳에 있을 때에는 태양빛이 안전하지 않을 수 있다. 일부 질병 또한 백내장을 일으킬 수 있다. 물론 노령에 의해서도 백내장이 발생할 수 있다. 시간이 지남에 따라 눈의 각 부분들이 약해진다. 한때는 의사들이 바늘을 이용해서 뿌연 부분을 제거했다. 현재에는 보통 수정체 전체를 플라스틱 렌즈로 대체한다. 대부분의 경우 환자들은 수술 당일에 퇴원할 수 있다.

Exercise 3 1 Ⓑ 2 Ⓒ 3 Ⓒ 4 Ⓐ p.152

해석

권리 장전

1789년에 미 헌법이 미국의 식민지들에 의해 채택되었다. 이로써 미합중국이 탄생했다. 미 헌법은 정부 부처의 다양한 역할들을 규정했다. 하지만 많은 미국인들은 그 이상이 필요하다고 생각했다. 그들은 사람들의 권리가 충분히 보장되지 않는다고 생각했다. 그래서 1791년에 권리 장전이 비준되었다. 여기에는 10개의 첫 수정 헌법 조항이 포함되어 있다. 이는 다수의 주요 권리들을 밝히고 있다. 가장 중요한 두 개는 언론의 자유와 무기를 소지할 수 있는 권리이다. 또 다른 수정 헌법 조항은 사람들이 신속한 재판을 받을 수 있는 권리를 부여한다. 사람들은 또한 종교 생활을 할 수 있는 권리를 갖는다. 사유 재산 역시 보호를 받는다. 권리 장전이 없다면 미합중국은 오늘날과 매우 다른 곳이 될 것이다.

Exercise 4 1 Ⓑ 2 Ⓒ 3 Ⓑ 4 Ⓐ p.153

해석

투우 경기의 말

매년 투우 경기에서 많은 말들이 부상을 당한다. 대개는 투우와 투우사에 관심이 집중된다. 관중들은 이들 각각의 용맹함과 기술에 찬사를 보낸다. 하지만 투우사가 말을 타는 경우도 있다. 말 역시 기술을 가지고 있다. 말은 투우사와 함께 경기에 참여하는 잘 훈련된 동물이다. 말과 투우사는 가장 간단한 명령만으로도 사방으로 빠르게 움직일 수 있다. 이는 성난 황소를 피할 때 필수적이다. 황소는 자기에게 고통을 주는 것이 인간이라는 점을 깨닫지 못한다. 말만 보일 뿐이다. 사람들은 말에 눈가리개가 씌워져 있다는 점과 귀에 귀마개가 들어 있다는 점을 모른다. 이로 인해 말은 황소를 보지도 못하고 황소의 소리를 듣지도 못한다. 만약 그런다면 말은 공포에 질리게 될 것이다. 경기장에서 말의 목숨은 투우사에게 달려 있다. 때때로 투우사가 민첩하지 못한 경우에는 황소가 말을 죽이기도 한다.

Exercises with Mid-Length Passages

Exercise 1 1 Ⓒ 2 Ⓐ 3 Ⓑ p.154

해석

보도의 기준

언론은 TV 뉴스 및 신문과 같은 뉴스의 출처이다. 언론은 사람들이 자유롭게 선택하고, 투표하고, 그리고 사고할 수 있도록 만든다. 언론은 정보가 유통되도록 만든다. 이러한 시스템이 작용하기 위해서는 기준이 있어야 한다. 좋은 보도는 피해, 진실, 프라이버시, 그리고 균형이라는 네 가지 개념을 통해 설명될 수 있다.

신문 기자는 피해에 대해 생각해야 한다. 기사 작성자는 자신이 질문을 함으로써 한 사람의 감정에 피해를 입힐 수 있다는 점을 유념해야 한다. 예를 들어 아이들은 감수성이 예민하기 때문에 주의해서 상대해야 한다. 기자는 사실을 수집할 때 아이가 어떤 영향을 받을지 생각해야 한다. 진실은 또 다른 문제이다. 기자는 사실을 보도할 때 가능한 실수를 하지 않도록 노력해야 한다. 사실은 의견과 다른 방식으로 말해져야 한다. 이로써 독자들이 더 나은 결정을 내릴 수 있다.

프라이버시 또한 문제이다. 기자는 대중들의 알 권리와 개인의 사생활에 대한 권리 사이에서 균형을 찾아야 한다. 정치인과 같은 공인들은 일반인과 동일한 권리를 갖지 않는다. 균형 역시 필요하다. 가능하다면 사건의 양쪽 당사자 이야기를 모두 들어야 한다. 사건의 한쪽 당사자 이야기만 듣는 경우, 해당 기자는 특정 인물의 편을 드는 것처럼 보일 수도 있다.

Exercise 2 1 Ⓐ 2 Ⓒ 3 Ⓓ p.156

해석

색맹

색맹은 대부분 남성에게 영향을 끼친다. 이러한 증상을 지닌 사람은 적색과 녹색을 같은 것으로 생각한다는 잘못된 인식이 있다. 그렇게 간단한 것은 아니다. 실제로 여러 가지 유형의 색맹이 존재한다.

눈의 한 부분인 망막 때문에 색깔을 볼 수 있다. 망막에는 두 가지 종류의 세포, 즉 간상체와 추상체가 들어 있다. 간상체는 약한 불빛에서 볼 수 있도록 해 준다. 추상체는 보통 불빛에서 볼 수 있도록 해 준다. 추상체는 세 가지 유형으로 존재하는데, 이들 각각은 빛의 종류에 따라 각기 다른 민감도를 지닌다. 이 세 가지 추상체가 함께 기능을 하면 여러 가지 색깔들을 보게 된다. 한 개 이상의 추상체가 제 기능을 하지 못하면 색맹이 나타난다. 드물기는 하지만, 세 가지 추상체 모두 제 기능을 못하는 경우도 있다.

때때로 눈을 다쳐서 색맹이 생기기도 한다. 하지만 대부분의 경우 색맹은 유전이다. 해당 유전자는 X 염색체에 있다. 여성은 두 개의 X 염색체를 가지고 있기 때문에 두 염색체 모두가 영향을 받아야 증상이 나타난다. 남성은 X 염색체 하나와 Y 염색체 하나를 가지고 있다. 남성들은 하나의 X 염색체만 영향을 받아도 그렇게 된다.

Exercise 3 1 Ⓐ 2 Ⓒ 3 Ⓓ p.158

해석

분열된 국가의 링컨

아브라함 링컨은 미국의 운명을 결정짓는데 일조했다. 그는 남북 전쟁을 통해 미국에 도움을 주었다. 전쟁 때문에 노예제가 끝났다. 하지만 이것이 남북 전쟁의 목적은 아니었다. 남북 전쟁은 주들을 하나의 정부 아래에 통합시키기 위한 것이었다.

링컨이 집권했던 당시 많은 주들이 아직 형성되지 않은 상태였다. 미국 정부는 넓은 땅을 소유했지만, 주들로 나뉘어져 있지는 않았다. 이러한 땅은 준주라고 불렸다. 남부의 주들은 준주가 주가 될 때 노예제를 도입해야 한다고 생각했다. 그렇게 되면 국내 정치에서 자신들에게 도움이 될 것이었다. 북부의 주들은 노예제를 도입한 주들이 많아짐으로써 남부의 정치 권력이 더 커지는 것을 원하지 않았다. 링컨은 노예제가 미국을 분열시키는 모습을 볼 수 있었다. 그는 분열을 막을 수 있는 최선의 방법이 미국 전역에서 노예제를 폐지하는 것이라고 생각했다.

인종 차별에 대한 링컨의 개인적인 신념이 어떠했는지는 분명하지 않다. 하지만 그가 통합된 국가에 대한 굳은 신념을 가지고 있었던 것은 분명하다. 미합중국에 대한 신념이 있었다. 그래서 그는 대통령이 되자 노예제 폐지를 결심했다. 이렇게 되면 남부 주들의 경제 시스템이 바뀌게 될 것이었다. 그러면 남부 주들이 북부의 주들과 비슷하게 되어서 미국은 통합을 유지하게 될 것이었다.

Exercise 4 1 Ⓑ 2 Ⓐ 3 Ⓒ p.160

해석

투우

투우는 여러 라틴 국가의 문화의 일부이다. 포르투갈, 스페인, 그리고 프랑스에도 이러한 전통이 있다. 미 대륙의 국가들도 투우를 한다. 고대 로마와 그리스에서도 투우사와 투우 간에 결투가 이루어졌다. 몇몇 결투들은 보다 잔인한 경우도 있었다.

투우에서는 용기와 스타일이 높이 평가된다. 이는 투우사와 투우에게 해당된다. 투우 역시 존중받아야 할 중요한 참가자로 여겨진다. 투지가 약하거나 체력이 떨어지는 투우는 투우의 주인 및 경기에 치욕을 가져다 준다. 투우사의 기술이 부족한 경우, 관중들은 투우를 응원할 수도 있다. 투우사는 한 방에 투우를 쓰러뜨리고 투우의 뿔 사이에 서 있음으로써 자신의 능력을 나타내야 한다.

동물 학대에 대한 우려가 오랫동안 존재해 왔다. 사회 내 많은 사람들은 동물에게 고통을 주는 것이 잘못된 일이라고 생각한다. 오락을 위해 동물을 죽이는 것은 더더욱 부당한 일이다. 전통을 유지하기 위해, 프랑스 및 미국과 같은 몇몇 나라에서는 치명적이지 않은 투우 경기가 이루어진다. 프랑스인들은 투우의 뿔에 있는 꽃을 잡아야 한다. 미국의 투우사는 벨크로를 사용해서 투우에 창이 붙게 만든다.

Building Summary Skills

p.162

A

Exercise 1 Standards in Reporting

1 TV news and newspapers are examples of the press, and they give information that helps people choose, vote, and think.

3 Reporters must be careful not to harm the person they are writing about.

2 There are standards for a good press.

5 A reporter must also consider a person's privacy and try to tell both sides of a story.

4 A reporter must try to report the facts as closely as possible.

Exercise 2 Colorblindness

1 Colorblindness is mostly found in men.

3 When the cones do not work properly, it results in colorblindness.

2 The parts of the eye called cones help people see certain colors of light.

5 Most of the time, this condition is genetic, and it is passed on to children through the X chromosome.

4 Sometimes colorblindness happens because of an injury.

Exercise 3 Lincoln in a Divided Land

1 Abraham Lincoln came to power at a time when the United States was trying to decide on slavery.

4 This issue divided the North and the South.

2 Many southern states wanted new states to have slaves.

3 It would help increase their political power, but northern states did not want this.

5 Lincoln thought it was best to end slavery in the whole country because he believed that the country should be united.

Exercise 4 Bullfighting

1 Bullfighting is an old tradition in some countries.

2 Courage, form, and style are very important in this sport for both man and bull.

5 Some countries have bullfights that do not hurt the bull.

4 Some people think this sport is cruel because it is not fair to make animals suffer.

3 If the bullfighter has poor skills, the crowd will cheer for the bull, so the bullfighter must show his skill by killing the bull quickly.

B

Exercise 1 Standards in Reporting

TV news and newspapers are examples of the press, and they give information that helps people choose, vote, and think. There are standards for a good press. Reporters must be careful not to harm the person they are writing about. A reporter must try to report the facts as closely as possible. A reporter must also consider a person's privacy and try to tell both sides of a story.

Exercise 2 Colorblindness

Colorblindness is mostly found in men. The parts of the eye called cones help people see certain colors of light. When the cones do not work properly, it results in colorblindness. Sometimes colorblindness happens because of an injury. Most of the time, this condition is genetic, and it is passed on to children through the X chromosome.

Exercise 3 Lincoln in a Divided Land

Abraham Lincoln came to power at a time when the United States was trying to decide on slavery. Many southern states wanted new states to have slaves. It would help increase their political power, but northern states did not want this. This issue divided the North and the South. Lincoln thought it was best to end slavery in the whole country because he believed that the country should be united.

Exercise 4 Bullfighting

Bullfighting is an old tradition in some countries. Courage, form, and style are very important in this sport for both man and bull. If the bullfighter has poor skills, the crowd will cheer for the bull, so the bullfighter must show his skill by killing the bull quickly. Some people think this sport is cruel because it is not fair to make animals suffer. Some countries have bullfights that do not hurt the bull.

Mini TOEFL iBT Practice Test

p.164

1 Ⓐ 2 Ⓑ 3 Ⓑ 4 Ⓓ 5 Ⓐ
6 Ⓐ

7 Ⓒ 8 Ⓒ 9 Ⓐ 10 Ⓓ 11 Ⓑ
12 Ⓓ

해석

[1-6]

FDA

FDA은 미국 식품 의약국의 통상적인 명칭이다. 이는 소비재의 안전을 책임지는 정부 기관이다. 식품 및 식품 유통을 규제한다. 건강 보조 식품도 규제한다. FDA는 의약품 및 의료 기기의 안전성과 효과를 확인하는 일도 담당한다.

의약품 및 의료 기기가 승인을 받기 위해서는 긴 과정을 거쳐야 한다. 여러 가지 엄격한 테스트가 존재한다. 우선, 인간이 사용하는 모든 것은 동물 실험을 거쳐야 한다. 최대 6년이 걸릴 수도 있다. 그 다음으로 소수의 사람들에게 테스트를 해야 한다. 15명에서 20명의 사람들을 대상으로 한 테스트는 최대 1년 반 동안 진행될 수 있다. 세 번째로 100명에서 500명 정도의 중간 규모의 그룹이 이용된다. 종종 2년 정도 걸린다. 마지막으로 3년에 걸쳐 대규모 그룹을 대상으로 한 테스트가 이루어진다. 개발된 5,000종의 약품 당 불과 5개만이 임상 시험을 거친다. 이 중에서 단 한 개만 시판이 된다.

인삼과 같은 식품 보조제는 다른 경로를 밟는다. 의약품의 경우와 달리 FDA는 이들에 대해 예비 테스트를 하지 않는다. 제품이 안전하지 않지만 이미 판매되고 있는 경우에만 기관이 이들 제품을 규제한다. 두 가지 예외는 유아용 식품과 환자용 식품이다. 이 제품을 사용하는 이들이 건강하지 못하기 때문에 이들 제품에 대해서는 FDA가 보다 신중을 기한다.

라벨링도 주요 사안이다. 라벨은 제품의 용도를 나타내야 한다. 의약품의 경우, 라벨은 의약품의 이름과 그 용도를 나타내야 한다. 또한 누가 약품을 복용해야 하는지를 상세히 알려 주고 부작용도 설명해 주어야 한다. 임산부, 아동, 혹은 노년층에 대한 지시 사항도 상세히 나타내야 한다. 또한 안전 정보도 포함하고 있어야 한다. FDA의 임무는 위험으로부터 대중들을 보호하는 것이다. FDA는 이를 규제와 라벨링을 통해 달성하고 있다. 의약품에 대해서는 효능에 관한 기준이 세워져 있다. 또한 정보가 공유되는 방식에 대해서도 기준이 세워져 있다.

[7-12]

장기 이식

1954년, 의사들이 전에 결코 해내지 못했던 일을 해냈다. 어떤 사람으로부터 신장을 꺼냈다. 그런 다음 이를 다른 사람의 신체에 이식했다. 이것이 최초의 장기 이식이었다.

장기 이식은 수술을 필요로 한다. 수술을 통해 건강하지 않은 장기가 건강한 장기로 대체된다. 건강한 장기는 다른 사람으로부터 나온다. 이 사람을 장기 제공자라고 부른다. 많은 경우, 이러한 사람은 최근에 사망한 사람이다. 하지만 신장 이식과 같은 일부 경우에는 살아 있는 사람일 수도 있다.

최초의 신장 이식이 이루어진 후, 의사들은 그러한 과정에 대해 매우 많은 것을 알게 되었다. 1960년대에는 간, 심장, 그리고 췌장 이식이 이루어졌다. 1980년대에는 폐와 장 이식이 이루어졌다. 모든 이식이 성공적인 것은 아니었다. 일부 경우, 수술을 받던 환자가 사망하기도 했다. 하지만 의사들의 숙련도가 높아짐에 따라 성공률도 높아졌다.

장기 이식의 주요한 문제는 수혜자의 면역 체계가 이식을 거부할 수도 있다는 점이다. 의사들은 수혜자와 제공자가 유전학적으로 거의 일치해야 한다는 점을 알아냈다. 만약 그렇지 않은 경우에는 신체가 이식을 거부할 것이다. 최근에 다양한 약품들이 개발되었다. 이들은 신체의 면역 체계를 억누를 수 있다. 따라서 신체가 장기를 거부하지 못한다. 하지만 면역 체계가 대처하지 못하는 감염병을 신체가 겪게 될 가능성이 높아진다.

2022년을 기준으로 미국에서는 백만 건의 장기 이식이 이루어졌다. 또한 보다 많은 사람들이 사망 시 장기 제공을 약속하고 있다. 그렇게 하면 신체의 일부가 도움이 필요한 사람들을 돕는데 사용될 수 있다. 의사들은 또한 동물들의 장기로도 실험을 하고 있다. 예를 들어 2022년에는 어떤 사람이 돼지의 심장을 이식받기도 했다. 이 환자는 두어 달 후 사망했다. 하지만 의사들은 미래에는 성공할 것으로 믿고 있다.

Vocabulary Check-Up p.168

1 Ⓒ	2 Ⓐ	3 Ⓓ	4 Ⓒ	5 Ⓑ
6 Ⓓ	7 Ⓑ	8 Ⓒ	9 Ⓐ	10 Ⓓ

UNIT 08 Insert Text

Basic Drill p.172

Drill 1 1

해석

괴롭힘은 비열한 행동이다. 이는 어떤 사람이 자신보다 약한 사람을 위협하거나 때릴 때 일어난다. [가해자들은 보통 계속해서 사람을 때린다.] 아이들의 경우 이러한 일은 보통 주변에 어른이 없을 때 일어난다. 가해자는 피해자에게 욕을 하고 이들이 하는 행동을 놀려 댄다. 피해자의 친구들에게 피해자에 관한 험담을 할 수도 있다. 심지어 피해자의 물건을 훔칠 수도 있다. 아이들이 이러한 행동을 계속 이어나갈 수 없도록 괴롭힘은 어린 나이에 중단되어야 한다.

Drill 2 1

해석

W.B. 예이츠는 아일랜드의 시인이었다. [그는 1865년에 태어났다.] 그는 사랑, 아일랜드 신화, 마법, 그리고 영혼에 관한 시를 썼다. 예이츠는 현대 영시에서 가장 중요한 시인 중 한 명이지만, 전통적인 형태의 시를 쓰는 것을 좋아했다. 그는 옛 시인들이 사용했던 압운과 운율을 사용하는 것을 좋아했다. 그의 시에서는 당당하고 세월이 흘러도 변함이 없는 느낌을 받을 수 있다. 예이츠는 인간의 경험을 이해할 수 있는 방법을 가지고 있었다. 그의 사상이 너무나 많은 추앙을 받았기 때문에 그는 정계에서도 영향력을 행사했다.

Drill 3 3

해석

인간 복제는 몇 가지 문제를 일으킨다. 우선, 유일하다는 것이 무엇을 의미하는지 생각해 보아야 한다. 유일하다는 것은 인간의 중요한 특징이다. [사실 그것은 모든 생물에게 필요한 특징이기도 하다.] 유일한 인간으로서, 자아에 대한 사람의 의식은 모든 것의 중심이 된다. 만약 어떤 사람이 다른 사람으로부터 복제된 경우, 정체성에 대한 그 사람의 개념은 바뀔 것이다. 이는 좋은 일이 아닐 수도 있다. 또한 관계에 대해서도 생각해 보아야 한다. 누군가가 복제되면 한 사람의 인생에만 영향을 미치는 것이 아니다. 주변 사람들의 인생 또한 영향을 받는다.

Drill 4 2

해석

관습법은 영국의 법률 체제이다. 관습법은 전 세계 여러 국가에서 사용된다. 법원의 판결은 과거의 판례에 기초한다. [다시 말해, 이러한 사법 시스템은 역사를 고려한다.] 관습법의 특징 가운데 하나는 배심원에 의한 재판이다. 한 그룹의 사람들이 다른 사람의 유죄 여부를 결정한다. 또 다른 특징은 어느 누구도, 심지어 대통령도, 법 위에 존재하지 않는다는 점이다. 대통령도 보통 사람들과 마찬가지로 법을 따라야 한다.

Drill 5 3

해석

이집트에 있는 알렉산드리아의 중요성을 둘러싼 논란이 존재한다. 이는 이 도시가 지식의 중심지로서 더 중요했는지, 아니면 상업의 중심지로서 더 중요했는지와 관련이 있다. 어떤 사람들은 이곳이 지식의 중심지로서 더욱 중요했다고 말한다. 이곳에는 유명한 도서관이 있었다. 한때 세계에서 가장 큰 도서관이었다. 각국의 학자들이 이곳으로 모여들었다. 현재 우리가 알고 있는 지식에 기여한 바가 크다. 이곳이 무역 때문에 보다 중요했다고 말하는 사람들도 있다. 이집트에서 생산된 많은 곡물들이 알렉산드리아에서 판매되었다. [이로써 굶주린 나라들에게 식량이 공급되었고 이 도시는 부유해졌다.] 이러한 점 때문에 이 도시는 막대한 힘을 얻게 되었다.

Exercises with Short Passages

Exercise 1 1 Ⓑ 2 Ⓐ 3 4 p.174

해석

윈스턴 처칠

윈스턴 처칠은 영국의 유명한 지도자였다. 그는 정치가 및 전쟁 영웅의 집안 출신이었다. 어렸을 때에는 학업 성적이 좋지 못했다. 하지만 나이가 들수록 군사학에 매료되었다. 그는 왕립 육군 사관 학교에서 학급 석차 8위로 졸업을 했다. 그 다음에는 인도에 주둔한 영국 육군에 입대해서 군인의 기술을 익혔다. 그에게는 좋은 경험이 되었다. 그 후에 제대를 해서 기자로서 남아프리카로 갔다. 그는 네덜란드와 영국 간의 전쟁을 취재하고 싶었다. 처칠은 자신이 군인이 아니었음에도 불구하고 전투를 하고자 했다. 그는 네덜란드 군대에 포로로 잡혔다. [감옥 생활은 그에게 힘든 경험이었다.] 한 달 후 그는 탈출을 했고, 수백 마일을 가로질러서 우방국에 도착했다. 그는 영웅이 되어 영국으로 돌아왔다. 처칠은 의원 선거에 출마해서 당선이 되었다. 이것이 그의 유명한 정치 경력의 시작이었다.

Exercise 2 1 Ⓑ 2 Ⓓ 3 4 p.175

해석

여성에 대한 사회적 압력

여성에게는 예뻐야 하고 성공해야 한다는 커다란 사회적 압력이 존재한다. 이는 여성들에게 많은 스트레스를 줄 수 있다. 이들은 미디어로부터 자신들이 영화배우처럼 예쁘게 보여야 한다는 점을 알게 된다. 아름다움은 자기 스스로가 결정하는 것이 아니라 다른 사람들이 결정하는 것이라는 것을 알게 된다. 이는 또 다른 메시지와 충돌한다. 여성들은 일에서도 독립적이어야 하고 성공해야 한다는 것이다. 기본적으로 여성들은 강하고, 똑똑하고, 그리고 자신의 업무를 매우 잘 해내야 한다. 16세에서 25세 사이의 많은 여성들이 이로 인해 커다란 압박감을 느낀다고 생각한다. [많은 경우, 이들은 우울해질 수도 있다.] 이들은 신경을 그처럼 많이 쓰고 싶지는 않지만, 신경을 쓰지 않는 것은 불가능하다고 말한다. 30세 정도가 되면 스트레스는 줄어든다. 여성들은 다른 사람이 생각하는 것에 그다지 신경을 쓰지 않게 된다.

Exercise 3 1 Ⓑ 2 Ⓓ 3 4 p.176

해석

에즈라 파운드

에즈라 파운드는 유명한 미국 시인이었다. 미국에서 자랐지만 유럽에서 여러 해를 보냈다. 그는 시각 예술가들과 중국의 고전 시가로부터 영향을 받았다. 그의 시는 복잡하면서도 섬세했다. 에즈라는 런던에서 몇 년간 생활했다. 그곳에서 자신의 영웅이었던 W.B. 예이츠를 만났다. 그들은 함께 시를 썼다. [이들은 서로의 작품에 막대한 영향을 미쳤다.] 에즈라 파운드는 또한 제임스 조이스, 그리고 T.S. 엘리엇과도 함께 작업을 했다. 1차 세계 대전이 끝나고 파운드는 이탈리아로 갔다. 그는 이탈리아 예술을 사랑했다. 또한 당시의 이탈리아 사회가 훌륭하고 도덕적인 사회라고 생각했다. 자본주의에 의해 파괴되지 않은 상태였다. 2차 세계 대전 당시 그는 미군에 체포되었다. 그들은 그가 미국에 적대적인 발언을 했다고 주장했다. 그 결과 그는 감옥에 수감되었다. 이 12년 동안 그는, 주변 삶에 대한 자신의 감상을 나타내는, 믿기 힘들 정도로 뛰어난 시들을 지을 수 있었다.

Exercise 4 1 Ⓑ 2 Ⓓ 3 3 p.177

해석

훌리거니즘

훌리건은 스포츠 경기에서 문제를 일으키는 사람들이다. 이들은 싸움을 유발하는 스포츠 팬이다. 종종 경기장 주변 지역에 피해를 입히기도 한다. "훌리건"이라는 용어는 1898년 런던 경찰의 보고서에서 처음 사용되었다. 이러한 폭력은 오랜 역사를 가지고 있다. 532년에는 일주일 간 계속된 싸움으로 수천 명이 목숨을 잃었다. 이는 한 경주의 팬들에 의해 시작되었다. 현대에는 축구팬들의 폭력이 가장 큰 문제가 되고 있다. 이는 1950년대 이후로 영국에서 계속되어 왔다. 이탈리아도 비슷한 문제를 겪어 왔다. 이러한 폭력은 다른 국가로도 확대되었다. [어떤 경우에는 이 때문에 국가 대표 경기를 거의 망칠 뻔했다.] 이로 인해 비폭력적인 팬들도 안전하게 스포츠를 즐길 수가 어렵게 되었다. 또한 폭력으로 인해 축구장 주변의 상점들도 안전하게 영업을 하기가 힘들다. 많은 국가들이 이러한 문제를 일으키는 팬들을 처벌하기 위해 엄격한 법을 마련해 놓고 있다.

Exercises with Mid-Length Passages

Exercise 1 1 A1 2 B1 p.178

해석

베티 프리던

베티 프리던은 미국 여성들의 권리를 주장했다. 그녀의 인생 경험과 교육 덕분에 그녀는 강력한 목소리를 낼 수 있었다. 그녀는 여성에 대한 사회의 인식을 변화시킬 수 있었다.

프리던은 1921년에 태어났다. 그녀는 스미스 대학에서 심리학을 공부했다. 또한 대학 신문사에서도 일을 했다. 프리던은 UC 버클리에서 대학원 과정을 밟을 수 있는 기회를 포기했다. [대신 노동자들의 권리에 관한 글을 쓰고 싶어했다.] 프리던은 결혼을 해서 세 자녀를 낳았다. 그녀는 주부들을 위한 잡지에 글을 쓰기 시작했다. 그녀는 지루해 했고 행복을 느끼지 못했다. 가정 생활에서는 자신의 능력을 발휘할 수 없었다.

1957년에 프리던은 삶에 대한 만족 여부를 알아보기 위해 스미스 대학의 대학원생들에게 질문을 했다. 그녀는 그중 다수가 만족하지 않는다는 점을 알게 되었다. [이러한 여성들은 자신의 중요성을 전혀 느끼지 못했다.] 그들의 삶은 단지 남편과 자녀의 성공을 위해 존재했다. 프리던은 사회가 여성들로 하여금 어떻게 가정에 머물도록 강요하는지에 대한 글을 썼다. 여성들은 가족을 위해 살아야 했고 흥미롭고 도전적인 직업을 가져서는 안 되었다. *여성의 신비*라는 그녀의 책은 매우 유명해졌다. 12년 후 그녀와 그녀의 남편은 이혼을 했다. 프리던은 여성의 새로운 이미지를 만드는 일을 계속했다. 그녀는 여성들이 단순히 아내가 되는 것에 머무르지 않고 더 많은 방법으로 사회에 참여해야 한다고 생각했다. 그녀는 여성과 남성이 동등한 관계에 있어야 한다고 주장했다.

Exercise 2 1 A3 2 B4 p.179

해석

소아 비만

많은 사람들의 경우 어렸을 때 보통 살이 찐다. 하지만 비만은 지방이 너무 많다는 의미를 나타낸다. 이러한 문제가 있는 아이들은 성인이 되어서도 이러한 상태에 머물러 있을 수 있다. 이는 장기간 지속되는 건강상의 문제를 야기한다. 미국에서는 약 15%의 아동이 비만이다. [이러한 수치는 1970년대 이후로 증가하고 있다.] 어떤 아이들은 다른 아이들에 비해 비만에 걸릴 위험성이 더 크다. 비만 가족력은 한 가지 위험 요소이다. 흡연이나 게으른 생활 방식 또한 위험 요소이다.

비만은 단순히 개인적인 문제가 아니다. 사회적인 문제이다. 비만인 사람은 물론 건강상의 문제를 겪는다. 하지만 비만 인구가 너무 많은 경우, 사회가 그 비용을 부담하기 시작한다. 의료 보험료가 더 많이 들고, 학교에서 더 많은 문제가 발생하며, 그리고 사람들의 생산성도 떨어진다.

비만의 일부 원인들은 사회적인 것이다. 학교에서는 건강한 생활을 선택할 수 없다. 학교 내에서 식품 회사가 정크 푸드를 광고하고 판매하는 것이 허용된다. 설상가상으로, 많은 학교들이 예산 문제로 체육 프로그램을 줄여야 한다. [그 결과, 아이들은 운동을 충분히 하지 못한다.] 집에서는 아이들이 TV를 너무 많이 시청하며 여러 가지 비디오 게임을 한다. 부모들 또한 잘 먹지 않는다. 부모는 좋은 생활 습관이 무엇인지 보여 주어야 한다. 좋지 않은 음식을 너무 많이 사서는 안 된다. 어렸을 때 건강한 습관을 기르도록 가르치는 것이 중요하다.

Exercise 3 1 A1 2 B3 p.180

해석

비극의 문학적 형태

비극은 희곡의 몇 가지 종류 중 하나이다. 이 문학 형식은 수천 년 동안 서양 문화의 일부를 이루어 왔다.

[비극에는 몇 가지 핵심 요소들이 있다.] 비극은 좋지 못한 일을 겪고 있는 영웅에 관한 이야기이다. 이러한 악재는 영웅의 행동과 관련이 있다. 이는 비극적 결함이라고 불리는 영웅의 성격상 약점 때문에 보통 발생한다. 많은 경우, 신들이 영웅 때문에 분노한다. 신들은 영웅으로 하여금 악재를 겪으며 살도록 만든다. 이는 특히 잔인한 것으로, 영웅은 고통을 겪어야 한다. 관객들이 영웅의 약점을 이해하기 위해서는 이러한 악재를 지켜보아야 한다. 또한 영웅의 고통도 지켜보아야 한다.

어느 시점이 되면 영웅은 자신의 잘못을 깨닫는다. 일종의 학습 과정을 거친다. 그렇게 되면 신들은 그에 대한 처벌을 멈추기로 결정한다. 희곡에서 신이 하늘로부터 내려와 계시를 내릴 수도 있다. 그래서 영웅을 고통에서 해방시켜 준다. 관객들은 공포감에서 안도감으로 감정의 변화를 경험한다. 이것을 카타르시스라고 한다. 이는 감정적 치유를 의미한다. [그리스 시인들은 이것이 훌륭한 비극에 필요한 부분이라고 생각했다.] 이러한 단순한 아이디어들이 수천 년 동안 계속되어 왔다.

Exercise 4 1 A1 2 B1 p.181

해석

패럴림픽

패럴림픽은 올림픽이 열리는 해마다 개최된다. [올림픽이 끝나고 3주 후에 시작된다.] 경기는 선수들이 자신의 기량을 선보일 수 있는 기회이다. 그러나 이 선수들은 다르다. 이들의 신체는 어떤 식으로든 장애를 겪고 있다. 선수들은 정규 올림픽의 선수들이 사용했던 경기장과 운동장을 그대로 사용한다. 접두사 *para*는 그리스어로 "곁에"라는 뜻을 나타낸다.

패럴림픽에 참가하기 위해서는 선수가 장애를 가지고 있어야 한다. 다섯 가지 유형이 있다. 일부는 팔이나 다리를 가지고 있지 않다. 일부는 뇌에 손상을 입었다. 이들은 균형 감각이 떨어진다. 일부 선수들은 휠체어를 타고 있다. 일부는 시각 장애인이다. 일부는 선천적인 장애를 지니고 있다. 이러한 경기에서 대단한 것은 기량에 관심이 모아진다는 점이다. 그들의 장애에 초점이 맞춰지지 않는다.

이 스포츠 대회는 영국에서 처음 시작되었다. 2차 세계 대전에서 부상당하고 돌아온 영국의 군인들을 위한 대회였다. [곧 다른 나라에서도 선수들을 보내기 시작했다.] 최초의 공식 패럴림픽은 1960년에 개최되었다. 400명의 선수들이 참가했다. 가장 최근에 열린 하계 올림픽에는 160여 개국에서 온 4,000명 이상의 선수들이 참가했다.

Building Summary Skills

p.182

A

Exercise 1 Betty Friedan

1 Betty Friedan was a feminist, and she argued for women to be treated fairly in society and in marriage.

3 She asked other female college graduates how they felt.

2 Friedan had a family, but she was not happy with her life as a housewife.

5 She said women should take part in society more actively and be seen as equal to men.

4 Friedan discovered that they felt the same way, so she wrote a book about it.

Exercise 2 Child Obesity

1 Children with obesity might have long-lasting health risks.

4 Obesity also affects society because it affects the cost of health care and creates social problems.

2 There are more children today with this problem than in the 1970s.

5 People can change how schools and companies operate to decrease the risk of obesity, and they should make better food choices and promote good behavior.

3 Some children are more likely to be obese than others.

Exercise 3 The Literary Form of Tragedy

1 A tragedy is a traditional form of theater.

4 The audience experiences a range of emotions while watching the play.

2 It has a hero who, because of his personality, gets put into a bad situation where he must suffer.

5 This emotional change is a key part of tragedy, and this form of drama has lasted for thousands of years.

3 The hero learns from his ways, and the gods stop his punishment.

Exercise 4 The Paralympics

1 The Paralympics give disabled athletes the chance to show their skills.

2 Only certain kinds of disabilities are permitted in the games.

4 The games first started in England after World War II with just a few people.

5 Years later, there are more than 4,000 athletes and 160 countries competing.

3 The important thing is that the disability is not the focus, but excellence in sports is the focus.

B

Exercise 1 Betty Friedan

Betty Friedan was a feminist, and she argued for women to be treated fairly in society and in marriage. Friedan had a family, but she was not happy with her life as a housewife. She asked other female college graduates how they felt. Friedan discovered that they felt the same way, so she wrote a book about it. She said women should take part in society more actively and be seen as equal to men.

Exercise 2 Child Obesity

Children with obesity might have long-lasting health risks. There are more children today with this problem than in the 1970s. Some children are more likely to be obese than others. Obesity also affects society because it affects the cost of health care and creates social problems. People can change how schools and companies operate to decrease the risk of obesity, and they should make better food choices and promote good behavior.

Exercise 3 The Literary Form of Tragedy

A tragedy is a traditional form of theater. It has a hero who, because of his personality, gets put into a bad situation where he must suffer. The hero learns from his ways, and the gods stop his punishment. The audience experiences a range of emotions while watching the play. This emotional change is a key part of tragedy, and this form of drama has lasted for thousands of years.

Exercise 4 The Paralympics

The Paralympics give disabled athletes the chance to show their skills. Only certain kinds of disabilities are permitted in the games. The important thing is that the disability is not the focus, but excellence in sports is the focus. The games first started in England after World War II with just a few people. Years later, there are more than 4,000 athletes and 160 countries competing.

Mini TOEFL iBT Practice Test p.184

1 Ⓐ 2 Ⓓ 3 Ⓑ 4 Ⓑ 5 Ⓓ
6 4

7 Ⓐ, Ⓓ 8 Ⓓ 9 Ⓑ 10 Ⓐ 11 Ⓑ
12 4

해석

[1-6]

윌리엄 스미스

윌리엄 스미스는 1700년대 후반에 살았다. 그는 엔지니어였다. 그의 단순한 발견이 평생의 업적으로 이어졌다. 그는 영국의 지질학 지도를 만들고 싶어했다.

스미스는 영국 서부에서 농사를 짓던 한 가정에서 태어났다. 그의 아버지는 그가 어렸을 때 사망했다. 스미스는 삼촌에 의해 키워졌다. 그가 기본적인 교육을 받기는 했지만, 지리학은 책을 보면서 독학을 했다. 그는 살던 곳 근처에서 자신이 발견한 화석에 일찍이 관심을 나타냈다. 스미스는 어른이 되어 엔지니어가 되었다. 토질을 검사하는 석탄 회사에서 일을 했다. 그는 물을 빼내고 그곳 땅을 파내기가 얼마나 쉬운지 알아내야 했다. [이러한 일로 그는 한 가지 발견을 하게 되었다.]

스미스는 석탄 회사를 위한 수로를 건설해야 했다. 그는 땅을 파다가 토양이 여러 층으로 이루어져 있다는 점을 알게 되었다. 각 층마다 특정 종류의 화석이 있다는 사실을 발견했다. 그는 영국을 돌아다니면서 동일한 특징들을 발견했다. 스미스는 영국 북쪽의 지층이 남쪽의 지층과 연결되어 있다고 믿었다. 그는 이러한 층들이 땅의 오래된 역사를 알려 준다는 점을 이해했다. 스미스는 곧 영국 각지를 돌아다녔다. 매년 지층을 관찰하기 위해 말과 마차로 수천 마일씩 여행을 하기도 했다.

스미스는 자신의 지식을 모든 사람들과 공유하기 위해 최선을 다했다. 그는 영국의 여러 지역에 어떤 종류의 바위, 흙, 식물이 분포하는지를 알려 주는 지도를 만들었다. 그는 농부들의 모임에서, 그리고 디너 파티에서 이야기를 했다. 또한 몇 권의 책도 썼다. 스미스는 기술이 매우 뛰어났다. 그가 지질의 특징을 관찰하기 위해 사용했던 여러 방법들은 오늘날에도 사용되고 있다. 그의 지도는 매우 정확해서 오늘날에도 사용이 가능하다. 그가 만든 많은 지질학 용어들 역시 여전히 사용되고 있다.

[7-12]

고대 이집트의 스포츠

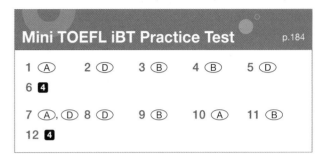

고대 이집트의 많은 스포츠들이 오늘날에도 실시되고 있다. 사실, 규칙 및 유니폼 같은 스포츠의 기본 요소 중 많은 것들이 이집트인들에 의해 처음 사용되었다. 스포츠는 사회에서 중요한 기능을 했다. 어떤 스포츠들은 재미와 건강 유지

를 위해 실시되었다. 보다 강력한 전사와 지도자를 배출하기 위해 실시된 스포츠도 있었다.

주로 재미를 위한 첫 번째 그룹의 스포츠에는 조정, 사냥, 그리고 높이뛰기와 같은 스포츠가 포함되었다. 사냥과 낚시는 왕과 일반 백성들도 즐길 수 있었다. 조정도 마찬가지였다. 조정에서는 강한 힘이 요구되었다. 여러 사람이 보트 안에 들어가 리더의 명령을 따랐다. 리더는 언제 노를 저어야 하는지를 알려 주기 위해 규칙적이면서도 날카로운 소리를 질렀다. 이러한 기술은 오늘날에도 조정팀에서 사용되고 있다. 또 다른 인기 종목은 줄다리기였다. 이는 두 팀이 줄 하나를 서로 자기 쪽으로 끌어당기는 경기이다. 앞으로 넘어지는 팀이 진다. 이 게임은 오늘날에도 여러 나라에서 실시되고 있다.

두 번째 그룹의 스포츠는 군대와 사원에서 쓸 인재를 기르기 위한 것이었다. 여기에는 권투, 승마, 달리기, 그리고 양궁이 포함되었다. 이들은 전투 기술을 익힐 수 있는 방법이었다. 또한 정신력 및 영력을 키울 수 있는 방법이기도 했다. 마라톤은 그에 대한 좋은 사례였다. [왕은 자신에게 나라를 이끌 정신력이 있다는 점을 나타내기 위해 달리곤 했다.] 하키는 또 다른 이집트의 경기였다. 사람들이 매장되어 있는 곳에서 이러한 경기를 나타내는 그림이 있다. 선수들은, 현대의 하키 스틱과 똑같은, 끝이 구부러진 나뭇가지를 들고 있었다. 이들은 밝은 색이 칠해진, 가죽으로 만든 공을 사용했다.

이러한 스포츠들은 이집트 문화의 일부였다. 스포츠 덕분에 사람들은 행복하고 건강할 수 있었다. 기본적인 규칙들은 수천 년 전에 만들어졌다. 이러한 규칙들은 오늘날에도 여전히 어떤 형태로든 존재한다.

Vocabulary Check-Up p.188

1 Ⓑ 2 Ⓐ 3 Ⓓ 4 Ⓒ 5 Ⓑ
6 Ⓐ 7 Ⓒ 8 Ⓑ 9 Ⓑ 10 Ⓓ

PART III Reading to Learn

UNIT 09 Prose Summary

Basic Drill p.194

Drill 1 2, 3

해석

희소성은 어떤 것을 충분히 가질 수 없음을 의미한다. 희소한 것이 필요한 경우에는 무엇을 해야 할지 결정해야 한다. 예를 들어 휘발유가 희소한 경우, 휘발유 가격은 올라간다. 그러면 인상된 가격을 지불할 것인지 결정해야 한다. 일부 경우, 인상된 가격을 지불하고 싶지 않을 수도 있다. 다른 곳에서 보다 저렴한 가격을 찾아볼 수 있을 것이다. 하지만 멀리 가야 할 수도 있다. 또한 휘발유 없이 사는 법을 익힐 수도 있을 것이다. 휘발유의 경우, 운전하는 횟수를 줄일 수 있을 것이다. 또한 자전거를 타거나 다른 사람들과 카풀을 할 수도 있다.

Drill 2 1, 3

해석

법의 철학을 법리학이라고 부른다. 이는 "법에 대한 지식"을 뜻한다. 이를 연구하는 사람들은 특정한 법이 존재하는 이유, 이들이 만들어지는 과정, 그리고 이들이 적용되는 방식을 이해하려고 한다. 법이 어떻게 사회에 영향을 미치는지 아는 것은 중요하다. 법을 공부하는 학생들은 현재 적용되는 법을 살펴볼 수 있다. 이로운 점 이외에도 예상하지 못했던 결과들이 나올 수 있다. 학생들은 또한 새로운 법의 개념도 공부할 수 있다. 범죄의 유형이 변하기 때문에 항상 새로운 법이 필요하다.

Drill 3 1, 2

해석

시중에서 사용되는 달러 지폐의 양은 통제되어야 한다. 정부가 화폐를 너무 많이 발행하면 물가가 오를 것이다. 처음에는 이것이 논리적으로 보이지 않는다. 하지만 돈이 많아지면 사람들이 쓸 수 있는 돈이 많아진다. 이러한 상황에서는 물가가 오르기 쉬운데, 그 이유는 사람들에게 구매력이 생기기 때문이다. 또 한 다른 효과도 나타난다. 화폐의 수량이 두 배로 증가하면 화폐 전체의 실제 가치는 절반으로 줄어든다. 그러한 경우, 고용주들이 전과 동일한 가치를 얻기 위해서는 노동자들에게 두 배의 임금을 지불해야 한다. 이러한 새로운 비용 때문에 물가는 오를 수밖에 없다.

Exercises with Short Passages

Exercise 1 1 Ⓒ 2 Ⓐ 3 1, 2 p.196

해석

음주 운전의 법적 책임

음주 운전은 교통 사고의 주요 원인이다. 술을 마신 운전자가 사고를 내면 여러 가지 일들이 일어난다. 운전자가 다른 사람을 다치게 하거나 재산상의 피해를 입히는 경우, 피해자는 운전자를 고소할 수 있다. 그 이유는 운전자가 자신의 행위에 대한 책임을 져야 하기 때문이다. 법률 용어로 "법적 책임"은 의무를 뜻한다. 하지만 법적 책임은 운전자에서 끝나지 않는다. 미국에서는 운전자가 술을 마신 술집에 대해서도 교통 사고의 피해자가 고소할 수 있다. 심지어 바텐더를 고소할 수도 있다. 술집은 운전자의 음주에 일조했기 때문에 사고와 관련해서는 술집에도 잘못이 있다고 생각되기 때문이다. 다시 말해 이러한 곳들은 매우 주의해야 한다. 사람들이 취하도록 만들어서는 안된다.

Exercise 2 1 Ⓐ 2 Ⓒ 3 [1], [3] p.197

해석

윤작의 이점

중세 시대 당시 윤작은 사회에 큰 발전을 가져다 주었다. 특별한 농법으로 농사가 이전보다 쉬워졌다. 이로써 인구가 증가했다. 그 원리는 간단했다. 식물은 종류에 따라 토양으로부터 흡수하는 양분이 서로 다르다. 또한 특정 종류의 곤충을 끌어들인다. 그렇기 때문에 농부가 항상 같은 장소에서 같은 작물만 키운다면 결국 토양에는 작물의 성장에 필요한 것들이 없어질 것이다. 자라는 것은 곤충들이 먹게 될 것이다.

중세 시대 사람들은 계절마다 같은 장소에 서로 다른 식물을 심으면 첫 번째 식물이 토양에서 가져간 것을 두 번째 식물이 보충해 준다는 점을 알게 되었다. 소가 잘 먹는 식물을 키우면 소의 ㅋ배설물이 토양에 추가적인 영양분을 가져다 주었다. 이는 새로운 발견이었다. 그래서 농사철마다 사람들은 서로 다른 작물을 심었다. 식물이 자라기에 더 좋은 토양이 만들어졌고, 식량 생산도 증가했다.

Exercise 3 1 Ⓐ 2 Ⓒ 3 [1], [3] p.198

해석

수면 장애

세 가지 유형의 수면 장애가 존재한다. 잠을 잘 수 없거나, 항상 잠을 자야 하거나, 혹은 호흡이 수면에 영향을 미치는 경우가 있다. 첫 번째 유형인 불면증은 잠을 잘 이루지 못하는 것을 의미한다. 수면에 들기가 어렵거나 혹은 계속 잠에서 깰 수도 있다. 낮 동안에는 졸음을 느끼거나 스트레스를 받을 수 있고, 집중하는데 어려움을 겪을 수도 있다. 두 번째 유형인 기면증은 수면병이라고 불린다. 이 경우 수면에 들어가는 시간을 제어할 수가 없는데, 심지어 낮에도 제어가 불가능하다. 실제로 흥분을 하는 경우에는 신체가 수면 상태에 들어가려고 한다. 깨어나면 움직이거나 말을 할 수 없다. 세 번째는 수면성 무호흡증이다. 이는 수면 시의 호흡 장애이다. 보통 목구멍이 닫히기 시작한다. 이는 알코올 섭취나 과다한 체중 때문에 일어날 수 있다. 근육이 충분히 제어를 하지 못한다. 뇌에서 호흡을 하라는 신호를 보내지 않는 경우도 있다. 그러다가 잠에서 깬다.

Exercise 4 1 Ⓑ 2 Ⓐ 3 [2], [4] p.199

해석

게임 이론

경제학자들은 선택의 사용을 연구한다. 이것을 게임 이론이라고 부른다. 결과는 관련된 모든 사람의 선택에 따라 달라진다. 때때로 사람들은 이기적인 결정을 내려야 한다. 그러한 결정으로 사람들의 삶은 더 나아질 것이지만 주변 사람들에게는 도움이 되지 않을 것이다. 심지어 그들에게 피해를 줄 수도 있다. 혹은 사람들이 모든 사람들에게 최선이지만 자신에게는 최선이 아닌 결정을 내리는 경우도 있다. 예를 들어 마을 전체에 쓰레기가 있다고 가정해 보자. 마을이 전혀 깨끗하게 보이지 않는다. 관광객들은 방문을 원하지 않는다. 상점 주인들은 야외에서 청소를 하는 것이 마을을 위한 최선책이라는 점에 동의한다. 한 가게의 주인이 청소를 해서 모두가 혜택을 받는다. 하지만 그 주인은 자신의 시간을 소비하고 있다. 그는 본인이 한 일에 대한 보수를 받지도 않으며, 아무도 그를 도와 주지 않는다.

Exercises with Mid-Length Passages

Exercise 1 [1], [2], [5] p.200

해석

미란다 원칙

미국의 법에 따르면 경찰이 자신에게 범죄에 대한 질문을 하는 경우 개인은 묵비권을 갖는다. 또한 범죄로 인해 감옥에 가야 하는 경우에는 변호사를 선임할 수 있는 권리도 갖는다. 이러한 권리를 갖는 이유는 간단하다. 경찰이 어떤 사람에게 그를 유죄로 만들 말을 하도록 강요할 수 없기 때문이다. 체포된 사람은 이를 알고 있어야 한다.

미란다 원칙은 어떤 사람이 체포된 경우에 경찰이 하는 말이다. 경찰은 "당신은 묵비권을 가지고 있습니다. 만약 그러한 권리를 포기한다면 당신이 하는 어떤 말도 법정에서 당신에게 불리하게 작용할 수 있습니다. 당신은 심문을 받는 동안 변호인을 이용할 수 있는 권리를 가지고 있습니다. 변호인을 선임할 여력이 없는 경우에는 국선 변호인이 선임될 것입니다. 심문을 받는 동안 원하는 경우 답변을 하지 않을 수도 있습니다."라고 말한다. 경찰은 체포된 사람에게 이를 확실히 이해시켜야 한다. 체포된 사람이 사용하는 언어로 미란다 원칙을 이야기해야 할 수도 있다.

경찰이 범죄자에게 그들의 권리를 제대로 알려 주지 않아서 범죄자들이 풀려나고 있다. 어느 사회에서나 기소된 사람들이 법과 자신의 권리를 아는 것이 중요하다. 이는 사회가 모든 사람들을 공정하게 대하도록 만들 수 있는 한 가지 방법이다.

Exercise 2 [1], [4], [6] p.201

해석

차 재배법

차는 많은 문화권에서 선호되는 음료이다. 이는 긴 역사를 가지고 있다. 한때는 중국의 남부와 인도의 북부에서만 차가 재배되었다. 지금은 전 세계에서 재배되고 있다.

차나무에서 차에 쓸 수 있는 좋은 잎이 나기까지 약 4년이 걸린다. 차나무는 보통 야생 상태에서 5미터에서 15미터 사이의 높이까지 자란다. 농장에서는 보통 2미터 높이로 유지된다. 이처럼 크기를 작게 하면 차나무에서 새로운 잎이 자주 나온다. 찻잎을 따는 시기는 3월부터 11월까지이다.

차나무는 다량의 물을 좋아한다. 이상적으로는 밤에 비가 내려야 한다. 그러면 차나무가 이를 흡수해서 다음날 햇빛을 받을 준비를 마친다. 낮은 길고 따뜻해야 하고 일조량이 많아야 한다. 햇빛과 물은 새잎이 지속적으로 자라나는데 필요한 것들에 차나무에 제공해 준다.

가장 좋은 찻잎들은 손으로 딴다. 대부분의 경우, 가장 부드러운 위쪽의 잎 두 개를 딴다. 차나무의 크기가 작기 때문에 어느 방향에서도 찻잎을 따기가 쉽다. 그 후 찻잎은 바구니로 옮겨져서 다음 단계를 밟게 된다.

Exercise 3 1, 4, 6 p.202

해석

비타민

비타민은 몸을 튼튼하게 만든다. 인체에 필요한 비타민은 13종류이다. 4개의 비타민은 지방을 통해 체내로 들어갈 수 있다. 나머지 9개는 물에 의해 섭취된다. 이들은 적절한 화학 반응이 일어날 수 있도록 만든다. 체내에 흡수된 음식을 신체가 이용할 수 있도록 만든다. 이러한 점은 성장기의 아이들에게 특히 중요하다. 성인들 역시 건강 유지를 위해 비타민을 필요로 한다.

아이들이 튼튼한 뼈와 조직을 갖기 위해서는 비타민이 필요하다. 아이들에게 비타민 D가 부족한 경우 뼈가 약해질 수 있다. 그러면 다리 뼈가 휘어질 수도 있다. 성인의 경우, 신경계가 작동하기 위해서는 비타민이 필요하다. 비타민을 섭취하지 않으면 여러 가지 질병에 걸릴 수 있다. 시력이 저하되고 심장 박동에 문제가 생길 수도 있다. 항상 무력감을 느낄 수도 있다.

사람들은 비타민 때문에 식단이 건강의 원인이라는 점을 백 년도 더 전에 알았다. 또한 나쁜 식단은 몇몇 질병의 원인이었다. 영국의 선원들은 괴혈병이라는 질병을 가지고 있었다. 피부에 반점이 생기고 입에서 피가 흘렀다. 이러한 일은 비타민 C가 부족했기 때문에 일어난 것이었다. 한 의사가 그 원인을 찾아내서 영국의 모든 선박에 레몬과 라임을 싣도록 했다.

Exercise 4 2, 4, 6 p.203

해석

펜실베이니아의 석탄

석탄은 막대한 에너지원이다. 국가들은 많은 돈을 들여 자국에 있는 석탄을 캔다. 미국의 동부 지역은 석탄 채굴의 전통이 있는 곳이다. 그러한 곳 중의 하나가 펜실베이니아이다. 이곳은 엄청난 양의 석탄이 나는 곳이지만, 또한 대규모 탄광 사고가 일어난 장소이기도 하다.

땅속에 묻힌 석탄을 캐내는 두 가지 방법이 있다. 첫 번째 방법은 지표면 아래에 구멍을 파는 것이다. 광부들이 길이가 수 마일에 이르는 터널을 판다. 두 번째 방법은 노천광이라고 불린다. 광부들은 원하는 곳에 도달할 때까지 넓은 지역의 지표면을 걷어낼 것이다.

펜실베이니아의 센트렐리아에는 품질이 매우 우수한 석탄이 생산된다. 다른 종류의 석탄보다 더 높은 온도로 연소된다. 이 도시에는 많은 노천광들이 있다. 불행하게도 오래된 노천 채굴장 근처에 시의 쓰레기 매립장이 있었다. 1962년, 쓰레기에 불이 붙었다. 이로써 노천광에도 불이 붙었다. 화재는 지하에서 시작되었는데, 이곳은 진화가 불가능했다. 우수한 품질의 석탄 때문에 사태는 더욱 악화되었다. 지하의 화재는 60년이 넘도록 꺼지지 않고 있다. 아무도 진압하는 법을 모른다. 전문가들은 250년 동안 계속해서 불이 꺼지지 않을 것이라고 생각한다.

Building Summary Skills p.204

A

Exercise 1 Miranda Rights

1 Miranda Rights remind people that they have the right to silence and a lawyer if police question them about a crime.

3 Criminals have been set free because the police failed to give them this warning.

2 The reason is that people do not have to say anything that will make them guilty of a crime.

4 All people—even criminals—must know their rights.

Exercise 2 How to Cultivate Tea

1 Tea is drunk all over the world.

4 The best tea is picked by hand.

2 The tea plant takes four years to mature and is kept small to ensure lots of leaves and easy picking.

3 It grows well in climates that are warm and wet.

5 The delicate top leaves are picked and carried in baskets to the next stage of processing.

Exercise 3 Vitamins

1 Vitamins are necessary for the body to build itself and to stay healthy.

5 Some diseases occur if people do not eat well.

2 Some are taken in through fat and others through water.

4 People have learned that their diets are the key to getting enough vitamins.

3 Children need vitamins to grow strong bones and organs, and adults need them for strong nervous systems.

Exercise 4 Pennsylvania's Coal

1 Pennsylvania has provided a lot of coal, which is an important fuel.

2 There are many coal mines there.

4 One of the coal mines caught fire and started burning underground.

3 Open mining was used in a town called Centralia, where there is high-quality coal.

5 It is impossible to put out the fire, and it may burn for 250 years.

B

Exercise 1 Miranda Rights

Miranda Rights remind people that they have the right to silence and a lawyer if police question them about a crime. The reason is that people do not have to say anything that will make them guilty of a crime. Criminals have been set free because police failed to give them this warning. All people—even criminals—must know their rights.

Exercise 2 How to Cultivate Tea

Tea is drunk all over the world. The tea plant takes four years to mature and is kept small to ensure lots of leaves and easy picking. It grows well in climates that are warm and wet. The best tea is picked by hand. The delicate top leaves are picked and carried in baskets to the next stage of processing.

Exercise 3 Vitamins

Vitamins are necessary for the body to build itself and to stay healthy. Some are taken in through fat and others through water. Children need vitamins to grow strong bones and organs, and adults need them for strong nervous systems. People have learned that their diets are the key to getting enough vitamins. Some diseases occur if people do not eat well.

Exercise 4 Pennsylvania's Coal

Pennsylvania has provided a lot of coal, which is an important fuel. There are many coal mines there. Open mining was used in a town called Centralia, where there is high-quality coal. One of the coal mines caught fire and started burning underground. It is impossible to put out the fire, and it may burn for 250 years.

Mini TOEFL iBT Practice Test

p.206

1 Ⓓ	2 Ⓐ	3 Ⓒ	4 Ⓓ	5 1, 3, 4
6 Ⓒ	7 Ⓐ	8 Ⓒ	9 Ⓑ	10 2, 3, 5

해석

[1-5]

유기 농업

유기 농업의 기본 개념은 화학 물질을 전혀 사용하지 않는 것이다. 농부들은 자연적인 방법을 이용해서 작물이 튼튼하게 자라도록 해야 하고 해충으로부터 작물을 보호해야 한다. 화학 물질을 사용하지 않으면 인간에게 보다 이로운 식품을 작물에서 얻게 될 것으로 생각된다. 하지만 이 개념은 그보다 더 크다. 유기 농업은 주변 환경에 있는 모든 동식물을 존중한다. 이러한 농업은 자연의 건강을 증진시킨다.

비료는 식물을 튼튼하게 만드는 화학 물질이다. 농부가 같은 장소에서 같은 작물을 반복적으로 심으면 그 토양에서는 작물이 양분을 공급받지 못하게 될 것이다. 농부는 토양에 도움이 될 수 있도록 비료를 사용해야 한다. 유기 농업을 하는 농부들은 비료를 사용하지 않는다. 대신 윤작을 하거나 동물의 분뇨 및 식물성 퇴비를 이용해 토양을 다시 비옥하게 만든다. 퇴비는 땅에 떨어져 썩은 식물로부터 만들어진다. 여기에는 식물의 성장에 필요한 모든 영양분이 들어 있다.

살충제 또한 쓰이지 않는다. 이들은 곤충과 같은 유해 생물들을 제거하는 화학 물질이다. 유기 농업을 하는 농부들은 다른 방법으로 해충을 상대하는데, 그 이유는 살충제가 식물을 보호해 주는 유익한 동물과 곤충들까지도 제거하기 때문이다. 여우와 뱀은 쥐를 잡아먹는다. 무당벌레와 같은 곤충은 유해한 곤충을 잡아먹는다. 그리고, 물론, 잡초가 있다. 이들은 유익한 작물의 재배 공간을 빼앗아간다는 점에서 농부들이 싫어하는 식물이다. 잡초를 제거하기 위해 유기 농업을 하는 농부들은 여러 차례 밭을 맬 수 있다. 결국 잡초는 없어진다.

일반적으로 유기 농업에서는 화학 물질을 대신하기 위해 인간의 많은 노동이 필요하다. 유기농 식품이 더 비싼 이유 중 하나가 바로 이러한 점 때문이다. 하지만 지구, 지구의 식물, 그리고 지구의 동물의 건강을 고려하면 아마도 그만한 가치는 있을 것이다. 결국 지구가 건강해지면 인간도 건강해질 것이다.

[6-10]

WTO

세계 무역 기구(WTO)에는 149개 이상의 국가들이 가입해 있다. 이들은 무역 증진을 기대한다. 무역이란 물건을 사고 파는 것이다. WTO는 회원국들이 서로 필요한 것에 대해 이야기할 수 있는 자리를 마련해 준다. WTO의 목표는 국가간의 법적인 장벽을 제거함으로써 무역을 확대시키는 것이다.

WTO는 여러 가지 방법으로 무역을 돕는다. 우선, 회원국들에게 서로를 평등하게 대할 것을 요구한다. 한 국가와는 특별한 무역 협정을 맺고 다른 국가와는 그렇지 않은 협정을 맺어서는 안 된다. 이들 국가들은 또한 한 나라에서 생산된 제품의 수입을 막으려 해서도 안 된다. 이러한 아이디어는 재화와 서비스가 국경을 쉽게 넘을 수 있어야 한다는 의미이다. 무역을 증진시키는 두 번째 방법은 관세를 낮추는 것이다. 관세는 사고 팔리는 물건에 대한 특별세이다. 무역을 촉진하기 위한 세 번째 방법은 원칙을 유지시키는 것이다. 사람들이 돈을 투자하기 위해서는 미래가 안전하다고 느껴야 한다. 네 번째 방법은 국가 간의 경쟁을 확대시키는 것이다. 이때의 핵심은 경쟁을 통해 경제가 더 튼튼해진다는 점이다. 무역을 증진시키는 마지막 방법은 가난한 나라를 돕는 것이다. 이들이 현대 국가의 수준으로 발전하기 위해서는 도움이 필요하다. 시스템을 구축할 수 있도록 이들에게 추가적인 시간을 줌으로써 이들을 도울 수 있다. 다른 나라와 무역을 하는 경우에는 이들에게 우선권을 줄 수도 있다.

자유롭고 순조로운 무역은 WTO의 목표이다. WTO는 부유한 국가들을 지원하고 가난한 국가들의 자립을 돕는다. 이는 전 세계 보다 많은 사람들의 삶을 향상시킬 수 있는 한 가지 방법이다. WTO는 국가들에게 이러한 과정에 도움이 될 수 있는 법 제정을 요구한다. 매년 더 많은 나라들이 WTO에 가입하고 있다. 이들은 회원국이 되는 것이 이로운 일이라고 생각한다.

Vocabulary Check-Up

p.210

1 Ⓓ	2 Ⓐ	3 Ⓑ	4 Ⓓ	5 Ⓒ
6 Ⓐ	7 Ⓑ	8 Ⓓ	9 Ⓐ	10 Ⓒ

UNIT 10 Fill in a Table

Basic Drill p.214

Drill 1 Interplate Quake: [2] Intraplate Quake: [3]

해석

지표면의 판이 움직이면 지진이 발생한다. 때로는 판들이 서로를 밀어내기도 한다. 이를 판 경계간 지진이라고 한다. 판들이 갑자기 미끄러지면 충격파의 형태로 에너지가 방출된다. 두 개의 판 모두 손으로 튕겼을 때의 기타줄처럼 흔들린다. 판의 가운데 부분에서 균열이 발생할 때에도 지진이 발생할 수 있다. 이를 판 내부 지진이라고 부른다. 이는 전혀 예상하지 못한 장소에서 발생하기 때문에 종종 과학자들을 놀라게 만든다.

Drill 2 Gaseous Nebula: [4] Dust Nebula: [2], [5]

해석

*성운*이라는 단어는 행성이나 혜성이 아닌 모든 물체를 지칭하는 말이었다. 이는 은하 및 성단도 일종의 성운이라는 의미였다. 하지만 오늘날 이 용어는 우주의 먼지 및 가스로 이루어진 구름을 가리킨다. 실제로 성운이라는 단어는 라틴어로 "구름"을 뜻한다. 성운의 한 종류는 가스로 이루어져 있다. 뜨거운 가스가 식으면 빛을 방출한다. 보통 이러한 성운들은 붉은 색을 띤다. 먼지로 이루어진 성운도 있다. 이들은 근처에 있는 항성의 빛을 반사한다. 먼지로 이루어진 성운 중에는, 자신의 뒤에서 빛을 내는, 천체의 빛을 가리는 것도 있다.

Drill 3 Before: [2] After: [4], [5]

해석

이리 운하는 뉴욕의 허드슨강과 오대호를 연결하는 수상 고속도로이다. 이 운하가 생기기 전에는 해당 지역에서의 여행과 무역이 어려웠다. 사람과 물건 모두 육지에서 수레를 타고 이동해야 했다. 때때로 강을 이용하기도 했지만, 날씨의 영향이 매우 컸다. 여행과 무역은 느리고, 비용도 많이 들고, 그리고 위험한 것이었다. 운하가 건설된 후에는 상황이 나아졌다. 첫째, 상품 운송에 드는 시간과 비용이 절약되었다. 이로 인해 무역이 활발해졌다. 서부에서 키운 농작물이 유럽으로 판매될 수 있었다. 둘째, 사람들이 서쪽으로 이주할 수 있었고 미국의 크기가 보다 쉽게 확대될 수 있었다.

Exercises with Short Passages

Exercise 1 1 Ⓑ 2 Ⓓ 3 First Way of Formation: [1], [4] Second Way of Formation: [3] p.216

해석

블랙홀

블랙홀은 잘 보이지 않는다. 중력이 모든 것을 빨아들이기 때문에 빛을 내지도 않고 빛을 반사시키지도 않는다. 물리학자들이 블랙홀의 존재를 알 수 있는 유일한 방법은 물체들이 그 안으로 빠져들어가는 것을 보는 것이다. 물체가 그 안으로 들어가면 수축이 일어나면서 열과 빛이 방출된다. 이러한 복사열은 관찰이 가능하다. 때로는 죽어가는 항성에서 블랙홀이 만들어지기도 한다. 크기가 큰 항성만이 블랙홀이 될 수 있다. 항성이 자신의 중심을 향해 붕괴를 하면 그 크기는 매우 작아지지만 여전히 중력은 존재한다. 이것이 블랙홀의 심장이다.

때로는 거대한 가스 구름에서 블랙홀이 형성되기도 한다. 기체 분자 사이에 생기는 중력 때문에 가스 구름이 수축된다. 허블 망원경이 이러한 종류의 블랙홀을 촬영했다. 과학자들은 그러한 블랙홀이 우리 은하의 한가운데에 존재한다고 생각한다.

Exercise 2 1 Ⓑ 2 Ⓓ 3 Agriculture: [3], [5] Military: [4] p.217

해석

수메르 문명

수메르인들은 많은 발전을 이루어 냈다. 먼저 농업을 발달시켰다. 나중에는 군대를 조직했다. 수메르인들은 바퀴를 발명한 것으로 생각된다. 바퀴는 처음에 도기에 사용되었는데, 도기는 곡물을 저장하는데 필수적인 것이었다. 그 다음에는 곡식을 빻는 일에 사용되었다. 마지막으로, 바퀴는 농사 및 군대의 수송 수단에서 사용되었다. 수메르인들은 처음으로 문자와 수학을 이용했다. 이집트인보다도 먼저였다. 이는 사회를 조직화하는데 도움을 주었다. 이러한 시스템은 식량 및 거래를 기록하려는 목적으로 사용되었다. 군대는 이를 이용해서 병사, 무기, 그리고 보급품에 대한 기록을 할 수 있었다. 수메르인들은 최초로 별과 태양을 본격적으로 연구했다. 이러한 연구를 통해 시간을 알 수 있었고, 이로써 언제 작물을 심어야 할지 결정할 수 있었다. 또한 별을 보고 언제 적을 공격할 것인지에 대한 계획을 세우기도 했다. 이들은 별들이 성공 또는 실패를 예측해 줄 수 있다고 믿었다.

Exercise 3 1 Ⓓ 2 Ⓐ 3 Queens: [2] Soldiers: [1] Workers: [3], [4] p.218

해석

흰개미

흰개미는 군락이라고 불리는 커다란 무리를 지어 산다. 수백만 마리의 흰개미들이 함께 살 수도 있다. 군락은 각기 다른 종류의 흰개미들이 서로 협력하기 때문에 유지될 수 있다. 각각의 개미집에는 최소 한 마리의 왕개미와 여왕개미가 있다. 이들의 역할은 군락의 삶을 지배하는 것이 아니라 보다 많은 흰개미를 낳는 것이다. 여왕개미는 하루에 수천 개의 알을 낳을 수 있다. 알을 지닌 경우 몸통이 10센티미터까지 커질 수 있다. 알은 유충이라고 불리는 어린 흰개미로 자란다. 일개미들은 앞을 보지 못한다. 이들은 먹이를 찾고, 병정개미와 어린 개미들에게 먹이를 주며, 개미집을 돌보는 일을 한다. 병정개미는 개미집을 방어한다. 이들의 머리에서는 보호 역할을 하는 덮개가 자란다. 하지만 턱이 매우 크기 때문에 일개미들로부터 먹이를 받아먹어야 한다. 이런 유형의 조직을 갖춘 군락은 한 마리의 개미가 할 수 있는 것보다 훨씬 더 많은 일들을 해낼 수 있다.

Exercise 4 1 Ⓐ 2 Ⓒ 3 Continental Drift: [2], [5] Plate Tectonics: [3], [4] p.219

해석

대륙 이동설

대륙 이동설은 오래된 지질학 이론이다. 판 구조론보다도 더 오래되었다. 초기의 과학자들은 각기 다른 땅덩어리들이 서로 들어맞는 모양을 하고 있다는 것을 알았다. 또한 이들의 지질학적 특성이 서로 비슷하다는 점에도 주목했다. 아프리카와 남아메리카 사이에는 유사성이 많았다. 두 곳에서 동일한 종류의 화석이 발견되었다. 심지어 현재에도 두 곳에서 동일한 종류의 지렁이가 발견되고 있다. 과학자들은 과거에 모든 땅이 함께 붙어 있었다는 점을 알게 되었다. 이 거대한 땅덩어리는 팡게아라고 명명되었다. 이 땅은 시간이 흐르면서 분리되었다. 문제는 어떻게 해서 이 땅덩어리들이 분리되었는지를 설명하는 것이었다. 과학자들은 어떻게 전체 대륙들이 해저의 암석을 통과해 이동할 수 있었는지 알 수 없었다. 마침내 그들은 해저 역시 특정 지역에서는 확장된다는 것을 알게 되었다. 이로써 판 이동과 판 구조라는 개념이 생겨났다.

Exercises with Mid-Length Passages

Exercise 1 Copernicus: 3, 5 Newton: 1, 2, 7 p.220

해석

우주에 대한 인류의 인식

인간은 수천 년 동안 밤하늘을 관찰했다. 이는 사람들의 상상력을 사로잡았고, 또한 사람들의 지식 탐구에 도움을 주었다.

오래전 인간의 조상들은 별들이 하늘에서 움직이지만 동일한 패턴을 유지한다는 점을 처음으로 알아냈다. 그들은 친숙한 형태로 별들의 무리를 구분했다. 이러한 형태는 여행을 하는 사람들에게 길을 알려 주었고, 사람들에게 언제 작물을 심어야 하는지도 알려 주었다. 이러한 형태는 또한 이야기와 신화의 주제가 되기도 했다. 수백 년 동안 사람들은 지구와 인간이 우주의 중심이라고 믿었다. 1543년, 니콜라우스 코페르니쿠스가 그러한 생각이 틀렸다는 것을 증명했다. 사실 지구가 태양 주위를 도는 것이다. 이로써 우주에 대한 이해가 깊어질 수 있는 길이 열렸다. 이후 갈릴레오 갈릴레이는 망원경을 이용하여 태양과 행성에 관해 보다 많은 것을 알게 되었다.

마지막으로 중력이라는 개념을 통해 우주가 하나로 합쳐졌다. 이는 아이작 뉴턴 덕분이었다. 중력으로 인해 작은 물체는 보다 큰 물체 쪽으로 이동한다. 중력은 태양계가 어떻게 형성되었는지 설명해 준다. 중력은 어떻게 행성들이 태양 주위를 도는지 설명해 준다. 중력은 어떻게 혜성들이 그처럼 태양계를 통과하여 이동하는지 설명해 준다. 중력에 대한 이해는 인간의 우주 탐사에 도움을 준다.

Exercise 2 Pros: 2, 7 Cons: 1, 5, 6 p.221

해석

루이스와 클락, 그리고 루이지애나 구매

제퍼슨 대통령은 1803년 프랑스의 통치자였던 나폴레옹에게서 미시시피강 서쪽 땅을 매입했다. 이는 그 당시 신생 국가였던 미국에게 몇 가지 문제를 가져다 주었지만, 이로 인한 이익은 엄청났다.

당시 많은 이들이 이러한 구매를 반기지 않았다. 어떤 사람들은 프랑스로부터 토지를 구입할 필요가 없다고 생각했다. 프랑스 군대가 북아메리카에서 없었기 때문에 이를 차지할 수도 있었다. 어떤 사람들은 대통령에게 토지를 구매할 권한이 없다고 생각했다. 이러한 토지 구매로 스페인이 분노할 것이라고 생각한 사람들도 있었다. 또 다른 사람들은 새로운 주들이 기존 주들의 권한을 빼앗아 갈 것이라고 우려했다.

그러한 우려에도 불구하고 이 구매로 인해 1803년에는 미국 국토가 두 배로 늘어났다. 하지만 처음에 제퍼슨 대통령과 미국인들은 이 새로운 토지에 대해 거의 아무것도 알지 못했다. 어떤 자원이 사용될 수 있는지 모르고 있었다. 결국 그곳에 풍부한 자원이 있다는 것을 알게 되었다. 광활한 토지는 농장으로 사용될 수 있었다. 채굴할 수 있는 광물도 묻혀 있었다. 무엇보다 경제 성장에 도움이 될 거대한 강들이 있었다. 대통령은 루이스와 클락이 이끄는 팀을 보내 그 지역을 탐사하도록 했다. 그들은 28개월간 8,000마일이 넘는 거리를 이동했다. 이 팀은 많은 지도를 제작하고 많은 기록을 남겼다. 이러한 정보는 미국의 미래를 계획하는데 이용되었다.

Exercise 3 Adaptability: 1, 6 Defenses: 2, 3, 7 p.222

해석

주머니쥐

유대 동물은 주머니를 가지고 있는 동물이다. 암컷은 새끼가 주머니 밖에서도 살 수 있을 정도로 충분히 자랄 때까지 새끼를 주머니에 넣어 키운다. 북아메리카에 있는 유일한 유대 동물은 주머니쥐이다.

주머니쥐는 커다란 고양이 정도의 크기이다. 털은 회색이며, 코와 발, 그리고 꼬리는 분홍색이다. 밤에도 볼 수 있는 크고 검은 눈을 가지고 있어서 밤에 가장 활발하게 움직인다. 50개의 매우 날카로운 이빨을 가지고 있지만, 매우 온순한 동물이다. 어떠한 싸움도 피하려고 한다.

주머니쥐는 적응력이 매우 뛰어나다. 나무속이나 지하를 비롯한 여러 장소에서 살 수 있다. 식물과 동물을 포함해서 온갖 종류의 먹이를 먹는다. 곤충, 쥐, 작은 뱀, 풀, 나뭇잎, 그리고 딸기류를 먹는다.

주머니쥐는 다양한 방어 수단을 가지고 있다. 일반적으로 뱀독에 대한 면역이 있다. 혈액 온도 때문에 위험한 질병인 광견병에도 잘 걸리지 않는다. 가장 잘 알려진 방어 기술은 죽은 척하는 것이다. 대부분의 동물들은 사체를 먹지 않기 때문에 이는 좋은 방어 기술이다. 주머니쥐는 등을 대고 누워 이빨을 보인다. 그리고 꼬리 주위에서 악취를 풍긴다. 보통은 다른 동물들이 자리를 떠나게 된다.

Exercise 4 Water at the Bottom: 1, 6, 7 Water at the Surface: 2, 5 p.223

해석

마리아나 해구

해구는 기다란 구멍이다. 하나의 지각판이 다른 지각판 밑으로 미끄러질 때 만들어진다. 바다 아래에는 22개의 거대한 해구가 있다. 세 개는 대서양에 있고, 한 개는 인도양에 있다. 18개는 태평양에 있다. 가장 큰 해구는 마리아나 해구이다. 이는 일본에서 멀지 않은 태평양에 위치해 있다.

마리아나 해구는 지구에서 가장 깊은 곳이다. 길이가 542킬로미터이고 폭은 69킬로미터이다. 깊이는 11,033미터이다. 지구에서 가장 높은 산도 이 해구 안에 넣으면 해수면에 닿지 못할 것이다. 산 위로 2킬로미터의 물이 더 있을 정도이다.

그곳 바닥은 수면 근처와 크게 다르다. 아래로 내려가면 수압이 해수면의 수압보다 1,000배 더 높다. 잠수정이 없으면 사람은 생존하지 못할 것이다. 그러한 환경에서 생물이 살 수 있을 것이라고 믿기는 매우 힘들다. 하지만 실제로 해구의 바닥에는 물고기와 새우가 살고 있다.

바닥에 있는 해수는 태양에 의해 데워지지 않는다. 지각에 난 틈 때문에 얼지는 않는다. 틈에서는 300℃의 열기가 분출된다. 수면에 있는 해수는 비교적 맑은 편이다. 아래로 내려가면 박테리아뿐만 아니라 예전에 살았던 동물들의 피부 및 작은 뼈들의 잔해들이 가득하다. 이 해수가 두꺼운 혼합층을 형성한다.

Building Summary Skills

p.224

A

Exercise 1 Humans' Perception of the Universe

1 Humans have tried to understand the night sky for a long time and have created many stories about it.

4 Newton came up with the idea of gravity.

2 For years, it was believed that humans were the center of the universe.

3 Copernicus and Galileo provided information to the contrary.

5 This helped explain the motion of all the objects in the universe.

Exercise 2 Lewis and Clark and the Louisiana Purchase

1 The Louisiana Purchase was a great addition to the United States, but it posed a few challenges.

3 Some were concerned about relations with other countries, and others were concerned about how it would affect political power in the U.S.

2 Politically, many people did not like the idea.

4 After buying the land, information about the people, the resources, and the rivers was needed to make use of it.

Exercise 3 The Opossum

1 The opossum is the only marsupial in North America.

4 It has a number of defenses.

3 It is adaptable in that it is an omnivore and can find a home in lots of places.

5 It is mostly immune to rabies and snake venom, and it can also play dead.

2 It is mostly nocturnal and, despite having many teeth, is very gentle.

Exercise 4 The Mariana Trench

1 The Mariana Trench is a long hole at the bottom of the sea.

4 The water has unique qualities: it does not freeze because of heat vents in the Earth, and the water is a thick mixture of bacteria and animal particles.

2 It is the deepest place on the Earth.

3 The pressure is huge at the bottom, but animals still manage to live there.

B

Exercise 1 Man's Perception of the Universe

Humans have tried to understand the night sky for a long time and have created many stories about it. For years, it was believed that humans were the center of the universe. Copernicus and Galileo provided information to the contrary. Newton came up with the idea of gravity. This helped explain the motion of all the objects in the universe.

Exercise 2 Lewis and Clark and the Louisiana Purchase

The Louisiana Purchase was a great addition to the United States, but it posed a few challenges. Politically, many people did not like the idea. Some were concerned about relations with other countries, and others were concerned about how it would affect political power in the U.S. After buying the land, information about the people, the resources, and the rivers was needed to make use of it.

Exercise 3 The Opossum

The opossum is the only marsupial in North America. It is mostly nocturnal and, despite having many teeth, is very gentle. It is adaptable in that it is an omnivore and can find a home in lots of places. It has a number of defenses. It is mostly immune to rabies and snake venom, and it can also play dead.

Exercise 4 The Mariana Trench

The Mariana Trench is a long hole at the bottom of the sea. It is the deepest place on the Earth. The pressure is huge at the bottom, but animals still manage to live there. The water has unique qualities: it does not freeze because of heat vents in the Earth, and the water is a thick mixture of bacteria and animal particles.

Mini TOEFL iBT Practice Test

p.226

1 Ⓓ 2 Ⓐ 3 Ⓓ 4 Ⓓ 5 Ⓒ

6 **Planets:** 1, 3, 5 **Asteroids:** 4, 7

7 Ⓑ 8 Ⓑ 9 Ⓐ 10 Ⓒ 11 Ⓒ

12 **Convergent Boundaries:** 2, 5 **Transform Boundaries:** 3, 4 **Divergent Boundaries:** 6

해석

[1-6]

태양계

태양계는 일정한 궤도로 태양 주위를 도는 천체들로 이루어져 있다. 하지만 항상 그런 것은 아니었다. 태양과 태양 주위를 도는 천체들은 서로 매우 다른 형태로 형성되었다.

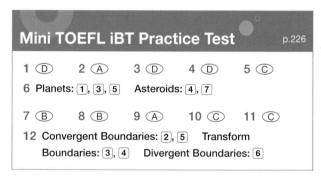

태양계는 가스와 먼지로 이루어진 거대한 구름에서 시작되었다고 생각된다. 구름은 둥근 형태였고 느리게 회전했다. 회전으로 인해 가스와 먼지가 납작해졌고 원반 모양이 만들어졌다. 중심부에 있던 가스와 먼지 덩어리가 태양이 되었다. 중력에 의해 가스와 먼지가 모이면서 핵반응이 시작되었다. 바깥쪽에 있던

나머지 먼지와 가스는 너무 느린 속도로 이동했기 때문에 곳곳에서 엉겨붙기 시작했다. 마침내 충분한 양의 물질이 서로 달라붙어서 행성이 만들어졌다.

태양계에는 여러 다양한 천체들이 존재한다. 물론 행성이 있다. 각 행성은 고유한 특성을 나타낸다. 어떤 행성은 암석이나 금속 성분으로 이루어져 있다. 수성, 금성, 지구, 그리고 화성이 그러하다. 가스나 얼음에 더 가까운 행성들도 있다. 목성, 토성, 그리고 나머지 행성들이 이러한 유형의 행성에 속한다. 이 행성들은 다수의 위성을 가지고 있다.

태양계에는 소행성대가 있다. 소행성은 기본적으로 암석이다. 가장 큰 소행성은 지름이 수백 킬로미터에 이를 수 있다. 이러한 수많은 암석들이 화성과 목성 사이에서 태양 주위를 돌고 있다. 때때로 소행성들은 서로 부딪치기도 하고 지구 쪽으로 이동하기도 한다. 지구 근처를 지날 때, 소행성은 가열이 되어 불에 탄다. 이는 별똥별로 관측된다.

마지막으로, 얼음과 가스로 이루어진 혜성이 있다. 이들 또한 태양 주위를 돌지만, 일반적인 경로를 따르지는 않는다. 태양 근처에 도달하면 녹기 시작해서 꼬리를 만들어 낸다. 태양에서 멀리 떨어진 곳, 즉 추운 우주에서는 혜성이 딱딱하게 얼어 있다.

[7-12]

판 구조론

판 구조론은 지질학 분야의 한 이론이다. 어떻게 지표면이 움직이는지를 설명한다. 지표면은 움직이는, 떠 다니는 판으로 이루어져 있다고 설명한다.

지구는 여러 개의 각기 다른 층으로 이루어져 있다. 맨 위층은 단단하지만 약 10개의 판으로 나뉘어져 있다. 두께는 100킬로미터 정도이다. 이 판들은 액체 상태인 아래쪽의 층 위를 떠다닌다. 아래층의 열기 때문에 판들이 이동하게 된다. 판들이 이동하면서 그 가장자리의 바다에 화산, 산, 그리고 해구가 만들어진다.

판은 세 가지의 각기 다른 방법으로 이동할 수 있다. 서로 떨어지면서 이동할 수 있다. 이를 발산형 경계라고 부른다. 해저에 이런 곳이 몇 군데 있다. 이런 방식으로 판이 움직이면 지구의 핵 안에 있는 액체가 위로 올라가서 지구(地溝)라는 공간을 채우게 된다. 지구 가장 가까이에 있는 암석은 지구에서 보다 멀리 떨어져 있는 암석보다 더 최근에 형성된 것이다. 지구는 보통 해마다 약 2센티미터씩 커진다. 보존형 경계는 두 개의 판이 나란히 이동할 때 생긴다. 이는 캘리포니아에서 많이 나타난다. 태평양판과 북아메리카판이 맞닿아 있는 부분은 거의 1,300킬로미터에 이른다. 이 판들은 해마다 약 0.6센티미터씩 움직인다. 이로 인해 산 안드레아스 단층이 만들어졌는데, 이 때문에 많은 지진이 발행하고 있다. 수렴형 경계는 두 개의 판이 서로를 향해 이동할 때 형성된다. 보통 하나의 판이 다른 판 아래로 들어간다. 이러한 일이 발생하면 위에 있는 판이 솟아오른다. 이러한 방식으로 산맥이 형성될 수 있다. 히말라야 산맥도 이러한 방식으로 만들어졌다. 히말라야 산맥은 세계에서 가장 최근에 만들어진 산맥 중 하나이다. 인도 아래쪽에 있는 판은 티베트 아래에 있는 판을 향해 계속 이동하고 있다. 이 거대한 산맥들은 해마다 5밀리미터씩 솟아오르고 있다.

Vocabulary Check-Up

p.230

1 Ⓒ	2 Ⓓ	3 Ⓒ	4 Ⓑ	5 Ⓓ
6 Ⓒ	7 Ⓓ	8 Ⓑ	9 Ⓐ	10 Ⓓ

Actual Test

Actual Test

p.234

1 Ⓐ	2 Ⓐ	3 Ⓓ	4 Ⓑ	5 Ⓒ
6 Ⓓ	7 Ⓒ	8 Ⓒ	9 2	
10 2, 3, 6				
11 Ⓑ	12 Ⓑ	13 Ⓓ	14 Ⓐ	15 Ⓓ
16 Ⓒ	17 Ⓐ	18 Ⓐ	19 3	

20 Problem: 3, 5 Solution: 2, 6, 7

해석

[1-10]

고대 동굴 벽화

선사 시대의 동굴 벽화는 기원전 40,000년부터 10,000년까지 해당되는 후기 구석기 시대 이후에 만들어졌다. 하지만 1879년이 되어서야 발견되었다. [최초로 발견된 벽화는 스페인의 한 동굴 안에 있었다.] 처음에는 이들이 조작된 것이라는 의심을 받았다. 하지만 전 세계의 다른 장소에서도 동굴 벽화가 발견되면서 진위가 확인되었다. 방사성 탄소 연대 측정법이라는 현대의 기술로 이들이 고대 유물이라는 점이 확인되었다. 프랑스, 이탈리아, 아프리카, 호주, 그리고 동남아시아의 동굴 벽에서도 기타 인상적인 작품들이 발견되었다.

1879년에 막달레니아인들의 작품이 발견되었다. 이들의 이름은 인근 도시인 스페인의 막달레니아의 이름을 따서 지어졌다. 이들은 대략 기원전 18,000년부터 10,000년까지 살았다. 막달레니아 미술은 독특하다. 주제와 스타일이 반복되는 특징이 있다. 가장 인기 있었던 대상은 동물이었다. 들소, 사슴, 말, 그리고 지금은 멸종한 매머드가 인기 있는 동물이었다. 실제 인간을 대상으로 삼는 경우는 드물었다. 인간의 추상적인 형태를 나타내는데 그쳤다. 하지만, 화가가 일종의 서명으로서 포함시켰을 수도 있는, 식별이 가능한 인간의 손은 찾아볼 수 있다.

동굴 벽화는 두 가지 요인 때문에 그처럼 오래 감추어져 있었다. 첫째, 화가들이 동굴 깊은 곳에서 작업을 했다. 이러한 곳에서는 동굴의 벽이 날씨로부터 보호를 받을 수 있었다. 이러한 장소는 고대 문명의 흔적을 찾는 현대의 학자들이 종종 접근할 수 없는 곳이었다. 둘째, 일단 동굴 벽화가 발견되어 호기심 많은 대중에게 알려지면 발굴 작업이 시작된다. 발굴이 되면 동굴 벽화는 사람 및 수천 년 동안 차단되었던 위험 요인들에게 노출된다. 그래서 1차 세계 대전 중 프랑스에서 발견된 그림들은 대중에게 소개된 후 6개월만에 사라져 버리기도 했다. 일부 장소들은 공조 장치로 보존되어 관람이 가능할 수 있다. 하지만 대부분은 관광객들에게 개방되어 있지 않다. 학자들도 들어가기 위해서는 신청을 해야 한다. 그런 다음 짧은 시간 동안에만 벽화를 관찰하는 것이 허락된다.

상대적으로 동굴 벽화에 대한 접근은 어렵지만, 과학자들은 고대 화가들이 썼던 방법이나 재료에 관해 많은 것을 알아낼 수 있었다. 최초의 작품은 손가락을 사용해 바위 표면에 부드러운 진흙으로 그린 그림이었다. 이들은 동물의 발톱을 묘사했다. 그 후에는 조각법을 채택했다. 돌로 된 도구를 사용해서 암벽에 모양을 새겼다. 화가들은 특수한 도구뿐만 아니라 자신만의 기술을 사용해 그림의 색조, 색깔, 그리고 농도를 변화시킬 수 있었다. 마지막으로 발달한 기술은 색칠이었다. 구석기인들이 자연 속에서 찾을 수 있는 것에는 한계가 있었기 때문에 사용할 수 있는 색이 별로 없었다. 색은 다양한 광물질과 나무로부터 얻었다. 예를 들어 빨간색은 산화철에서, 흰색은 운모에서 얻었다. 나무가 불에 타면 나오는 탄소로부터 검정색을 얻었다.

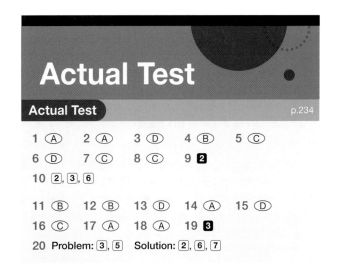

재료는 원시적이었지만, 화가들은 색을 섞고 바르는 일에서 솜씨를 발휘했다. 거의 200개나 되는 색깔을 내는 광물질이 만각류 껍질에서 발견되었는데, 여기에 안료들이 혼합되어 있었다. 한 화가는 인간의 두개골을 이용해 색깔을 혼합하기도 했다. 칼슘이 포함되어 있는 동굴 속 물이 혼합제로 사용되었다. 동물성 기름과 식물성 기름이 안료를 뭉치게 했다. 색칠용 붓은 발견된 바 없지만, 완성된 작품에는 붓을 사용했던 흔적이 뚜렷하게 남아 있다. 때때로 미리 준비한 스텐실로 덮은 표면에 물감을 분사하기도 했다. 입으로 부는 속이 빈 막대가 페인트 스프레이로 사용되었다.

그림을 그리는 일은 전문적인 기술이었다. 사냥 및 생존을 위해 모든 시간을 바쳐야 하는 평범한 아마추어들이 하기에는 너무나 어렵고 비용이 많이 드는 일이었다. 한 가지 어려움은 어두운 동굴 벽을 밝히는 것이었다. 과학자들은 고대 화가들이 동물성 지방을 연료를 이용한 횃불을 사용해서 작업을 했다는 이론을 제시한다. 또 다른 문제는 일부 벽면에 손을 닿기가 쉽지 않았다는 점이었다. 좁은 공간에서 누운 채로 그림을 그렸을 것으로 보이는 그림들도 있었다. 동굴 바닥에서 너무 높은 곳에 있어서 발판이 필요했을 것으로 보이는 그림들도 있었다.

벽화가 그려진 장소를 통해 인류학자들은 후기 구석기인들의 생활 방식에 관한 중요한 단서를 얻을 수 있다. 동굴 사람들이라고 종종 불리는 구석기인들은 동굴 안에서 살지 않았다. 공기에 노출될 경우 그림이 빨리 사라져 버리는 것을 막기 위한 실용적인 이유에서 동굴 벽을 캔버스로 사용한 것이었다. 따라서 동굴은 그림을 보호해 주고 보존시켜 주었다. 그들은 그림이 오래 지속되기를 바랐다. 즐거움을 위해서뿐만 아니라 그림이 수행하는 문화적 기능 때문에 오래 지속되기를 바랐다. 그림은 선사 시대 문명들이 역사를 전하고 전통과 조상을 기리는 매개체였다.

[11-20]

시간대의 역사

지구가 태양 주위를 공전하면서 자전하기 때문에 시간대가 필요하다. 지구는 24시간마다 자전을 한다. 따라서 지구의 각 지점은 아침에 태양 쪽으로, 그리고 저녁에는 태양 반대쪽으로 계속 움직인다. 지구에서 서쪽 방향으로 가는 경우 각각의 지점마다 태양이 머리 위에 오는 시각, 즉 정오가 달라진다. 따라서 한 도시의 정오는, 동쪽으로 100마일 떨어져 있어서 이미 태양이 머리 위를 지나가 버린, 한 도시의 정오와 다르다.

산업화 시대 이전에는 이러한 점이 문제가 되지 않았다. 이때는 기술로 인해 장거리 간 빠른 커뮤니케이션이 가능하지 않았다. 시간 계측은 지역적인 일이었다. 각 마을은 태양이 그 지역에서 가장 높은 위치에 도달할 때 정오로 시간을 맞추면 되었다. 다른 도시로 여행을 가는 사람은 자신의 회중 시계를 현지 시각에 맞도록 조정해야 했다.

19세기가 되자 철로가 놓였다. 또한 전신이 보편화되었다. 처음으로 사람들이 하루에 수 마일을 이동할 수 있었다. 또한 전신으로 전국적인 사업을 벌일 수 있었다. 불규칙한 기존의 시간 계측 시스템은 상업과 통신을 어렵고 혼란스럽게 만들었다. 정거장마다 서로 다른 현지 시간을 사용했기 때문에 통일된 열차 시간표가 존재할 수 없었다. 각 철도 회사들은 자신들만의 표준시를 사용했다. 이는 대부분 본사가 있는 곳이나 중요한 역이 있는 지역의 시간이었다. 어떤 기차역에는 그 역을 이용하는 각각의 철도를 위한 별개의 시계들이 갖추어져 있었다. 그래서 주요 도시에 정차한 여행객은 기차 승강장에서 6개의 시계를 볼 수도 있었다. 각각은 서로 다른 시간을 나타내었다. 철도의 효율적인 운영을 위해서는 시간을 표준화해야 했다.

1878년 캐나다의 기관사인 샌포드 플레밍 경이 해결책을 내놓았다. 그는 지구를 시간대로 표시하자고 제안했다. 이는 지구의 경도선에 의해 구분될 수 있었다. 각 시간대의 폭은 15도였다. 따라서 지구의 360도는 15도로 이루어진 24개의 시간대로 구분되었다. 이 시스템에 의하면 지구는 자전으로 한 시간에 15도, 즉 지구의 1/24에 해당되는 시간대를 이동하게 된다.

미국의 철도 회사들은 1883년에 플레밍 시스템을 사용하기 시작했다. 하지만 전 세계에서 효율적으로 사용되기 위해서는 하나의 경도 시작선을 기본선으로 지정해서 하루를 측정해야 했다. 1884년 이 문제 해결을 위해 워싱턴 D.C.에서 국제 본초 자오선 회의라는 국제 회의가 열렸다. 여기에서 영국의 그리니치를 통과하는 자오선을 본초 자오선, 즉 경도가 0인 선으로 지정했다. 이 경도에서의 시간은 그리니치 평균시 또는 GMT라고 알려져 있다. 각 경도선들은 북극과 남극을 연결하며 적도와 수직을 이룬다. 이론상 경도선은 직선이다. 하지만 실제로는 현지인들의 요구에 부응하여 구부러져 있는 경우가 많다.

모든 국가들이 곧바로 이 시스템을 채택한 것은 아니었다. 미국 대부분의 지역에서는 1895년 이후가 되어서야 채택되었다. 1918년 미 의회에서 표준시법이 통과되기 전까지는 의무 사항도 아니었다. 심지어 오늘날에도 이러한 통일성에서 벗어나 있는 국가들도 있다. 이스라엘의 경우 오전 12시가 아니라 오후 6시에 하루가 시작된다. 중국에는 5개의 시간대가 존재해야 하지만, 중국 정부는 중국 전역에 하나의 시간대만 적용하기로 했다. [이는 일부 지역에서 때때로 오후 2시에 해가 질 수 있다는 점을 의미한다.] 기타 일부 국가들은 반시간대를 채택하기도 한다. 시간대를 조정하는 일반적인 방법 중 하나는 일광 절약 시간이다. 일부 국가에서는 서머 타임이라고 불린다. 해당 국가들은 봄에 한 시간을 앞당긴다. 가을까지 이러한 시스템을 유지한다. 이로써 하루가 끝날 때 낮 한 시간이 추가된다. 주된 목적은 에너지 절약이다. 한 시간 늦게 어둠이 내리면 사람들이 잠에서 깨어 전기를 소비하는 시간이 한 시간 줄어든다. 또 다른 이점은 날씨가 따뜻한 시기에 사람들이 야외에 있을 수 있는 시간이 늘어난다는 점이다.

GMT는 지구의 자전 속도에 기반해 있는데, 지구의 자전 속도가 항상 일정한 것은 아니다. 따라서 시간이 지나면서 GMT에 약간의 오차가 발생한다. 이에 따라 1972년에 GMT와 초정밀 원자 시계를 일치시켰는데, 초정밀 원자 시계는 행성의 자전에서 비롯되는 차이만큼의 "윤초"를 포함하고 있다. 이러한 새로운 시스템은 협정 세계시 또는 UTC라고 불린다.

MEMO

MEMO